Rethinking Elementary Education

EDITED BY:

Linda Christensen

Mark Hansen

Bob Peterson

Elizabeth Schlessman

Dyan Watson

A Rethinking Schools Publication

RETHINKING ELEMENTARY EDUCATION

Edited by Linda Christensen, Mark Hansen, Bob Peterson, Elizabeth Schlessman, Dyan Watson

A Rethinking Schools Publication

Rethinking Schools Ltd. is a nonprofit educational publisher of books, booklets, and a quarterly magazine on school reform, with a focus on issues of equity and social justice. To request additional copies of this book and/or a catalog of other publications, or to subscribe to *Rethinking Schools* magazine, contact:

Rethinking Schools
1001 East Keefe Avenue
Milwaukee, WI 53212
800-669-4192
www.rethinkingschools.org

FIRST EDITION

Cover and book design: Mary Jane Karp
Cover photo: Getty Images/Jamie Grill
Curriculum Editor: Bill Bigelow
Proofreading: Lawrence Sanfilippo
Business Manager: Mike Trokan

Library of Congress Cataloging-in-Publication Data
Rethinking elementary education / edited by Linda Christensen ... [et al.].—1st ed.
p. cm.
"A Rethinking Schools Publication."
ISBN 978-0-942961-52-2
1. Elementary school teaching—United States. 2. Social justice—Study and teaching
(Elementary)—United States. I. Christensen, Linda. II. Rethinking schools.
LB1556.5.R48 2012 372.1102—dc23
2012011680

Contents

Introduction

Barbara Miner

In the best of times elementary teachers are thoughtful surrogate parents, nurses, counselors, social workers, listeners, disciplinarians, teachers, and preachers. In the worst of times we are all those things too, but perhaps not so thoughtful, more quick tempered, and overwhelmed with the demands of our jobs and the problems of those who we teach and care for.

We believe that teaching elementary school children is one of the most challenging occupations in the world—among the most rewarding under good conditions, and one of the most frustrating under poor ones. What amazes us is that even with massive budget cuts and rising class sizes, even with the gutting of the arts, physical education, and libraries, even with all the mandated testing and scripted curriculum, staff at elementary schools still welcome each new school year with fresh anticipation. There's an almost naive hopefulness that despite the many problems, the upcoming school year will somehow bring new opportunities to teach creatively and help our students to grow and mature.

Why do most elementary teachers have such hopeful notions at the beginning of each school year? What gives elementary school teaching such powerful potential?

The stories, lessons, and testimonies in *Rethinking Elementary Education* answer those questions and many others with such vitality that readers should be left with no doubt that teaching elementary school children is a venerable occupation.

All teaching matters. And all levels of teaching offer unique challenges and opportunities. But the stories in this book reveal that there is something especially powerful and essential about elementary teaching.

First, it's the children. Their curiosity. Their energy. Their sense of fairness. And the fact they've not yet been conditioned to all of the habits and prejudices of adulthood.

Their inquisitiveness is amazing. Questions are endless.

And elementary teaching offers especially rich opportunities to integrate the curriculum. Teaching all subjects with a single class of students lends itself to weaving together math and writing, science and reading, social studies and drama. By doing so, disciplines are not imprisoned in segregated silos, but blended as they are in the real world. Of course, there still needs to be explicit and sequential instruction in core subjects, but those same subjects are most engaging, most motivating to students when they are integrated together—as so many of the articles in this volume explore.

Another feature that makes elementary school teaching so compelling is that young children tend to wear their lives on their sleeves, being only too willing to tell their teacher or educational assistant the burdens—perceived or real—that they carry in the classroom. This makes the important task of connecting to students' lives relatively easy. And connecting children's lives with those of their families and their families' heritages in turn motivates students, and deepens educators' relationships with students and families.

Young children's minds are like sponges, soaking up the most obscure, profound, (and sometimes erroneous!) things imaginable. The challenge for teachers is to engender the disposition and the skills required to critically look at all that bombards our students daily—from the endless stream of advertising, to their dull textbooks, to one-sided news reports, to the video games and TV shows, to racist and prejudicial jokes and comments they might hear.

Moreover such critical dispositions and questioning can set the stage to encourage children to act on what they've learned—to have "civic courage," to act as if we live in a democracy. We are not talking about telling students how a teacher thinks their parents should vote, but rather to create a learning community in the classroom that models and thinks hard about values of justice and empathy.

The powerful potential of teaching in elementary school, in fact the very craft of teaching, has never been as endangered as it is now. If there ever has been a time when we need to rethink what is going on in elementary education, it is now.

Federal and state mandates, often developed by people decades away from the classroom, and enforced by administrators who have either forgotten or compromised what they know is right for children, are directly assaulting the teaching profession. Whether it's absurdly rigid pacing guides or lifeless scripted curriculum, or an unnatural obsession with testing, our craft is under attack. These policies discourage curriculum integration, problem-posing curriculum, linking teaching to students' needs and interests, creative projects and performances, and the acknowledgement that "teachable moments" arrive at the most unexpected times.

Just as public space in our society shrinks as the forces of privatization seek to destroy the public sector, so too does the pedagogical space shrivel as policy makers attach their futures to flawed quick fixes and scapegoating of teachers, our unions, and our students.

We need child-driven teaching—not data-driven instruction. We need to create the spaces in our classrooms and our schools for engaging projects, role plays, dramas, and experiments. We need to help children talk back to textbooks, examine what's going on in their community and talk together about what role they can play to make their classroom, their community, and the world a more just and democratic place. The articles in this book are powerful examples of how to do just that.

But as we create those spaces—and, we hope, entire schools—that rethink elementary education, a huge challenge for teachers is to remain hopeful in these turbulent times. Too often, elementary teachers comply with unsound mandates and do not defend the craft of teaching, fearful of being isolated from colleagues or being called out by an administrator. This is particularly a problem for new teachers who have experienced little else than the yoke of scripted curriculum. This yoke not only inhibits more creative and critical approaches to teaching, but it also warps new teachers' perception of what good teaching is all about. In too many cases, the stress of such unsound practices pushes them out of the teaching profession.

We know that the only way to sustain hope over a long teaching career is to recognize that we cannot do it alone. Part of "rethinking elementary education" entails rethinking how we nurture ourselves as thoughtful, critical, and committed educators. We've done this through involvement in book circles, union caucuses, teacher social justice groups, parent-teacher collaboratives, and broader movements for social justice. Some of us have been involved in teacher collectives, like the Oregon Writing Project, where we work on developing social justice curriculum. And some of us have been involved in starting innovative public schools, like La Escuela Fratney in Milwaukee—a two-way bilingual, social justice school—where the learning community of caring staff, parents, and students has sustained committed teaching for years.

We also stay positive through reveling in and celebrating the amazing things the children do—the role plays, the projects, the poetry readings, the thinking, and ultimately their excitement in learning and trying to change the world. Every time a child's curiosity and sense of justice blossoms in the classroom we are reassured that the current regime of data-drenched, scripted, narrow curriculum will eventually fall.

Human sensibility will prevail and we will once again strive to educate the whole child, engaging students in meaningful education, treating young children as they deserve to be treated.

As we rethink the ways of teaching that are currently being pushed by educational corporations, policy makers, and many administrators, we must rehearse our craft in all the spaces we can secure. We need to show what is good, what motivates students, and what helps all students, especially those who in the past have been too quickly abandoned. We need to demand that our unions and professional associations fight so that schools can be more than just places to train students to "compete in the global economy." We need engaging, caring classrooms where children acquire the love of learning, the habit of carrying a book (paper or digital) at all times, the "skill" of being able to name what is just—to dig deeply to see behind the statements of government officials and corporate apologists. We want children to come to stand with their friends, their neighbors, and those around the planet who they may never meet, in our common quest to realign our human societies with the natural world, and seek justice for all. ■

Rob Lewine

1.

Building Classroom Community

Building community is not a straightforward task. There's no checklist to be ticked off in the opening days of the school year with a few name games and a set of rules. Building community takes time and a willingness to pay attention to students as they work and play and talk, listening in to determine places where a story or a writing assignment or a unit might be needed. Constructing safe classrooms for children requires a curriculum that bends to students' needs as issues about race, class, gender, death, and difference arise.

The Challenge of Classroom Discipline

Involving students in decision-making helps build a cooperative community

BOB PETERSON

One of the most challenging tasks in any elementary classroom is to build a community where students respect one another and value learning. Too often, children use put-downs to communicate, resolve conflicts violently, and have negative attitudes toward school and learning. These problems often are based in society. How can one tell students not to use put-downs, for example, when that is the predominant style of comedy on prime-time television?

But schools often contribute to such problems. Approaches based on lecturing by teachers, passive reading of textbooks, and "fill-in-the-blank" worksheets keep students from making decisions, from becoming actively involved in their learning, and from learning how to think and communicate effectively.

Involving Students in Decision-Making

If a teacher wants to build a community of learners, a number of things have to happen. Students need to be involved in making decisions. They need to work regularly in groups. They need a challenging curriculum that involves not only listening but actually doing as well. They need to understand that it is OK to make mistakes, that learning involves more than getting the "right" answer.

At the same time, teachers need to make sure that students are not set up for failure. Teachers need to model what it means to work independently and in groups so that those who have not learned that outside of school will not be disadvantaged. Teachers need to be clear about what is and what is not within the purview of student decision-making. And teachers need to learn to build schoolwide support for this kind of learning and teaching.

The parameters of students' decision-making range from choosing what they write, read, and study, to deciding the nature of their collaborative projects, to helping establish the classroom's rules and curriculum.

Each year I have students discuss their vision of an ideal classroom and the rules necessary in such a classroom. I explain how certain rules are made by the state government, by the school board, by the school itself, and by the classroom teacher. I let kids know that I will be willing to negotiate certain rules, but that my willingness to agree to their proposals (because ultimately I hold authority in the classroom) is dependent on two things: the soundness of their ideas and their ability as a group to show that they are responsible enough to assume decision-making power. I also tell kids that if they disagree with rules made outside of the classroom, they should voice their concerns.

Things don't always go smoothly. One year while discussing school rules the kids were adamant that anybody who broke a rule should sit in a corner with a dunce cap on his or her head. I refused on the grounds that it was humiliating. Eventually we worked out other consequences including time-outs and loss of the privilege to come to the classroom during lunch recess.

The cooperative learning technique of the "T-Chart" is helpful in getting kids to understand what a community of learners looks like during different activities. The teacher draws a big "T" on the board and titles the left side "looks like" and the right side "sounds like." Kids brainstorm what an outside visitor would see and hear during certain activities. For example, when we make a "T-chart" about how to conduct a class discussion, students list things like "one person talking" under "sounds like" and "kids looking at the speaker" and "children with their hands raised" under "looks like." We hang the T-chart on the wall; this helps most children remember what is appropriate behavior for different activities.

A well-organized class that is respectful and involves the students in some decision-making is a prerequisite for successful learning.

Classroom organization is another essential ingredient in building a community of learners. The desks in my class are in five groups of six each, which serve as "base groups." I divide the students into these base groups every nine weeks, taking into account language dominance, race, gender, and special needs, creating heterogeneous groups to guard against those subtle forms of elementary school "tracking."

Dividing Students into Base Groups

Throughout the day children might work in a variety of cooperative learning groups, but their base group remains the same. Each group has its own bookshelf where materials are kept and homework turned in. Each group elects its own captain who makes sure that materials are in order and that his or her group members are "with the program." For example, before writing workshop, captains distribute writing folders to all students and make sure that everyone is prepared with a sharpened pencil.

Sometimes the group that is the best prepared to start a new activity, for example, will be allowed to help in dramatization or be the class helpers for that lesson. This provides incentive for team captains to get even the most recalcitrant students to join in with classroom activities.

By organizing the students this way, many of the management tasks are taken on by the students, creating a sense of collective responsibility. Arranging the students in these base groups has the added advantage of freeing up classroom space for dramatizations or classroom meetings where kids sit on the floor.

When students use their decision-making power unwisely, I quickly restrict that power. During reading time, for example, students are often allowed to choose their own groups and books. Most work earnestly, reading cooperatively and writing regularly in their reading response journals. If a reading group has trouble settling down, I intervene rapidly and give increasingly restrictive options to the students. Other students who work successfully in reading groups model how a reading group should be run: The students not only conduct a discussion in front of the class, but also plan in advance for a student to be inattentive and show how a student discussion leader might respond.

A well-organized class that is respectful and involves the students in some decision-making is a prerequisite for successful learning. Cooperative organization and student involvement alone won't make a class critical or even build a community of learners, but they are essential building blocks in its foundation. ∎

....

Bob Peterson (REPMilw@aol.com) was a co-founder and 5th-grade teacher at La Escuela Fratney in Milwaukee for 22 years, a founding editor of Rethinking Schools *magazine, and serves as president of the Milwaukee Teachers' Education Association. He has co-edited numerous books including:* Rethinking Columbus, Rethinking Our Classrooms, Rethinking Globalization, *and* Rethinking Mathematics.

Maya Christina Gonzalez

Inner and Outer Worlds

Building community through art and poetry

ANN TRUAX

How does a teacher bring a complicated mix of personalities, backgrounds, ethnicities, abilities, and attitudes into a climate of mutual respect? No pat answer solves every classroom problem, but the key to building community is a deeper knowledge of each other beyond the facades as well as recognition of commonalities within the group. Activities that allow personal disclosure in a nonthreatening way and promote sharing in a safe environment help bridge the gap between individuals. As the Rethinking Schools editors noted in the introduction to *Rethinking Our Classrooms*, "We need to design activities where students learn to trust and care for each other. Classroom life should, to the greatest extent possible, prefigure the kind of democratic and just society we envision and thus contribute to building that society."

During the summer of 2011, I faced the challenge of building community with a diverse group of students when I taught a group of academically challenged 5th and 6th graders in an intensive, five-week writing program. I met with students for five hours four days a week for five weeks as part of a partnership between Portland Public Schools and the Oregon Writing Project. Our students came from various schools in southeast Portland. Among the 22 students, there were two Latinos, five were of Vietnamese descent, five African Americans, 10 European Americans. In that mix, there were 11 girls and 11 boys, nine SPED students, one student with an anxiety disorder, four English Language Learners, one student with serious diabetes, two students diagnosed with attention deficit/hyperactivity disorder, and one student whose mother was in jail. Twenty out of the 22 were eligible for free and reduced lunch. Most had never met each other before. On the first day, the girls chose to sit close to each other, and the boys chose tables dominated by their own gender. Most seemed awkward and unsure of themselves. On the first day, the student with the anxiety disorder broke down in tears and needed to call home for reassurance.

The task was to teach students to write effectively in five weeks, but I knew that I had to build a community before I could get students to take the kinds of risks needed to push their writing forward. I had to move them beyond the safety of fill-in-the-blank worksheets that too often dominate the writing curriculum for struggling students. All the students had writing challenges, as demonstrated in the required pre-assessments. Generally, the boys wrote minimally, rarely more than a paragraph, with few concrete details, no metaphors, clichéd and repetitious verbs, and a lack of sentence fluency. The girls wrote more, but their writing was also vague with lackluster leads, tedious word choice, and anemic verbs. The questions I faced included how to unleash their stories, how to overcome resistance to writing at the same time teaching the craft of writing, how to foster students' confidence as writers, and how to create an environment of mutual support and appreciation.

Self Portraits:
Art as the First Step in Writing

Instead of starting with writing, I opened my instruction with art. As an ESL teacher, I have discovered that images lead to talking and talking leads to writing. Art and conversation are time well spent because they build community, validate the individual, forge new links between students, and ultimately move students into writing. The combination of art and writing is dynamic. Creating art calms students, requires intense focus, and opens a channel for language learning. From the visible, concrete image, students—ELL as well as mainstream—can discuss what they see, ask questions, formulate and expand ideas, learn new vocabulary, and think abstractly. For many students, talking about an image is an important precursor to writing. My first two lessons: "Self-Portraits, Inner and Outer Worlds" and "The Outside/Inside Poem" did just that in a low-stakes environment with multiple opportunities for students to talk to each other and share pieces of their personal histories.

I introduced students to a self-portrait done by the artist Maya Christine Gonzalez.* It is a brightly colored image of a smiling woman dressed in purple and white polka dots with paintbrushes stuck in her hair. A red frame surrounds the self-portrait; two lines of words circle the frame. Gonzalez writes: "The words around the border are things I love, like polka dots and fire, and ways that I feel, like loud and hungry." Gonzalez's self-portrait is an invitation for students to create their own. I put her self-portrait on the document camera and asked students: "What do you notice in her portrait?" Students shared ideas with a partner, then the whole class. Nayisha commented: "She's wearing earrings shaped like hands with eyes on them." Steven said, "Maybe that's because she works with her hands and her eyes." Jenny pointed to what she thought were feathers painted at the bottom, but Julian thought it was a light or fire showing her energy. Then together we read the artist's narrative accompanying her self-portrait. She explained:

One night when I was 5 years old, I woke up and saw a light shining brightly in the corner of my

* Selected art from *Just Like Me* copyright © 1997 by Maya Christina Gonzalez. Permission arranged with Children's Book Press, an imprint of Lee & Low Books, Inc.

room. Some people said it was an angel. Some people said it was a ghost. All I know is it made me feel really happy, like I was special.... In my painting I show the light shining from my heart.

After students read Gonzalez's narrative, I asked: What do you notice about the artist's story? What symbols does she use in her painting? What do you think the symbols mean? Students again shared responses with a partner first, and then with the whole group. I directed students to look at the words around the portrait. I asked, "What kind of words are on the inside line?" Steven immediately noticed they showed her feelings.

I pushed again to provoke more discussion, "What do these words tell us about her?"

Kendra responded, "Sometimes she has different feelings like loud and quiet and happy and sad."

Then I said: "Read the words on the outside line with a partner. What kind of words are they?" Students were quick to determine the words named things she likes: love, green, pencils, dogs, words.

When we finished discussing the pictures, I told students, "Now, you are going to create your own self-portraits combined with words." The students seemed eager to get going.

Word Lists

Before starting the self-portrait, students needed to create two word lists—one for the inner world and one for the outer world—using Gonzalez as a model. I gave a few examples of mood adjectives: sad, lonely, joyous, and so on. Then students added to the list of adjectives as I wrote their suggestions on the overhead. Jenny added, "Crazy." Jorge said, "Mysterious." I shared some of my feeling adjectives (adventurous, anxious, busy, creative, dorky, envious) to show that even the teacher has a mix of positive and negative feelings. Also, I hoped that sharing who I am added incrementally to the level of trust within the room. After the students created their own lists, they shared with a small group.

Then we started the second "outside" list consisting of nouns showing what students like or enjoy. Students again shared their lists, ranging from hoodies to puppies to hanging out to volleyball to go-carts to tank tops. Many students needed a few more minutes to add ideas ignited by their classmates. Conversations

began loosening up as students discovered information about each other. We learned that Chris and Peter loved football, Nyasha lived in a big household with an extended family, Maira was an incurable Justin Bieber fan, Cristy wanted to learn to ice skate, John frequently went fishing with his father, Danny wanted to be a chef, Alicia lived with her grandfather, Lasandra's grandmother had recently died.

Personal Symbol

At this point, we returned to the model and discussed the artist's choice of symbols. I showed my students my self-portrait that incorporated two symbols: snow and wolves. I told the story about my symbols: "I love the energy that snow, the outdoors, and the fresh air give me. Recently, I was on a cross-country ski trip to Yellowstone in winter, where I saw wolves resting after a big meal of elk they had hunted down. I admire these animals for their independence, intelligence, and ability to work together. Now go back to your list of things you love and choose one or two to use as your own personal symbol. Briefly sketch your own symbol or symbols, and then share the image and the story with your small group."

Jamil described his love of basketball and the times he spends with his older brother at the park playing basketball. John's symbol was a sturgeon; he told about going fishing on the Columbia River with his dad and uncle. Danny's symbols were a barbecue and a steak; he loves to barbecue for his family. This continual sharing slowly built students' confidence and comfort level; the groups became more animated, their laughter and noise level demonstrated that they connected. The student with the anxiety disorder appeared comfortable and involved. Jenny and Carla laughed and chatted like long-lost friends even though they had only just met.

The Self-Portrait

I gave students a black-and-white copy of a photo of themselves, which I had taken the day before. I told them to incorporate a personal symbol(s) into the photo. Some students decided to draw their symbols on the photo, and others drew theirs on a separate piece of paper, cut them out, and glued them on top of the photo. The variety of approaches and designs that sprang from this activity was impressive.

Once students completed the self-portraits, they selected a piece of light-colored construction paper (18"x12" is a commonly available size) and glued their portraits onto this background. (The key is to choose construction paper at least two inches wider and taller than the self-portrait—enough space for the inside line of adjectives and the outside line of nouns.) The high level of concentration continued as students wrote their words around the portrait in the frame. Lasandra and Andre laughed with Maira about her obsession with Justin Bieber. Julian didn't like his photo, so he chose to draw his self-portrait instead, impressing his tablemates with his drawing skills.

Gallery Walk

In order to continue building community, language, and confidence, I hosted a gallery walk. I like to give students an opportunity to see and appreciate all the artwork as well as give positive feedback to the artists and make connections between students. I set up the gallery walk with the portraits displayed in the hall. I handed out multiple Post-it notes. To avoid the generic, meaningless statements like "I like it" or "It's great," I modeled specific appreciative statements: "I like how you put musical symbols around your self-portrait." "Playing basketball is important to me, too." "The flower you added to your hair really stands out." "Your self-portrait conveys so much energy and joy." Each student stood in front of a different portrait, wrote the name of the artist on the Post-it, composed a specific, positive comment, signed the Post-it and handed it to me. At a signal, they moved one portrait to the right and repeated the process. I continued this process until their interest and focus began to wane. After I reviewed the comments, I handed them to the appropriate student artists, who were eager to read the responses.

The Poem

The self-portrait provided the perfect catalyst for the subsequent lesson: "The Outside/Inside Poem," which continued our community building, but moved us more squarely into writing. I like this poem because it springs from an immigrant culture, portrays a unique family, has a simple yet strong pattern, and paints a night at home with powerful imagery. I began by reading "The Outside/Inside Poem" by

Sarah Chan. I used different voices for the outside vs. the inside. The students did a choral reading of the poem—one half of the class read the outside lines, and the other half the inside lines. Choral reading is especially helpful for the English Language Learners in the classroom because they can practice the language without feeling self-conscious.

THE OUTSIDE/INSIDE POEM*

By Sarah Chan

Outside the night sneaks up with cat feet.
Inside my sisters listen to Chinese love songs
on the radio and sing along like movie stars.
Outside the snow rests on cars like thick rugs.
Inside my mother rubs circles in my brother's back
telling him stories of how she collected peanuts
from the riverbank after the spring floods in Lion
    Village.
Outside the stars climb into the cold winter sky.
Inside my father wraps our holiday presents,
newspaper and scotch tape crunching behind the
    door.
Outside the crescent moon hangs between the
    branches of a tree.
Inside I help my grandma make dumplings,
    pressing
my hands into the warm dough, shaping it into
    moon-smiles.
Outside the wind talks stories to the streets.
Inside my family stands at the window, holding
    hands,
listening to whispers. The night rubs against the
    glass,
trying to get in.

"Raise the Bones"

After the students became familiar with the poem, we "raised its bones," a term we use in the Oregon Writing Project to mean looking at a poem's skeleton. How did the writer build the poem? I want students to learn to "raise the bones" as they approach new pieces of writing, so they can see how writers approach different genres. After we read the poem

---

*Ada, Alma Flor, Violet J. Harris and Lee Bennet Hopkins, eds. *A Chorus of Cultures Anthology: Developing Literacy Through Multicultural Poetry*. Des Moines, Iowa: Hampton Brown, 1994.

together, students highlighted lines that resonated and then shared with a partner. When we returned to the whole group, a few students shared a favorite line, like "Outside the snow rests on cars like thick rugs." Peter noticed the comparison of the night to cat in the first and last lines. I was able to discuss how the poet used similes and metaphors in the context of the poem. We also looked at how Sarah Chan structured her poem, using repeating lines that begin outside or inside. Students noted the contrast between the coziness of the inside and the cold night outside. Inside the family was busy and interacting; outside it was lonely and dark.

To prepare students to write their own poems, I had students experiment with writing metaphors. I referred them back to their self-portraits and directed them to take one of their nouns from the outside line. "Let's take Jamil's word 'basketball,'" I said as I wrote the phrase "Outside I am a basketball" on the document camera. "Notice how I extend the metaphor by adding a verb phrase, such as 'Outside I am a basketball pounding on the concrete.' Now let's look at Andre's lion. I might add, 'Outside I am a lion dreaming in the shade.' In my self-portrait I wrote, 'Outside I am a wolf.' I added the verb phrase 'loping across the snow.'" After the students wrote one or two metaphors or added verb phrases, a few students volunteered to read theirs aloud. Caitlyn wrote, "Outside I am snow dropping like leaves." Lasandra wrote, "I am a bubble trying to pop." An wrote, "Inside I am a pink shirt living in the closet."

Again, the movement between writing and sharing is an important piece of building a classroom community where students see each other more fully, but where they also learn with and from each other. The best moments are when students crowd together, sharing their lines, laughing or nodding at each other's wisdom.

Write the Poem

As we moved into writing the poem, I modeled my process first on a T-chart, listing inside pieces on one side and outside on the other. As students began their own writing, I reminded them, "Don't judge your ideas. Just let them flow and let one idea lead into the next." After the T-chart brainstorming session, they composed the poem in the Outside/Inside format, using some of the metaphors and verb phrases from their previous brainstorming.

When students finished the first draft, I handed out the poetry checklist and asked them to highlight in one color all the specific details that created a clear image and in another color an example of a metaphor or simile. I asked for volunteers to share their poems on the document camera. Because of the sharing we had already done, many students were willing to place their poems in full view. I reminded them that we were looking for and appreciating specific details and figurative language. We were not judges or critics. I then gave students time to revise, followed by a final read-around. Again, we only applauded students' efforts because a focus on individual strengths builds the confidence and cohesion of the entire community.

At a time when teachers are forced to do whatever it takes to improve test scores, we must pause to remember that when we systematically construct a classroom around students' lives and cultures, we can raise academic expectations while we build a community where students feel both safe and significant. These two lessons serve many purposes: as an icebreaker, as a writing craft lesson, as a grammar lesson, and, most importantly, as a community builder. Students forged connections with peers; they laughed together; others listened to them; and they moved beyond stereotypes and shared their real selves in a safe, appreciative environment. They also revisited grammar and figurative language in the context of genuine writing and made revisions according to clear criteria. From this small opening lesson, our class took an important step toward building a community of writers and learners who support and inspire each other in an atmosphere of acceptance and respect. ▪

....

Ann Truax retired from teaching ESL in Portland Public Schools and works as a writing coach with the Oregon Writing Project.

Abe Herzog-Arbeitman, 2nd grade, Northampton, Mass.

Heather's Moms Got Married

Second graders talk about gay marriage

MARY COWHEY

Last spring, my 2nd graders gathered on the rug, discussing the impending 50th anniversary of the historic *Brown v. Board of Education* decision. I asked how their lives would have been different without *Brown*.

"I wouldn't have all these friends ... 'cause I wouldn't know them," said Sadie.*

Michelle raised her hand and said, "I wouldn't exist." Michelle is a biracial girl, with an African American mother and white, Jewish father. Her mother Barbara had stayed for morning meeting that day, and she elaborated:

"Because of *Brown*, I was able to get a good education and went to a college that was integrated. That's where I met Michelle's dad. We fell in love and decided to get married."

Samuel, who is Panamanian and Pakistani, said, "My mom is brown and my stepdad is white, and they got married." He turned to ask Barbara, "In those days could a brown person and a white person get married?" Barbara said they got married in Massachusetts in 1985, and it wasn't a problem.

Angela, an African American girl, had quietly been following the discussion and finally raised her hand. "Because of that [the *Brown* decision], things are more fair, like I can go to this school and have all different friends. Still, not everything is fair, and that makes me sad."

Sadie asked Angela what still wasn't fair. "Well, your parents could get married, because you have a mom and a dad, but I have two moms and they can't get married. That's not fair."

Sadie considered this for an instant before asking, "Who made that stupid rule?"

With the honesty and incisive thinking I cherish in 2nd graders, Angela and Sadie had cut to the chase. When it comes to discussing gay marriage in 2nd grade, these are the

---

*Most students' names have been changed, except for those with last names. They asked to have their real names published in the interest of modeling family pride to others.

questions that matter most: Is it fair to exclude some families from the right to marry? Who made that rule (and how is it changing)?

I should pause here to say that I don't teach in Anytown, U.S.A. I teach in Northampton, a small city of 29,000 in western Massachusetts, which has been known as a haven for women and for lesbians. Northampton's status as a refuge from homophobia has been profiled in dozens of newspapers and media outlets around the country and around the world.

While the numbers vary from year to year, I have always had at least one child in my class with lesbian parents. That spring, one-third of my students had lesbian parents. While I probably have more lesbian-parented families than most teachers, the reality is that teachers may not know by looking if they have a child with gay or lesbian parents, aunts, uncles, grandparents, or family friends.

I teach at Jackson St. School (JSS), a public elementary school with about 400 students. Our school is a celebration of economic, racial, linguistic, and family diversity. Families speak a variety of home languages including Albanian, Spanish, Khmer, Vietnamese, Chinese, French, and Hindu. About 39 percent of the students are children of color, with the largest share of those being Puerto Rican. Forty percent of the students receive free or reduced lunch.

The school welcomes family involvement, with a weekly family newsletter and regular potluck dinners. It has a Family Center, which hosts a weekly Parents' Hour with coffee and conversation, as well as a family portrait project, in which a professional photographer takes free family portraits at Open House. These photos are displayed in the front hallway, heralding for all visitors the breadth of the school's diversity. Over the years, many parents have told me that even before speaking to anyone in the school, just looking at those family photos in the front lobby made them feel welcome, like they could fit in.

An Eye-Opener

I began teaching at Jackson St. School eight years ago, fresh out of my teacher-preparation program. I decided to start the school year with home visits to my new students and their families. At one of the first homes I visited, a parent greeted me wearing a button that said, "We're here. We're gay. And we're on the PTA." Beth and

Karen Bellavance-Grace began talking about being foster parents for the state Department of Social Services and being adoptive parents. As we began talking about family diversity issues, I asked if they would be willing to advise me on good books and teaching ideas. My education in teaching family diversity and learning from my families began on the first day of my teaching career, before I even set foot in my classroom.

> ## When I speak to teachers and future teachers about gay and lesbian issues in elementary schools, they often ask how I can "get away with that."

When I speak to teachers and future teachers about gay and lesbian issues in elementary schools, they often ask how I can "get away with that." This is particularly ironic in Massachusetts, which was one of the first states to recognize the rights and needs of gay and lesbian youth in schools. In 1993, during the administration of Republican Gov. William Weld, the Massachusetts Governor's Commission on Gay and Lesbian Youth recommended that:

- high schools establish policies protecting gay and lesbian youth from harassment, violence, and discrimination.

- teachers and counselors receive professional development to respond to the needs of these students.

- schools establish support groups (gay-straight alliances).

- schools "develop curriculum that incorporates gay and lesbian themes and subject matters into all disciplines, in an age-appropriate manner."

Despite that progressive policy, established under a Republican governor, teacher self-censorship, often based on the fear of raising potentially controversial topics, remains the status quo in many schools. Another problem, as progressive as the Weld commission's report was, is that it focused solutions primarily at the secondary level, with gay-straight alliances and so forth. Most people still get queasy talking about gay and lesbian issues at middle or—heaven forbid—elementary levels.

Teaching About Same-Sex Couples

In my classroom, issues of family diversity often arise spontaneously. Once a group of my 1st-grade readers decided to act out *The Carrot Seed*, a simple story about a boy who plants a carrot seed and cares for it diligently, despite the discouragement of his brother, mother, and father. After the skit, all the other students wanted a chance to act it out too. I said we could do it once more before lunch. I began pulling sticks with student names at random from a cup, to assign the four roles. After I pulled the first three sticks, a boy had already claimed the part of the brother. One girl had taken the role of the mother and another girl had taken the role of the kid who plants the seed. The last stick I pulled was Natalie's, and the remaining role was for the father. A boy quickly said I should pull another stick. Natalie sprang to her feet without hesitation. "That's okay!" she said, "I'll be the other mom!"

In 2003, same-sex marriage became legal in Massachusetts. Heidi and Gina Nortonsmith, parents of one of my students, had been plaintiffs in the *Goodridge v. Mass. Department of Public Health* landmark lawsuit that resulted in the legalization of same-sex marriage in our state. They were given the first place in line at Northampton's crowded City Hall on the morning of May 17 to get their marriage license.

After the court's decision, my students got "marriage fever." During "sharing time" Maggy reported on how she was the flower girl and her sister was the "ring barrier" at their friends' wedding. Avery Nortonsmith proudly showed the silver ID bracelet that he, his brother, and his moms all got on their wedding day, inscribed with the historic date. Sarah talked excitedly about preparations for her moms' wedding, how she and her sister and six of their girlfriends would be flower girls. I went to the wedding with my daughter and saw about half the families from my class. It was one of the most joyous and supportive celebrations I have ever witnessed.

My 5-year-old daughter caught the fever too, and conducted wedding after wedding in her imaginary play. Each night she'd say, "Come on Mom and Dad, you're getting married tonight." "We got married eight years ago," my husband would remind her. Undeterred, my daughter would say, "No, that was your commitment ceremony, but this is gonna be your wedding."

Even snack time conversations raise the issue of gay marriage. Beth Bellavance-Grace, who now works as an aide at our school, told me about a kindergarten conversation she heard. A girl announced to her table, "I know who I'm gonna marry when I grow up. I'm gonna marry Ella."

"You can't marry a girl," a boy at her table replied.

"That was just in the olden days," she replied. "But now I can."

Discussing Diversity

When we discuss family diversity, I define family as "the circle of people who love you." After I showed *That's a Family* one year, Marisol responded, "Yuck, that is so weird to have two dads!"

James turned to her and spoke with an air of sophistication. "What's the big deal about two dads?" he asked. "I got two dads. I got one in my house and one in the jail. Lots of kids gots two dads."

Marisol considered this a moment, then said, "Oh, I didn't think of that. I have two moms. I have my mom at home and a stepmom at my dad's house."

"See?" James said with a shrug of his shoulders. "I told you it's not so weird."

I had one student who was co-parented by three women. One morning we were having a math exhibition and the students had invited their parents. Thomas' three moms came in one at a time, each from their different jobs. James knew that his parents wouldn't be attending, but he kept looking to the door whenever another parent entered. He finally went over to Thomas and asked, "It be OK if I could borrow one of your moms?"

I wish many Americans would approach the issue of same-sex marriage with the same openness as my 2nd graders. The refusal to extend equal rights to families with gay and lesbian parents hurts children like my students, giving them the message their families are not equal, are somehow inferior. And, as my 2nd graders will tell you: That's not fair. ▪

....

Mary Cowhey teaches Title 1 Math at Jackson St. School. She is the author of Black Ants and Buddhists: Thinking Critically and Teaching Differently in the Primary Grades.

Creating a Gay- and Lesbian-Friendly Classroom

MARY COWHEY

When it comes to issues of family diversity, teacher self-censorship remains the status quo in many schools. Often this is based on the fear of raising potentially controversial topics. When schools do get involved in promoting gay-straight alliances and so forth, it is usually at the secondary level. Most people still get queasy talking about gay and lesbian issues at middle or — heaven forbid — elementary levels.

Based on my experiences over the course of eight years of teaching, here are some of my recommendations for teachers in elementary schools:

Do not presume that students live in traditional families with both married heterosexual birth parents. Name a wide variety of configurations possible in the diversity of human families. Part of that naming process includes using books and resources that portray family diversity, including the video *That's a Family*. (See p. 14 for more resources.) Invite students to respond to the question "Who is in your family?" Allow students to share and display their family stories and pictures.

Explore and challenge gender stereotypes with your students. Use children's books such as *Amazing Grace, William's Doll, Oliver Button Is a Sissy, China's Bravest Girl: the Legend of Hua Mu Lan, Riding Freedom,* and *Beautiful Warrior* as springboards for discussions. Activities can include students brainstorming lists of stereotypical behavior for boys and girls, then making captioned drawings of boys and girls engaging in nonstereotypical behaviors. These can be made into a class book or hallway display: "Boys Can/Girls Can." Once students learn to question gender stereotypes, they can recognize and reflect on stereotypical characters and behaviors in other books and media. They can extend their understandings of stereotypes to recognize and challenge other forms of bias.

Teach a lesson on teasing and name-calling. Children's literature, such as *Oliver Button Is a Sissy* or *The Hundred Dresses* can be an excellent point of departure for discussion and activities. These can help establish a baseline of classroom expectations that we are all respected members of this classroom community and that no put-downs will be tolerated.

Answer students' questions about gay and lesbian issues in a straightforward, educational manner. Do not ignore or quash their curiosity. Remember that the two main points of reference are respecting differences and equality for all people. Elementary children are not asking about sexuality. When they ask what "gay" means, it's sufficient to say, "Gay is when a woman loves a woman or a man loves a man in a romantic way."

Replace the phrase "moms and dads" with "parents and guardians" in your classroom and in your school. Do this in informal conversation, classroom teaching, and official school documents such as registration forms and emergency cards. Not only is this phrase more inclusive for students with gay or lesbian parents, but also for those being raised by foster parents, grandparents, aunts, and others. It accepts and affirms all of the families in your school.

Consider showing a video like *Oliver Button Is a Star* as part of a professional development workshop for faculty and staff. *Oliver Button Is a Star* is a documentary that weaves a reading and musical production of *Oliver Button Is a Sissy* with interviews with adults like arctic explorer Ann Bancroft, author/illustrator Tomie dePaola, and dancer Bill T. Jones, who recall their childhood experiences. It includes scenes (some from my classroom) where 1st and 2nd graders do activities about name-calling and challenging gender stereotypes. *That's a Family* and *It's Elementary* are good choices too.

In the event that you encounter an intolerant colleague, administrator, or parent, keep the following points in mind:

- The diversity of families in our school is more beautiful and complex than any one of us could presume to know. Whether we have any self-identified ("out") gay- or lesbian-parented families in our school community or not, it is safer to assume that they are here than not.

- An estimated one in 10 students may grow up to be gay or lesbian adults.

- All of our students deserve a safe and supportive school experience.

- Gays and lesbians are entitled to the same rights as others. We are talking about equal rights, not special rights.

- We are not talking about "sexuality" when we discuss gay and lesbian issues any more than we are discussing sexuality when we read Cinderella or any other story with all heterosexual characters.

Resources on Family Diversity

All Families Are Different
Nonfiction
By Sol Gordon
Prometheus Books, 2000, 50 pp.

Written by a clinical psychologist, this illustrated book for readers 7 and older defines families in multiple ways, considering economic and racial factors as well as including same-sex, divorced, and foster parents.

All Families Are Special
Fiction
By Norma Simon
Albert Whitman and Company, 2003, 32 pp.

A teacher tells her students she is going to be a grandmother, initiating a conversation about family diversity in which students share how their home lives are similar or different. Colorful illustrations complement an appropriately sensitive book for young readers.

Families All Matter Book Project
Curriculum
aMaze, PO Box 17417, Minneapolis, MN 55417
www.amazeworks.org

This literature-based elementary school curriculum includes annotated lists of children's books, creative activities, and a teachers' guide. Many aspects of family diversity are covered.

That's a Family: A Film for Kids About Family Diversity
Nonfiction, VHS and DVD
Women's Educational Media, 2180 Bryant St., Ste. 203, San Francisco, CA 94110
www.groundspark.org

Children's voices are central to this gentle approach to talking about and developing respect for family diversity.

Katherine Streeter

It's OK to Be Neither

Teaching that supports gender-variant children

MELISSA BOLLOW TEMPEL

Allie arrived at our 1st-grade classroom wearing a sweatshirt with a hood. I asked her to take off her hood, and she refused. I thought she was just being difficult and ignored it. After breakfast we got in line for art, and I noticed that she still had not removed her hood. When we arrived at the art room, I said: "Allie, I'm not playing. It's time for art. The rule is no hoods or hats in school."

She looked up with tears in her eyes and I realized there was something wrong. Her classmates went into the art room and we moved to the art storage area so her classmates wouldn't hear our conversation. I softened my tone and asked her if she'd like to tell me what was wrong.

"My ponytail," she cried.

"Can I see?" I asked.

She nodded and pulled down her hood. Allie's braids had come undone overnight and there hadn't been time to redo them in the morning, so they had to be put back in a ponytail. It was high up on the back of her head like those of many girls in our class, but I could see that to Allie it just felt wrong. With Allie's permission, I took the elastic out and re-braided her hair so it could hang down.

"How's that?" I asked.

She smiled. "Good," she said and skipped off to join her friends in art.

"Why Do You Look Like a Boy?"

Allison was biologically a girl but felt more comfortable wearing Tony Hawk long-sleeved T-shirts, baggy jeans, and black tennis shoes. Her parents were accepting and supportive. Her mother braided her hair in cornrows because Allie thought it made her look like Will Smith's son, Trey, in the remake of *The Karate Kid*. She preferred to be called Allie. The first day of school, children who hadn't been in Allie's class in kindergarten referred to her as "he."

I didn't want to assume I knew how Allie wanted me to respond to the continual gender mistakes, so I made a phone call home and Allie's mom put me on speakerphone.

"Allie," she said, "Ms. Melissa is on the phone. She would like to know if you want her to correct your classmates when they say you are a boy, or if you would rather that she just doesn't say anything."

Allie was shy on the phone. "Um … tell them that I am a girl," she whispered.

The next day when I corrected classmates and told them that Allie was a girl, they asked her a lot of questions that she wasn't prepared for: "Why do you look like a boy?" "If you're a girl, why do you always wear boys' clothes?" Some even told her that she wasn't supposed to wear boys' clothes if she was a girl. It became evident that I would have to address gender directly in order to make the classroom environment more comfortable for Allie and to squash the gender stereotypes that my 1st graders had absorbed in their short lives.

Gender Training Starts Early

Gender is not a subject that I would have broached in primary grades a few years ago. In fact, I remember scoffing with colleagues when we heard about a young kindergarten teacher who taught gender-related curriculum. We thought her lessons were a waste of instructional time and laughed at her "girl and boy" lessons.

My own thoughts about gender curriculum shifted when I became a mother. As I shopped for infant clothes for my first daughter, I was disgusted that almost everything was pink and there was no mistaking the boys' section of the store from the girls'. I refused to make my baby daughter fit in the box that society had created for her. "What if she doesn't like pink?" I thought. "What if she likes tigers and dinosaurs?"

As my two daughters grew, I talked with them about gender stereotypes. I let them choose "boys'" clothes if they wanted to (and often encouraged them because they are more practical). The first week of kindergarten, my younger daughter's teacher told me that she had a heated argument with a boy while they played dress up. "She insisted that boys can wear dresses if they want to," the teacher told me. I beamed with pride.

Unfortunately, it wasn't until I had a child dealing with gender variance (defined as "behavior or gender expression that does not conform to dominant gender norms of male and female") in my classroom that I realized how important it is to teach about gender and break down gender stereotypes. Why did I wait so long? I should have taken a hint from that kindergarten teacher years ago. As I thought about how to approach the topic, I realized that the lessons I was developing weren't just for Allie. She had sparked my thinking, but all the children in my class needed to learn to think critically about gender stereotypes and gender nonconformity.

We started off with a lesson about toys because it's a simple topic I knew my students thought they had clear ideas about. The class gathered on the carpet and I read *William's Doll*, which is about a boy who, against the wishes of his father, wants a doll more than anything.

After we read the story, I taped up two large pieces of paper and wrote "Boys" on one and "Girls" on the other. "Students," I said, "what are some toys that are for boys?" Eagerly, the students began to shout out their answers: "Legos!" "Hot Wheels!" "Skateboards!" "Bikes!" The list grew quite long. "OK," I said, "now tell me some toys that are for girls." "Baby dolls!" "Nail polish!" "Barbies!" "Makeup!"

When we had two extensive lists, I read both lists out loud to the class and then studied them carefully.

"Hmm," I said. "Here it says that Legos are for boys. Can girls play with Legos?"

"Yes!" most of them replied without hesitation.

"I wonder if any of the girls in our class like to play with Hot Wheels?"

"I do! I do!" blurted out some of the girls. We continued with the rest of the items on our "Boys" list, making a check mark next to each one as it was declared acceptable for girls.

Then we went on to the "Girls" list. We started with baby dolls. Because we had just read and discussed *William's Doll*, the children were OK with boys playing with dolls. "It's great practice for boys who want to be daddies when they grow up," I mentioned.

But when we got to nail polish and makeup the children were unsure. "There are some very famous rock 'n' roll bands," I said, "and the men in those bands wear a lot of makeup." Some of the children gasped.

Then Isabela raised her hand: "Sometimes my uncle wears black nail polish." The students took a moment to think about this.

"My cousin wears nail polish, too!" said another student. Soon many students were eager to share examples of how people pushed the limits on gender. Our school engineer, Ms. Joan, drove a motorcycle. Jeremy liked to dance. I could see the gears turning in their brains as the gender lines started to blur.

Supporting Gender Variance Every Day

I knew that broadening my students' ideas of what was acceptable for boys and girls was an important first step, but to make Allie feel comfortable and proud of herself, I was going to have to go further.

For example, as teachers, we often use gender to divide students into groups or teams. It seems easy and obvious. Many of us do this when we line students up to go to the bathroom. In one conversation that I had with Allie's mother, she told me that Allie did not like using public bathrooms because many times Allie would be accused of being in the wrong bathroom. As soon as she told me I felt bad. By dividing the children into two lines by assigned gender, I had unintentionally made the children whose labels aren't so clear feel uncomfortable in more ways than one.

When we lined up to go to the bathroom, I kept my students in one line until we reached the bathroom, and then let them separate to enter their bathrooms. Allie usually said she didn't need to use the bathroom. The few times that she did, I offered the bathroom around the corner, a single-stall bathroom that was usually unoccupied. When the kids came out of the bathroom, they wanted to line up as most classrooms do, in boys' and girls' lines. Instead, I thought up a new way for them to line up each day. For example: "If you like popsicles, line up here. If you like ice cream, line up here." They loved this and it kept them entertained while they waited for their classmates. Here are a few more examples:

Which would you choose?
- Skateboard/Bike
- Milk/Juice
- Dogs/Cats
- Hot day/Snow day
- Fiction/Nonfiction
- Soccer/Basketball
- Beach/Pool

I also became very aware of using the phrase "boys and girls" to address my students. Instead, I used gender-neutral terms like "students" or "children." At first, the more I thought about it, the more often I'd say "boys and girls." I tried not to be too hard on myself when I slipped, and eventually I got out of the habit and used "students" regularly.

Around the same time, another child's mother told me that her son had been taunted for wearing a Hello Kitty Band-Aid. She mentioned that his sister was also teased at school for having a lunch bag with skulls on it. I planned more lessons to combat gender stereotypes in our classroom.

"It's OK to Be Different"

In order to deepen our discussion of gender, I selected another read-aloud. Before we read, I asked my students: "I would like to know—how many of you like to dance?" Most raised their hands.

"How many of you have been told you can't do something because it was 'only for boys' or 'only for girls'?" Many hands went up.

Then I read *Oliver Button Is a Sissy*. In the book, Oliver is bullied because he prefers dancing to sports.

The students quickly realized that this was not fair and empathized with Oliver Button.

The following day we read *It's Okay to Be Different* by Todd Parr. Parr's books are quite popular in the primary grades because they include an element of humor and simple, colorful illustrations. We read:

It's OK to wear glasses.
It's OK to come from a different place.
It's OK to be a different color.

As we read, I asked questions to empower the students: "Who used to live in a different place?" Students proudly held up their hands. "Awesome!" I replied. "My mom comes from a different place, too. She used to live in Hong Kong."

Then I guided the direction of the conversation toward gender. As a class, we brainstormed a list of things that students thought were "OK" even though they might challenge society's gender norms. Monica told us very matter-of-factly, "It's OK for a girl to marry a girl," and Jordan said, "My dad carries a purse and that's OK!" At that point I explained that my father and my friend Wayne both call their man purse a "murse." The children were fascinated.

Toward the end of the discussion I explained: "People make all kinds of different decisions about gender. Sometimes, as we grow, we might not want to pick one or the other, and that's OK; we don't have to." I wanted them to begin to see that our lessons were not only about expanding the gender boxes that we've been put into, but also questioning or eliminating them altogether.

Afterward, I had the students do a simple write-and-respond exercise. I asked them to pick one activity that they associated with girls and one associated with boys to write about and illustrate. Monica drew two brides in beautiful wedding gowns. Miguel drew a man with a purse slung over his shoulder. I showed off the pictures on the hallway bulletin board around the words "It's OK to Be Different."

Although things were getting better for Allie, she still faced many challenges. At the end of the school year, Allie's mother told me a heartbreaking story. She said that for Allie's recent birthday party, her grandmother had bought her colorful, formfitting clothes and then demanded them back when Allie did not like them. "Does she know she is a girl?" she yelled, and announced she would never buy her clothes again.

It was so sad to hear this. I visualized Allie on her special day, excitedly ripping open gifts in front of her family and friends only to find, again and again, the gifts were things that she would never be comfortable with. As a mother, the feeling of extreme disappointment was unbearable for me to imagine.

I have just begun to empathize with the challenges that gender-variant children deal with. For some it may seem inappropriate to address these issues in the classroom. My job is not to answer the questions "Why?" or "How?" Allie is the way she is (although asking those questions and doing some research in order to better understand was definitely part of my process). My job is not to judge, but to teach, and I can't teach if the students in my class are distracted or uncomfortable. My job is also about preparing students to be a part of our society, ready to work and play with all kinds of people. I found that teaching about gender stereotypes is another social justice issue that needs to be addressed, like racism or immigrant rights, or protecting the environment.

Later in the year, I opened my inbox one morning and read: "Andrew says he wants a Baby Alive doll and he doesn't care if it's for girls. Thank you, Ms. Melissa!" ▪

....

Melissa Bollow Tempel (meljoytempel@gmail.com) works as a teacher for the students of the Milwaukee Public Schools and is an editor of Rethinking Schools.

Resources

dePaola, Tomie. *Oliver Button Is a Sissy*. Orlando, Fla.: Sandpiper Books, 1979.

Parr, Todd. *It's Okay to Be Different*. New York: Little, Brown Books for Young Readers, 2007.

Zolotow, Charlotte. *William's Doll*. New York: Harper & Row Publishers, 1985.

For more information: http://www.acceptingdad.com/supportive-book-media-for-gender-variant-non-conforming-kids.

Alain Pilon

Peers, Power, and Privilege

The social world of a 2nd-grade classroom

LAUREN G. MEDNICK

I vividly remember standing at the door of my classroom on the first day in my new school, a highly regarded urban magnet school. I was 8 years old, and I looked around at my classmates — they were so different from those at my old private school where everyone had pretty much looked like me. Here were kids with a wide variety of skin colors, hairstyles, and clothes. I wanted to throw myself into the classroom and become friends with them all!

Unfortunately, it did not turn out that way. There were confusing barriers. I remember one day on the playground walking over to a group of black girls and watching them play a hand game that was unfamiliar to me and listening to them talk, using many words that I did not understand. I hovered for a while, hoping that someone would invite me in, but I felt awkward and invisible and slowly walked over to the other side of the playground where a group of mostly white kids were playing games that I did know.

Gradually my circle of friends (all girls) coalesced and included four white girls, one biracial (Puerto Rican/white) girl, one black girl (often teased by other black kids, who called her an "oreo"), and a student whose family was from India. What I did not realize at the time was that they were all from middle-class families. Our families lived in similar neighborhoods; our parents became friends. For the kids, it translated into frequent play dates and carpools to gymnastics and soccer, places where I never saw my classmates from low-income families.

I enjoyed my schooling, but at some level, I always felt troubled by the racial divisions in my elementary and secondary schools and the fact that teachers did not seem to be concerned about them. These unsettled questions and the desire to help out in the schools led me to volunteer as a teaching assistant in a similar magnet elementary school throughout high school and college. I became aware of the gap between the rhetoric and reality of "desegregated" schools. I heard administrators and teachers congratulate themselves on having achieved a "balanced" and "diverse" population in their school. In contrast to my childhood experiences, they seemed to assume that all they had to do was to put children together and integration would magically happen because, after all, young children are "colorblind." I saw attempts to "keep white families in the schools" with enrichment programs and "gifted and talented" classes. Although these initiatives satisfied some parents, they widened the racial and social class divisions among the children.

As a volunteer teaching assistant, I became aware of the gap between the rhetoric and reality of "desegregated" schools.

Based on these experiences I decided that the culprit was "ability grouping." As researchers such as Jeannie Oakes have described, the white middle-class children were in the higher groups while their low-socioeconomic-status (SES) peers of color were assigned to the lower groups.

The kids, of course, immediately figure out which are the "smart" and "dumb" groups—despite cheerful nonhierarchical group names (e.g., Giraffes, Lions). When I was in 3rd grade, the teacher let us choose our own names. My "high" group settled on Whiz Kids, whereas a "lower" group called themselves Cool Cats. In 4th grade, I was put in a "low" spelling group with several of the black kids that I had so eagerly wanted to befriend when I first came to the school. However, by then I equated this placement with being "stupid." I felt ashamed, and my main goal was to work hard enough to get back up to the higher group (which I did). At the time, I was only conscious of my own humiliation, but now I see the devastating effects of ability grouping on children.

As I spent time in different classrooms, I realized that it was not just the ability grouping per se that caused the divisions, because children still clustered in their own racial and social class groups at

other times. Segregation seemed to be propelled by other forces as well, and I wanted to understand what went on in children's interactions that reflected and reinforced these divisions and why these dynamics seemed to be "invisible" to teachers. So with the help of my advisor Patty Ramsey, who has been a longtime advocate for social justice and for multicultural antibias education, I examined these patterns for my senior thesis at Mount Holyoke College.

With the permission of the teachers and parents of the children in the classroom where I was volunteering, I systematically observed and recorded the children's contact patterns and conversations in different activities. The school where I made these observations was a racially and economically diverse urban magnet school located in the Northeast. (I'm not naming the school here, because I promised anonymity in order to record these observations.) The classroom of 28 children had a fairly even balance between white and black children, with three biracial children and one Latino child. Race and social class almost completely overlapped with the exception of two middle-class black boys and two middle-class biracial girls. (Estimates of social class were based on available information on family income, household size, and residential neighborhood.)

I realize that this is just a snapshot of one class of students, and so I don't want to overgeneralize based on my observations. Nonetheless, what I found helped me to reframe my own childhood experiences and to rethink the kind of teacher I'd like to be.

The ways that social class divides children were evident in my observations of the children's interactions, making cross-group conversations and play difficult. The white middle-class children often talked about books they were reading with their parents, structured after-school activities, and expensive family vacations in conversations that excluded their low SES peers.

In a fast, high-pitched voice, with a smile on her face, Megan (a middle-SES, white female) says to Amy (a middle-SES, white female), "Are you going skiing this weekend?" In a low voice Amy responds, "Noo." Cody (a low-SES, Latino male) walks over and says in a slow voice with a small smile on his face, "I'm going ice skating this weekend." Amy and Megan continue talking about skiing as they giggle. They do not respond to Cody.

In contrast, the low-SES children talked about neighborhood and family events and were more likely to interact with humorous, physical actions such as playfully bumping into each other, which often led to reprimands from the teachers.

It is lunchtime, and Summer, Andrea, and Arianna (all low-SES, African American females) are sitting next to each other. Andrea is in the middle and is sliding back and forth, bumping into each girl. She is giggling and saying in a high-pitched voice, "Tornado, tornado." Summer and Arianna begin to laugh and sway their bodies back and forth. After a few minutes, the teacher on lunch duty yells at them over the microphone.

When I started to observe what actually occurred in children's conversations and play, the biggest and most disturbing surprise was the extent to which the white girls and one biracial girl (all middle class) dominated the low-SES boys and girls of color, with threats of reprisal including reporting their actions to teachers or principal.

The children are finishing breakfast and the teacher has just announced to the entire class that they had 10 minutes to finish eating. Liza (a middle-SES, white female) turns to Ricki (a low-SES, African American male) who is sitting next to her eating his breakfast, and, in a harsh tone, she says, "All breakfasts must be thrown away before specials," as she rolls her eyes. The boy replies in a quiet voice, "I'm almost done." The girl then says in a very stern tone, "You better be … or I am getting the principal." The boy looks around the room, then gets up and throws away his container, leaving cereal in the bowl.

The boy complied, suggesting that the hierarchy was well entrenched by this time (January–March) of the school year. The classroom teachers — both very experienced and sensitive — and I were stunned that we hadn't noticed this pattern before. Even more disturbing was the realization that the teachers (and undoubtedly I, too) frequently reinforced this hierarchy, sometimes punishing based solely on a white girl's report.

The teachers also frequently put these middle-SES girls into positions of authority by asking them to do special jobs (e.g., hand out papers, stack chairs, run errands to the office). Over one three-day period the teachers assigned 21 tasks to members of the class. Almost 90 percent of their choices were middle-SES females, who, in turn, often used these responsibilities to dominate or intimidate their peers.

Over one three-day period the teachers assigned 21 tasks to members of the class. Almost 90 percent of their choices were middle-socioeconomic-status females.

On the rare occasions when low-SES children of color tried to make demands on a middle-SES white child, the teachers often undermined them.

Todd (a low-SES, biracial male), while looking at the nearby teacher, says in a loud voice to Amy (a white, middle-SES female who has taken his marker), "Give me my marker back!" Amy continues to look at her paper and draw with the marker. Once again Todd says, "Come on!" Amy still continues writing. The teacher then tells Todd to sit down and be quiet.

As others have found, and I had observed in many classrooms, the white middle-class children were placed in the highest ability groups and in the "talented and gifted" program. They also were chosen most often to read aloud when the whole classroom was reading together. However, what surprised me, when I observed children's interactions more closely, was how frequently they flaunted their academic skills by belittling the work and interests of their low-SES peers (e.g., "I've already written two pages! … How come you've just started?").

During free time in the library, Daisy (a low-SES, African American female) says excitedly, "Oh, look at this!" as she lifts up a book and shows it to Amy (a middle-SES, white female). Amy answers in an abrupt tone, "I read that in 1st grade." Daisy puts the book back on the shelf, turns her back to Amy, and walks away slowly, looking down at the floor.

Often the assumption of authority and academic superiority converged.

Lindsay (a middle-SES, white female) walks up to Randal (a low-SES, African American, male), and says in a stern voice, "Why are you still writing about your small moment? Everyone else finished days ago."

Randal looks at Lindsay with wide eyes, then looks back at his paper and continues to write.

In this incident, Lindsay got out of her seat and walked over to Randal to reprimand him for being behind on his work. He didn't overtly resist Lindsay's criticism. The teacher, who was within hearing distance, did not say anything.

The message about academic superiority appeared to have been absorbed by all the children. In several observations, low-SES African American children went out of their way to ask middle-SES white girls about assignments, frequently bypassing peers of color.

Although the divisions and hierarchy of the classroom seemed fixed and tacitly accepted by children and teachers alike, there were some positive and equitable cross-group interactions. These were more likely to occur when teachers explicitly conferred equal power on all the children involved. One time a teacher asked Megan (a middle-SES, white female who often dominated her peers of color) and Carla (a low-SES, African American female) to work together to organize a bookcase and they collaborated quite well.

Megan takes a pile of map placemats from the bookshelf and says, "A little help please…" with a gentle smile on her face and a high-pitched voice and a slight giggle. Carla takes the maps and places them on a lower shelf with wide eyes and a big smile. She puts one of the maps on the table, looks down at it and with a smile on her face says, "Look…I found Connecticut." Megan looks and in a high-pitched voice says, "Cool!" Carla replaces the map on the shelf and then takes a pile of books, which Megan is handing her. Then Megan turns around and says (to the observer), "Miss L., look at how good it looks. Me and Carla did this all ourselves." Carla has a huge smile on her face as Megan talks about how well they had worked.

The children also had positive and balanced cross-group interactions when they were engaged in physically active play, such as playing tag at recess, or when they were all interested in a novel event or object.

During recess, Isabella (a middle-SES, biracial female), Summer and Andrea (both low-SES, African American females), Lindsay (a middle-SES, white female), and Pete (a middle-SES, white male) are all intently looking at a tree. Isabella and Pete are touching it and then slowly pulling their hands away. In a piercing voice Isabella says, "Ahh, it's sticky." In a loud voice and a smile on her face Summer says, "Cool…that's sap." Pete and Summer then call over to the teacher, and Pete says, "Look, Mrs. M…. There's sap on this tree!" All of the children are talking animatedly with one another and most of them are smiling.

Interestingly, given the prevailing assumptions about the white middle-SES girls' academic superiority, it is Summer who appears to be the most knowledgeable about the sap.

In retrospect, the same dynamics and power differentials existed in the classrooms that I attended as a child. My friends and I enjoyed being the "best" students and the recipients of praise and privileges. I now realize that despite my long-term concerns about the racial segregation in classrooms, I have not fully appreciated the divisive effects of social class nor "seen" the power differentials among the children. Thus, it is not surprising that teachers, preoccupied with the many pressures of running a classroom and meeting multiple expectations, are often unaware of these dynamics and ways that they unwittingly reinforce them.

> **It is not surprising that teachers, preoccupied with the many pressures of running a classroom and meeting multiple expectations, are often unaware of these dynamics and ways that they unwittingly reinforce them.**

The racial segregation and power inequities that I observed are deeply rooted in the divisions in the larger society. In the past year and a half, I have worked in a couple of other classrooms and have seen these patterns emerge in different dimensions. For example, in a classroom of refugee children, the students who spoke more English were clearly at an advantage both academically and socially. Teachers tended to talk more to English-speaking students and frequently bestowed responsibilities on them, and thereby supported the existing hierarchy.

By learning to observe the nuances of children's behaviors, I have become better at monitoring my own decisions and reactions. I see clearly how the social norms of children from middle-class families are aligned with the expectations in the classroom and, as a result, how easy it is to put more advantaged students in positions of leadership. Often these decisions are driven by the need to get a job done with the least disruption — in other words "convenience." However, now I try to consciously equalize power and ensure that all children have opportunities to hold positions of responsibility. Likewise, I discourage children from reporting on others' misbehavior and am especially careful not to act on white middle-class children's negative comments about peers of color.

Encouraged by the positive cross-group interactions that I did observe, I try to create opportunities for children of different groups to work together in cooperative situations where power is explicitly shared. So we put on plays, do collaborative murals, and play cooperative games at recess, to name a few activities. My goal is not only to equalize power but also to help children reach out across economic, racial, and cultural barriers and to find and develop common interests.

Observing children's interactions — closely and systematically — expanded and deepened my understanding of peer relationships and how they are influenced by the larger society. Because children often mask their discriminatory and exclusive behaviors, we need to learn to see "below the surface" so that we can identify and challenge children's assumptions about different groups. Armed with this information, we can monitor our decisions about program structure and our moment-by-moment responses to specific situations to be sure that we are challenging, rather than reinforcing, the racial and economic divisions and hierarchies of our larger society. ▪

....

Lauren G. Mednick is founder and executive director of Elm City International. She is assistant to the CEO of Achievement First.

Patricia G. Ramsey is professor of psychology and education at Mount Holyoke College. She is the author or co-author of several books on multicultural education, including What If All the Kids Are White? Anti-Bias Multicultural Education with Young Children and Families *(2006, 2011).*

Barbara Miner

Helping Students Deal with Anger

Finding constructive ways to handle negative emotions in and out of the classroom

KELLEY DAWSON SALAS

"Let me go! LET ME GO!!!" Michael's screams fill the entire second floor hall-way. I imagine the noise bolting like lightning down the stairway, forcing its way through the double doors at the bottom, and arriving abruptly in the principal's office.

Arms flail and a fist connects with my teaching partner's ribs. I speak in what I hope is a soothing voice, although I know it is tinged with tension: "Michael, it's gonna be OK. As soon as you settle down we can let you go."

By the time Michael is allowed to bring his hoarse voice and his 3rd-grade body back into our classroom the next morning, I have decided that I need to teach my young students some strategies for dealing with anger.

Earlier in the year, after Michael's first few outbursts, I had sought help for him from people outside of our classroom. I was in my first year of teaching, learning what kids were all about for the very first time. I was going to school twice a week to meet the requirements of my alternative certification program. I simply didn't feel I had the time or the experience to help Michael respond to his emotions more appropriately.

"What can we do to find out what is behind Michael's angry behavior? Can he receive counseling from the social worker or psychologist?" I asked our Collaborative Support Team. Michael did see the psychologist a few times after that. Both the social worker and I made calls to the family. But the flare-ups continued, and I was not the only person to notice. More than once, the students saw Michael fly into a tantrum. They saw how he put his head down on his desk and covered it up with his coat from time to time. They took a step backward as he pushed a chair out of the way or hit another student on the playground and called it an accident. They had seen me give him a choice of "cooling down" and getting back to work or leaving the classroom.

Other staff also were aware of Michael. One day, I heard a specialist who had stepped in to supervise my students say: "We have to be real careful of Michael when he comes back to the classroom. We don't know what he'll do, do we?"

I didn't like the sound of that. I, the teacher, was Anglo, almost all of the students were Latino, and Michael was one of three African American boys. I did not want our classroom to be a place where students or staff were allowed to reinforce stereotypes that link anger with boys and men, especially African American boys and men.

In fact, Michael was normally an outgoing, upbeat kid who was well liked by his classmates and teachers. But the emotionally charged interactions that took place fairly regularly in our classroom indicated that something needed to change. As I tried to help Michael through a long process of learning how to identify his feelings and emotions and respond constructively, I also went through an important learning process.

Classroom Dynamics

I had to consider all the factors that contributed to our classroom dynamic. I had to examine my own beliefs, attitudes, and responses to Michael's behaviors. I had to consider how my actions as a white teacher of students of color affected Michael's emotions and responses. I had to try different approaches. These responsibilities weighed on me as I planned my course of action, and I continue to consider them as I reflect on what I did and what I might do differently

next time. For example, at the time I characterized Michael's outbursts as anger. Whether that is the appropriate emotional term, I am not sure; perhaps he was expressing frustration, or loneliness, or pain. I realize, in retrospect, that I used the term "anger" to describe strong emotional outbursts that may have had their origin in any number of emotions.

> **I realize, in retrospect, that I used the term "anger" to describe strong emotional outbursts that may have had their origin in any number of emotions.**

Teaching about anger immediately after a conflict with Michael didn't make sense. All eyes were on him. If I taught about anger during these moments, I would only be singling Michael out and escalating the problem. The rest of the students would pick up on my cue and would probably label him as an angry person. I might send an incorrect message that the only people who feel angry are those who act out the way Michael did.

Instead, I tried to plan a few simple lessons that would help all students consider what anger is, what other emotions or experiences it is linked to, and how we can respond. Over the course of the next four weeks, I developed and taught four short lessons. I drew upon my own personal experiences with anger and tantrums to put the lessons together. The resources I used were minimal. I am sure there are much more extensive curricula on this topic. The important thing for me and my students was that these lessons helped us create a common framework for thinking about anger. Later I would refer to this framework in crisis moments or in interventions with Michael.

I wanted my students to be able to identify the experiences and emotions that lead to what might be described as angry behaviors. I wanted them to recognize different responses to anger that they and others use. Most important, I wanted students to consider the choices we have for responding to strong emotions such as anger. I wanted them to recognize that when we are upset, we can either choose a course of action that is unsafe or unhealthy for ourselves and others, or we can choose a course of action that is safe and healthy. I hoped this discussion would lead students not only to see that it is unacceptable to allow anger and strong emotions to explode in outbursts, but also to identify and practice safe responses when they feel angry.

I led three discussions with my students. First, we made a list of "things that make us angry." Students cited a great many sources of anger, from the trivial to the unjust. Some of their responses: "I get mad when I can't find the remote"; "when people treat me like I'm stupid"; "when we lose part of our recess"; and "when my mom hits me."

Second, we made a list of "things people do when they're mad." I encouraged the students to share examples of things they personally do when they're mad, and allowed them to share things they'd seen other people do. Many student responses were negative, hurtful, or unsafe, such as: "I punch the nearest person"; "hurt myself"; "bang my own head against the wall"; "kick or slam a door as hard as I can"; and "yell at the person who's making me mad."

A couple of students offered what I would categorize as "safe" responses to anger: "I go for a bike ride to blow off steam"; "I go in my room and read until I'm not mad anymore"; and "I talk to my mom about what's making me mad." I asked the students, "Can you think of any other things like that, things that would help you to cool down or solve the problem?"

They suggested a few more: "You could talk to an adult you trust"; "go for a walk or go outside and play"; and "tell the person who's making you mad how you feel."

Finally, we made a large poster to hang in the classroom that showed different responses to anger. The students each made their own copy of the poster for their own use. In the center, the question "What can you do when you feel angry?" prompted kids to remember the responses we had brainstormed in the previous activity. The top half of the poster was reserved for writing in safe or healthy responses to anger, while the bottom half was labeled "unsafe/scary." While completing this activity, we had a chance to discuss the idea that each person must make a choice when she is angry about what course of action she's going to take. I again reminded students that some responses to anger are safe and some are not.

Several complexities surfaced in our discussions. Michael, who in addition to his tantrums had also been known to crumple his papers in frustration or to put his head down and "drop out" during class time, asked about how to classify these kinds of actions. "Is it safe to crumple up your paper? You're not hurting anyone if you do that."

> **Students should be encouraged to see the difference between a response that simply helps them blow off steam, and one that actively seeks to address the cause of their anger and solve the problem.**

"Well, let's think about that one," I responded. "It might not be physically dangerous to anyone, but is it hurting you in any way? Does it hurt you when you put your head down for hours and decide not to learn or do your work?" My hope was that Michael would slowly come to realize that he was hurting himself with some of his behaviors.

Michael participated during these sessions just as any other student. I did not single him out or use him as an example; in fact, I tried hard not to allow myself or other students to refer to his behavior in our discussions. I did keep a close eye on him, and noticed that he participated actively. His brainstorming worksheets also gave me an idea of some things that made him angry, and some of his usual responses to anger at school and at home. This was important to my work with Michael because it allowed me to think about possible causes of his behaviors without having to do it in a moment of crisis, and without making him feel like he was being singled out.

Looking back on these discussions, it seemed necessary to discuss with students some of the complexities of responding to feelings of anger. Rather than just telling students to respond "safely" to a situation that makes them mad, they need to be taught to consider the source of their anger and to develop a response that is not only safe but also effective. Routine bickering with a sibling might be effectively solved by some time apart, but a series of name-calling incidents or physical bullying by a classmate will not be resolved just by walking away one more time. Students should be encouraged to see the difference between a response that simply helps them blow off steam, and one that actively seeks to address the cause of their anger and solve the problem.

Our discussions around anger focused mostly on interpersonal relationships, and sought to understand what an individual can do when he or she feels angry. Looking back at this focus on individual interactions, I see that I missed an opportunity to guide students in an inquiry into other types of anger. I think it is important to help students understand that anger exists not only on an individual level, but can be related to societal issues of oppression and injustice as well.

This in turn could lead to a discussion of the role anger can play in the fight for social justice. As an activist for social justice, I use my anger at injustice to guide my own actions on a daily basis. Students can and should be aware that emotions often described as anger are not categorically "bad." Just as anger on an individual level can compel us to address a problem or make a change, the anger we feel when we witness injustice on a societal level should guide us toward changing unjust and oppressive systems. Rosa Parks comes quickly to mind as an example any 3rd grader can understand.

Adult Behavior

It was during our talks about anger that students' questions provided a springboard to an additional discussion that could have turned into a whole unit of its own. As we looked together at the abundance of unsafe or violent responses to anger, a few students began to ask, "If we're not supposed to throw tantrums, why do so many adults do it?"

They're right, I thought. How can I tell them that they should choose safe responses to anger when so many adults choose verbal outbursts or even physical violence? I allowed my teaching to take a brief detour in pursuit of an answer to the students' important question: How and when can we hold adults responsible for their angry behaviors?

I designed a lesson in which I talked about my own experiences with adults and anger, and shared a poem about a parent's angry outbursts. Together we discussed a few key concepts about adult anger and tantrums. We discussed the fact that adults, just like kids, must make choices about how to act when they

are angry. Some adults make poor choices, I said. I also wanted to make sure that my students didn't internalize feelings of guilt over an adult's anger, as if they were somehow to blame for the outburst. I pointed out that it is not a child's fault if an adult they know responds to anger in a way that hurts others. I referred back to a previous unit we had done on human rights and asserted that as human beings, we have a right to live free from the threat of angry outbursts and violence. We agreed that it is important for us to talk with someone we trust if someone is threatening that right. Adults can change their behaviors, and may need help to do so.

These affirmations provided a very basic introduction that could have easily turned into a much more profound examination of anger and violence in families. Our discussion only scratched the surface.

I did not assume or suspect that Michael was dealing with anger or violence in his own family. Rather, I planned this lesson in order to address the students' concerns and to give students a clear message that adults are responsible for making safe choices when faced with anger. By helping students see the connection between their responses to anger and adults' responses, I tried to encourage them to understand that each of us has a lifelong responsibility to resolve anger appropriately and safely. It is not appropriate to use our feelings as an excuse to lash out at others.

> **I allowed my teaching to take a brief detour in pursuit of an answer to the students' important question: How and when can we hold adults responsible for their angry behaviors?**

The school year went on. Michael did not miraculously change overnight, but he did make some changes, and so did I. In situations where he resorted to angry behaviors, we had a language to talk about his feelings and his choices for responding to them. I also had developed more sensible and effective strategies for helping Michael through tough times.

Later in the year when Michael was angry, he was no longer as likely to say to me: "Look what you made me do." He knew I would respond by saying, "You choose what you do." Many times, I said to him: "It's clear to me that you're feeling frustrated or angry. Are you choosing to deal with your feelings in a safe way?" Things got easier. The cooling-down periods got shorter. He seemed to be taking more responsibility for his actions and developing some strategies for what to do when he felt frustrated or angry.

For my part, I tried to become more flexible and to stop trying to force Michael to respond exactly as I wanted him to when he felt angry. I gave him more time to cool down. I always tried to get to what triggered his discontent and to acknowledge his feelings. Perhaps most important, I learned not to touch Michael while he was angry, or to try to move him physically. I had seen that that simply did not work.

Workable Solution

I was relieved that we had found a somewhat workable solution to Michael's behavior in our classroom. Part of me continued to wonder whether there were circumstances in Michael's life that were causing

anger and frustration to build up. I kept working with his family and advocating with school support staff for additional help for him. I talked with Michael often about his feelings and tried to be alert to signs of a more serious problem without making unfounded assumptions.

Michael and I worked together for a year and I think each one of us made some progress. As I struggled to become an effective teacher in my first year on the job, I was willing to learn from anyone who wanted to teach. Michael proved to have a lot of lessons in store for me. How little I would have learned had I simply written him off. For his part, Michael could have just as easily turned his back on me. I am thankful to him for giving me a chance to be his teacher and to learn from him. ▪

Kelley Dawson Salas is a teacher at Milwaukee Spanish Immersion School in Milwaukee and an editor of Rethinking Schools *magazine.*

Jean-Claude Lejeune

Staying Past Wednesday

Helping students cope with death and loss

KATE LYMAN

I remember the first time that death took a seat in my classroom. Jessica, a kindergartner in my class, and her brother had died over the weekend in a fire at a babysitter's house. I prepared to return to school on Monday, to face the empty seat at her table, answer the inevitable questions, and deal with my students' fears and grief.

When I got to school, the staff was told to go to the library for a brief meeting. The principal announced the tragedy and warned teachers not to broach the subject. "Trained personnel" (the school psychologist and social worker) would talk with the children. Teachers could answer questions but were to get on with school business as soon as possible.

"I'm giving this until Wednesday," whispered the teacher of my student's sibling. "After Wednesday, we won't talk about it anymore."

Death — like sex, AIDS, genocide, racism, and poverty — is silenced in the elementary classroom. That silence sends a strong message to children: This may be your reality but it is not the truth that we honor in this institution. You must set aside your classmate's death or your ancestor's history or your 13-year-old sister's pregnancy. You are here to discuss and write and learn about matters of more importance.

The Monday after Jessica's death, my students gathered on the rug. Many had heard about the fire. They burst out with facts (many erroneous), questions, and feelings. There was an undertone of fear for their own safety.

I took the students' lead and, ignoring the principal, I moderated a sharing session. After about 30 minutes, the tone switched from curiosity and fear to sadness. What about Jessica? Where was she now? How could we remember her and tell her that we miss her? I asked the students for ideas. They wanted to decorate her table space, to write about her, to draw pictures of her, and to send something to her family. I told them I would clear off a bulletin board for remembering Jessica and sent them to their tables to draw and write.

The bulletin board stayed up until the end of the school year. Questions, stories, and projects about Jessica did not end on Wednesday.

Death and Loss

Since then, I have often included a unit of several weeks on death and loss in my curriculum. Some years, especially when I taught kindergarten, the unit was precipitated by the death of a classroom guinea pig or by a robin found dead on the playground. Books, such as *The Tenth Good Thing About Barney*, sparked student discussions on a range of topics: the loss of a favorite pet (Barney was a cat), the death of a grandparent, and the many different views on afterlife.

More recently, when teaching 1st through 3rd grade, I have incorporated the unit as a regular part of my curriculum, sometimes as part of a discussion on AIDS awareness. The unit's immediacy invariably becomes clear. One year, for example, while I was preparing for the unit, a student who had been in my classroom the year before died in a car accident. A few years later, the mother of a girl in my class came in to tell me that her cousin was dying of AIDS and probably would not survive the night. Several days later, as part of our unit, this student solemnly shared her eulogy of her mother's cousin.

One year, in my 2nd/3rd-grade classroom, I planned for the class to create a "death and loss quilt" as a follow-up to a field trip to view panels from the NAMES Project (AIDS Memorial) Quilt. For students who

had several stories to tell, we talked about whom they would choose for their quilt panel; we discussed hard questions like who had meant the most to them and whom they missed the most. For several students, the loss of a parent through separation was akin to death because the parent had dropped out of their lives.

On that particular day, Lisa came in late, which was not atypical. She is often quiet and withdrawn, but she appeared unusually upset and on the verge of tears. She sat down at her seat and laid her head on her arms. With some coaxing, she agreed to meet with me in the hall.

"What's the matter?" I asked.

"Nothing."

"You seem to be feeling very sad." No response. "Did something happen at home?"

"Yeah, but it's nobody's business," Lisa said, her body wracked with sobs. I sat with her a while and asked how I could help. She blurted out, "Well, my aunt killed herself last night, but my mom says it's nobody's business."

I suggested that Lisa speak with a counselor but she didn't want to. She wanted to go back to the classroom. Feeling as if I were in a movie, I told her what the class was writing about. She sat down and wrote about her dog who had run away. Being unsure myself if it were too soon, I tentatively suggested she write about her aunt.

"No. Too hard," was her tearful answer.

Then I noticed that Mariah was also in tears. Usually a prolific writer, she had written only her name and the date. I went over to talk to her.

"I want to write about my mom, but it makes me too sad," she confided.

I told her that Lisa was having a similar problem and suggested they share their feelings. They went to the bench in the hall. When they came back, they were both ready to write. Lisa quickly wrote her story:

My aunt, Linda, lived in Stevensville for a long time, since she was a kid. When my grandma moved out, she had to move out. She got an apartment. And it was very small. It was one room. Everybody said she was a slob because she left cigarette wrappers around. Everybody said she was crazy. She died and I miss her.

When Mariah finished her story, she shared it with the class:

Brenda was my mom. I will never see her again. I loved her and I still do. I always will. Whenever I came over she gave me sea shells because I hadn't seen her for too long.

When they got divorced I was 4. We went out for ice cream from Dairy Queen. We don't know where she lives. That's why I'll never see her again. I have to stay with my dad. I want to stay with her, but I can't.

She loves Cheetos. I know she loves me. My mom couldn't take care of me. But my dad could. My mom and dad probably had a fight over me. But I don't know. I was only 4. I wished it never happened.

I wished on a star. It was the first one; I know it. I wished on Lauren's sea shell that was painted.

I know she loves me. I know it. I just know it. She is a friend and a special mom. She is special because she's my mom, and I love her. And she's part of my family.

I love you mom!!

Struggling Through

I was having a hard time handling the intensity of the girls' feelings. I struggled through the day and the rest of the year. Students worked on their quilt squares in art class. They wrote and decorated acrostics (poems or short stories formed around the letters of a person's name) about their loved ones. I read the chapter book *Words of Stone* by Kevin Henkes, which paralleled Lisa's and Mariah's issues. In this book, two children who have experienced the loss of a parent (one through death and the other through abandonment) discover what they have in common and become friends.

Lisa and Mariah also became friends and continued to write about their losses. While Lisa's writing seemed to serve as a private emotional outlet, Mariah asked again and again to read her stories to the class. She welcomed questions and input from classmates. She seemed relieved to discover that her loss was not unique.

"Oh, that's just like me," contributed Jamie. "But my mom's in jail. I hardly ever can see her."

The support that Mariah gained from the class enabled her to begin to heal from her loss. Lisa, however, went on an emotional spiral downward, was treated for depression, and was briefly institutionalized. As the school, her family, and her therapists struggled to deal with her mental illness, writing was one of the few activities that sustained her. She wrote stories about her aunt at every opportunity, even on paper towels used to serve snacks.

> **I wondered what would have happened if I hadn't made room for their stories. Would they and the other children have learned that grieving, compassion, and working through loss have no place in school, perhaps no place in life?**

For both girls, writing had become necessary and cathartic. As I watched them write about their pain and grief, I wondered what would have happened if I hadn't made room for their stories. Would they and the other children have learned that grieving, compassion, and working through loss have no place in school, perhaps no place in life?

I have always believed that the most powerful lessons are those relevant to the students' lives. Death, tucked away in the "life cycle" part of our science standards, has never been a major part of our official curriculum. But ever since Jessica's death 15 years ago, it has forced its way into my classroom. It has taken a seat and proclaimed its presence. It refuses to move out on Wednesday. ▪

....

Kate Lyman teaches in Madison, Wis.

10 Ways to Move Beyond Bully Prevention

(and why we should)

LYN MIKEL BROWN

Years ago, I helped found a nonprofit organization committed to changing the culture for girls. Our work is based on the health psychology notion of "hardiness"— a way of talking about resilience that not only identifies what girls need to thrive in an increasingly complex and stressful world, but also makes clear that adults are responsible for creating safe spaces for girls to grow, think critically, and work together to make their lives better.

As a result of this work, I've grown concerned that "bully prevention" has all but taken over the way we think about, talk about, and respond to the relational lives of children and youths in schools. So, from our group's strength-based approach, I offer 10 ways to move beyond what is too often being sold as a panacea for schools' social ills, and is becoming, I fear, a problem in and of itself:

1. Stop labeling kids.

Bully prevention programs typically put kids in three categories: bullies, victims, and bystanders. Labeling children in these ways denies what we know to be true: We are all complex beings with the capacity to do harm and to do good, sometimes within the same hour. It also makes the child the problem, which downplays the important role of parents, teachers, the school system, an increasingly provocative and powerful media culture, and societal injustices children experience every day. Labeling kids bullies, for that matter, contributes to the negative climate and name-calling we're trying to address.

2. Talk accurately about behavior.

If it's sexual harassment, call it sexual harassment; if it's homophobia, call it homophobia, and so forth. To lump disparate behaviors under the generic "bullying" is to efface real differences that affect young people's lives. Bullying is a broad term that de-genders, de-races, de-everythings school safety. Because of this, as sexual harassment expert Nan Stein explains, embracing antibullying legislation can actually undermine the legal rights and protections offered by antiharassment laws. Calling behaviors what they are helps us educate children about their rights, affirms their realities, encourages more complex and meaningful solutions, opens up a dialogue, invites children to participate in social change, and ultimately protects them.

3. Move beyond the individual.

Children's behaviors are greatly affected by their life histories and social contexts. To understand why a child uses aggression toward others, it's important to understand what impact race, ethnicity, social class, gender, religion, and ability has on his or her daily experiences in school — that is, how do these realities affect the kinds of attention and resources the child receives, where he fits in, whether she feels marginal or privileged in the school. Such differences in social capital, cultural capital, and power relations deeply affect a child's psychological and relational experiences in school.

4. Reflect reality.

Many schools across the country have adopted an approach developed by the Norwegian educator Dan Olweus, the Olweus Bullying Prevention Program, even though it has not been effectively evaluated with U.S. samples. Described as a "universal intervention for the reduction and prevention of bully/victim problems," the Olweus program downplays those differences that make a difference. But even when bully prevention programs have been adequately evaluated, the University of Illinois' Dorothy Espelage argues, they often show less-than-positive results in urban schools or with minority populations. "We do not have a one-size-fits-all school system," she reminds us. Because the United States has a diversity of race, ethnicity, language, and inequalities between schools, bully prevention efforts here need to address that reality.

5. Adjust expectations.

We hold kids to ideals and expectations that we as adults could never meet. We expect girls to ingest a steady diet of media "mean girls" and always be nice and kind, and for boys to engage a culture of violence and never lash out. We expect kids never to express anger to adults, never to act in mean or hurtful ways to one another, even though they may spend much of the day in schools they don't feel safe in, and with teachers and other students who treat them with disrespect. Moreover, we expect kids to behave in ways most of us don't even value very much: to obey all the rules (regardless of their perceived or real unfairness), to never resist, refuse, or fight back.

It's important to promote consistent consequences — the hallmarks of most bully prevention programs — but it's also critically important to create space for honest conversations about who benefits from certain norms and rules and who doesn't. If we allow kids to speak out, to think critically and question unfairness, we provide the groundwork for civic engagement.

6. Listen to kids.

In her book *Other People's Children*, Lisa Delpit talks about the importance of "listening that requires not only open eyes and ears, but also hearts and minds." Again, consistent consequences are important; used well, they undermine privilege and protect those who are less powerful. But to make such a system work, schools have to listen to all students. It's the only way to ensure that staff members are not using discipline and consistent consequences simply to promote the status quo.

7. Embrace grassroots movements.

There's nothing better than student-initiated change. Too many bully prevention programs are top-heavy with adult-generated rules, meetings, and trainings. We need to empower young people. This includes being on the lookout for positive grassroots resistance, ready to listen to and support and sometimes channel youth movements when they arise. We need to listen to students, take up their just causes, understand the world they experience, include them in the dialogue about school norms and rules, and use their creative energy to illuminate and challenge unfairness.

8. Be proactive, not reactive.

In Maine, we have a nationally recognized Civil Rights Team Project. Youth-led, school-based preventive teams work to increase safety, educate their peers, and combat hate, violence, prejudice, and harassment in more than 250 schools across the state. This kind of proactive, youth-empowerment work is sorely needed, but is too often lost in the midst of zero-tolerance policies and top-down bully prevention efforts. Yet such efforts work. According to a study conducted by the Gay, Lesbian and Straight Education Network, or GLSEN, youth-led gay/straight alliances make schools safer for all students.

9. Build coalitions.

Rather than bully prevention, let's emphasize ally- and coalition-building. We need to affirm and support the definition of coalition that activist Bernice Johnson Reagon suggests: work that's difficult, exhausting, but necessary "for all of us to feel that this is our world."

10. Accentuate the positive.

Instead of labeling kids, let's talk about them as potential leaders, affirm their strengths, and believe that they can do good, brave, remarkable things. The path to safer, less violent schools lies less in our control over children than in appreciating their need to have more control in their lives, to feel important, to be visible, to have an effect on people and situations.

Bully prevention has become a huge for-profit industry. Let's not let the steady stream of training sessions, rules, policies, consequence charts, and no-bullying posters keep us from listening well, thinking critically, and creating approaches that meet the unique needs of our schools and communities. ▪

....

Lyn Mikel Brown, is Professor of Education at Colby College in Waterville, Maine, and co-creator of the non-profit Hardy Girls Healthy Women. A version of this article appeared in Education Week.

Randall Enos

Bad Signs

ALFIE KOHN

You can tell quite a lot about what goes on in a classroom or a school even if you visit after everyone has gone home. Just by looking at the walls — or, more precisely, what's on the walls — it's possible to get a feel for the educational priorities, the attitudes about children, even the assumptions about human nature of the people in charge.

A chart that I created more than a decade ago called "What to Look for in a Classroom" listed some Good Signs along with Possible Reasons to Worry (Kohn, 1999, appendix B). Among the latter: walls that are mostly bare, giving the building a stark, institutional feel; and posted displays that suggest either a focus on control (lists of rules or, even worse, punishments) or an emphasis on relative performance (charts that include grades or other evaluations of each student).

Because I've done so elsewhere, I won't take time here to explain why such lists and charts make me shudder. Instead, I'd like to consider a few signs and posters that are generally regarded as innocuous or even inspiring.

"No Whining"

This sign — which sometimes consists of the word "whining" with a diagonal red slash through it — sends a message to students that seems to be "I don't want to hear your complaints about anything that you're being made to do (or prevented from doing)." To be sure, this is not an unusual sentiment; in fact, it may be exactly what your boss would like to say to you. But that doesn't mean it's admirable to insist, perhaps with a bit of a smirk, that students should just do whatever they're told regardless of whether it's reasonable or how it makes them feel. If we might respond with frustration or resentment to receiving such a message, why would we treat students that way? "No whining" mostly underscores the fact that the person saying this has more power than the people to whom it's said.

Of course, the sign could be read more literally. Perhaps it's just a certain style of complaining, a wheedling tone, that's being targeted. Frankly, I don't love that sound either, but should someone's tone of voice really take precedence over the content of whatever he or she is trying to say to us? I'm less annoyed by whining than I am by the disproportionate reaction to it on the part of adults. It's fine to offer an occasional, matter-of-fact reminder to a child that people tend to be put off by certain ways of asking for something, but our priority should be to make sure that kids know we're listening, that our relationship with them doesn't depend on the way they talk to us. Besides, young children in particular need to have some way of expressing their frustration. We don't let them hit, scream, or curse. Now we're insisting that they can't even use a tone of voice that's, well, insistent?

Regardless of how whining is defined, going to the trouble of posting a sign about it suggests that our own convenience is what matters most to us (since it's obviously easier for anyone in a position of authority if those being ordered to do something comply without question). It also implies that we're unwilling to reconsider our own actions and uninterested in

having students question authority — despite the fact that education at its best consists of helping them to do precisely that.

"Only Positive Attitudes Allowed Beyond This Point"

I've seen this poster on classroom doors in a public school in Minnesota, a Catholic school in Indiana, and a quasi-progressive Friends school in Massachusetts. Each time I came across it, I found myself imagining how its message might be reworded for satirical purposes. Once I came up with "Have a Nice Day … or Else." Another time I fantasized about secretly removing the poster at night and replacing it with one that reads "My Mental Health Is So Precarious That All of You Had Better Pretend You're Happy."

I've long been convinced that dark stuff sometimes lurks just behind the huge, brittle smiles and the voices that swoop into unnaturally high registers in front of little children. Even apart from the treacly style in which it's often delivered, the compulsive tendency to praise kids when they do something helpful may reflect the pessimistic assumption that the action was a fluke: Children must be marinated in "Good job!"s whenever they happen to do something nice; otherwise they'll never act that way again. The more compulsive (and squeaky) the use of positive reinforcement, the bleaker the underlying view of children — or maybe of our species.

Putting students on notice that their attitudes had better damn well be positive tells us less about what makes for an optimal learning environment than it does about the needs (if not neediness) of the person who sends this message. Kids don't require a classroom that's relentlessly upbeat; they require a place where they'll feel safe to express whatever they're feeling, even if at the moment that happens to be sad or angry or scared. They need a place, in other words, where negativity is allowed. Bad feelings don't vanish in an environment of mandatory cheer — they just get swept under the rug where people end up tripping over them, so to speak. What you or I may describe as a negative attitude, meanwhile, may be an entirely appropriate response to an unfair rule, an intimidating climate, or a task that seems pointless or impossible. To exclude such responses from students is to refuse to think seriously about what may have given rise to their negativity.

Inspirational Posters

Far more common than any specific message, including the two I've mentioned here, is a whole class of posters that might be described as "inspirational." Taped up in elementary, middle, and high schools across the country—outside the main office, in the cafeteria and the library, on individual classroom walls—we find these earnest, interchangeable calls to greatness, typically superimposed on gorgeous, fading photographs. "You can if you think you can!" "Reach for the stars!" "Achievement is within your grasp!" "Winners make the effort!" "This year I choose success!" And on and on.

> **Show me a school that adorns its walls with posters created by distant corporations, and I'll show you a school where it's possible the same could be said of its curriculum.**

At this point I should probably confess that I don't much care for posters on school walls, period. It may seem like a harmless way to cover up painted cement blocks, but there's something impersonal and generic about items that weren't created by, or even for, the particular individuals who spend time in this building. Show me a school that adorns its walls with posters created by distant corporations, and I'll show you a school where it's possible the same could be said of its curriculum.

But if commercial posters in general don't gladden the heart of a visitor, there's something uniquely off-putting about these posters, which show up in all sorts of workplaces, not just schools. And it seems I'm not alone in this reaction, judging by the popularity of a series of parodies marketed under the name "Demotivators." One of these posters features a dramatic image of the pyramids along with the caption: "ACHIEVEMENT—You can do anything you set your mind to when you have vision, determination, and an endless supply of expendable labor." Another depicts a leaping salmon about to wind up in the jaws of a bear: "AMBITION—The journey of a thousand miles sometimes ends very, very badly."

Let's not just satirize, though; let's analyze. The exhortatory slogans found on motivational posters, like those in motivational speeches and books, tend to offer a combination of strenuous uplift and an emphasis on self-sufficiency. They tell us that, individually, we can do anything if we just set our minds to it.

Here's the first problem: The assurance that you can achieve anything you desire through hard work stretches the truth beyond recognition. And it's in the neighborhoods where children are most likely to hear about the wondrous results that await anyone with perseverance and a dream that the claim is hardest to defend.

"You can be the valedictorian!" It's not just that being the valedictorian is an unrealistic expectation for most students; it's that this status, like so much else in our schools and our society, is set up as a zero-sum game. If I become the valedictorian, then you can't, and vice versa. In a competitive environment, our dreams are mutually exclusive. This fact the posters somehow neglect to mention.

"You can get into Harvard!" And what happens when I, like 93 percent of the other self-selected and mostly super-qualified applicants, receive my rejection letter from Cambridge? What if I choose success and reach for the stars and stay true to my goals—only to wind up with nothing? Some students will become angry—concluding, not unreasonably, that they have been lied to. But others will blame themselves.

And that's problem No. 2: "The flip side of positivity is thus a harsh insistence on personal responsibility," Barbara Ehrenreich observed in her recent book *Bright-Sided: How the Relentless Promotion of Positive Thinking Has Undermined America*. If you fail, "it must [be] because you didn't try hard enough, didn't believe firmly enough in the inevitability of your success."

And who benefits when the have-nots are led to think that way? Suffice it to say that nothing maintains the current arrangement of power more effectively than an approach that ignores the current arrangement of power. Rather than being invited to consider the existence of structural barriers and pronounced disparities in resources and opportunities, we're fed the line that there are no limits to what each of us can accomplish on our own if we just buckle down.

Notice, too, that inspirational posters are almost always generic, the implication being that "success" or "achievement," per se, is desirable; it doesn't matter what one wants to achieve. Any dream will do. But is that a conviction we're really prepared to endorse? And again, as they say in Latin, *cui bono?* Whose interests are served when we look at things that way?

"You can get an A!" For example, what if success is defined in terms of high grades, as is the case in traditional schools? The available research suggests that there are three predictable effects when students are led to focus on bringing home better report cards: They tend to become less interested in the learning itself, to think in a more superficial fashion, and to prefer the easiest possible task. But who is going to bother rethinking the value of rating students with letters or numbers — or the value of the specific tasks involved, like memorizing facts for a test or filling out worksheets, that determine who gets which grades — if the goal is just success, and that's equated with getting an A? Do we want to send the message that this objective is more meaningful than, say, coming up with a novel solution to a meaningful intellectual challenge? (Kohn, 1993, 1999)

The message of the self-help movement has always been: Adjust yourself to conditions as you find them because those conditions are immutable; all you can do is decide on the spirit in which to approach them (hint: We recommend a can-do spirit). To do well is to fit in, and to fit in is to perpetuate the structures into which you are being fit.

Am I being too hard on, or expecting too much from, a simple poster? Well, precisely because they're so pervasive — and accepted so uncritically — I think it's worth digging into the hidden premises of their chirpy banalities. Just because something is generally regarded as uncontroversial doesn't mean it's value-neutral. Imagine if a very different sort of poster appeared in your local high school — one that said, for example, "Some children are born into poverty; others are born with trust funds" — and picture what the accompanying illustration might look like. Or suppose we put up a sign that featured this remark by the late George Carlin: "It's called the American dream because you have to be asleep to believe in it." Undoubtedly some people would complain that these sentiments were too controversial. But where is the outrage over the subliminal values of a poster that airily assures us "The sky's the limit!"?

One measure of the ideological uses to which inspirational slogans are put is the fact that they seem to be employed with particular intensity in the schools of low-income children of color. Jonathan Kozol has incisively pointed out the political implications of making African American students chant "Yes, I can! I know I can!" or "If it is to be, it's up to me." Such slogans are very popular with conservative white people, he notes, because "if it's up to 'them,' the message seems to be, it isn't up to 'us,' which appears to sweep the deck of many pressing and potentially disruptive and expensive obligations we may otherwise believe

> **"Auto-hypnotic slogans" such as "I'm smart! I know that I'm smart" are rarely heard in suburban schools where "the potential of most children is assumed."**

our nation needs to contemplate." He adds: "Auto-hypnotic slogans" such as "I'm smart! I know that I'm smart" are rarely heard in suburban schools where "the potential of most children is assumed."

I'd love to see a research study that counted the number of motivational posters (along with other self-help, positive-thinking materials and activities) in a school and then assessed certain other features of that school. My hypothesis: The popularity of inspirational slogans will be correlated with a lower probability that students are invited to play a meaningful role in decision-making, as well as less evidence of an emphasis on critical thinking threaded through the curriculum, and a less welcoming attitude toward questioning authority. I'd also predict that the schools decorated with these posters are more likely to be run by administrators who brag about the school's success by conventional indicators and are less inclined to call those criteria into question or challenge troubling mandates handed down from above (such as zero-tolerance discipline policies or pressures to raise test scores).

Good Signs

It would seem unsporting, and perhaps unduly negative, to conclude this essay without suggesting what might replace all of those mass-produced exhortations. Perhaps we can begin with phrases that seem suitable for posting to someone with a more progressive sensibility—for example, "Question authority." Or imagine a principal's office with a framed copy of this reminder from researcher Linda McNeil: "Measurable outcomes may be the least significant results of learning." Similarly, what could be more refreshing than the large sign tacked up in a Washington state classroom that said "Think for yourself; the teacher might be wrong"?

I'd be happy to wander the halls of a middle school where every student has a sign on his or her locker that says "[Name of student] is currently reading…" accompanied by a photocopy of the cover of the book in question (Frost). Beyond the specific information being conveyed, compare the cumulative impact of hundreds of such announcements with those well-meaning but insipid reminders to "Read!" that appear in libraries. In fact, I like to see school walls filled with all sorts of information about, and personal mementos of, the people who spend their days there. (And that includes the adults. When Deborah Meier was its principal, the central corridor of the Mission Hill School in Boston filled a large bulletin board with childhood photos of the school's teachers.)

When I visit traditional classrooms, grimacing at so much of what's on the walls, I find myself wondering why they're not filled with stuff done by the students. The answer to that question, unfortunately, may be that the students haven't been allowed to do much that's worth displaying. Hence my original hypothesis, that the room decor may speak volumes about the theory and practice of instruction. I once spent time in a Long Island elementary school classroom where elaborate animal habitats were being created, and students had posted lists of "problems we faced when designing and constructing" these habitats. The displays gave evidence of complex thought, perseverance in overcoming those problems, classwide cooperation—and the fact that the teacher's priority was to help these kids learn to think like scientists rather than just memorizing scientific facts for a test.

The broader moral is that the best classrooms, regardless of age level or academic discipline, often feature signs, exhibits, or other materials obviously created by the students themselves. And that includes students' ideas for how to create a sense of community and learn together most effectively—as opposed to

a list of rules imposed by the teacher (or summarized on a commercial poster).

We're ultimately led to ask a meta-question: "Who decides what goes on the walls?" I'd be willing to bet that just about all of the signs and posters about which I've been raising concerns here were put up by the adults without even consulting the students. (What kid would suggest "No Whining"?) In fact, the exclusion of the people we're there to teach may be the most significant, though invisible, implication of what usually goes on the walls. To reverse this, we'd need not only to rethink what we're posting but also whether the school in which these items are displayed is one that invites students to participate in thinking about what they do as well as the look of the place where they do it. ▪

Notes

Ehrenreich, Barbara. *Bright-Sided: How the Relentless Promotion of Positive Thinking Has Undermined America.* New York: Metropolitan Books, 2009.

Frost, Shari. "Creating a Culture of Literacy." Choice Literacy. www.choiceliteracy.com/public/1062print.cfm

Kohn, Alfie. *Punished by Rewards: The Trouble with Gold Stars, Incentive Plans, A's, Praise, and Other Bribes.* Boston: Houghton Mifflin, 1993.

Kohn, Alfie. *The Schools Our Children Deserve.* Boston: Houghton Mifflin, 1999.

Kozol, Jonathan. *The Shame of the Nation: The Restoration of Apartheid Schooling in America.* New York: Crown, 2005.

....

Alfie Kohn is the author of 12 books, including The Schools Our Children Deserve, Punished by Rewards, *and, most recently,* Feel-Bad Education…and Other Contrarian Essays on Children and Schools.

Barbara Miner

Tracking and the Project Method

Reflections on alternatives to tracking

BOB PETERSON

Children enter my 5th-grade classroom at so many levels that at times I feel I'm teaching in a one-room schoolhouse in the 1800s. A few of my students who are learning-disabled struggle with basic sounds and letters, while other students read at close to a high school level. The same is true with math, writing, artistic, athletic, and verbal skills — although not all students remain at one end of the spectrum. Sometimes, for instance, I will have a student who has difficulty reading but is quite adept at math.

This range of skills is one of the most difficult dilemmas that I grapple with as a teacher. To deal with it, I draw not only on my years of classroom practice, but also my own experience as a student and my grounding in progressive educational philosophy. The result is an approach that combines curricular projects with an eclectic grouping of students, with the twin goals of promoting equity within my classroom and of pushing each child to perform their best.

The issue, however, is much broader than how I, as an individual teacher, decide to organize my classroom. Fundamentally, the issue involves important questions of how schools, especially schools in urban areas, can provide equal educational opportunities to all, and avoid the tracking and ability grouping that are all too popular despite their stereotypical assumptions and their disastrous consequences.

My Student Experience

I grew up in Madison, Wis., and I recall how some of my teachers dealt with the varied skill levels in their classrooms. In elementary school, we were placed by "ability" in reading and math groups named after birds and animals, a thinly veiled attempt to mask who the teacher thought was smart and who was not. There was virtually no chance of moving from one group to another, a rigidity I remember well because my best friend and I were always in different groups.

As we moved into junior high, this tracking became more pronounced. Every kid in the school knew where they fit in the intellectual pecking order, and teachers held different expectations for different groups.

There were five gradations for the 7th-grade student body — 7–1 being "the best and the brightest," with the "losers" grouped in 7–5. Each gradation started the day together in homeroom and traveled as a group to all classes, except gym and industrial arts. Interestingly, during this time my family moved overseas for 18 months, and upon my return I was placed into the lowest track. School officials quickly changed my academic classes, but left me in the lower-track homeroom. It was there that I made my first African American friends — not surprisingly, since then as now, racist assumptions about intelligence led to a tracking system in which African Americans were often segregated and grouped into the lower tracks.

By high school, the tracks were even more rigid: vocational, general education, and college bound. It's not hard to guess which kids were in the top track at my school, Madison West High School — the middle-class and upper-middle-class whites.

During my sophomore year, in a fit of progressivism, Madison West detracked the social studies courses. I have no clue whether school officials deemed the effort "successful," but one incident in particular made me realize the negative impact of tracking on some of my friends. While I was leaving my 10th-grade U.S. history class one day, a "lower-track" student — a cheerleader — approached me and apologized for being in the class. She told me she was sorry for "slowing down the class with her questions"

and wondered why they put all the "smart and dumb" kids together in the same history class. I was taken aback by her comments, but recovered enough to tell her the problem wasn't her lack of smarts, but the less-than-capable teacher that bored all the students to tears every day.

The teacher took the dreary but pervasive approach that students are empty vessels who need to be "filled up" with "facts" about names, dates, and places, so they can regurgitate those "facts" on tests filled with true and false, multiple choice, and short-answer fill-in-the-blank questions. In fact, according to researcher John Goodlad in his seminal work, *A Place Called School*, less than 1 percent of instructional time in high school is spent on discussion that requires students to form an opinion or use any reasoning skills.

Criticisms of Tracking

In the late 1970s and early 1980s, there was a growing awareness of the negative consequences of ability grouping in the elementary grades and tracking in secondary schools. Research by Robert Slavin of Johns Hopkins University, and books such as Jeannie Oakes' *Keeping Track: How Schools Structure Inequality* and Anne Wheelock's *Crossing the Tracks: How "Untracking" Can Save America's Schools*, helped alert educators and policy makers to the problems with tracking; they also pointed toward potential alternatives. People such as Slavin, Oakes, and Wheelock argued that in many schools, tracking institutionalizes inequality and leads to lower expectations and less rigorous course work for students in the bottom tracks. They also found that such tracking does not benefit the students in the upper tracks, as is commonly assumed. As Oakes, an assistant dean in the Graduate School of Education and Information Studies at UCLA, wrote: "No group of students benefits consistently from being in a homogeneous group."

At the same time, community groups in some areas took up the issue, even to the extent of going to court. In essence, they viewed the struggle against tracking as a continuation of the movement to abolish separate but unequal schools — although in this case the focus was on nominally integrated schools that were highly segregated by classroom. In both cases, the unequal and segregated schooling denied African Americans full access to equal opportunities.

Today, with the stress on "high standards" and "back to basics"— and decreased emphasis on issues of equity and multiculturalism — the pendulum appears to be swinging back to tracking as an acceptable way to group students.

The influential Thomas B. Fordham Foundation (headed by conservative education guru Chester Finn) published a 27-page report arguing that tracking isn't really all that bad, and in fact may be good. The report, "The Tracking and Ability Grouping Debate," was written by Tom Loveless, an associate professor of public policy at Harvard. In the report, Loveless argues that criticisms of tracking are "mostly unsubstantiated by research" and that "evidence does not support the charge that tracking is inherently harmful."

This swing back toward tracking is complemented by trends such as increased reliance on standardized testing, an obsession with phonics-based reading instruction, attacks on multicultural and bilingual education, and attempts to "decertify" the teaching profession and undermine schools of education, which are seen as bastions of child-centered pedagogy.

What unifies these shifts is a conservative conception of education itself — a view that education is little more than a transfer of subject matter and facts from the adult society to the next generation, best done through drill and rote memorization. The conservative approach stands in stark contrast to a progressive view of education, perhaps most notably articulated by John Dewey at the turn of the century. Dewey held that schools should start with the child, build on his or her interests, and link them to broader intellectual and social concerns through a curriculum that poses problems and actively involves the student.

If one's conception of education is the "subject matter set out to be learned" approach (as the conservative approach has been characterized), then it's understandable why ability grouping and tracking might be viewed as the most efficient and easiest way to "deliver" an education. If, on the other hand, one's educational goal is to develop independent thinkers who can look critically at the world and solve real-world problems, heterogeneous groupings might make more sense. To cite just one reason: The more social diversity there is in a class, the more the classroom mirrors the real world, and the more students learn to draw upon each other's strengths to analyze and solve problems.

Let me explain by looking at my own classroom.

Grouping in My Classroom

I admit that I group students. I can't imagine a teacher who has two or three dozen children in a classroom who never does so. But my groups vary a lot. Some are homogenous — kids who need work on certain skills or kids who are dominant in Spanish or English (I teach in a two-way bilingual school). But most often the groups are heterogeneous, with kids of varying skill levels working in cooperative groups on a common project such as a role play, dramatization, critique, or discussion. Sometimes students work in pairs, such as in peer conferences in which they give feedback on each other's writing. Occasionally, I allow the students to choose their own groups.

But the most important thing is that the groups are always changing. No student is forever "stuck" in a "lower" group, as my best friend was in elementary school.

Take my reading groups. Every two weeks or so, we start a new children's novel as part of my guided reading instruction. I show the children four or five different books of varying levels, and they write their top three choices on a file card. I make up two or three groups based on student interest, my assessment of their reading skills, and their background knowledge about the book's subject.

The composition of the groups changes every two weeks, and the activities vary as well. Sometimes the groups are self-directed "literature circles." Other times I take a more active role and use the time to reinforce basic reading and vocabulary skills. I usually make sure that all the books for any two-week period have a common theme that relates to something else we are studying (for example, homelessness, the American Revolution, the Underground Railroad, immigration experiences of Asian Americans, and so forth). This way, the groups can adopt additional projects that extend into other parts of the curriculum, and can discuss common themes regardless of which book they are reading.

I take a similar approach in math, sometimes working with the entire class, sometimes in small groups, sometimes with pairs of students, and sometimes one-on-one. I especially use a varied approach when introducing a new topic, such as fractions, to ensure that students get as many opportunities as possible to understand the new concept. Depending on the concept and skill being taught, I might group by "ability" for a week or two (for instance when reviewing long division and it becomes clear that some students need extra help) and then rearrange both the groups and my approach. Sometimes the students do group math projects, such as using data they collect from their classmates to make graphs or solve problems.

In other curriculum areas, I group kids depending on the purpose, whether it's brainstorming ideas, critiquing, or discussing. In social studies, for example, as we start studying a topic such as the American Revolution or the abolition movement, groups of three to five might generate a list of things they know about the subject, or what they'd like to learn. Often when I have an assignment for the children — such as writing a dialogue poem or doing a book report — we look at examples of similar assignments by my previous students. Afterward, the students break into different groups to evaluate what they think of the previous students' work and generate ideas on how they will evaluate their own work. Students working in groups have also critiqued things like the bias in children's books about Columbus, or the number of put-downs and stereotypes on popular TV shows.

These varied approaches to grouping and class-

I believe that cooperative groups done well, especially when there is a component of individual accountability, can boost academic achievement and improve the classroom's sense of community.

room organization are a beginning step toward dealing with the "range of skills" dilemma. I believe, for example, that cooperative groups done well, especially when there is a component of individual accountability, can boost academic achievement and improve the classroom's sense of community. If done in a slipshod fashion, however, cooperative groups can lead to a situation in which the harder working, more committed students do most of the work and little learning takes place for the students who might need it the most.

Even if done well, however, cooperative grouping is insufficient as a teaching strategy. My goal is not just to push each student to learn to the best of their ability, or to have students understand the value of working together. I also want to promote an anti-racist, social justice curriculum that encourages children to critically think about — and help change — the world. Cooperative learning is a worthwhile method, but we need to ensure that it isn't used to more effectively teach a traditional curriculum replete with Eurocentric biases and stereotypes.

Structured-Project Approach

Perhaps the most useful curricular approach that I have found is what I call the structured-project approach.

The projects are interdisciplinary assignments in which each student must make a booklet using reading, writing, geography, research, and other skills. Throughout the year, my 5th-grade students make a total of five magazine-size booklets; they follow a prescribed outline developed over the past several years by my partner teacher, Jesús Santos, and me.

The projects include a student autobiography, a report on an endangered animal, a bilingual poetry anthology, a report on a famous person who fought for social justice, and a report on the student's journey through elementary school. The topics allow for significant student input so that the specific theme of each book is generated by the student. Although each student is expected to complete an individual project, many components of the project are approached collaboratively in groups. For example, one part of the student autobiography is to write about their neighborhood. In groups, students will list all the things they might look for in their neighborhood — such as the type of buildings, the different kinds of people, and what they like and don't like about their neighborhood — then write a draft in the evening and come back the next day and share their drafts in their group.

For the project on a famous person who worked for social justice, the students start by interviewing family and friends for suggestions of who might fit the category. As a class, we compile lists and I use mini-lectures to teach children about dozens of possible choices. Continuing as a class, we read parts of biographies on a few people. Then we break into groups and the students take notes on what we've read. Each student has to write down at least three things they've learned, but the whole group must compile a master list. Each group then shares its notes with the entire class and we draw lessons about how to take good research notes. Eventually we do the same kind of activity for turning notes into rough drafts.

The modeling and group practice help teach all students basic research and writing skills. The process also challenges the most skilled and assists the least skilled — so that no child is left behind, and no child is left bored.

> **The modeling and group practice challenge the most skilled and assist the least skilled — so that no child is left behind, and no child is left bored.**

Ultimately, the completed projects are shown at student-led parent-teacher conferences in fall and spring, and also at an end-of-year 5th-grade exhibition. These demonstrations of their work provide additional motivation for the students to do quality work.

Interestingly, it was not until I was well into the third year of using this project approach that I recalled — and ultimately recovered from my parents' attic — some similar projects I had done while in 5th and 6th grade. My favorite was on jet airplanes, and I had written to a range of corporations and officials, from North Central Airlines to the U.S. Air Force, to get photos. I show the 84-page report to my students when we start our work on projects. (They seem to comment most on the impeccably neat cursive handwriting, which is in sharp contrast to my current scrawl. More than one of my students has asked whether I had a serious accident with my hand at some point after 6th grade, which might account for my current handwriting.)

Other Projects

Students do their book projects in the context of other project-like activities in my classroom. I try to make sure that some of those projects are more group-based than the books. I also try to ensure that some of the projects don't take very long, so that students can see immediate results and build their self-confidence.

In the first few days of school, for example, each of my students does a name poem in which they reflect on how they were named, their name's significance, and how they feel about their name. I do the poem in the context of a social studies lesson about the power of naming, and how enslaved Africans and many immigrants were forced to take on new names as they arrived in the Americas. Working in pairs, the students edit, type, and print their poems, which are then framed on colored paper, laminated, and displayed. Later, a version of that poem will be incorporated into their autobiography and their bilingual poetry booklets.

Students also do lots of drama and role plays in my classroom. Drama projects range from reenactment of scenes from the literature books we are reading, to problem-posing situations where groups of students show how they might peacefully resolve peer conflicts, such as a playground quarrel or who gets to use a computer first.

In our study of U.S. history, I use more involved role plays to highlight key conflicts. Such role plays have specific parts and involve several days of student preparation. Some of my most successful role plays have been a trial of Columbus, a mock Constitutional Convention that includes groups not invited to the original convention, and a trial of a runaway slave.

Projects have also emerged out of discussions of current events. One year, for example, a few students were particularly concerned after reading a *Weekly Reader* article about child labor. They did more research, writing, and discussing, which led to a couple of them speaking at a community rally against child labor and NAFTA. As a spin-off, I helped them form a Stop Child Labor Club that met weekly during lunch hour.

These various projects help me deal with students who are at different skill levels. First, because of the combination of group and individual activities, the more-skilled students can help the lesser-skilled students, and in so doing both benefit. The student who is a good writer, for example, can help to revise and edit a weaker writer's essay, and in the process learn more about writing. Second, because the book projects are individualized, each student can be challenged according to my assessment of their capabilities. For example, the learning-disabled or English language learner might write considerably less in English than another student. Nonetheless, both projects can challenge those students to the maximum. Third, because I do a variety of projects in my classroom and not all the projects are writing-based, students have a chance to shine in different contexts. For example, students who have difficulty writing sometimes are among the best verbal acrobats in the class. They are sought after by other students to be in their groups when we do dramas or role plays. I remember how one year, a student with a learning disability who could barely write excelled in social studies because in the group work, role plays, and dramatizations he was among the most articulate. Had I just expected him to show what he learned through "end of chapter tests," he would have been perceived as a poor student and quite likely would have been turned off to learning.

Final Reflections

I am convinced that tracking and rigid ability grouping lower expectations unfairly for many students and channel them away from rigorous classwork. But proponents of equality must not only work to end tracking. We must also ensure that teachers in untracked classrooms use techniques that are effective with all students. Tracking and ability grouping can't be ended overnight with dictates from above. We must create school cultures and staff development programs that help teachers deal effectively with their students' wide-ranging level of skills. It should be unacceptable for teachers to rely on traditional whole-class approaches which use the textbook as a crutch and a substitute for good teaching. Such approaches either bore the more-skilled students or leave the less-skilled students behind.

If we don't boldly confront this issue, dissatisfied parents and students will fall prey to the idea that the best way to resolve such problems is to promote admission standards for schools, increase tracking within schools, and use strict ability grouping within classes.

Our students demand more of us, and we must rise up and meet that demand. ▪

Bob Peterson (REPMilw@aol.com) was a co-founder and 5th-grade teacher at La Escuela Fratney in Milwaukee for 22 years, a founding editor of Rethinking Schools *magazine, and serves as president of the Milwaukee Teachers' Education Association. He has co-edited numerous books including:* Rethinking Columbus, Rethinking Our Classrooms, Rethinking Globalization, *and* Rethinking Mathematics.

Barbara Miner

2.

Reading and Writing Toward a More Just World

In elementary schools the loudest battles seem to be fought over reading and writing. Whole Language or Phonics? Balanced Literacy or basals? But social justice educators also grapple with the desire to help students find a vision of themselves within literature and history and "talk back" to it. Critical literacy is threatened by subtle and not so subtle messages in packaged curriculum that hijack the language of social justice movements — employing a language of equity and justice to push schemes that are anything but. When teachers and students read and write to find and make their own meaning, the liberatory power of the page and pen materialize.

Barbara Miner

Teaching for Social Justice

One teacher's journey

BOB PETERSON

It's November and a student brings in a flier about a canned food drive during the upcoming holiday season. The traditional teacher affirms the student's interest — "That's nice and I'm glad you care about other people"— but doesn't view the food drive as a potential classroom activity.

The progressive teacher sees the food drive as an opportunity to build on students' seemingly innate sympathy for the downtrodden, and, after a class discussion, has children bring in cans of food. They count them, categorize them, and write about how they feel.

The critical teacher does the same as the progressive teacher — but more. The teacher also uses the food drive as the basis for a discussion about poverty and hunger. How much poverty and hunger is there in our neighborhood? Our country? Our world? Why is there poverty and hunger? What is the role of the government in making sure people have enough to eat? Why isn't it doing more? What can we do in addition to giving some food?

Participating in a food drive isn't the litmus test of whether one is a critical teacher. But engaging children in reflective dialogue is.

Unfortunately, a lack of reflective dialogue is all too common in American schools. Less than 1 percent of instructional time in high school is devoted to discussion that requires reasoning or an opinion from students, according to researcher John Goodlad in his study of American schooling. A similar atmosphere dominates many elementary classrooms, where worksheets and mindless tasks fill up children's time.

Divisions between traditional, progressive, and critical teaching are often artificial and many teachers use techniques common to all three. As I attempt to improve my teaching and build what I call a "social justice classroom," however, I have found it essential to draw less on traditional methods and more on the other two.

What follows is an outline of lessons that I have learned as I have tried, sometimes more successfully than others, to incorporate my goal of critical/social justice teaching into my classroom practice over the past 25 years.

There are five characteristics that I think are essential to a critical/social justice classroom:

- A curriculum grounded in the lives of our students.
- Dialogue.
- A questioning / problem-posing approach.
- An emphasis on critiquing bias and attitudes.
- The teaching of activism for social justice.

A well organized class based on collaboration and student participation is a prerequisite for such a program. I'd also like to add that such "characteristics" are actually goals — never quite reached by even the best teachers, but always sought by good teachers.

Curriculum Grounded in the Lives of Our Students

A teacher cannot build a community of learners unless the lives of the students are an integral part of the curriculum. Children, of course, talk about their lives constantly. The challenge is for teachers to make connections between what the students talk about and the curriculum and broader society.

I start the year with a six-week unit on the children's families and backgrounds. To begin the unit I have students place their birthdates on the class timeline — which covers nearly 600 years (an inch representing a year), and which runs above the blackboard and stretches around two walls. Students write their names and birthdates on 3x5 cards and tie the cards with yarn to the hole in the timeline that corresponds to their year of birth. On the second day we place their parents' birthdates on the timeline, on the third

day those of their grandparents or great-grandparents. Throughout the year, students add dates that come up in our study of history, literature, science, and current events. The timeline provides students with a visual representation of time, history, and sequence, while fostering the understanding that everything is interrelated.

The weekly writing homework assignment during this family background unit consists of children collecting information about their families — how they were named, stories of family trips, favorite jokes, an incident when they were young, a description of their neighborhood. Students share these writings with each other and at times with the whole class. They use these assignments as rough drafts for autobiographies which are eventually bound and published. The assignments also inspire classroom discussion and further study. For example, one of my students, Faviola Perez, wrote a poem about her neighborhood, which led to discussions about violence and what we might do about it. The poem goes:

MY STREET AT NIGHT

My mom says, "Time to go to bed."
The streets at night
are horrible
I can't sleep!
Cars are passing
making noise
sirens screaming
people fighting
suffering!
Suddenly the noise goes away
I go to sleep
I start dreaming
I dream about people
shaking hands
caring
caring about our planet
I wake up
and say
Will the world be
like this some day?

In the discussion that followed, many students shared similar fears and gave examples of how family members or friends had been victims of violence. Others offered ways to prevent violence.

"We shouldn't buy team jackets," said one student.

"The police should keep all the criminals in jail forever," was another suggestion. Needless to say, the students don't have a uniform response, and I use such comments to foster discussion. When necessary or appropriate, I also interject questions that might help the students deepen or reconsider their views. I also try to draw connections between such problems and conflicts that I witness daily in the class. When a student talks about a killing over a mundane argument or a piece of clothing, for instance, I ask how these differ from the conflicts in our school and on our playground, and how we might solve them.

Focusing on problems in writing and discussion acknowledges the seriousness of a child's problem; it also fosters community because the students recognize that we share common concerns. Ultimately, it can help students to re-examine some of their own attitudes that may in fact be a part, albeit small, of the problem.

Throughout the rest of the year I integrate an examination of children's lives and their community into all sections of the curriculum. In reading groups, children relate contemporary and classic children's books to their own lives. For example, I have students divide their paper vertically: On one side they copy an interesting sentence from a book they are reading; on the other side they write how that reminds them of something in their own lives. The students then share and discuss such reflections.

In math we learn percentages, fractions, graphing, and basic math through examining their own lives. For example, my 5th-grade class keeps logs of the time that they spend watching television, graph it, and analyze it in terms of fractions and percentages. As part of our school's nine-week theme called "We Send Messages When We Communicate," they surveyed all the classes in the school to see how many households had various communication equipment, from telephones to computers to DVD players.

Such activities are interesting and worthwhile but not necessarily critical. I thus tried to take the activity a step further — to help them question if watching television is always in their best interests. For instance, we found that some of our students could save over 1,000 hours a year by moderating their TV watching.

"I can't believe I waste so much time watching TV," one girl stated during a discussion.

"You're not wasting it," replied one boy. "You're learning what they want you to buy!" he said sarcastically.

Similar discussions helped children become more conscious of the impact of television and even led a few to reduce the hours they watched.

One problem, however, that I have encountered in "giving voice" to students is that the voices that dominate are sometimes those of the more aggressive boys or those students who are more academically skilled. I try to overcome this problem by using structures that encourage broader participation. During writing workshop, for example, I give timed "free writes" where children write about anything they want. Afterward they share their writing with another student of their choice. Students then nominate classmates to share with the entire class, which often has the effect of positive peer pressure on those who don't normally participate in class. By hearing their own voices, by having other students listen to what they have to say, children become more self-confident in expressing their own ideas, and feel more a part of the classroom community.

Dialogue

The basic premise of traditional teaching is that children come to school as empty vessels needing to be filled with information. "Knowledge" is something produced elsewhere, whether by the teacher or the textbook company, and then transferred to the student.

This approach dominates most schools. "Reform" usually means finding more effective ways for children to remember more "stuff" or more efficient ways to measure what "stuff" the students have memorized.

I agree that children need to know bunches of stuff. I cringe any time one of my 5th graders confuses a basic fact like the name of our city or country. But I also know that the vast bulk of stuff memorized by children in school is quickly forgotten, and that the empty vessel premise is largely responsible for the boring, lecture-based instruction that dominates too many classrooms.

The curriculum that I want the children to learn will be best remembered if it relates to what they already know, if they have some input into what is actually studied, and if it is studied through activities rather than just listening.

To initiate dialogue I may use a song, poem, story, news article, photo, or cartoon. These dialogue triggers are useful for both classroom and small-group discussion. I often use them as starting points in social studies, writing, or math lessons. I have a song, word, poster, and quotation of the week which, whenever possible, are related to our curriculum topics.

For example, during the study of the American Underground Railroad, I used the song "New Underground Railroad," written by Gerry Tenney and sung by Holly Near and Ronnie Gilbert. The song compares the Underground Railroad in the United States to the movement to save Jews during World War II and to the sanctuary movement to help "illegal" Salvadoran refugees in the 1980s. My student from El Salvador connected immediately to the song. She explained to the class the problems of violence and poverty that her family had faced in El Salvador. This one song raised many more questions, for example: Why did the Nazis kill people? What is anti-Semitism? Who runs El Salvador? Why does the United States send guns to El Salvador? Why are people from El Salvador forced to come to the United States secretly?

I also use provocative newspaper or magazine photographs. For example, for a poetry lesson during writing workshop, I used a *New York Times* photograph taken during a winter cold spell that showed piles of snow-covered blankets and cardboard on park benches near the White House. (See photo below.) Many students initially thought the piles were trash. When I told them that they were homeless people who had been snowed upon while asleep, my students were angry. The discussion ranged from their own experiences seeing homeless people in the community to suggestions of what should be done by the president.

"That's not fair," one student responded.

"Clinton said he'd take care of the homeless people if he got elected and look what he's done," said a second student. "Nothing."

"I didn't vote for him," said a third. "Us kids never get to do anything, but I know that if we were in charge of the world we'd do a better job."

"Like what?" I asked.

"Well, on a day that cold he should have opened up the White House and let them in," responded one student. "If I were president, that's what I'd do."

One of my students, Jade Williams, later wrote a poem:

Bettman/Reuters

Homeless people sleep under blanket-covered park benches across the street from the White House. By making transparencies of news photos such as this, teachers can spark discussion about contemporary social issues.

HOMELESS

I walk to the park
I see homeless people lying
on a bench I feel sad
to see people sleeping outside
nowhere to go I felt
to help them let them stay
in a hotel
give them things
until they get
a job and
a house to stay
and let them
pay me back
with their love

A Questioning/Problem-Posing Approach

Lucy Calkins, director of the Teachers College Reading and Writing Project, argues that teachers must allow student viewpoints to be part of the curriculum. "We can't give children rich lives, but we can give them the lens to appreciate the richness that is already there in their lives," she writes in her book, *Living Between the Lines.*

But even that approach is not enough. We should also help students to probe the ways their lives are both connected to and limited by society. This is best done if students and teachers jointly pose substantive, challenging questions for the class to try to answer.

Any time a student poses a particularly thoughtful or curious question in my class, we write it down in the spiral notebook labeled "Questions We Have" that hangs on the board in front of the room. Not every question is investigated and thoroughly discussed, but even the posing of the question helps students to consider alternative ways of looking at an issue.

In a reading-group discussion, for example, the question arose of how it must have felt for fugitive slaves and free African Americans to fear walking down the street in the North during the time of slavery. One student said, "I sort of know how they must have felt." Others immediately doubted her statement, but then she explained.

"The slaves, especially fugitive slaves, weren't free because they couldn't walk the streets without fear of the slave masters, but today are we free?" she asked. "Because we can't walk the streets without fear of gangs, violence, crazy people, drunks, and drive-bys."

In reading groups a common assignment is to pose questions from the literature that we read. For example, while reading *Sidewalk Story* by Sharon Bell Mathis, a children's novel in which the main protagonist, a young girl, struggles to keep her best friend from being evicted, my students posed questions about the ethics of eviction, failure to pay rent, homelessness, discrimination, and the value of material possessions over friendship.

"Is it better to have friends or money?" a student asked, which formed the basis of a lengthy discussion.

Other questions that students have raised in our "Questions We Have" book include: Who tells the television what to put on? Why do geese fly together in an angle? Did ministers or priests have slaves?

How many presidents owned slaves? Why haven't we had a woman president? How do horses sweat? If we are free, why do we have to come to school? When did photography start? Who invented slavery? Why are people homeless? What runs faster, a cheetah or an ostrich? How many children died in the 1913 massacre that killed 73 people in Calumet County, Michigan? (in reference to the Woody Guthrie song about a tragedy that grew out of a labor struggle).

Some questions are answered by students working together using reference materials in the classroom or school library. (Cheetahs can run up to 65 miles an hour while ostriches run only 40 mph.) Other questions are subjects of group discussion; still others we work on in small groups. For example, the question "What is the difference between the master/slave relationship and parent/child relationship?" developed one afternoon when a child complained that his parent wouldn't allow him out in the evening for school story hour. A girl responded that we might as well all be slaves, and a third student posed the question. After a brief group discussion, I had children work in groups of three or four and they continued the debate. They made two lists, one of similarities and one of differences, between the master/slave relationship and the parent/child relationship. They discussed the question in the small groups, then a spokesperson from each group reported to the class.

The fascinating thing was not only the information that I found about their lives, but also how it forced children to reflect on what we had been studying in our unit on slavery and the Underground Railroad. When one student said, "Yeah, it's different because masters whipped slaves and my mom doesn't whip me," another student responded by saying, "All masters didn't whip their slaves."

When another student said that their mothers love them and masters didn't love their slaves, another girl gave the example of the slave character Izzie in the movie *Half Free, Half Slave* that we watched, in which Izzie got special privileges because she was the master's girlfriend. Another girl responded that that wasn't an example of love; she was just being used.

In this discussion, students pooled their information and generated their own understanding of history, challenging crude generalizations typical of children this age. It was clear to all that the treatment of slaves was unjust. Not so clear was to what extent and how children should be disciplined by their parents. "That's abuse!" one student remarked after hearing about how one child was punished.

"No, it's not. That's how my mom treats me whenever I do something bad," responded another.

While no "answers" were found, the posing of this question by a student, and my facilitating its discussion, added both to kids' understanding of history and to their sense of the complexity of evaluating what is fair and just in contemporary society.

Emphasis on Critiquing Bias

Raising questions about bias in ideas and materials — from children's books to school texts, fairy tales, news reports, song lyrics, and cartoons — is another key component of a social justice classroom. I tell my 5th graders it's important to examine "the messages that are trying to take over your brain" and that it's up to them to sort out which ones they should believe and which ones promote fairness and justice.

To recognize that different perspectives exist in society is the first step toward critiquing materials and evaluating what perspectives they represent or leave out. Ultimately it helps children see that they, too, can have their own values and perspectives independent of what they last read or heard.

"Whose point of view are we hearing?" I ask.

One poem that is good to initiate such a discussion is Paul Fleischman's dialogue poem, "Honeybees," from *Joyful Noise: Poems for Two Voices* (included in *Rethinking Our Classrooms, Volume 1*). The poem is read by two people, one describing the life of a bee from the perspective of a worker, and one from the perspective of a queen. Children love to perform the poem and often want to write their own. They begin to understand how to look at things from different perspectives. They also start to identify with certain perspectives.

After hearing the song of the week, "My Country 'Tis of Thy People You're Dying," by Buffy Sainte-Marie, one of my students wrote a dialogue poem between a Native American and a U.S. soldier about smallpox-infected blankets the U.S. government traded for land. In another instance, as part of a class activity when pairs of students were writing dialogue poems between a master and a slave, two girls wrote

one between a field slave and a house slave, further deepening the class's understanding about the complexity of slavery. During writing workshop six weeks later, three boys decided to write a "Triple Dialogue Poem" that included the slave, a slave master, and an abolitionist.

Students also need to know that children's books and school textbooks contain biases and important omissions. I find the concept of "stereotypes" and "omission" important to enhance children's understanding of such biases.

For example, around Thanksgiving time I show my students an excellent DVD called "Unlearning Native American Stereotypes" produced by the Council on Interracial Books for Children (available at www.rethinkingschools.org). It's narrated by Native American children who visit a public library and become outraged at the various stereotypes of Indians in the books. One year after I showed this, my kids seemed particularly angry at what they had learned. They came the next day talking about how their siblings in 1st grade had come home with construction paper headdresses with feathers. "That's a stereotype," my kids proudly proclaimed. "What did you do about it?" I asked. "I ripped it up," "I slugged him," came the chorus of responses.

After further discussion, they decided there were more productive things they could do than to hit their siblings. They scoured the school library for books with Indian stereotypes and found few. So they decided to investigate the 1st-grade room. They found a picture of an Indian next to the letter I in the alphabet strip on the wall. They came back excited, declaring that they had "found a stereotype that everybody sees every day!" They decided they wanted to teach the 1st graders about stereotypes. I was skeptical, but agreed, and after much rehearsal they entered the 1st-grade classroom to give their lesson. Returning to my classroom, they expressed frustration that the 1st graders didn't listen as well as they had hoped, but nonetheless thought it had gone well. Later the two students, Paco Resendez and Faviola Alvarez, wrote in our school newspaper:

We have been studying stereotypes of Native Americans. What is a stereotype? It's when somebody says something that's not true about another group of people. For example, it is a stereotype if you think all Indians wear feathers or say "How!" Or if you think that all girls are delicate. Why? Because some girls are strong.

The emphasis on critique is an excellent way to integrate math into social studies. Students, for example, can tally numbers of instances certain people, viewpoints, or groups are presented in a text or in mass media. One year my students compared the times famous women and famous men were mentioned in the 5th-grade history text. One reaction by a number of boys was that men were mentioned far more frequently because women must not have done much throughout history. To help facilitate the discussion, I provided background resources for the students, including biographies of famous women. This not only helped students better understand the nature of "omission," but also generated interest in reading biographies of women.

In another activity I had students tally the number of men and women by occupation as depicted in magazine and/or TV advertisements. By comparing their findings to the population as a whole, various forms of bias were uncovered. Another interesting activity is having students tally the number of biographies in the school library and analyze them by race, gender, and occupation.

One of my favorite activities involves comparing books. I stumbled on this activity one year when my class read a story about inventions in a reading textbook published by Scott Foresman. The story stated that the traffic light was invented by an anonymous policeman. Actually it was invented by the African American scientist Garrett A. Morgan. I gave my students a short piece from an African American history book and we compared it with the Scott Foresman book. We talked about which story we should believe and how one might verify which was accurate. After checking out another book about inventions, the students realized that the school text was wrong.

The Teaching of Activism for Social Justice

The underlying theme in my classroom is that the quest for social justice is a never-ending struggle in our nation and world; that the vast majority of people have benefited from this struggle; that we must under-

stand this struggle; and that we must make decisions about whether to be involved in it.

I weave the various disciplines around this theme. When I read poetry and literature to the children, I often use books that raise issues about social justice and, when possible, in which the protagonists are young people working for social justice. In math, we will look at everything from the distribution of wealth in the world to the percentage of women in different occupations. The class songs and posters of the week also emphasize social struggles from around the world. I also have each student make what I call a "people's textbook"—a three-ring binder in which they put handouts and some of their own work, particularly interviews that they conducted. There are sections for geography, history, current events, songs, poetry, and mass media. I also have a gallery of freedom fighters on the wall—posters of people we have studied.

In addition to studying movements for social justice of the past, students discuss current problems and possible solutions. One way I do this is by having students role-play examples of discrimination and how they might respond.

I start with kids dramatizing historical incidents such as Sojourner Truth's successful attempt to integrate street cars in Washington, D.C., after the Civil War, and Rosa Parks' role in the Montgomery, Ala., bus boycott. We brainstorm contemporary problems where people might face discrimination, drawing on our current events studies and interviews children have done with family members and friends.

One day in the spring of 1993, my class was dramatizing contemporary examples. Working in small groups, the students were to choose a type of discrimination—such as not being allowed to rent a house because one receives welfare, or not getting a job because one is a woman—and develop a short dramatization. Afterward, the kids would lead a discussion about the type of discrimination they were acting out.

After a few dramatizations, it was Gilberto, Juan, and Carlos' turn. It was a housing discrimination example—but with a twist. Gilberto and Juan were acting the part of two gay men attempting to rent an apartment, and Carlos was the landlord who refused to rent to them. I was surprised, in part because in previous brainstorming sessions on discrimination none of my students had mentioned discrimination against gay people. Further, as is often the case with 5th graders, in the past my students had shown they were prone to uncritically accept anti-gay slurs and stereotypes. But here were Gilberto, Juan, and Carlos transferring our class discussion of housing discrimination based on race to that of sexual orientation.

The dramatization caused an initial chorus of laughs and jeers. But the students also listened attentively. Afterward, I asked the class what type of discrimination had been modeled.

"Gayism," one student, Elvis, yelled.

It was a new word to me, but it got the point across. The class then went on to discuss "gayism." Most of the kids agreed that it was a form of discrimination. During the discussion, one student mentioned a gay rights march on Washington a week earlier. (Interestingly, Gilberto, Juan, and Carlos said they were unaware of the march.)

Elvis, who coined the term "gayism," then said: "Yeah, my cousin is one of those lesi... les..."

"Lesbians," I said.

"Yeah, lesbian," he said. He then added enthusiastically: "And she went to Washington to march for her rights."

"That's just like when Dr. King made his dream speech at the march in Washington," another student added.

Before long the class moved on to a new role play. But the "gayism" dramatization lingered in my memory.

One reason is that I was pleased that the class had been able to move beyond the typical discussions around gay issues — which had in the past seemed to center on my explaining why students shouldn't call each other "faggot." More fundamentally, however, the incident reminded me of the link between the classroom and society, not only in terms of how society influences the children who are in our classrooms, but also in terms of how reform movements affect daily classroom life.

It's important not only to study these progressive social movements and to dramatize current social problems, but to encourage students to take thoughtful action. By doing this they see themselves as actors in the world, not just things to be acted upon.

One of the best ways to help students in this area is by example — to expose them to people in the community who are fighting for social justice. I regularly have social activists visit and talk with children in my classes. I also explain the activities that I'm personally involved in as an example of what might be done.

I tell students they can write letters, circulate petitions, and talk to other classes and children about their concerns. My students have gone with me to marches that demanded immigrant rights. Two of my students testified before the City Council, asking that a Jobs With Peace referendum be placed on the ballot. Another time students testified with parents in front of the City Council that special monies should be allocated to rebuild our school playground.

If we neglect to include an activist component in our curricula, we cut students off from the possibility of social change. We model apathy as a response to the world's problems.

Such apathy is not OK. At a time when cynicism and hopelessness increasingly dominate our youth, helping students understand the world and their relationship to it by encouraging social action may be one of the few antidotes. Schools are a prime place where this can take place. Teachers are a key element in it happening. ▪

....

Bob Peterson (REPMilw@aol.com) was a co-founder and 5th-grade teacher at La Escuela Fratney in Milwaukee for 22 years, a founding editor of Rethinking Schools *magazine, and serves as president of the Milwaukee Teachers' Education Association. He has co-edited numerous books including:* Rethinking Columbus, Rethinking Our Classrooms, Rethinking Globalization, *and* Rethinking Mathematics.

Jose Luis Pelaez Inc.

Writing for Change

Persuasion from the inside out

MARK HANSEN

Once, a principal remarked to me, "Whenever I come into your classroom, you're on the carpet, talking." I took it as a compliment because it has always been a point of pride for me as a teacher how much time I set aside for my students to share their lives. Much of the most profound and memorable learning and teaching I've been a part of started with a student's remark — either joyous or troubling. We do spend a fair amount of time simply sharing news from our lives, but I also try to push their reaction to the "news" in a more editorial direction.

One year, some third graders were incensed that the parents of some students from our school had been detained by ICE (Immigration and Customs Enforcement) officers after a raid on the Del Monte factory where they worked. They wrote letters to the mayor, to ICE, and created a petition that they then had the whole school sign. Another class was both excited and nervous about the redevelopment of the public housing where some of our class lived. After exploring the proposed plans and meeting some of the officials and architects, they submitted their own plans for what the community should look like. All of these examples emerged from classroom conversations and from urgent issues that rose up in the community.

During one of our weekly current events conversations, I showed footage of the aftermath of the Gulf oil spill. Later, Kaylee came across some pictures of environmental catastrophes around the world while doing her own research on her grandma's computer. She and her grandma were both shocked by the garbage island in the North Pacific Gyre, much of which is plastic water bottles. Kaylee brought her concern, along with some printed photos of the garbage floating in the ocean, to a class meeting. Her passion was palpable, and other students were swept into her concern. I asked for students to discuss their reactions with a neighbor and the room exploded with talk. Before pulling them back together I listened in to a few conversations. Some kids seemed saddened, and so I asked them to think about what could be done.

"We should stop using water bottles," said Antonio, "and just use the fountain."

Kaylee agreed, "We could also make posters to tell people about this."

A few days later it was raining during recess so the class stayed in, playing board games and teasing me about eating my lunch and emailing at the same time. Kaylee and a few others asked if they could use my computer to get some more information from the internet. I helped them find some images of ocean trash to inspire their drawing. One rainy Oregon week later, they'd drawn up some posters and placed them around the school.

It was a great example of meaningful social justice and academic work coming through a routine of discussing what matters.

So it started to feel odd that my students were channeling their passion and curiosity into persuasive writing, when my intentional teaching of persuasive writing was yielding relatively rote and flat results. For example, assigning my writers a persuasive letter on a given topic, like asking the principal to make school

different—usually more recess—may have taught them some effective ways to make an argument and back it up with evidence and analysis, but it went nowhere, either with the principal or with the learning. It was an exercise, not a learning opportunity. Because both reader and writer perceived it as an empty gesture, there was the sad hidden lesson that writing is not an effective way to advocate or to make change.

> ## I asked myself how I could shift my students from merely working on persuasive pieces to actually writing to persuade.

I asked myself how I could shift my students from merely working on persuasive pieces to actually writing to persuade. How could I strike a balance between the passion of their concerns, the difficulty of writing well, and their fragile sense of power in the world? How could I juggle my goals for their growth as individuals, as writers and as citizens? I wanted them to think about the change they wanted and to explore the best way to address it.

Starting Out

I believe that listening and speaking, reading and writing, reflecting and advocating are reciprocal processes. If I want to effect change, then I need to account for my influences and explore how others have brought about change. For students, I know that careful modeling is the linchpin of any new learning. To begin a unit on persuasive writing, I asked my students to think how they came to their beliefs and to explore the strategies others have used in working for justice.

I started by telling a story from my life that illustrated what I wanted them to do. I told them that my mom worked at my high school and my friend, Amina, was her student aide. "Amina was my friend in 4th grade, and we still keep in touch. She is Muslim and chose to start covering her head with a scarf our senior year. As we got ready for graduation, the principal let her know that she would not be able to march if she had anything else covering her head beside her mortarboard. My mom was furious and dashed off a letter to the principal. This led to some big arguments, but in the end Amina was left to choose how she wanted to participate. This experience taught me that you have to take a stand when people are being treated unfairly." I then put the question to my students, "When have you learned a lesson like that from somebody else—about what you should do when you face a problem?"

Divonne talked about how her dad had helped her feel better about a problem with a friend by joking around. I said, "Great example. I'm going to start a poster with these examples to help us remember." I wrote, "Divonne learned to laugh at her problems from her dad."

Veronica said her brother had shown her a new way to do division and also taught her to breathe deeply when she felt stressed. We added that to the poster, too. Some students could not think of an example right away, but as their friends shared their ideas, the light bulbs started to go on.

Shelby asked, "So does it count if I learned something from school? I learned that reading helps me understand the world."

"I think it's a great idea to list how you use your school learning in the rest of your life," I said, adding her idea to the list.

Over the next week we returned to the chart during class meetings, adding new ideas. Not all of the ideas were earth-shattering political awakenings. In fact, many were simple things like, "I learned to tie my shoes from my cousin." I included every idea, though, because I wanted students to take pride in all of the ways they had learned from the people they cared about. I wanted them to situate themselves within a community of learning and influence.

This is important because I often find myself pushing my students to a level of insight or critical thinking that is beyond their grasp developmentally. When the insight doesn't come, I feel like my lesson has failed or I haven't tried hard enough. What I've discovered, though, is that patience is key. I can't will a conversation to go deeper—it just takes time. Often, they are really just offering something they think is acceptable to the group or pleasing to me. And as their teacher, I'm happy they feel safe sharing the tenderly specific experiences that are emotionally resonant for them as children.

But these first ideas are not just a way to get on the list. For Michael, learning to tie his shoes from his cousin needed to go on the list because his cousin had moved away, and he missed her. There is often a deeper idea hiding behind the first thing that comes to mind. As homework, I asked my class to talk to their families and think of what else they might add to the list. The next morning, as they trickled to their seats, I asked them if they had thought of anything else to add to our chart. Michael grabbed a sticky note and a marker from his supply tub and wrote, "I learned that it's important to call people you miss on the phone, like my cousins." When I asked him where his idea came from, he said, "Well, I talked to my sister and she said we should call them and it felt good to talk to them."

"That's great, Michael. How could we turn that into a lesson that everyone could use in their life?"

He puzzled for a moment. Veronica offered, "We should stay in touch with the people we love so we have good connections."

Michael agreed that was an important thing he had learned. As a teacher with a concern for justice, I know the conversation needs to go deeper. But if I drag them along, stressed by the pace of our go-go curriculum, my teaching about persuasion becomes yet another assignment, herding them into a flat "correct" idea. Small first ideas have a way of becoming smarter second or third ideas when they have a chance to breathe and live in a community of influence.

I included every idea because I wanted students to take pride in all of the ways they had learned from the people they cared about.

To keep their ideas dancing and start to prioritize their lessons learned, I asked everyone to collect their thoughts on a graphic organizer that has spaces for them to list the people who have influenced them and the ways in which they were influenced (see p. 64).

Next, I wanted them to see how these influences, the lessons I had learned, had prompted me to take a stand at different times in my life. I also wanted to demystify the process by which people decide to act for fairness—to help them see that standing up is not just something that exceptional, heroic people do. I want them to see that the courage to act often springs from awareness. So again, I shared stories from my life, but this time about times where I had acted for fairness.

I told them, "In 5th grade my friend Mary was excluded from an 'all boys' football game. After the teachers blew off her concerns, she asked me to practice throwing with her instead of playing with the boys. I wanted to keep playing with the boys but after I thought about it, I realized that she was right to feel left out, so I joined her. Soon enough, other boys and girls joined us and we had our own game."

Students shared their own stories of being left out of games at school. Kevin told a story of helping some younger students who didn't know how to join a game. "They were just standing there," he said, "so I asked them if they wanted to play kickball. Then I told everyone to let them play."

To expand the scope of influence we were thinking about, we spent a few days re-reading some of the justice fighter biographies and memoirs we'd read at the beginning of the year. Using picture books such as *César Chávez: Champion and Voice of Farmworkers*, by Suzanne Slade, we talked about what we could learn from people who had acted for justice. After reading the book, I asked students what lessons we could learn from César Chávez. There were perplexed looks. I tried another tack, "Well, what did he do that was important?"

"He helped farmworkers!" Lidia said.

"How? Can you find a page in the book that shows that?" I asked, handing the book to Lidia. She turned to the middle of the book. "Right here it says he started the union to get the farmers to listen to the workers."

"So what can we learn from that, everybody?"

After a number of attempts to get a good phrasing, we agreed that a lesson we could take from him was that, "If you stick together and support each other, then people will listen to you." We looked further into the book and talked about how he fasted and went to jail. From this my students decided that "sometimes you need to take a risk and do something brave to make a change."

For their persuasive writing pieces, I wanted them to tackle a big issue or idea. I gathered the class on the floor and asked them which of the life lessons they thought were the most important ones. Edwin said, "I think it was important that Ariana showed Divonne

how to use her lunch card in the cafeteria, but I think it was more important what she learned from her dad." When I asked him why, he said, "The lunch card is just about how to do something that you only do in one place. What her dad taught her is something that she can use anytime in her life."

Taking up his smart idea, I reworded the question as: "What are the lessons up here that we could use anywhere? That shape who you are?" I asked them to share the ones they thought fit those criteria with a neighbor and then asked them to make a list of those in their writing notebooks. Some students found only one or two from the long list on the poster, but most had a good list of "learnings." I told them to keep this list in their memory because they were going to use it to write a poem.

For a writing lesson, this was a lot of talking and thinking, which is crucial, but it's not a lot of writing. So to help students organize their thoughts around the question of influences and life lessons, and to keep the pencils moving, I asked them to share what they learned in a poem. I gave them an example to work from by creating a repeating line poem on the projector.

I used this pattern, "From _____, I learned _____," using my thoughts on the posters to build the lines. I started, "From my mom, I learned that sometimes you have to speak up if you're going to do what's right." Then I asked them to help me add a few lines, based on our biography studies.

WHAT I LEARNED

From Wilma Rudolph I learned to keep on trying, even when you're tired.

From my dad I learned to laugh at your problems like they're silly.

From Harriet Tubman I learned to leave no one behind.

From my brother I learned to play just enough.

From Ar'Nea I learned that a smile tells you that you aren't alone and that time is tickin' and we better get this poem done.

From my teachers I learned to read and write, which is everything.

— Divonne (4th Grade)

After sorting through what they believe and who they look to for guidance, it was time to flip the focus, to return to the question of how influence becomes inspiration, how learning becomes action. I wanted them to use this grounding to articulate what they thought was important, what they thought should change. Still, I had to guide students in identifying issues that matter—that matter to them and will matter to a lot of people. This is a delicate balance, moving beyond their own sphere of knowledge and concern while claiming their place in the world around them.

"Now it is time for you to think about what you want to teach people. You can take a turn telling the world how things should be." I asked them to think about things they wished were different about the world, things they wished people would do and things they wish people would stop doing (see organizer, p. 65). Some students struggled here, so I prompted them to reflect on their experiences and to think about what they talked about in their "What I learned" poem.

Some students needed guidance honing in on an idea that was neither unique to their experience or out of the realm of their expertise. I asked them questions like, "Is this an issue that affects a lot of people or just a few?" and "How much do you know about this topic? Would you have a lot of smart ideas to share about this or just a few?" Many students were worried about pollution, some wanted to address health risks like smoking or drugs, and many wanted to change what schooling was like.

Making a Poster

From teacher-writer Stephanie Parsons' book, Second Grade Writers, I got the idea of having students make posters to clarify their thinking before they write their persuasive letter or essay. She has students pick a topic to explore and create a poster that explains their thinking. This becomes a rudimentary thesis, or central argument. The crux, though, is that they create a message on the poster explaining what they want people to do. After looking at some images of posters from different political and health campaigns, we talked about some of the elements they saw in the posters.

"They all had some way of getting our attention," said Max, "like the way the words were big or there was a picture that looked interesting."

Sarah added to that, "A lot of them were silly or scary to make you really focus on the idea." We discussed how in every one, the message was clear.

"Right! You have to make sure they can understand what you're trying to say," I said. Using copier paper to make first drafts, students revised, edited, and then moved to bigger sheets of paper to make a version for public display.

Martin wrote, "Be smart, make art. Don't spend too much time watching TV!" under a two-panel picture showing a child with a TV for a face, in one, and a girl making art with smiling family members behind her, in the other. Juan drew a zombie-like class of students and a furious looking teacher underneath. "Parents, make sure your kids get a good night's sleep. Their teacher will thank you." Ari's poster showed a smiling tree around whose branches was written, "Compost! Starve a landfill! Feed a tree!"

Putting it All Together

From there, we had a great launching pad for creating a written piece. I told them that they were now going to back up the message on their posters with a longer written message. Some of my students jumped right in to it, using what they remembered from working on a personal essay to structure a persuasive essay.

> **They were now going to back up the message on their posters with a longer written message.**

Many of my writers needed some careful guidance. I gathered small groups at our group table with their posters, some markers and some sentence strips. Using D'Andre's poster about pollution in the ocean as a model, we brainstormed arguments that would back up his message of "The ocean is filling with plastic bottles. Use a water bottle or drink from the tap!" I asked them what we could say that would help people understand the problem. D'Andre said, "Well, fish and birds are dying from all the plastic pieces." I wrote that down on a sentence strip. "There's a huge island of trash in the Pacific," he continued, and I wrote that down, too. We went on for a bit, stacking up arguments. Not all of them were very sound, but I took them all in anticipation of weeding out the weak ones later. Then I asked students to work with a partner to develop some supporting sentences of their own.

The next day we met again and I helped them arrange the sentence strips together with their posters and asked students how they could take all their ideas and turn them into a written message that would help people understand what they were trying to say. D'Andre was ready to write a longer piece so I used his ideas again, pointing out that each sentence could grow into part of a persuasive essay if we explained the evidence even further.

I asked him to take his argument about the garbage patch in the North Pacific Gyre and go back to a newspaper article we'd read together earlier in the year. He found a part that described the garbage island and read it to the group.

I asked, "So how can you use that to say more? Can you use that information to back up your argument, here?" He grabbed a marker and started adding to his first sentence:

> There's a huge island in the Pacific Ocean. It is mostly plastic trash that floats on the water. Some scientists say it is as big as Texas. Chemicals from the trash gets into the ocean and it's poisonous to living things. Some of the trash is from boats but most is from land.

We watched him write, erase, cross out, and circle back to find the best phrasing. I said, "He made such smart moves when he was writing, didn't he? He kept reading that section again and again, turning it over in his head to make the ideas his own. What did you see him doing?" They described what I had seen him doing: grabbing information from the article, thinking about it, and then wording it so that it suited his argument.

"He had to keep going back to the article and in his own writing," said Veronica.

"It's kind of like drawing or building," said D'Andre. "When I got to the last sentence, I realized I needed to change something from the beginning."

I was glad that they could see that the process did not proceed from top to bottom in a single pass, but came out of many attempts. I hope that my students, especially the ones for whom writing is hard, know that good arguments don't spring out of your mind fully formed—that they emerge from revision. With some conferencing and help from partners, most students developed their evidence into a handful of paragraphs. I held special lunchtime revision sessions to help small groups grow their ideas and asked some kids finish their writing as homework. Some students ended up with only one or two developed paragraphs, but they satisfied my requirement—that they have a clear message, backed up with evidence and explanation.

For the message to resonate with a broad community, they need to be able to manipulate the conventional tools and structures of writing.

As a teacher, I needed to make a decision about how much choice I allow and how much structure I impose on their writing because there were many formats their pieces could take. Finding the balance is difficult, especially when I am required to evaluate their writing by a rubric or set of traits. For the message to be meaningful and memorable to students, they need some control over both content and process. For the message to resonate with a broad community, they need to be able to manipulate the conventional tools and structures of writing. Of course, guiding students to make a smart decision can be a lengthy process and requires a lot of thoughtful exploration of the possibilities. Maybe it will be a poster with an attached paragraph, maybe it will be a blog post, maybe it will be an op-ed in our class newsletter and maybe it will be a traditional essay.

Some years, I have had the time and freedom to let students explore different formats, some years I have prioritized academic writing and directed everyone toward moving into an essay. With every group of students, though, the key for building strong pieces has been to have strong models that my students can analyze and emulate. All good writing is made up of the "bones" of other pieces. Some of my models were from former students, but I pulled some opinion pieces from student publications: *YouthRadio.org*, *IndyKids.org* and *TeenInk* magazine. We read the models repeatedly—highlighting arguments and evidence, teasing apart the magic of a lovely sentence or surprising word.

A few weeks after students had finished their pieces, we were back on the carpet, in a circle. They had their persuasive pieces in front of them, ready for a final read around. Before we started, I asked them what they'd learned in this unit. Martin spoke up first, "I learned a lot about my friends from this, like who is important in their lives and what they've learned from those people."

Jessica picked up on his thought, "I think I learned most about everyone's opinions, like what they want to change."

I tried to get them to talk about what they had learned about writing, and they had some teacher-pleasing things to say about arguments and evidence. They wanted to talk about each other, though, and how they had been influenced. To accompany their writing in the hall display we added this statement: "We're not just writing to change the world. We're writing to change each other and ourselves. It's about writing to change who we are in the world." ▪

....

Mark Hansen teaches in a combined 3rd- and 4th-grade classroom at Peninsula K-8 in Portland, Ore. He is a co-director of the Oregon Writing Project.

My Influences

People who influenced you	How did they change you?

Books that influenced you	How did these change you?

What I Want to Talk About

Things I wish we could change

Things I wish people would do more often

Things I wish people would stop doing

Diana Craft

Patterns and Punctuation

Learning to question language

ELIZABETH SCHLESSMAN

"Look, Teacher! Moss! I see moss!" Ana exclaims as we cross the street during our 5th-grade class field trip. My eyes follow Ana's index finger past the grates of a storm drain. "Where?" asks Daniel. "Oh! I see it, too! Moss!"

Moss is not new to my students. It has been a part of their lives in the Pacific Northwest since they were born 11 years ago. We can find moss growing around the perimeter of the rubber seal of car trunks and the base of car windows. We can find moss in sidewalk cracks and curb joints. Moss proliferates in Oregon.

Punctuation is not new to my students' lives, either. The books they have been reading since kindergarten are full of capital letters, periods, commas, quotation marks, and exclamation points. We can find punctuation on signs, in letters, and on labels. Punctuation proliferates in text, though not always in student writing.

There are more than 20,000 species of moss on Earth. Most of us, however, have only one word to describe moss. So "moss" is what we see. We pass by the green without noticing or thinking about the patterns.

Whether or not we are asked to notice and question patterns in the world around us can depend on who we are. A well-known study by Jean Anyon contrasted the education at a school in which students' families were working class with a more affluent school. It showed that students in the working-class school were asked to complete mechanical and routine tasks while students in an affluent school were invited to problem-solve, develop, and elaborate on ideas. Many years later, Jonathan Kozol described a similar phenomenon and dubbed it "educational apartheid" in his book *The Shame of the Nation*.

The majority of students I work with carry society's labels working class and Latina/o. Our school often toes the slippery Adequate Yearly Progress line where the word *not* leeches itself onto the word *met*. In today's educational context, the mechanical and routine tasks observed in Anyon's study can easily translate into a simplified educational vision for working-class students: Follow the rules and pass the tests. As we plan instruction—even instruction about punctuation—we have the opportunity to engage students' minds and create new labels: question-asking, problem-solving. How we teach embeds a vision of who we think our kids are and what we think they are capable of. Are they destined for a future of critical thinking, questioning, revising the rules—or a future of compliance and rule-following?

Seeing the Layers

"Look, Teacher, moss! I see two different types!" Mayra exclaims on the playground as she picks up a storm-blown sycamore branch. I think I found some lichen, too!" She is beginning to see the layers of nature—the patterns and complexities that differentiate lichen from moss. I, too, am beginning to see the layers—of punctuation.

I found myself in the middle of a "Look, Teacher, moss!" moment one mid-September afternoon. I was reading *The Dangerous World of Butterflies,* by Peter Laufer, when a sentence stopped me short: "Incredible: gray sky to blue sky to orange sky."

A single adjective before a colon. Who knew you could do that? Some 10 pages later, there it was again. The adjective colon technique pranced across the page: "Amazing: He grabs a cell signal and calls the El Paso ejido."

When my students were 4th graders about to take the state writing test, their teachers did the best they could to prepare them for success; they taught them to add a colon to their writing by mentioning the time of day. Almost every narrative I read in the fall of 5th grade included a reference to a specific time. "It started at 6 p.m. and ended at 7:02 p.m.," Joel wrote in his narrative writing assessment at the end of October.

Hurling a colon into a personal narrative may help boost the double-weighted conventions score on the Oregon state writing test. Yet the sight of colon after colon formulaically flung into writing made my teaching heart hurt. I saw obedient students submitting to the rules of the red pen, trying to conform to an invisible power. Meaning was compromised to serve the punctuation mark and the state test score. It was painful to watch students dutifully insert colons based on their trust that test scores are a definitive and valid measure of good writing.

I learned punctuation through rules and exercises and red pen corrections. And I learned to trust those rules over my own thinking. As we marveled over a sentence in our bilingual 5th-grade classroom, I felt obligated to explain it away as an anomaly. "This is something that doesn't follow the rule," I said as I read some of my favorite parts aloud from Jerry Spinelli's *Maniac Magee:* "Bodies. Skin. Colors. Water. Gleaming. Buttery. Warm. Cool. Wet. Screaming. Happy." Or one of my favorite paragraphs: "Apparently not."

Whether or not the sentences conform to the simplified rules I learned, there is no doubt that Spinelli's writing works. It not only works, it shines. The period beckons the reader to slow down and honor each of the words. The choices to use periods over commas and single words over sentences serve the author's purpose. Although students need to understand the ways their writing will be analyzed on the state test (and perhaps know they will receive a higher mark for including a colon), they also need to understand that the purpose of punctuation is to express oneself more powerfully and imaginatively, to better communicate, not merely to be "correct."

I still can't identify moss species, but I can go for a hike and see 20 varieties where I used to see only one. I walk trails asking questions and searching for patterns. Why does this particular moss species thrive in this particular place? Can I predict its location by better understanding the patterns of its adaptations? Can we apply this notice-the-mark and search-for-pattern inquiry to our study of the dash and the comma?

Teacher-Guided Inquiry

I decided to try collective and individual inquiry as a part of our classroom study of punctuation. I wanted my students to know that there were patterns beyond—and exceptions to—the rules they already knew. I wanted them to trust their own thinking to reason about those patterns. Even if we ended up discovering the so-called "rules," I wanted students to start from a place of inquiry and empowerment. I wanted them to see that placing punctuation on the page is a decision-making process and that the teacher or the textbook and the "rules" created by others can be questioned.

In the classroom, I often use familiar content to teach a new process or a familiar process to teach new content.

In the classroom, I often use familiar content to teach a new process or a familiar process to teach new content. As we gathered on the rug in the front of the room to begin our punctuation inquiry, I reminded students that they were in a familiar place by referring to the diagram of the inquiry cycle that was posted on the wall: "Today we will apply the inquiry cycle we've been using in science to explore questions about punctuation. We will ask a question about a particular type of sentence, make a prediction or hypothesis about what we think is happening, and see if we can collect examples of similar sentences to support our hypothesis. For now we will all work with the same question, but soon you will think of your own."

Eventually I wanted students to notice marks and ask open-ended questions, so I decided to start by

modeling inquiry from question to application in one anchor lesson. I began by modeling an I-notice-and-now-I-wonder process. I chose a model sentence and question that would make the inquiry process accessible to students at all levels of reading and English language learning: "I was reading *Chicken Sunday*," I said, "and I noticed this sentence: 'When we passed Mr. Kodinski's hat shop, Miss Eula would always stop and look in the window at the wonderful hats.'

"Now I am wondering about the comma. Here is my question: Is there always a comma in the middle when a sentence starts with when?"

I wrote the example sentence and question on the board. Then I asked, "Can you find any other examples that follow the same pattern?"

Students set to work with partners, paging through Patricia Polacco's *Chicken Sunday*—detectives on a search. I wanted students to be able to hold on to meaning as they asked questions about the author's punctuation choices, so I had picked a book we had read together a few times the previous week.

"I found one," volunteered Laura. "'When it was time for her solo comma, we knew she was singing just for us,'" she read. Picking up the red and black markers, I began color-coding the examples to help students see the pattern. I wrote the word when in red and continued filling in the rest of the words of the sentence in black. When I was done, I added a red comma.

I had hardly finished writing Laura's example when Jessica shared another: "'When we finally got the courage to ask about doing odd jobs to earn some extra money comma, he apologized and told us that there was no work.'"

Once we had five examples on the board, we looked for a pattern and tried to make a generalization: What do we notice about these sentences? How do they start? Where is the comma? Why did the writer put it there? I was hoping that students would begin to understand that they could infer the function of a punctuation mark by analyzing its effect on the meaning of the text. I wanted to remind them that their analytical brains could create "Look, Teacher, moss!" moments—that they could make generalizations about punctuation patterns in the world around them. I asked students to explain what they were noticing to a partner and then asked a few to share their thinking with the class.

Jason tried to explain: "It's like you put a comma when one thing happens while another thing is happening."

"When a sentence starts with when, you put a comma after the first part," suggested Julia. I wrote the generalizations on the board and wondered aloud if the pattern would be the same in other books or if we might be able to find some counterexamples.

Since my goal in the anchor lesson was to model the inquiry process from question to application, I referred back to the inquiry diagram and invited students to move beyond analysis and interpretation to application.

"Can you think of a sentence with this pattern you might use in your own writing?" I looked at students gathered on the floor, chairs, and stools. They looked back, hands in laps, twisting hair, and scraping pencils. Had I pushed through the analysis too quickly? Should we have taken the time to play with words, flip the clauses, see how the sentence reads when we remove the comma? "Here, I will start you off with my own example," I offered. "When we come to school the day after evening conferences comma, the students and teachers are sleepy."

Slowly the water started to bubble. "When I went to my conference comma, my mom told me she was proud of me," shared David as other hands slid into the air.

"When my dad saw my work comma, he was impressed," Angela volunteered.

I wrote color-coded student examples on the board under the examples we had found in the book. As I set the red and black markers on the marker board sill, I asked students to share one more example orally with their partner. I listened in as a few pairs shared their examples and then encouraged students to find other examples or counterexamples in the books they were reading.

Student-Generated Inquiry

And so we began. We had named our process, tried it together, and now I wanted to see whether I could help students form their own questions about other punctuation patterns on the page. I chose open-ended over guided inquiry because I wanted students to

realize they could learn about punctuation outside of teacher-initiated lessons. I wanted them to notice and question punctuation in their own reading. I knew there would be times when we would work together on a specific use of punctuation, but I wanted to create a space for students to generate their own questions and trust their own thinking.

> **We had named our process, tried it together, and now I wanted to see whether I could help students form their own questions about other punctuation patterns on the page.**

I invited a group of seven students to the rug the next day during reading workshop. We settled into a circle on the floor, and began paging through *Chicken Sunday*. "What do you observe? What do you notice about the punctuation? What questions do you have?"

Students slowly flipped pages, minds churning.

Joel pointed at a sentence in the middle of the book: "Why does it have two commas in the air and a comma under?" I recorded his question on a piece of notebook paper for him. I wanted student energy to stay focused on thinking, not writing.

By the time I finished, Ana glanced up. "Why does it have a dialogue mark and then a comma after the person's name?"

I was surprised by the range of questions and the tendency to use descriptions instead of formal names. Hadn't we already talked about quotation marks during our study of dialogue? Is there a correlation between student use of formal terminology and the degree to which they apply punctuation in their writing? Is punctuation awareness a continuum in which students move from noticing and describing to naming and applying?

"Here it says 'hatbox dot dot dot gift-wrapped.' Why does it have dots?"

"Why does *Chicken Sunday* start with a capital letter in the middle of the sentence?"

I continued recording questions and asking for more. Once everyone in the group had generated at least one question, I invited students to pick one to investigate for the day and handed out an inquiry guide to help them through the process. As students began recording their questions and collecting examples in a three-column chart, I was thankful I had chosen to do the individual inquiry as a small group activity. Students stumbled —"What was my question again?" They needed direction —"I think there might be another example of that pattern in this paragraph." "Does the author of this book use dashes in the same way as that author?" There were opportunities for collaboration —"You two have the same question; maybe you want to work together."

Students were beginning to analyze and explain patterns. Daniel collected examples as he investigated his question: How do authors use dashes? Next to each example, Daniel analyzed the author's use of the dash in the My Thinking column on his Punctuation Inquiry guide (see p. 72).

"I think you use dashes to give more information," he wrote in the box next to the sentence he collected from *Those Shoes* by Maribeth Boelts: "We shoot baskets — a loose piece of tape on Antonio's shoe smacks the concrete every time he jumps."

As students found examples and began to draw conclusions, I invited some of them to ask a new question. In the midst of the momentum, I forgot to loop the inquiry back to applying the learning to our own writing.

Applying

As the small group gathered around a pile of familiar classroom library books a few days later, I had a sense that question-generation and pattern-searching could deepen and expand indefinitely. I wanted to honor student needs, yet I also wanted to press toward application in student writing. I turned to Joel, who had collected three examples of ellipses. He was busy writing a conclusion. "I think you use them, like, when you want to show a pause," he explained.

A handful of students had tried this: research a safe question —one with an already known answer. "I bet you are used to pausing for ellipses when you read." Joel nodded. "Do you already use ellipses in your writing?" Joel shook his head. "Go get your journal and try. See if you can find a place to use ellipses in something you already wrote, or start something new."

"It was a cold day it was the last game of the seson and I yeld 'pas me the … soccer bal.' I was gonna fall."

"Did you really pause when you said that?" I asked, wondering if he had forced ellipses into a place where they didn't belong.

"Actually, I fell when I said that, right there," Joel pointed at the ellipses. "I couldn't talk because I was falling."

I often mine student writing for great examples of character description or narrative openings so that students can learn from each other and try out a classmate's technique in their own writing. I asked a few students to post their color-coded sentence strip examples and conclusions on a bulletin board to encourage other students to think about the patterns and leave tracks of our process so we could reference our learning.

Looking Back

As I listened to student questions and watched the search for examples, I realized that open-ended inquiry was a valuable —and inefficient —process. The opportunity to ask questions certainly helped students delve into the layers of print and the purposes of punctuation. Yet sifting through sentences in search of examples was time-consuming, and with so many inquiries happening at the same time, it was difficult to facilitate the deep discussion needed to solidify learning. Although open-ended inquiry infused wonder and freedom into our study of punctuation, I knew I still needed to create space for collective inquiry, discussion, and teaching about the ways punctuation choices affect meaning.

Empowerment Through Inquiry

"Why does your class always stop to look at that tree? Is it a part of what you are doing in science?" a colleague asks as we cross the asphalt to our portable classrooms. Her simple question has a layered answer that begins with appreciating moss and changing leaves, and branches to critical thinking about the world and the word. Why is it worthwhile for students to notice patterns, ask questions, and pay attention to detail?

My students helped me answer that question as we spent time reflecting on learning at the end of the year. "I used to just read and I ignored the punctuation," Laura told me. "Now I notice the punctuation marks. I used to keep reading on, but now I know they count."

Daniel reminded me to balance open-ended inquiry, teacher-guided inquiry, and direct teaching: "Maybe the students won't recognize the punctuation. Maybe if you teach it, when they are reading they will recognize it."

Open-ended inquiry certainly isn't the only way to teach punctuation. But it can help build a powerful context.

Mayra recognized the value of discovery, the value of constructing knowledge with scaffolds and support: "You won't learn that much if someone just tells you that's how you do it. I like using the book to look for clues. If I use a book, I can figure it out myself."

Open-ended inquiry certainly isn't the only way to teach punctuation. But it can help build a powerful context. By beginning a study of commas and quotation marks with student observations and thinking, we can empower children to think critically as they notice patterns and ask questions about the world around them. Teaching is always about nurturing the capacities of our students to imagine and create a better world—it begins with commas and ellipses, but that's not where it ends. ∎

References

Anyon, Jean. "Social Class and the Hidden Curriculum of Work," *Journal of Education.* 162.1. (Fall 1980).

Boelts, Maribeth. *Those Shoes.* Somerville, Mass.: Candlewick Press, 2007.

Kozol, Jonathan. *The Shame of the Nation.* New York: Crown, 2005.

Laufer, Peter. *The Dangerous World of Butterflies: The Startling Subculture of Criminals, Collectors, and Conservationists.* Guilford, Conn.: Lyons Press, 2009.

Polacco, Patricia. *Chicken Sunday.* New York: Scholastic Inc., 1992.

Spinelli, Jerry. *Maniac Magee.* New York: Scholastic Inc., 1990.

Wall Kimmerer, Robin. *Gathering Moss: A Natural and Cultural History of Mosses.* Corvallis, Ore.: Oregon State University Press, 2003.

....

Elizabeth Schlessman teaches bilingual 4th grade in Woodburn, Oregon She is a teacher-consultant with the Oregon Writing Project. All students' names have been changed.

Punctuation Inquiry

MAKE AN OBSERVATION AND ASK A QUESTION:

Choose one page of the book. What do you notice about punctuation? What punctuation marks grab your attention? Do you see anything you haven't noticed before? Do you notice any patterns?

QUESTION:		
COLLECT DATA:		
Punctuation Mark	**Example**	**My Thinking**
CONCLUSION:		

APPLY:

Go back to one of your journal entries or your writing notebook, and apply what you have learned.

Orlando Sierra

Confronting Child Labor

An elementary teacher discovers that her students' best work emerges from a unit on child labor

KATHARINE JOHNSON

The best work I have seen from my students came as a result of a two-month-long research project into child labor. The work my students created during this social justice research project showed passion, creativity, and academic rigor. Keeping justice at the center of my curriculum did more than heighten students' awareness of social issues; it offered them an opportunity to expand their academic skills by engaging with something meaningful.

Boise-Eliot is a public school in Portland, Ore. Most of Boise-Eliot's students are African American (nearly 80 percent) and come from working-class and working poor families.

The rest are from immigrant or low-income white families. The school is proudly multiracial, multilingual, and academically rigorous.

When I designed my child labor unit, I had a few key goals in mind. I wanted students to gain an understanding that goods are produced by labor. I wanted them to see that children perform that labor in many parts of the world, including the United States. I wanted them to develop personal connections with real children trapped in child labor. I wanted them to learn about effective strategies for resistance. And I wanted them to create polished work around the issue of child labor. I found the child labor chapter in *Rethinking Globalization: Teaching for Justice in an Unjust World* to be a valuable guide in helping to align teaching goals and classroom activities.

Seeing Labor

To help my students start to think about the origins of the goods we purchase in U.S. stores, we began with a "label hunt." Students worked in pairs to identify the countries of origin for their shoes and their shirts. I made a list of the countries where our

> **To help my students start to think about the origins of the goods we purchase in U.S. stores, we began with a "label hunt."**

clothes were manufactured and together we tallied the number of articles made in each country. Most of the clothing was manufactured throughout Southeast Asia; the shoes primarily came from China. Then I gave them world maps and asked them to highlight all the countries from our list.

"I have a bunch of highlighting down here by India," noted Irina.*

"Yeah, me too. How do you say this place Bon... Bang..."

"Bangladesh," I answered.

"Dang, that's far," said Deja. "I bet it took her shirt like a week to get here."

Through this exercise, students were beginning to understand that labor often takes place far from where the products of that labor are consumed. Later

*All students' names have been changed.

I would regret beginning with a focus on international rather than U.S. labor, but at the time I was elated at their enthusiasm.

Seeing Child Labor

The next day I asked them what they thought child labor was. They responded with a litany of household chores they were responsible for doing. Kalvin has to watch his baby sister sometimes and always has to take out the trash. Frank and Ben have to work safety patrol before and after school. Elizima has to stay home from school to help her mom when the babies are sick. After I learned what they thought child labor was, we began to read about and discuss child labor: what it looks like, who is involved, who benefits, who is hurt.

Over the course of the next weeks, we spent time reading background articles that discussed various aspects of child labor. (See "Useful Resources on Child Labor," p. 77.) As the students read and discussed the articles, the conversation grew richer.

We analyzed the U.N. Declaration on the Rights of the Child and discussed why parts of this international document are ignored in different contexts. Students created their own versions of the declaration and shared these with classmates by making posters that we hung from the window blinds.

Making Personal Connections

An important shift in my students' thinking came when we read "Everywhere on Earth," by Eduardo Galeano. (See p. 84.) This stirring piece illustrates various jobs children around the world are forced to do.

The classroom, normally filled with murmured questions and blurted observations, was very quiet as we read this piece. I asked students to tell me what they felt as we were reading. "Sad" was the most common response, along with "That's whack," and quite a bit of tongue clicking and lip smacking. I asked my students to call out some of the jobs Galeano mentions. I listed the jobs on chart paper, and then we compared the list to the household chores my students had listed earlier. When I asked for an analysis of the jobs child laborers do versus the chores my students do, hands went flying.

"I wouldn't want to pick fruit all day, especially with those pesticides on it." Maria began.

"Yeah and what if you had to work in a diamond mine? That's messed up. I'd take me some diamonds and run away," Leon added. The students were beginning to understand that child labor is not helping around the house but aching work performed all over the world by children even younger than they are.

The Tea Party

To deepen my students' connections to real child laborers, I used two amazing books: *We Need to Go to School: Voices from the Rugmark Schools* and *Stolen Dreams: Images of Child Labor*. The books are filled with photographs, descriptions, and personal narratives from actual child laborers. I used these materials to develop a "tea party." (See "Child Labor Tea Party Notes," p. 80, and "Child Labor Tea Party Participants," p. 81.) I copied or transcribed short biographical sections from the books, passed the biographies out randomly to the class, and asked the students to read them as many times as they could. As they read, I shared the pictures of the children they were reading about. They read and reread the biographies and spent a long time looking at the photos to memorize information about the child laborers. Finally they spent an afternoon in character as these laborers. Students walked around the room talking to each other and sharing details from their characters' lives. The knowledge I was asking my students to work with was painful and hard to comprehend. Being able to talk together and literally move away if it felt too overwhelming helped sustain the learning over a longer time than if I had simply had them at their seats reading biographies of child laborers.

Debating Child Labor

My students had already been developing strong reading and research strategies by reading articles and responding in research journals and discussion groups. I knew I wanted them to write persuasive essays by the end of the unit, but I hadn't planned how to do that yet. Fortunately, Karen Cosper, our English Language Learning teacher (who spends 45 minutes a day in my classroom) came up with the idea of having debates. She had held debates before in another class and promised they would strengthen students' knowledge. We planned to use debates to solidify the students' understanding and meet state benchmarks for formal speaking. These same debates would then act as springboards for organizing persuasive essays.

"What should we do about child labor?" I asked the class a few days later. Most of my class wanted to make it impossible for child labor to occur. But I reminded them that some child laborers we had read about didn't want it to end. They just wanted it to be safe and to earn a living wage. After some small-group and whole-group time devoted to the question of what should be done, we eventually agreed upon two main options for dealing with child labor: to make it stop right away or to make rules so it would be more fair. Karen hung two pieces of chart paper — one labeled "Abolish" and the other "Regulate" — and we divided the class into groups of three or four to generate ideas to support both positions.

We planned to use debates to solidify the students' understanding and meet state benchmarks for formal speaking. These same debates would then act as springboards for organizing persuasive essays.

They had their research folders out, and the teams searched for reasons why to abolish or regulate child labor. Karen and I passed out two colors of Post-It notes, which the students used to post their support of one of the positions on the chart papers. As a class we negotiated whether ideas belonged on one list or could be used to support either position. "Children get hurt or die," belonged on both lists. But the fact that children are needed to help support their families belonged on "Regulate."

By having the students in small groups discussing and reviewing the articles in their research folders, we were able to get a broad base of supporting details for the two positions. Students developed evidence from both the factual information in articles about international child labor and stories of real children living in child labor.

After the students shared their posted ideas, Karen and I recorded their Post-It note ideas onto the chart paper with bold black marker to make them easier to read. These chart papers hung at the front of the room and became both the support for our debates and a source of further information for students who still struggled to find their positions.

At first we did organized debates as part of our research time. Two students stood in front of the class and each took a position. (They didn't have to agree with the position.) They followed a formula for initiating the debate. Each student stood in front of the chart paper that listed the reasons to abolish or regulate and began by stating, "I believe child labor should be regulated/abolished because _____." Then they stated what they believed to be the strongest reasons for their positions. The two debaters went back and forth, giving reasons to support their positions and responding to their opponents' positions. Students pulled ideas from the chart paper. Karen and I modeled the debating process, overacting and turning to look at the chart paper for our ideas. At the end of our debate, we smiled and shook hands. Karen told the class that everyone would debate sometime in the next week then asked who was willing to start. Hands flew up.

At first, the debates lasted only two or three minutes and the students relied heavily on the ideas posted on the chart paper. But after a few days, they started improvising and the debates grew to three or four minutes. After each debate, Karen asked members of the audience what new ideas they had heard and encouraged everyone to return to their research folders and journals to get their own new ideas. Students hunted for great facts or vignettes to make their points. Mai studied the gnarled hands of an eight-year-old carpet factory laborer while Ken read and reread the article about child activist Iqbal Masih. Sarah circulated around the room asking for more evidence when she got stuck. Soon what had been "Kids get hurt when they work" became "Kids get hurt, like Benta, whose hands burn from the pesticides. Her hands should be protected."

Students who supported abolition began by saying, "No one makes the factory owners follow the law." By the end of the debates, someone said, "There are rules already, but they don't get followed and look at what happened to Iqbal Masih when he tried to make it change. He got murdered."

Students changed their positions as the debating continued. Some days, a student would debate very effectively for a position and a few kids would shift to that position. I did not want to force students to occupy either position; the debates were supposed to stir up ideas and solidify them through talking and listening. After about a week, most students stopped changing positions and had added ideas of their own to the initial ones we had listed on chart paper. We were almost ready to write persuasive essays.

During the final stage of the debates, I required each student to stake out and maintain one position. I gave them a day to decide finally where they stood and why. Again, I offered them time to discuss in small groups or with partners using the resources we had available. These final debates were the formal speeches students needed to give to meet the state benchmark. Students were prepared to present a fairly lengthy formal speech with a clear thesis, vivid details, and a strong conclusion.

Persuasive Essays

To help my students turn their oral arguments into persuasive essays, I passed out graphic organizers — pages with a large box at the top for a main idea and several smaller boxes below for details. I asked each student to record his or her position and several strong reasons for holding that position. I modeled completing the graphic organizers for both positions with an overhead transparency of the graphic organizer. I demonstrated the process, not because the form itself was difficult to complete, but because I wanted to show them how to pick four or five reasons that could best support their positions. Students took two class sessions to complete their graphic organizers. This large chunk of time allowed students to really think about which evidence they would choose to support their positions. It also allowed me a chance to give small group support to students who were overwhelmed by the vast amount of information we had collected. Some graphic organizers were the beginnings of eloquent essays with passion and voice already emerging. Others were simple lists of reasons to regulate or abolish. The important thing was that each student now had a map, crude or elegant, to guide the essay writing.

The persuasive essays would be the academically rigorous product I had hoped would come of the valuable process of this work. The debates supported the writing in a few ways: Students had already identified their strongest reason for holding their positions; they had already practiced responding to opposing views (counterpoint); and they had already practiced supporting their positions with evidence during the debates.

I used a variation on Linda Christensen's introduction examples from *Reading, Writing, and Rising Up* (startling fact, quote, scene, questions) to teach ways to introduce persuasive essays. I found examples from books and wrote a few myself to give students ideas of different types of introductions. I pointed out how each example had a position on child labor somewhere in the introductory paragraph.

Each student tried writing each type of introduction over two days of writing time. After trying each type, students chose one introduction they thought strongest for their essay. Some students used knowledge from the tea party to practice writing "character description" introductions. Roberto wrote:

> I know somebody who needs your help. Her name is Akash. She works in a carpet factory. The work is hard. The pay is little. She wants to go to school; mostly she wants time to play. Because of Akash and the other 125,000,000 child laborers child labor should be abolished so Akash can go to school and have time to play.

Hannah used a "startling fact" introduction:

> Did you know child labor doesn't only happen in the Third World? It happens in the United States, too. 120,000,000 children aged between four and 14 work around the whole world.

Using descriptions he had read of various types of work child laborers do, Karl wrote a "scene" introduction:

> Smoke rises from the dimly lit factories. The floor is musty; the air is dirty. The walls are filthy … and nobody is ever happy in there. Kids ranging from age four to 15 from all over the world work endless hours in these conditions for little money each day. Sad hmmmmmm? Well, what you just read about is child labor and every word of it is true.

Trevor used questions in his introduction:

> Why do some kids work? Why can't they go to school? Child labor should be abolished so kids can go to school.

Useful Resources on Child Labor

Harvest, by George Ancona (Marshall Cavendish Corp., 2001). A color photography book detailing the experience of migrant farm workers, including children in the United States.

Rethinking Globalization: Teaching for Justice in an Unjust World, edited by Bill Bigelow and Bob Peterson (Rethinking Schools, 2002). An excellent collection of resources, articles, and teaching ideas for all levels.

Stolen Dreams: Portraits of Working Children, by David Parker, with Lee Engfer and Robert Conrow (Lerner Publications, 1997). I used this for the tea party because of the terrific black-and-white photographs and brief captioned descriptions of working children.

We Need to Go to School: Voices of Rugmark Children, compiled by Tanya Roberts-Davies (Groundwood Books, 2001). First-person narratives of former child laborers who attend Rugmark-funded schools. Includes artwork and schoolwork done by the students.

The introductions varied in sophistication, but the variety of categories made this less glaring than if every child had written an identical introduction. Experimenting with different kinds of introductions also made it possible for my students to focus on the aspects of child labor that mattered most to them.

Once we had introductions, we returned to our graphic organizers. I used the overhead to show how to take an idea listed on the organizer and wrap explanatory sentences around it to make a paragraph. Students spent three days writing the body paragraphs of their essays. Each day we began and ended writing time with students sharing paragraphs they were confident about or ones they were stuck on and wanted their classmates to help them with. A few students needed one-on-one support to focus all the information into clear paragraphs. Others relied heavily on the chart papers still hanging at the front of the room for their details. But they all wrote.

Getting Active

I posted the essays on the bulletin board outside our classroom door and thought educating our school community could be the activist component of the unit. But I soon learned the bulletin board was nowhere near good enough for my kids. They wanted to do something more direct. Mel wanted to send all our school supplies to schools that educate former child laborers. Sandy wanted to bring former child laborers to the United States as adoptees. Gary wanted to go to the factories and get the kids. I needed to remind students of our earlier conversations about the larger context. I talked about shifting power and not just helping individual kids. They needed my help to decide how we could be effectively activist instead of impotently outraged. We decided to raise not just awareness but also money.

After an Internet search of various groups working to end child labor, I chose to affiliate with the Rugmark Group. The Rugmark Group liberates children from carpet factories and certifies factories as "child-labor free." Rugmark runs schools that educate former and current child laborers. I thought my students would be able to identify with the Rugmark schools.

> **I thought educating our school community could be the activist component of the unit. But I soon learned the bulletin board was nowhere near good enough for my kids. They wanted to do something more direct.**

We decided to continue our community outreach by creating a display booth for the Boise-Eliot Multicultural Fair, an event that happens once a year. And we agreed to raise money for Rugmark by making magnets to sell.

For the display, we left the persuasive essays up and added student poems for two voices (one voice a student at Boise-Eliot, the other a child laborer). (See p. 83.) For the magnet project, the students spent hours at home and school precisely coloring in motifs common in rugs woven by child laborers, which we then laminated and affixed to magnets.

The students practiced and role-played educating adults and kids who approached our display about child labor. I gave small groups scenarios they might encounter the night of the fair. What if a little kid keeps touching the magnets and messing up the display? What if an adult claims that you are doing child labor by selling magnets?

By the night of the fair we had created about 100 magnets. We set up a schedule of 15-minute shifts that teams of three kids would work. The bulletin board was covered with essays, photos, and poems about child labor. The students arrived eager to sell some magnets, most wearing their "church clothes." I practically had to kick kids out of the booth at the end of their 15-minute shift so that everyone got a chance to work. I hovered near the booth, monitoring but not interfering.

While the students' conversations couldn't be scored or sent into the school district's research and evaluation department, they offered me the evidence I needed to feel confident about my students' learning. Juan and Ned tried hard to sell the magnets for more than a dollar. "They cost a dollar but if you give more we'll send that, too."

Jameala and Aida got serious with their customers: "Did you know some kids have to work 14 hours a day for only $1?" Some kids were nervous and hardly spoke, but most could articulate that we were raising money for a school for children who used to be child laborers.

People were surprised to see what we were doing. A few seemed put off, but most asked the kids lots of questions, read some of their essays, and bought magnets. The last three kids were still selling magnets as the last families left the evening event.

The next morning when we counted our $125 to send to the Rugmark Foundation, every face in my classroom was bright. We shared joy in knowing that we had seen injustice and we had worked to stop it.

Looking Back

I would change many things about this unit. I would begin by analyzing child labor in the United States so that my students understand that child labor isn't something that just happens far away. I would try to make the activism closer to home, like supporting the school serving the agricultural workers I see every summer right outside of town. Or we might try to influence our school district in deciding who grows, picks, and packages the school lunches. I would try to put my students in touch with students at one of the schools serving students coming out of child labor.

Overall, I was extremely pleased with the academic skills my students developed during this unit. They honed geography skills when we did the label hunt; math applications when we sold magnets; reading and research strategies throughout the unit; speaking and writing skills during the debates and essays. They experienced collaborative learning and negotiated with each other through some meaningful disagreements. I was even able to turn in scores to the research and evaluation department of Portland Public Schools for their debates and essays.

I am certain that the quality of my students' work and their commitment to struggling through difficult material was born not just out of a dedication to learning, but from the meaningful, provocative content of child labor. ▪

....

Katharine Johnson teaches in Portland, Ore. She is co-director of the Oregon Writing Project.

Child Labor Tea Party Notes

Use the spaces below to write down notes about the other child laborers you meet during our tea party. First, work with your small group to fill in information about the child laborer you will be for the tea party.

	#1	#2	#3	#4	#5
What is the child laborer's NAME?					
WHERE does she/he work and live?					
What KIND OF WORK does he/she do?					
How OLD is he/she?					
WHY does she/he need to work?					
How does he/she FEEL about working?					
What is one DETAIL that stands out to you?					

Child Labor Tea Party Participants

AAKASH   I am 10 years old and I work every day in the carpet factory. All day and often into the night, I work at the looms, weaving row after row into carpets. My work is not very good because I am so young. Sometimes I get punished. I am always afraid of losing my job. I need to work to help feed my family in a village near Kathmandu. I want go to school, but how? I am small now, but I will grow bigger. When I am big, I will leave the factory. I will go to school. I will grow. I will learn. We all know drops of water make the ocean.

BENTE   All day long I pick coffee beans under the hot sun. My country, Kenya, is famous for its coffee. But harvesting the coffee is very hard work. The beans are covered in pesticides to kill the bugs. The pesticides burn my hands and leave me with painful sores. I don't mind working. I like being able to help my family. Even though I am only eleven, it makes me feel good to help my family. I only wish I could work in safety. Work is not bad, but the long hours and the painful sores all over my skin make me very sad. What can I do, though? If I don't work, my family won't eat.

ELMER   I am 15 years old. I moved to the United States with my family three years ago. We had a hard time finding work. Then we heard about the meat packing plant. We all got jobs there, even me. The work is difficult, carving animal carcasses and sending the pieces into packages. Sometimes the equipment scares me, it is so big and sharp. Once I cut my elbow badly on the giant saw we use to carve up cows. The supervisor told me to get fixed up and get back to work. He knows I do not have all the papers I need to be in the United States. He knows I can't report how mean he is or how dangerous the factory is because I might get sent back to El Salvador if I do.

MANOJ   All day I carry gravel and clay in the hot sun. I shape it into bricks that the builders use to make new buildings all around India. I have a special basket for carrying my loads on my head. Some days I carry loads of gravel and clay for as much as 14 hours. Then I collapse into bed, too tired to even eat. Back and forth, back and forth all day long I walk. Each load seems to get heavier as my legs get more tired and my head gets more sore.

CHEN   For most of my life, I lived with my family on our farm in rural China. One day, my parents told me we couldn't afford to feed everyone in the family anymore. I offered to go to the city to find work and send the money home to them. It felt good to be able to help my family. My sister and I both moved to the city. It was easy to find work in the factory that makes T-shirts. The work was easy to find, but hard to do. We are not allowed to leave the factory, sometimes for 12 or 14 hours a day. After work, we go back to the tiny apartment we share with 10 other people. The clothing company owns the apartments, too.

Student Essay: Abolish Child Labor

URIEL

I know someone who needs your help. Her name is Aakash and she works in a carpet factory. The work is hard and the pay is little. She wants to go to school, mostly she wants time to play. Aakash and thousands of other children want to stop working and go to school. Because of Aakash, I believe child labor should be abolished.

Child labor should be abolished so kids can go to school. Going to school will help them get smarter so they can have better jobs when they grow up. Kids should be in school, not at work.

Kids should get to play and not work in dangerous jobs. If kids were out of the jobs, adults could have them. Grown-ups can work more and not get hurt as much as kids do. Kids need to play and joke around with their friends.

I know some people think child labor should just be regulated so kids can still work. They think kids will work for a few hours and go to school or play for the rest of the day. But what if the child laborers had to do a dangerous job and got hurt or even killed? That would be really sad. Regulation is not enough. Child labor needs to be abolished.

Kids should go to school, but it is hard not to work. One worker said, "My dream is to graduate from high school. However, if my family ever needs me to go out in the fields, that's where I'll be." Child labor needs to be abolished so kids can go to school.

If kids go to school now, they can help their families more in the future by getting a better job. The knowledge they learn in school can even be used to fight child labor. Is child labor right or wrong? That is the question you have to answer.

Student Poems for Two Voices

I AM A CHILD

*I am a child who has a family who comforts
   him when he needs them.*
I am a child who spins silk to survive.

*Early in the morning I wake up, brush my
   teeth, and play with my friends.*
Early in the morning I wake up and go to work.

During the day I play with my friends.
During the day I spin silk until late at night.

*In the evening I brush my teeth and watch
   television.*
In the evening I sew silk until I am very tired.

Late at night I go to sleep.
Late at night I go home to sleep.

Usually I play with my friends.
Usually I do nothing but work.

I am happiest when I play with my friends.
I am happiest when I can see my family again.

It hurts me when people have arguments.
It hurts me when I stand and spin silk.

I am a child.
I am a child.

— Malcolm Rouse, 4th grade

A POEM FOR TWO VOICES

I am a child who gets an education by going
   to school.
*I am a child who works 12 hours a day to be
   able to eat and drink.*

I hope everyone can get an education.
*I hope someday I can go to school to learn
   about people, the world, and math.*

Early in the morning I wake up and take
   a shower.
I get dressed and my dad takes me
   to school.
*Early in the morning I get up and go to work
   barefoot.*

During the day I learn how to write and do
   math at school.
During the day I fish in the hot sun.

When I grow up I want to be a teacher and
   help kids learn.
*When I grow up I want to go to school and
   get a better job.*

Late at night I sleep in my bed dreaming of
   good things.
*Late at night I come home with aching feet
   and sleep only three hours.*

I am a child who is lucky.
I am a child who has to work to survive.

— Angela Williams, 4th grade

These poems were written by Katharine Johnson's students at Boise-Eliot Elementary in Portland, Ore.

Everywhere on Earth

EDUARDO GALEANO

Everywhere on earth, these kids, the children of people who work hard or who have neither work nor home, must from an early age spend their waking hours at whatever breadwinning activity they can find, breaking their backs in return for food and little else. Once they can walk, they learn the rewards of behaving themselves — boys and girls who are free labor in workshops, stores, and makeshift bars, or cheap labor in export industries, stitching sports clothes for multinational corporations. They are manual labor on farms and in cities or domestic labor at home, serving whoever gives the orders. They are little slaves in the family economy or in the informal sector of the global economy, where they occupy the lowest rung of the world labor market:

In the garbage dumps of Mexico City, Manila, or Lagos they hunt glass, cans, and paper and fight the vultures for scraps.

In the Java Sea they dive for pearls.

They hunt diamonds in the mines of Congo.

They work as moles in the mine shafts of Peru, where their size makes them indispensable, and when their lungs give out they end up in unmarked graves.

In Colombia and Tanzania they harvest coffee and get poisoned by pesticides.

In Guatemala they harvest cotton and get poisoned by pesticides.

In Honduras they harvest bananas and get poisoned by pesticides.

They collect sap from rubber trees in Malaysia, working days that last from dark to dark.

They work the railroads in Burma.

In India they melt in glass ovens in the north and brick ovens in the south.

In Bangladesh they work at over 300 occupations, earning salaries that range from nothing to nearly nothing for each endless day.

They ride in camel races for Arab sheiks and round up sheep and cattle on the ranches of the Rio de la Plata.

They serve the master's table in Port-au-Prince, Colombo, Jakarta, or Recife in return for the right to eat whatever falls from it.

They sell fruit in the markets of Bogotá and gum on the buses of São Paulo.

They wash windshields on corners in Lima, Quito, or San Salvador.

They shine shoes on the streets of Caracas or Guanajuato.

They stitch clothes in Thailand and soccer shoes in Vietnam.

They stitch soccer balls in Pakistan and baseballs in Honduras and Haiti.

To pay their parents' debts they pick tea or tobacco on the plantations of Sri Lanka and harvest jasmine in Egypt for French perfume.

Rented out by their parents in Iran, Nepal, and India they weave rugs from before dawn until past midnight, and when someone tries to rescue them they ask, "Are you my new master?"

Sold by their parents for $100 in Sudan, they are put to work in the sex trade or at any other labor.

Reprinted from *Upside Down: A Primer for the Looking-Glass World* (New York: Metropolitan Books, 2000).

Teaching Ideas for 'Everywhere on Earth'

This short piece can be used to show students how geographically widespread child labor is, and the diversity of jobs it encompasses.

Ask students what kinds of jobs or chores they have to do and how much time those jobs take. Tell them that together you will read a list from a famous Uruguayan writer who is concerned that in many parts of the world children work for little money in unsafe situations, instead of doing educational things such as going to school or learning from elders.

Distribute copies of the list to each student and read it together. Help students find some of the locations on a wall map. After going through the list, have students number each item. Working in pairs and using an atlas, have students mark the numbers on a world map indicating where child labor exists.

Another approach is to give each student a small Post-It note and have her draw a symbol representing the type of work and the name of the place. Then have students place the Post-It notes on a large wall map.

Ask students what they notice about the distribution of child labor. Ask them why they think child labor is so widespread. Have students generate more questions as a basis for future study of child labor issues.

Ask students to match Galeano's written descriptions with photos of child labor from around the world. Collect several books and photocopies depicting child labor. Have students in groups try to match photos with the written descriptions. This encourages observation and discussion skills. After groups have worked on making comparisons, have each group report back to the whole class on what it found, noting similarities and differences. As a follow-up, students could draw their own pictures based on Galeano's descriptions and display them on a bulletin board entitled "Everywhere on Earth." They also could add to Galeano's list, based on their own study.

After students examine child labor more thoroughly, Galeano's list could be used to generate ideas for poetry, interior monologue assignments, or short improvisations.

For a comprehensive list of the kinds of jobs that child workers have in different countries, check out the U.S. Department of Labor report "By the Sweat and Toil of Children," at www.dol.gov/ILAB/media/reports/iclp/sweat/overview.htm.

— *Bill Bigelow and Bob Peterson*

Reprinted from *Rethinking Globalization: Teaching for Justice in an Unjust World.*

University of Washington Special Collections / Clifford Howard

Learning About the Unfairgrounds

A 4th-grade teacher introduces her students to Executive Order 9066

KATIE BAYDO-REED

The Puyallup Fair, 35 miles south of Seattle, Wash., ranks as one of the 10 largest fairs in the world. When I was growing up, every September my mom, dad, brother, sister, and I drove the 20 minutes from our house to the fairgrounds to spend the day. We kids looked forward to cotton candy and bumper car rides. Mom and Dad held our hands as we ooh-ed and ah-ed over 200-pound pumpkins. There were magic shows, animals to pet, cows to milk, and the World Famous Earthquake Burger.

Up until several years ago, local school districts released children early on the second or third Wednesday of the school year with free tickets to attend the Puyallup Fair. Even today districts distribute free admission tickets to schoolchildren. For people who grow up in this area, the fair is a tradition.

I'm sure I was not more than 2 years old the first time I attended the fair. Still, it was another 10 years before I learned some of the fairgrounds' history. In middle school, I was close friends with a girl whose father was Japanese American. In 1988, she told me that her grandmother would receive several thousand dollars from the government as part of an apology for detaining her and her family at the Puyallup fairgrounds during World War II. I couldn't believe that she had the story straight and convinced myself that she must have misunderstood her father. It was impossible that my fairgrounds, those hallowed grounds of tradition, had been used for something unjust. It was not until college that I realized that she was right. During World War II, the land on which the fairgrounds stood was dubbed the Puyallup Assembly Center, or, as some referred to it in an attempt to mask the nature of the place, Camp Harmony.

Executive Order 9066

Following the bombing of Pearl Harbor on Dec. 7, 1941, U.S. officials issued a series of proclamations that violated the civil and human rights of the vast majority of Japanese Americans in the United States — ostensibly to protect the nation from further Japanese aggression. The proclamations culminated in Executive Order 9066, which gave the secretary of war the power to "prescribe military areas" wherever he deemed necessary for the security of the nation. This order provided license to incarcerate more than 110,000 Japanese Americans in internment camps (as well as several thousand Italian Americans and German Americans). Most of the people held in the camps were taken from the West Coast, where the feds believed "the enemy within" might be able to alert the Japanese military of U.S. vulnerabilities via a short wave radio or perhaps a lit cigarette.

Camp Harmony was one of 18 Civilian Assembly Centers — temporary holding areas for the Japanese Americans who were rounded up for incarceration. More than 7,000 people were held at Camp Harmony. Most were from the Seattle area, but some were brought from as far away as Alaska. It did not take long for the new residents to realize they were living in stalls that had previously housed livestock.

Once the government completed construction of the more permanent War Relocation Centers (commonly referred to as "internment camps"), authorities boarded those being held in the assembly centers onto buses and trains and shipped them to the internment camps. In all, 10 War Relocation Centers were built between March and October of 1942, located as far west as Tule Lake, Calif., and as far east as Desha County, Ark. Many people were held until 1945, three years after the first camps opened.

Civil Rights in the Northwest

When the day came in early September for me to distribute Puyallup Fair tickets to my 4th-grade class, I asked if any of them knew the history of the fairgrounds beyond its use as a place to display large vegetables. No one raised a hand. I took this as an opportunity to investigate with my class some of the local roots of a national injustice.

> **Teaching about civil rights struggles as only occurring Someplace Else disempowers students. I wanted my 4th graders to understand that injustice has played a role in the shaping of our community.**

There is something mythological about the Civil Rights Movement. Over the years I've discovered that most children in my classes think that civil rights struggles were fought long ago in far away places. Here in the Northwest, the movement is often revered as a unique time in our nation's history when brave souls spoke truth to power in distant places like Montgomery, Birmingham, and Selma. However, teaching about civil rights struggles as only occurring Someplace Else disempowers students. I wanted my 4th graders to understand that injustice has played a role in the shaping of our community, and that the responses of people being treated unfairly do not always look the same. I wanted them to see that sometimes activism against injustice can be as quiet as refusing to answer a question. My hope was that the class would understand that it was unfair to assume that Japanese Americans as a group were a threat to the safety of the country, based on an attack by a foreign nation. Further, I wanted them to see that blanket incarceration was a violation of human rights.

Resources

Patneaude, David. *Thin Wood Walls*. New York: Houghton Mifflin, 2004.

De Graaf, John. *A Personal Matter*. (DVD documentary). The Constitution Project. Available from the Center for Asian American Media, 1992.

Yamaguchi, Jack. *This Is Minidoka* (VHS documentary). Nagai Printing, 1989.

The Densho Project. An online archive of original sources for the study of the internment of Japanese Americans (www.densho.org).

We began by reading several children's books (see box above). These all provided an accessible way for the children to see how fundamentally unfair it was for thousands of people to be persecuted based solely on their ancestry. We discussed how the families' civil rights were violated. We also looked at how the voices of those incarcerated were hopeful and resistant.

To provide the class with a deeper understanding of the issues, I wanted to include a longer work of literature. I found the book *Thin Wood Walls* by local author David Patneaude. I read the novel and found it to be a valuable look at the many ways incarceration affected people in the Northwest. The protagonist is Joe Hanada, an 11-year-old boy living in Auburn, Wash. during World War II. The FBI takes his father prisoner and holds him, away from his family, for two years. Eventually the government sends the remaining Hanada family—Joe, his mother Michi, his paternal grandmother, and his older brother Mike—to the Tule Lake internment camp. While the novel focuses on Joe's experiences, Patneaude does an excellent job of showing how, even within the Japanese American community, people reacted differently to government actions.

A Tea Party to Introduce a Challenging Novel

The book has a recommended reading level of age 12 and up, and my class included 9- and 10-year-olds. To help them better understand the nuanced differences in how the characters reacted to Executive Order 9066, I held a "tea party" (for instructions on tea parties, see "The U.S.-Mexico War Tea Party" in Rethinking Schools' *A People's History for the Classroom*). A tea party takes a novel or historical event and assigns each student a literary or historical character. Students circulate in the classroom and initiate conversations, introducing themselves (in role) and asking questions of other characters.

I picked out 21 characters from the novel and wrote up "persona cards." Here are a few examples:

JOE HANADA

I am 11 years old and live in Auburn, Wash., in the early 1940s. My parents are Japanese. I was born in the United States, so am a U.S. citizen. I enjoy playing basketball, baseball, and marbles. My best friend is Ray O'Brien—an Irish American boy who is in my class at school. I love to write and hope to be an author when I get older. I am Nisei (second generation Japanese in America). When Japan bombed Pearl Harbor, the government arrested my father and moved my family to two different camps. I keep a journal to write about my feelings.

MICHI HANADA

I am the mother of Joe, 11, and Mike, 16. I was born in Japan but came to the United States 20 years ago with my husband. While by law I cannot become a citizen, my children are citizens because they were born on U.S. soil. I have worked hard to make sure that my household is beautiful and to provide what my family needs. I do everything I can to keep my spirits up and fill the shoes of my husband, who has been arrested by the FBI. The government has still not charged him with any crime. I do not know when he will return to our family.

DAVID OMATSU

They call me a No-No Boy. Let me tell you why: The government gave a questionnaire to all of the Japanese Americans at the camp. Question 27 asked if we would agree to fight for the United States in the war. I said no — how could I be in the Army when my whole family is jailed in this camp? Question 28 asked if we would "forswear any form of allegiance to Japan." I answered no because I was born in the United States — I'm an American! But anyone who answered no to both questions is called a No-No and sent to a special prison camp.

MR. LANGLEY

I live on the same block as the Hanada family. I am not surprised to hear that Japan has attacked the United States. I knew they were a no-good country. I think all the Japanese should be rounded up and sent back to Japan. My son Harold goes to school with one of the Hanada boys and I told him to stay away from that traitor's family. I don't want my own son to catch any of that disloyalty.

SERGEANT SANDY

I joined the army because I knew it would help my future. I have a wife and I'm excited to begin building a family. I have been stationed as a guard at the Tule Lake Relocation Camp in Northern California. I'm sad because I think that the government has made a bad decision to lock up so many innocent people. However, I have my orders and I will not disobey. I try to get to know as many of the families at the center as I can.

I handed out the persona cards and gave the children a worksheet to guide their interactions during the tea party. Then I had them write, from their characters' standpoints, answers to the following questions: "How do you feel about the war with Japan?" and "What is your opinion about how Japanese Americans were treated by the U.S. government? Why do you feel that way?"

Once the children finished writing, we began the tea party. I asked the students to find other individuals who could help them answer the questions on their worksheets. For example: "Find someone who feels the same way you do about the Japanese American experience during World War II. Who is this person? What do you agree about? Why do you think this person feels similarly to you?" "Find someone who feels differently than you do. Who is this person? How is this person's opinion different than yours? Why do you think you feel differently?"

Following the tea party, I asked students to reflect in writing about what they had learned.

As I circulated throughout the activity, I overheard snippets of conversations and wrote down key phrases. I was pleasantly surprised that several children seemed able to internalize aspects of their characters:

Shawna *(as Michi Hanada):* "This is sad because they took my husband away."

Henry *(as Mrs. O'Brien, a family friend):* "I am sad and sorry about what happened to the Hanada family. I wish there was something I could do to help, but I can't think of anything to help them."

Kim *(as David Omatsu):* "I am angry because I was treated like dirt, just because I am Japanese American."

Karen *(as Sergeant Sandy):* "I think what we are doing to the Japanese Americans is wrong, but I am doing what is right for my future by staying in the army."

The tea party was invaluable in introducing the children to some of the complexities of the period. It helped equip most students to comprehend *Thin Wood Walls* as I read it aloud to them. The variety of roles in the book allowed the children to realize that there were many, many ways people reacted to what was happening. Some of the Japanese Americans, despite being forced to leave their homes and livelihoods, felt it was their duty to do as their government asked. Some felt their rights were being violated, but did not know how they could resist alone. Others felt that the best way to prove loyalty was to enlist and fight in the war for the United States. Still others openly resisted the policies of incarceration and discrimination.

Throughout our reading, the children engaged in a series of activities and reflections. As I read, they sketched scenes I described, "drawing along" to increase comprehension. Joe Hanada saw himself as a writer and kept a journal, so I had the children write from the perspective of various characters in the book. I tried to provide enough concrete information to make these types of activities accessible to all children. Several children in the class spoke English as a second or third language and needed more support than I initially provided in terms of vocabulary and context.

Over the next few weeks, I incorporated aspects of what we were learning into as many lessons as possible. For example, we used data from the incarceration camps to do plot and line graphs in math. I obtained the numbers of people held in the various camps and wrote the names of the camps on the x-axis of a graph and the numbers up the y-axis. The children then worked to construct tables and graphs that showed population distribution in the camps throughout the western United States. This activity opened up opportunities to discuss big numbers and led to a deeper understanding of place value. Here was a direct connection for my students between important mathematical concepts and a chapter in U.S. history.

A Mock Trial

During the Japanese American incarceration, there were three attempts to find Executive Order 9066 unconstitutional. I chose two of the cases to conduct mock trials in my class: the cases of Gordon Hirabayashi, whose story is told in the documentary *A Personal Matter*, and Fred Korematsu. Hirabayashi and Korematsu were convicted in federal court of violating curfew and refusing to relocate in 1942 and 1943, respectively. Both men were re-tried over 40 years later: Hirabayashi's conviction was overturned; Korematsu's case was vacated and his name cleared.

The children wanted to find the men not guilty, and they conducted their court based on their beliefs of what was right and wrong. It took a lot of coaching to get them to see the cases from the perspectives of government agents, lawyers, and the Supreme Court of the early 1940s. Ultimately the class found both men not guilty, and defended their judgments based on the Constitution. They were stunned to find that the U.S. government had been so negligent in its dispensing of justice more than 60 years earlier. I told them that it wasn't until the passing of the Civil Liberties Act of 1988 that the government admitted that "racial prejudice, wartime hysteria, and failure of political leadership" fueled the mass incarceration of innocent people during World War II.

The unit culminated with a trip to the Wing Luke Asian Museum in Seattle. I prefaced this trip by sharing stories about Wing Luke, who fought for equal housing rights in Seattle from the 1950s until his death in 1965. Although Luke's name is not as well known as that of Martin Luther King Jr. or Rosa Parks, the work he did to combat anti-Asian discrimination was groundbreaking. Prior to his activism, Asian Americans were confined to living mostly in Seattle's Beacon Hill neighborhood, much as African Americans were restricted to the Central District.

Luke ran for and was elected to the Seattle City Council in 1962 and was instrumental in passing the 1963 Open Housing Ordinance, which established punitive provisions for racial discrimination in the selling or leasing of real estate. A special exhibit at the museum about World War II helped my students build on what they had learned and broadened their understanding of the impact of racism on the community.

Ultimately, this curriculum taught several valuable lessons. The first lesson was that, even though the signs of past discrimination are not obvious when we walk down the street, the history of our region holds evidence of injustice. The second lesson was a deeper understanding of human rights and the need that we all have to be treated with respect and justice. Students who had never experienced racial discrimination themselves learned that it exists even in their own backyards. Finally, students learned that there are many ways people react to and resist injustice: sometimes overtly by challenging laws in court, sometimes quietly by refusing to comply, sometimes by an act of kindness or empathy.

The notion that our nation's struggles for civil rights took place only in the South was replaced with the knowledge that people here in the Northwest, too, have been active in creating the world we live in today. I hope that students in my class learned that, even though we say we are "the land of the free and the home of the brave," the U.S. government has acted against its people. The unit's lesson was that we must demand justice when rights are being violated. ▪

....

Katie Baydo-Reed (k.baydo.reed@gmail.com) currently teaches 6th grade in Lacey, Wash. The Thin Wood Walls *tea party is available at www.zinnedproject.org/posts/11995.*

Reuters/Andrew Winning

Crossing Borders, Building Empathy

BOB PETERSON

As we shared a meal of beans and rice at the Casa del Migrante, a migrant shelter in Tijuana, Juan Torres told me how badly he missed his two daughters — 3rd and 4th graders who were born in the United States and are U.S. citizens. In a soft voice he spoke of being arrested in California a few days earlier for driving without a license, a license he can't legally obtain because he is undocumented. He explained that he made his first crossing to the United States years ago as a teenager; after 12 years of not being able to visit Mexico, he had few friends or family back in his homeland.

Juan's eyes moistened as he told me of his recent phone call to his daughters, who pleaded for him to return and said, "We miss you, Papi." My mind raced, thinking of my own two daughters and how horrific a forced separation would be. I also thought of my 5th-grade students in Milwaukee, some of them separated for various reasons from their parents. I realized that when I taught about immigration in the future, I would try to help students look beyond the statistics and see the human realities.

Later, back in Milwaukee, I reflected on my trip to Tijuana. I also thought of writer Alfie Kohn's admonition after the Sept. 11 attacks: "Schools should help children locate themselves in widening circles of care that extend beyond self, beyond country, to all humanity." One story that can help do this is Pam Muñoz Ryan's "First Crossing" (see p. 96). In the story, 14-year-old Marco attempts to cross the Tijuana–San Diego border with his father. As they embark on their dangerous journey, they encounter coyotes (people smugglers), the Border Patrol, and Marco's fear of separation from his father and his family in Mexico.

I teach in a two-way Spanish-English bilingual elementary school and many of my 5th graders belong to immigrant families. I decided to use "First Crossing" at the beginning of the year to initiate our year-long discussion of immigration and to begin to break down the barriers of "self" and "country" that Kohn warns against. Like Kohn, I want my 5th graders to regard themselves as part of a broader human family and to think critically about the border and the way it legitimates "us" and "them" divisions. I thought that "First Crossing" might be a good way to honor the experiences of some of my immigrant students, and perhaps be an invitation to them to share their stories in a supportive environment.

Before we read Muñoz's story, I asked the students what they knew about immigration, and if they had any questions we might address throughout the year. The students' knowledge ranged broadly. They knew there were lots of immigrants, "especially Hispanics and Russians" (there's a growing Russian immigrant community in Milwaukee), that some were "illegal," some "without papers," and some stayed and some returned home. One immigrant student explained that "the migra kicks people out of the country." I asked what he meant by "the migra" and he said, "the border police." I noted that for many people "the migra" referred to any government official involved in immigration enforcement and was not limited to just border officials.

When I asked why they thought people left their home countries, students said that people wanted "more space," "jobs," "a home," "because they don't get paid a lot [in their home country]" and "to start new lives."

The questions they had about immigration were varied and thoughtful. They ranged from "Why is there a border between Mexico and the United States?" to "What are documents for?" to "How many people immigrate to the United States?"

I told students that the story we would read over the next three days wouldn't answer all their questions, and in fact might elicit more. I explained that we'd start by looking at immigration from the point of view of a boy about their age. We could have read

the story more quickly, but I wanted to give my students time to enter into the difficulties and choices faced by Mexican immigrants. I hoped that the longer my students spent with Marco and his father, the greater the likelihood of nurturing their empathy.

I explained that Marco's father has crossed the border into the United States illegally several times to make money to support his family in Mexico. This time he is

> **I want my 5th graders to regard themselves as part of a broader human family and to think critically about the border and the way it legitimates "us" and "them" divisions.**

taking his son with him. It could be dangerous.

I then said, "I want you to pretend that you are Marco. Get inside his thoughts and write down what he might be thinking. Write as if you were Marco, so use the word 'I' in your writings." I also asked them to predict what might happen, reminding them, "When you make predictions and think about a character, your reading comprehension — your understanding of the story — improves."

The students wrote in their reading-response journals and then shared in pairs. Many wrote that they were "scared" and already "miss home." Many predicted the police or Border Patrol would catch Marco. One wrote: "I don't know if I really want to be here. But what choice do I have? I need to go with my papa so we can have a better life. I'm scared."

I distributed copies of "First Crossing" and we started reading together as a class. Early on, Marco explains that his father originally left Mexico to help his family survive. Marco thinks back to the time when "six days a week, Papá had carried 50-pound bags of rock and dirt from the bottom of a crater to the top of a hill" for a "pitiful $5 for his nine hours." We paused and figured out how much per hour Marco's father earned in Mexico and then compared it to Marco's father's statement that in the United States he makes "$30, $40, $50 a day, maybe more."

I had students calculate the difference between the two wages in terms of a day, a week, and a year — at first by themselves and then as a class. The students figured out that in the United States Marco's father could earn in one day what it took him a week to earn in Mexico.

"That's not fair!" exclaimed one student. "No wonder people want to come here," said another.

Stopped by the Border Patrol

Marco and his father travel standing up in the back of a van so full of people they can barely breathe. I paused to point out Muñoz Ryan's descriptive language, "Their bodies nested together, faces pressed against faces, like tightly bundled stalks of celery. Marco turned his head to avoid his neighbor's breath and found his nose pressed against another's ear."

I had taped off an area in the classroom to demonstrate the approximate dimensions of the van. I asked a dozen student volunteers to stand in the "van" while we reread that part. I then asked for a few more volunteers to act out the van being stopped by Border Patrol agents, the migrants being taken in and fingerprinted. The students particularly enjoyed giving false names as Marco did in the story.

In the short story, the Border Patrol sends Marco and his father to Tijuana where they find their way back to the coyote. They now try a different way to cross the border, one even more brazen than the first. They are to hide under the hood of a car that has a platform inserted next to the engine. They must travel one at a time and are to meet across the border.

Again, I paused and asked students to write a brief interior monologue.

Mario* wrote, "I feel very scared because I want to see my dad again. Maybe the migra will send him to a different place and then where am I going to go?" Tonya wrote: "I am scared because I might get burned by the engine, or I could get caught by the migra, I am also scared because my dad might not be there when I get there, if I can get there. I wonder if I am ever going to see my hometown and my mom and sisters again. . . . I wish I could go home to see my mama and sister and never come back."

A student who speaks limited English and whose family has had immigration problems wrote in Spanish: "Marco tiene miedo de crusar la frontera porque puede estar la migra y lo puede regresar a México y su familia tambien tiene mucho miedo." [Marco is afraid to cross the border because the migra might be there and they might return him to Mexico and his family is very afraid too.]

Miguel referred back to the time Marco was waiting in the coyote's house watching an *Aladdin* video and wrote, "I feel nervous my dad is going to get caught; I wish I had a magic carpet too."

Others were optimistic. Jaime wrote, "I feel good 'cause we're going to the United States. I will be happy because we gonna live more, save, and work and we can go shopping for clothes and some shoes and go to parties."

"Scrunched Like Sardines"

When we got to the section of the story when the coyote demands that Marco lie quietly in the car next to the motor, I asked for a volunteer to do the same in a taped off section on the floor. While we read this excerpt very slowly, Jaime lay absolutely silent. The children watched Jaime lie without motion and followed along in their copies.

After getting up from the floor, I asked Jaime how he'd felt. Jaime said it was hard to lie that still and that he had pretended to hear the car engine. "It would have been worse," he told some kids, "if I had been really inside that car." Time didn't permit the many other volunteers who wanted to lie silently on the floor, although I did compliment Jaime again and playfully reminded other students that such stillness could be practiced any time in a seated position during a lesson.

After we completed the story, for homework I asked students to choose an event in the story, draw a picture of it, and write a caption.

Many children drew the van and coyote when they "were scrunched like sardines." One student wrote: "I drew Marco and his dad when they were going to cross the border but the police caught them." Others drew "when Marco was to hide in the engine."

Others stressed the positive: "This is the dad crossing the border [where he is] going to make more money." One Mexican American student drew a picture of a car with a Mexican flag in the wind, with the caption, "This is when they get to buy a new car in the United States."

I found it interesting that while students seemed to express real empathy for Marco—either in writing or in discussion—students of immigrant families were more likely to speak about the economic benefits of coming to this country. As a final in-class activity, I asked students to write Marco a letter of advice. I encouraged those who had come to this country as immigrants or moved to a new school to draw on their own experiences.

Students' advice ranged from how to get along in school, to dealing with a new language and how to deal with the migra. Some students clearly recognized that undocumented families must be vigilant. The personal nature of the letters and the sensitive advice showed that students cared for Marco.

A Mexican American girl whose family immigrated to the United States wrote, "My advice for you is to fake to be somebody else and try not to get caught. And if you do just take a break and wait for a couple of weeks or months. After that you can go back and fake you are somebody else and if you get past I would be really happy for you. Good luck. Sincerely, your friend."

Lucy, who has complained about living with her strict grandfather after her mother abandoned her, wrote, "Dear Marco, You are a brave and courageous boy. You did not cry when you were in the hood of the car. Let me tell you now I would have cried until my eyes were swollen. You are just like me, I wonder when

> **As we concluded our reading of the story, the students were indignant not only at Marco's treatment at the hands of the Border Patrol, but also at me when they realized that it was the end of the story.**

my magic carpet will come!"

Tonya, who is African American, wrote, "Dear Marco, I hope you don't get caught. I am rooting for you and I also support you. Do you want to go home to see your mama? How did you feel when you finally crossed the border? If I were you I'd want to go home. I wish you good luck, Marcos and Papa! Buena suerte!"

Roberto, who had pointed out that as a Puerto Rican he didn't have trouble going back and forth to "my country," wrote, "I think [your story] was great. I

David Bacon

was sometimes sad, sometimes happy and sometimes anxious. Don't you wish your family had papers?"

Jaime related his own immigration story to Marco's writing: "I've been thru those problems too. I don't have papers but I came here thru the desert. There was hot water [to drink] but I really didn't care. Then I almost got caught with a coyote in a van with seats and they told me and my mom to stay quiet under them. The coyote had them covered so they won't see us. They asked the coyote what is that [the seat covers] for and he said so the seats stay clean."

New Respect

After Jaime shared part of his story, it seemed that students gained new respect for him, as other class members encouraged him to share more. He declined, at which point one girl, hoping for more stories, said, "Why don't we have all the people in the class who don't have papers raise their hands?" A few students agreed saying, "Yeah!" I quickly vetoed the idea, pointing out that it was a personal matter for each student and their family and there was no need for people to share that information if they didn't want to. I said, "In our classroom we treat people the same regardless of whether they have papers or not." One student seated close to where I was standing said to students seated nearby, "The government oughta do the same."

As we concluded our reading of the story, the students were indignant not only at Marco's treatment at the hands of the Border Patrol, but also at me when they realized that it was the end of the story. Because I had shown students the whole book, entitled *First Crossing*, they had assumed that we had read only the first chapter, and would be able to continue the story in subsequent chapters.

As I mentioned earlier, I had limited goals in using "First Crossing." Later in the year, we would explore some of the causes of migration from Mexico and look at aspects of the origins of the border. And we would look more at the immigrant experience in the United States. I wanted to begin this inquiry with a story that gently but profoundly calls into question the outlawing of people who were born on the "wrong" side of a national boundary. Should Marco and his father (who, of course, represent millions of other undocumented migrants) be captured and deported to Mexico? That's a political and a moral question that students would confront later in the year. But answering it should begin from an appreciation of our shared humanity. ■

....

Bob Peterson (REPMilw@aol.com) was a co-founder and 5th-grade teacher at La Escuela Fratney in Milwaukee for 22 years, a founding editor of Rethinking Schools *magazine, and serves as president of the Milwaukee Teachers' Education Association. He has co-edited numerous books, including* Rethinking Columbus, Rethinking Our Classrooms, Rethinking Globalization, *and* Rethinking Mathematics.

Rick Reinhard

First Crossing

An immigration story

PAM MUÑOZ RYAN

Revolution Boulevard in downtown Tijuana swarmed with gawking tourists who had walked over the big cement bridge from the United States to Mexico. Shop owners stood in front of their stalls calling out, "I make you good deal. Come in. I make you good price." Even though it was January, children walked the streets barefooted and accosted shoppers, determined to sell gum or small souvenirs with their persistent pleas: "Come on, lady, you like gum? Chiclets? Everybody like gum." Vendors carried gargantuan bouquets of paper flowers, hurrying up to cars on the street and trying to make sales through open windows. It appeared that no one ever accepted the first rebuff from tourists. The Mexicans simply badgered them until they pulled out their wallets. With its shady, border-town reputation, Tijuana maintained an undeniable sense of mystery, as if something illegal was about to transpire.

Marco added up the hours he'd been riding on buses from his home in Jocotepec, Jalisco, in order to reach Tijuana. Eighteen hours? Twenty-three hours? It was all a blur of sleeping and sitting in stations and huddling as close to his father as possible so he wouldn't have to smell the sweat of strangers. Now, even though they were finally in

---

the border town, their journey still wasn't over. Papá pointed to a bench in front of a liquor store, and Marco gratefully dropped onto it. Even though it wasn't dark yet, a neon sign flashed TEQUILA and KAHLÚA in the liquor store window. Marco felt conscious of himself, as if everyone who passed by knew why he was there. For some reason he felt guilty, even though he hadn't yet done anything wrong.

"No te apures. Don't worry," said Papá, reaching into a brown bag for a peanut. He calmly cracked and peeled it, letting the shells drop onto the sidewalk.

Marco looked at him. Papá had an eagle's profile: a brown bald head with a bird-of-prey nose. Once, when he was a little boy, Marco had seen a majestic carved wooden Indian in front of a cigar store in Guadalajara and had said, "Papá, that's you!" Papá had laughed but had to agree that the statue looked familiar. Marco looked just like Papá but with 10 times the hair. They had the same walnut-colored skin and hooked noses, but Papá's body was muscular and firm while Marco's was skinny and angular, all knees and elbows.

"How do we find the coyote?" asked Marco.

"Do not worry," said Papá. "The coyote will find us. Like a real animal stalking its next meal, the coyote will find us."

Marco took off his baseball cap and ran his fingers through his thick, straight hair. He repositioned the hat and took a deep breath. "Papá, what happens if we get caught?"

"We have been over this," said Papá, still cracking peanuts. "We will have to spend a few hours at the border office. We stand in line. They ask us questions. We give them the names we discussed. They take our fingerprints. Then we come back here to Tijuana. The coyote will try to move us across again, tomorrow or the next day or even the next. It could take two attempts or a dozen. Eventually, we make it. It's all part of the fee."

"How much?" asked Marco.

"Too much," said Papá. "It is how it is. They are greedy, but we need them."

Stories of Danger

Marco had heard stories about coyotes, the men who moved Mexicans across the border. Sometimes they took the money from poor peasants, disappeared, and left them stranded in Nogales or Tecate with no way home. Coyotes had been known to lead groups into the desert in the summer, where they would later be found almost dead and riddled with cactus thorns. And then there were the stories about scorpion stings and rattlesnake bites after following a coyote into a dry riverbed. Just last week, Marco overheard a friend of Papá's tell about a group of people who hid in a truck under a camper shell, bodies piled upon bodies. The border patrol tried to stop the truck, but the coyote was drunk and tried to speed away. The truck overturned, and 17 Mexicans were killed. Since then, Marco's thoughts had been filled with his worst imaginings.

Papá saw the wrinkle in Marco's forehead and said, "I have always made it across, and I wouldn't keep doing this if it wasn't worth it."

Papá saw the wrinkle in Marco's forehead and said, "I have always made it across, and I wouldn't keep doing this if it wasn't worth it."

Marco nodded. Papá was right. Everything had been better for the family since he'd started crossing. His father had not always worked in the United States. For many years, before Marco was 10, Papá had gone to work at a large construction site in Guadalajara, 30 miles away from their village of Jocotepec. Six days a week, Papá had carried 50-pound bags of rock and dirt from the bottom of a crater to the top of the hill. All day long, up and down the hill.

Marco had asked him once, "Do you count the times you go up and down the hill?"

Papá had said, "I don't count. I don't think. I just do it."

Papá's frustration had grown as the years went by. He was nothing more than a burro. When the hole in the ground was dug and the big building finished, he had been sent to excavate another hole. And for what? A pitiful $5 for his nine hours? The day that one of los jefes spat on his father as if he was an animal, Papá set the 50-pound bag down and began to walk away.

The bosses laughed at him. "Where are you going? You need work? You better stay!"

Papá turned around and picked up the heavy bag. He stayed for the rest of the day so that he could collect his pay and get a ride home, but he never went back.

He told Mamá, "My future and the children's future are marked in stone here. Why not go to the other side? There, I will make $30, $40, $50 a day, maybe more."

For the past four years, Marco had seen Papá only twice a year. He and his mother and younger sisters had moved into another rhythm of existence. He woke with the roosters, went to school in the mornings, and helped Mamá with Maria, Lilia, and Irma in the afternoon. During harvest, he worked in the corn or chayote fields and counted the days until Papá would come home.

The money orders always preceded him. They made Mamá happy and made Papá seem godlike in her eyes. They still did not own a house, but now they were able to pay the rent on time and had plenty left over for things like a television and the clothes and games Marco's sisters always wanted. They had money for the market and food, especially for the occasions when Papá came home and Mamá cooked meat and sweets every day. The first few nights were always the same. Mamá made birria, goat stew, and capirotada, bread pudding. Then Papá went out with his compadres to drink and to tell of his work in Los Estados, the States. The family would have his company for a month, and then he would go back to that unknown place, disappearing somewhere beyond the vision of the departing bus.

"What is it like, Papá?" Marco always asked.

"I live in an apartment above a garage with eight messy men. We get up early, when it's still dark, to start our work in the flower fields. In the afternoon, we go back to the apartment. We take turns going to the store to buy tortillas, a little meat, some fruit. There is a television, so we watch the Spanish stations. We talk about sports and Mexico and our families. There is room on the floor to sleep. On weekends we sometimes play fútbol at the school and drink a few cervezas. Sometimes we have regular work, but other times we go and stand on the corner in front of the gas station with the hope we will be picked up by the contractors who need someone to dig a ditch or do some other job a gringo won't do. It goes on like this until it's time to come back to Mexico."

For several years, Marco had begged to go with Papá. His parents finally decided that now that he was 14, he was old enough to help support the family.

With both Marco and Papá working, the family could buy a house next year. Mamá had cried for three days before they left.

When it was time to board the bus to Guadalajara, Marco had hugged his mother tight.

"Mamá, I will be back."

"It will never be the same," she'd said. "Besides, some come back and some do not."

Marco knew he would return. He already looked forward to his first homecoming, when he would be celebrated like Papá. As the bus pulled away from Jocotepec, Marco had waved out the small window to the women, and for the first time in his life, had felt like a man.

Marco leaned back on the hard bench on the Tijuana street and closed his eyes. He already missed Jocotepec and his sisters playing in the corn fields behind the house. He even missed the annoying neighbor's dog barking and Mamá's voice waking him too early for mass on Sunday morning when he wanted to sleep.

Papá nudged him. "Stay close to me," he said, grabbing Marco's shirtsleeve.

Marco sat up and looked around. There was nothing unusual happening on the street. What had Papá seen?

The Coyote

A squat, full woman wrapped in a red shawl came down the sidewalk with a determined walk. Marco thought her shape resembled a small Volkswagen. Her blue-black hair was pulled back into a tight doughnut on the top of her head, not one strand out of place. Heavy makeup hid her face like a painted mask, and her red mouth was set in a straight line. As she passed, she glanced at Papá and gave a quick nod.

"Let's go," he said.

"That's the coyote?" said Marco. "But it is a woman."

"Shhh," said Papá. "Follow me."

Papá weaved between the tourists on the street, keeping the marching woman in his sight. She pulled out a beeping cell phone and talked into it, then turned off the main avenue and headed deeper into the town's neighborhood. Others seemed to fall in with Papá and Marco from doorways and bus stops until they were a group of eight: five men and three women. Up ahead, the coyote woman waited at a wooden gate built into the middle of a block of

Reuters / Jeff Mitchell

apartments. She walked in and the little parade followed her. They continued through a dirty callejón between two buildings, picking their way around garbage cans until they reached a door in the alley wall.

"In there," she ordered.

Marco followed Papá inside. It seemed to be a small basement with plaster walls and a cement floor. Narrow wooden stairs led up one wall to someplace above. A light bulb with a dangling chain hung in the middle of the room, and in a corner was a combination television and video player with stacks of children's videotapes on the floor. The woman came inside, shut the door, and bolted it. The men and women turned to face her.

"Twelve hundred for each, American dollars," she said.

Marco almost choked. He looked around at the others, who appeared to be peasants like him and Papá. Where would they have gotten that kind of money? And how could Papá pay $2,400 for the two of them to cross the border?

The transients reached into their pockets for wallets, rolled up pant legs to get to small leather bags strapped around their legs, unzipped inside pouches of jackets, and were soon counting out the bills. Stacks of money appeared. The coyote walked to each person, wrote his or her name in a notebook, and collected the fees. Papá counted out 120 bills, all 20s, into her chubby palm.

In his entire life, Marco had never seen so much money in one room.

"*Escucha.* Listen. Since Sept. 11, I have had trouble trying to get people across with false documents," she said, "so we will cross in the desert. I have vans and drivers to help. We'll leave in the middle of the night. If you need to relieve yourself, use the alley. The television does not work, only the video." Her cell phone beeped again. She put it to her ear and listened as she walked up the stairs, which groaned and creaked under her weight. Marco heard a door close and a bolt latch.

It was almost dark. Marco and Papá found a spot on the concrete floor near the video player. Marco put his backpack behind him and leaned against it, protecting himself from the soiled wall, where probably hundreds of backs had rested.

One of the women, who was about Mamá's age, smiled at Marco. The others, tired from their travels, settled on the floor and tried to maneuver their bags for support. No one said much. There was murmuring between people sitting close to each other, but despite the obligatory polite nods, anxiety prevented too much interaction.

A man next to Papá spoke quietly to him. His name was Javier, and he'd been crossing for 12 years. He had two lives, he said: one in the United States and one in his village in Mexico. The first few years of working in the States, he dreamed of the days he would go home to Mexico and his family, but now he admitted that he sometimes dreaded his trips back. He wanted to bring his wife and children with him to work and live in the U.S., but they wouldn't come. Now he went home only once a year. What worried him was that he was starting to prefer his life on the other side to his life in Mexico.

Papá nodded as if he understood Javier.

Marco said nothing because he knew that Papá was just being polite. He would never prefer the United States to Mexico.

Marco was too nervous to sleep. He reached over and took several videotapes from the pile. They were all cartoon musicals, luckily in Spanish. He put one in the machine, *The Lion King*, and turned the volume down low. Trancelike, he watched the lion, Simba, lose his father.

"*Hakuna matata,*" sang the characters on the video. "No worries."

A series of thoughts paraded through Marco's mind. The desert. Snakes. The possibility of being separated from Papá. Drinking beer with the men in Jocotepec after eating goat stew. A woman coyote. Scorpions. He closed his eyes, and the music in the video became the soundtrack of his piecemeal nightmare.

Hours later, Papá woke Marco. "Now, *M'ijo.* Let's go."

Marco, jarred from sleep, let Papá pull him up. He rubbed his eyes and tried to focus on the others, who headed out the door.

Crammed Together

A man with a flashlight waited until they all gathered in a huddle. He wore all black, including his cap, the brim pulled down so far that all that was apparent was his black moustache and a small, narrow chin.

They picked their way through the alley again, following the direction of the man's light. At the street, a paneled van waited, the motor running. The door slid open, and Marco could see that the seats had been removed to create a cavern. It was already filled with people, all standing up. Men and women held small suitcases and had plastic garbage bags next to them filled with their belongings.

There didn't seem to be an inch of additional space until the flashlight man yelled, "¡Mueva!" Move!

The people in the van crammed closer together as each of the group of eight climbed inside.

"¡Más!" said Flashlight Man. The people tried to squash together. Papá jumped inside and grabbed Marco's hand, pulling him in, too, but Marco was still half out. The man shoved Marco as if he were packing an already stuffed suitcase. The others groaned and complained. The doors slid shut behind Marco. When the van surged forward, no one fell because there was no room to fall. Their bodies nested together, faces pressed against faces, like tightly bundled stalks of celery. Marco turned his head to avoid his neighbor's breath and found his nose pressed against another's ear.

The van headed east for a half hour. Then it stopped suddenly, the door slid open, and Flashlight Man directed them into the night. His cell phone rang to the tune of "Take Me Out to the Ballgame," and he quickly answered it.

"One hour. We will be there," he said into the phone. Then he turned to the small army of people and said, "Let your eyes adjust to the night. Then follow me."

Marco and Papá held back. They were the last in the group forming the line of obedient lambs walking over a hill and down into an arroyo. There was no water at the bottom — just rocks, dirt, and dry grasses. Visions of reptiles crowded Marco's mind. He was relieved when they climbed back up and continued to walk over the mostly barren ground. They crossed through a chainlink fence where an opening had been cut.

> **When the van surged forward, no one fell because there was no room to fall. Their bodies nested together, faces pressed against faces.**

"Are we in the United States?" asked Marco.

"Yes," said Papá. "Keep walking."

They walked along a dirt road for another half hour, and in the distance, headlights blinked. Flashlight Man punched a number into his cell phone. The headlights came on again.

"That's it," said Flashlight Man, and they all hurried toward the van, where they were again sandwiched together inside.

That wasn't so bad, thought Marco, as the van sped down a dirt road. A tiny bud of relief began to flower in his mind. No worries.

Within five minutes, the van slowed to a crawl and then stopped. Marco heard someone outside barking orders at the driver. Suddenly, the van door slid open and Marco met la migra.

Four Border Patrol officers with guns drawn ordered them out and herded them into two waiting vans with long bench seats. A small consolation, thought Marco. They rode back to the Border Patrol station in silence. Inside, it was exactly as Papá had said. They stood in line, gave false names during a short interview, were fingerprinted, and released.

"Now what?" asked Marco, as they stood in front of the Border Patrol building on the Mexico side.

"We walk back to *la casa del coyote*," said Papá.

It was seven in the morning as they walked down the narrow streets. Most shops weren't open yet, and bars and fences enclosed the vendors' stalls, which were filled with piñatas, leather goods, ceramics, and sombreros. Papá bought premade burritos and Cokes inside a corner tienda before they turned down the street that led to Coyote Lady's house.

Many of their group had already found their way back to the basement room off the alley. Papá and Marco found a spot against the wall and fell asleep. They woke late in the afternoon, went to the taco vendor on the corner for food, and came back and watched the video *The Little Mermaid*.

Marco listened to the fish maiden's song. She wanted to be free to go to another world. *Like me*, he thought. It seemed everyone wanted to get to the other side.

In the middle of the night, they were roused and put in a van for another attempt to cross over. Again, the Border Patrol sat in wait and ambushed them, as if they had known they were coming. Each night the van took them a little farther east into the desert, but after five attempts, they were no farther into the United States than they'd been the first night.

Early Sunday morning, Coyote Lady came down the stairs into the basement room. She wore a dress like the ones Marco's mother wore for church, a floral print with a white collar, although it was much bigger than any dress his mother owned. Her face was scrubbed clean of makeup, and she looked like someone's aunt or a neighborhood woman who might go to mass every day.

"Today is a big football game, professional, in San Diego. La migra will be eager to get people into the U.S. in time for the game. We start moving you in one hour, one at a time. The wait will not be bad at the border this morning. But later today, closer to game time, it will be horrible."

Marco looked at Papá. He did not want to be separated from him.

Papá said, "How?"

"In a car," said Coyote Lady. "We hide you. If I take only one across at a time, the car doesn't ride low in the back and does not look suspicious. I drive in a different lane each time. As you can see, we are having trouble with the usual ways, so we try this. It has worked before, especially on a busy day."

Marco didn't like the idea of being away from Papá. What would happen if Papá got across and he didn't? Or what if he couldn't find Papá on the other side? Then what would he do? He didn't like this part of the journey. Suddenly, he wished he'd stayed home for another year in Jocotepec.

Suddenly, Marco wished he'd stayed home for another year in Jocotepec.

As if reading his mind, Papá said, "I will go before you, Marco. And I will wait for you. I will not leave until you arrive. And if you don't arrive, I will come back to Tijuana."

Marco nodded.

Coyote Lady gave orders and told a woman to get ready to go. Every hour she stuck her head inside the room and called out another person.

Papá and Marco were the last of the group to go. They walked outside.

In the alley, the trash cans had been pushed aside to make room for an old car, a sedan. Flashlight Man waited beside the car, but he wasn't wearing his usual black uniform. Instead, he had on jeans, a blue-and-white football jersey, and a Chargers cap. He lifted the hood.

Inside, a small rectangular coffee table had been placed next to the motor, forming a narrow ledge. Two of the wooden legs disappeared into the bowels of the car and two of the legs had been cut short and now provided the braces against the radiator and motor.

"OK," he said. "You lie down in here. It only takes a half hour. There is a van waiting for you in Chula Vista that will take you to your destinations.

Papá's Turn

Papá climbed up. Flashlight Man positioned his feet and legs so they would not touch the motor. Papá put his head and upper body on the tiny tabletop, curling his body to make it smaller. For an instant before the hood was closed, Papá's eyes caught Marco's.

Marco turned away so he wouldn't have to see his father humbled in this manner.

"*Vámanos*," said Coyote Lady, and she wedged into the driver's seat. Flashlight Man sat on the passenger side. A Chargers football banner and blue pompoms sat on the dashboard as further proof of their deception. The car backed out of the alley and left. Marco closed the gate behind them.

He paced up and down the alley. They had said it would take an hour roundtrip. The minutes crawled by. Why did Papá agree to do this? Why did he resign himself to these people? "It is the way it is," Papá had said. Marco went back into the basement room and walked in circles.

After one hour, he put in a tape, *Aladdin*, and tried to pay attention as the characters sang about a whole new world. It was so easy in the video to get on a flying carpet to reach a magical place. *Where is this new world? Where is Papá? Did he get through?* Marco had never once heard a story of someone crossing over under the hood of a car. He tried to imagine being inside, next to the engine. His stomach churned. *Where is my magic carpet?*

The door opened suddenly. Flashlight Man was back. "Let's go," he said.

The car was already positioned in the alley with the hood up. Coyote Lady took Marco's backpack and threw it in the trunk. Marco climbed up on the bumper and swung his legs over the motor, then sat on the makeshift ledge. Flashlight Man arranged Marco's legs as if he were in a running position, one leg up, knee bent. One leg straighter, but slightly bent. Marco slowly lowered himself onto his side and put his head on the tabletop. Then he crossed his arms around his chest and watched the sunlight disappear to a tiny crack as the hood was closed.

"Don't move in there," said Flashlight Man.

Don't worry, thought Marco. *My fear will not permit me to move.*

The motor started. The noise hurt his ears, and within minutes it was hot. The smell of motor oil and gasoline accosted his nostrils. He breathed through his mouth, straining his lips toward the slit where the light crept through for fresh air. The car moved along for about 10 minutes until they reached the lanes of traffic that led to the border crossing. Then it was stop and go. Stop and go. Marco's legs began to cramp, but he knew not to move one inch. He tried

not to imagine what would happen if he rolled onto the inner workings of the car.

The car lurched and stopped, over and over. Marco wanted to close his eyes, but he was afraid that he would get dizzy or disoriented. He watched the small crack between the car and hood as if it were his lifeline. A flash of color obliterated his line of sunlight as a flower vendor stopped in front of the car, trying to make one last sale to those in the car next to them "¡Flores, flores! You buy cheap."

The line of cars started to move again, but the flower vendor continued to walk in front of their car. Coyote Lady pressed on the horn. Marco's body trembled as the sound reverberated through his body. He inched his hands up to cover his ears. The vendor stepped out of the way, and the car began to move faster.

Marco never knew when they actually crossed the line. He only knew when the car began to speed up on the freeway. His body pulsed with the vibrations of the car. Afraid to close his eyes, he watched beads of moisture move across the radiator, as if they had the ability to dance. Marco could not feel his right foot. It had fallen asleep. Panic crept into his chest and seized his muscles. He slowly pressed his hand back and forth across his chest to relieve the tightness. "No worries," he whispered. "No worries."

The car stopped and shook with a door being slammed. Marco heard someone fiddling with the hood latch. Light streamed into his eyes, and he squinted. Flashlight Man pulled him from the car and handed over his backpack. Marco stumbled from his dead foot, and his body still rocked with the feeling of the moving car. He looked around. He was in a parking lot behind an auto shop. Papá was waiting.

"We made it," said Papá, clapping Marco on the back. "We're in Chula Vista."

Marco said nothing. He couldn't hear what Papá had said because of the noise in his ears, as if they were filled with cotton and bees. He felt as if he'd been molested, his body misappropriated. He pulled away from Papá's arm and climbed into the waiting van, this one with seats and windows. The door slid shut. Marco turned his face to the window and saw Coyote Lady and Flashlight Man driving away.

The others in the van smiled and talked as if they'd all just come from a party. The relief of a successful crossing seemed to have unleashed their tongues. Marco listened as they talked of their jobs in towns he'd never heard of before: Escondido, Solana Beach, Poway, Oceanside. Papá told them that he and his son were going to Encinitas to work in the flower fields and that it was his son's first time crossing over. Faces turned toward Marco.

Marco cringed, his discomfort showing. *Why did he have to mention me?*

One of the men laughed out loud. "At least you were not rolled in a mattress like I was on my first time!"

"Or like me," said a young woman, grinning. "They dressed me as an *abuelita*, a grandmother, with a wig and old clothes and had me walk across with another woman's identification. I was shaking the entire time."

Marco could only force a smile, but everyone else laughed.

Stories spilled from their lips about their first times or their friends' or family members': hiding inside hollowed-out bales of hay, cramped inside a hide-a-bed sofa from which the bed frame had been removed, buried in the middle of a truckload of crates filled with cackling chickens. Marco found himself chuckling and nodding in co-misery. An almost giddy air seemed to prevail as they all reveled in one another's bizarre stories and sometimes life-threatening circumstances.

He found himself eager to hear of each exploit and began feeling oddly proud and somehow connected to this unrelated group. A strange camaraderie seemed to permeate the air, and when one man told how he was hidden in a door panel of a truck, smashed in a fetal position for one hour, and thought he might suffocate, Marco laughed the hardest.

As the people were dropped off in towns along the way north, they shook hands with Marco and Papá and left them with the words *"Buena suerte,"* good luck. When Papá and Marco were the only ones left in the van and the driver finally headed up Freeway 5 toward Encinitas, Papá grinned at him. "OK now?"

Marco nodded. "OK." He looked out the window at the people in the cars on the freeway. They were all headed somewhere in the United States of America. Marco wondered how many were headed to a whole new world. ▪

....

Pam Muñoz Ryan's maternal grandparents immigrated to the United States from Aguascalientes, Mexico, during the Great Depression. Her grandmother's life was the inspiration for Ryan's book Esperanza Rising. *Ryan's other books include the historical* Riding Freedom, *the biography* When Marian Sang, *and several picture books, among them* Amelia and Eleanor Go for a Ride, Mud Is Cake, *and* Hello, Ocean.

Image Productions

The Trial

How one teacher explores issues of homelessness

KATE LYMAN

"Hey, what would you do?" Brandon asked. "They are innocent. Their mom was only trying to find a safe place for the family to sleep for the night. Hey, what would you do if you was homeless?"

Brandon was passionate in his plea to his fellow jury members — part of a mock jury trial that culminated a two-month unit on shelter. The students in my 2nd/3rd grade classroom were role-playing the parts of the judge, lawyers, bailiffs, witnesses, and jury members in a trial of a homeless family arrested for vagrancy.

I had done mock trials with my students before, but the year of this trial there was a new tone of urgency in the voices of Brandon and the other jurors.

Brandon was one of seven students in my class (out of 24) who had been in and out of shelters and/or homes of friends and relatives while his family's desperate search for housing continued. Some 75 percent of my students were at the poverty level, as defined by qualifying for free or reduced-price lunch. Many of their families, if not homeless, were just a missed paycheck away. Even the more financially secure students had talked about seeing homeless people in the streets of Madison, Milwaukee, or Chicago. During the year, in fact, students had encountered a homeless man sleeping in the underground bypass that crosses under the highway on the way to our school.

Developing the Unit

Our shelter unit began with a discussion of basic animal and human needs. We then explored concepts commonly studied in the primary grades: the variety and ways that wild animals find or create shelter, and the proper care of domesticated animals. We learned about the plight of abandoned or abused animals in our city and raised money to sponsor a "crate" at the local Humane Society. Even before we moved away from a focus on animals, my students' empathy with the homeless dogs and cats that we sponsored or read about indicated to me that they were personally invested in the topic.

When we did our initial activity of talking about what the kids already knew about homelessness and drawing a visual "web" that listed and linked their knowledge, just about everyone contributed.

"I saw a homeless person when I was coming to school with my mom," Stephanie said. "She had a sign that said, 'No job, no food.' I asked my mom if I could give her a dollar from my allowance."

Jamel, who was living in a foster home, said he became homeless when neither his mom nor dad could take care of him. Robert related that his family had lived in a city shelter before moving to the school's neighborhood.

Students also talked about difficulties of life on the streets: getting food, keeping clean, being safe, and finding protection from threatening weather. They spoke with indignation about ways that people could

become homeless. Typical comments were, "Landlords kick you out for no good reason," or, "Your boss doesn't like you and he fires you. Then you can't pay the rent." One student shared that her mother had become homeless as a child when her family's house had burned down.

I looked at the student-generated "web" and pondered how to go on. Interest was high. The children had a lot of knowledge. And students like Jamel and Robert, who were as often shooting rubber bands as raising their hands to volunteer information, had been leaders in the discussion.

I was concerned, however, about the very thing that made this topic so compelling — we weren't talking about a distant "other" such as endangered rainforest animals or the heroic travelers on the Underground Railroad. We were talking about the students and their families. I knew that I had to be very careful not to create a dichotomy of "us" (the lucky ones who have housing) vs. "them" (those homeless people). I wanted to support the experiences of the students who had been homeless, as well as to promote empathy and compassion among the others. I wanted to encourage all the students to speak up about issues generated by the topic.

I decided to use a book on the United Nations' Children's Bill of Rights to spark a discussion on basic human rights. Then I planned to use books with photos, drawings, stories, and poetry by homeless children to facilitate discussions and writing. I also used our district's Transitional Education Program to find speakers and books written by homeless children in our district. Most of the fictional stories that I selected for use were written from the point of view of the homeless character; I wanted to avoid books that conveyed a "they need our help" attitude. (See the Resources list on p. 108).

The students responded to the stories, poems, and guest speakers with their own writing. After reading a poem in an anthology that began "If I were President . . . ," students wrote their own versions. Some students decided to address their concerns directly to the President.

We also visited a Salvation Army shelter — a trip that immediately took on a personal note when Keisha saw her aunt waiting in the lobby. Then Robert, who had been living at the shelter before coming to our school and who was always ready to take charge of the class, seized the opportunity to be the tour guide. Our official guide quickly stepped back as Robert showed the class the laundry room, explained the rules of the dining and TV areas, and showed us the drawers where he had kept his toys. Robert's way of prefacing his comments with, "Hey, guys, you'd like this," or, "But this ain't so good," gave the students a balanced view of life in a shelter.

The Trial

After the visit to the Salvation Army came the culmination of the unit—the mock trial. My partner, a legal services attorney, came to explain what an advocate does and to share work he has done in protecting the rights of the homeless. After straightening out some terms and clarifying how our legal system works (many students had knowledge from television as well as experience in court), I asked why a homeless family might need legal representation. One student who had paid close attention to a presentation about the rules governing our city's shelter system had a suggestion.

"They might need a lawyer because their 30 days are up at the shelter," Melanie said. "They might have no place to go, and what if they had a sick kid and didn't want to be out on the streets?"

I used Melanie's idea, along with the incident that had occurred the previous year, to create the scenario for the trial. I asked if any students remembered encountering the homeless person in the tunnel. Several did. For the sake of the drama, we altered the story so that it was about a family who had reached their 30-day limit, and then were arrested for vagrancy when found sleeping in the tunnel.

The students were very excited to be able to play out a "real trial." However, we reminded them that although their role play would have aspects of a real trial, the legal system was much more complicated than we could explain in a short time.

Students volunteered to take parts in the role play and with some prompting carried out the drama. The "judge," played by a student who often has to be reminded to listen to others, took every opportunity to pound the gavel (a hammer) and demand, "Order in the court!" The defense and prosecuting attorneys questioned the witnesses. After the closing statements,

> ## Facts on Homelessness
>
> - Families with children are the fastest growing segment of the homeless.
>
> - Nationwide, more than two million households confronted foreclosure in 2007 and at least an equal number was projected in 2008–09.
>
> - In Seattle, one of the most "livable" cities in the United States, more than 400 people died homeless between 2000 and 2011.
>
> - A conservative estimate of the combined costs of the wars in Iraq and Afghanistan places the cost at more than a trillion dollars as of 2011. The same amount of money could have built 8 million housing units.
>
> - A 2009 report by the National Coalition for the Homeless is filled with accounts of homeless people assaulted or killed for sport. The report documents 880 assaults against homeless people between 1999 and 2008, including 244 murders.

the trial participants went out for recess, leaving the jury members in the classroom.

The Jury Deliberation

Turning their chairs—placed in double rows of six—to face each other, the members of the jury solemnly began their task. Jeremy, the foreperson, took charge and asked for initial verdicts.

"The homeless people are guilty—no!" said Keisha, who was passionate about her ideas, but couldn't always find the right words to express herself. "What's that word that means they didn't do it? Yeah, that's right, innocent!"

Ten others proceeded with "innocent" verdicts. Melanie, a sly smile revealing her willingness to stand out on her own, asserted, "Guilty!"

"But Melanie, what if they are thrown into jail?" asked Brandon, a quiet, thoughtful boy. "The whole family will be sleeping on hard, cold floors. And they might get beaten up."

"Yeah," agreed Greg. "I know about that. My dad got beaten up in jail."

"Give them a chance," said Jamie, a student whose voice is rarely heard in group discussions, but whose family I know had been homeless for months. "They just need a roof over their heads."

"What was they supposed to do?" agreed Tasha. "They wasn't hurting nobody. They was just minding they own business."

Silent, with arms crossed against her chest, Melanie held her ground. "Still guilty," was all she said.

Greg, normally quiet and unassertive in class, became vehement: "You've got to have a good reason. You can't just do this to this family. What did they do to you?"

Then, two other students joined in on the guilty charge, saying that the homeless family was scaring the kids walking to school.

"What?" said Brandon, now shouting, "Did they have weapons — a knife or anything? Did they try to hurt the kids? They were just taking care of themselves."

After several more minutes of debate, Jeremy took a final vote: Eleven said "innocent" and only one (still Melanie) voted "guilty."

As the rest of the class filed in from recess, the judge took his seat. "Order in the court," he demanded, pounding the hammer on his desk. The jury's foreperson announced the verdict: 11-1, "not guilty." The class cheered.

Epilogue

The trial was over, but not the tribulations of the families in my class. Some found housing; for one family of seven, it amounted to one room in a transitional housing shelter. The family of Keisha, who was finally beginning to make some progress in school after two years of absenteeism and "attitude problems," had been evicted from their apartment and was living in the YWCA. Her family joined the ranks of the homeless, moving back and forth from the YWCA to relatives' apartments, finally to transitional housing. The district paid for Keisha to be taxied to our school for 30 days; then, still without permanent housing, she was forced to bid our school — the only place of permanency for her over the last month — a tearful farewell. Brandon also moved to another school, his fifth within the last two years.

Several months later I heard a voice call out my name in the parking lot of a shopping mall. I looked around, but before I could locate the voice, a body bounded into my arms.

"Keisha! How have you been doing?" I asked as we hugged.

Keisha said she was now living in an apartment and going to another new school. "I miss you," she said, still hanging on to me. "I miss the class."

I missed her, too, and didn't even let myself wonder about how many steps backwards she had taken academically and behaviorally in her journey from school to school. I could only hope that our trial and related activities had removed some of the stigma of being homeless, and that our classroom had become a place where the homeless were not viewed as criminals and where housing was seen as a basic right. ▪

....

Kate Lyman teaches in Madison, Wis.

Resources on Homelessness

NONFICTION

A Kids' Guide to Hunger and Homelessness: How to Take Action! by Cathryn Berger Kaye. Minneapolis: Free Spirit Publishing Inc., 2007.

Amazing Grace: The Lives of Children and the Conscience of a Nation, by Jonathan Kozol. New York: HarperCollins, 1995.

Criminal of Poverty: Growing Up Homeless in America, by Lisa, aka Tiny, Gray-Garcia. San Francisco: City Lights, 2006.

No Place to Be: Voices of Homeless Children, by Judith Berck. New York: Houghton Mifflin, 1992.

No Room of Her Own: Women's Stories of Homelessness, Life, Death, and Resistance, by Desiree Hellegers. New York: Palgrave Macmillan, 2011.

Shooting Back: A Photographic View of Life by Homeless Children, by Jim Hubbard. New York: Chronicle Books, 1991.

Sidewalk, by Mitch Duneier. New York: Farrar, Strauss & Giroux, 1999.

Street Child: An Unpaved Passage, by Justin Reed Early. New York: Authorhouse, 2008.

FICTION/POETRY

A Chance to Grow, by E. Sandy Powell. Minneapolis: Carolrhoda Books, 1992.

A Safe Place, by Maxine Trotter. Morton Grove, Ill.: Albert Whitman, 1997.

Beloved Community: The Sisterhood of Homeless Women in Poetry. A WHEEL Anthology. Seattle: Whit Press, 2007.

Cooper's Tale, by Ralph da Costa Nunez. New York: Homes for the Homeless Inc., 2000.

Fly Away Home, by Eve Bunting and Ronald Himler. New York: Clarion Books, 1991.

The Homeless Hibernating Bear, by Kids Livin' Life (a group of homeless, post-homeless, and low-income children changing the images of homelessness and of poverty). Placerville, Calif.: Gold Leaf Press, 1993.

Sidewalk Story, by Sharon Bell Mathews. New York: Puffin Books, 1971.

Rick Reinhard

Someplace to Go, by Maria Testa. Morton Grove, Ill.: Albert Whitman and Co., 1996.

This Home We Have Made/Esta casa que hemos hecho, by Anna Hammond and Joe Matunis; Spanish translation by Olga Karman Mendell. New York: Crown Publishers, 1993.

We Are All in the Dumps with Jack and Guy: Two Nursery Rhymes with Pictures, by Maurice Sendak. New York: HarperCollins, 1993.

Uncle Willie and the Soup Kitchen, by Dyanne Disalvo-Ryan. New York: Murrow Junior Books, 1991.

VIDEOS

Fly Away Home. A Reading Rainbow Video, 1996.

Home at Last: Stories for Children About Homelessness, by Ralph da Costa Nunez. New York: Institute for Children, Poverty, and Homelessness, 2007.

Diana Craft

Fairness First

Martin Luther King Jr. and Ruby Bridges help set the stage for learning about injustice

STEPHANIE WALTERS

It was story time and my 1st graders and I were reading the book *Virgie Goes to School with Us Boys*. Set in the South shortly after the Civil War, it is about a young girl whose parents do not want to send her to school. One of my students raised her hand and asked, "Ms. Walters, how can they do that? We know that isn't fair."

I explained that Virgie's parents did not think she was ready to make the long trek to school and that a century ago, many people believed girls would not benefit from learning in the same way as boys. And I felt cautiously optimistic that this student was transferring her understanding from a unit we had done on "fairness" to our everyday shared reading.

When I decided to teach a social studies unit on "fairness" as a jumping-off point for talking about justice, I was conflicted.

On the one hand, I believe it is important for young children to understand they have a role in creating a more just society — and that children have been present in movements to stamp out injustice, with the Civil Rights Movement and the anti-apartheid movement in South Africa being just two examples.

On the other hand, I lacked confidence that the unit could be a success. Although I had good rapport with my 16 students, all of them African Americans like myself, I was new to teaching first grade. I was not convinced I could convey the concepts that would get across my two key goals. My first goal was to help my students understand that children can work for change despite their ages. My second goal was to underscore that fairness and justice are not just global concepts, but that students can take action in their own corner of the world to right wrongs.

I was also nervous because my social studies curriculum and teacher's guide had nothing whatsoever on this topic; I knew I would have to develop all the materials myself. It would have been so much easier to have done a unit on "goods and services," since all the materials I needed were in the teacher's guide.

After reflection, I decided to go ahead with the unit on fairness and justice. I kept reminding myself that it's okay to stray from the pre-packaged curriculum.

Classroom Community

Since the beginning of the school year, I had tried to build a sense of community in our classroom. For example, we held daily meetings where we shared what was going on in our lives. The students paired up and told each other what they did the night before and what they planned to do after school. We then wrote a summary of these "news" reports, with each person reporting on their partner's news. (I modeled several times for my students what it would look and sound like to be eager, respectful listeners.) We had also done lessons about friendship and had begun a reading buddy program with a fourth-grade classroom.

In addition, we often talked openly in class about why some people are treated differently than others. I didn't pretend to know why, but I think it is important to be honest about the fact, since my students will face prejudice and racism during their lives.

I knew my students were aware of the ideas "fair" and "unfair" and decided to start the two-week unit with those concepts rather than the words "justice" and "injustice."

> **I knew my students were aware of the ideas "fair" and "unfair" and decided to start the two-week unit with those concepts rather than the words "justice" and "injustice."**

In our first lesson, we discussed what it meant to be fair. I wrote their answers on a piece of chart paper labeled, "Fairness."

"Letting everyone get a turn," was Tammy's example.

"Sharing your toys with your friends," was Bryan's idea.

Andre's contribution was that we have to make sure everyone has room in the circle.

I took down more of their examples, but I was a little concerned. My students were not giving the answers I wanted, which were answers dealing with the concept of "justice" in a broader social context. I took a step back and realized my expectations were unrealistic, and that my students' answers were important because they were from their own experiences and set the stage for deeper understandings as they mature.

We repeated the exercise with a paper headed, "Unfairness."

"Not letting someone play with your favorite game," Quincy said.

"Pushing in front of somebody in line," was Nathaniel's suggestion.

"Not letting other children play with you or sit or come to your birthday party with you because of the way they look," said Inez.

While I appreciated all the responses, Inez's answer excited me. It began to get at the idea that whether people are treated "fairly" is not necessarily random or arbitrary, but may be related to something about the person's identity. And because I did not have to explain what she meant to the other students, I was hopeful that my students might intuitively have a deeper understanding of the concept of "fairness" than I had originally credited them for.

At the end of this first lesson I asked my students, "Are people always fair? What should we do when we see people treated unfairly?"

They were stumped by the questions but I was encouraged enough overall to move on.

Young Martin Luther King Jr.

I then tried to make the bridge from "fair" and "unfair" to "justice" and "injustice"— which, even for older students, is somewhat of a stretch. Although the transition was not always smooth, I wanted to move beyond "unfair" in the individual sense of being pushed around on the playground, to issues such as discrimination and prejudice on a social level.

I proceeded to do two lessons on Martin Luther King Jr. Immediately, I had doubts. Was King the right choice? Would it be better to focus on a leader who does not get such attention? Still, I forged ahead. For one thing, I had several high-quality, age-appropriate books about King. Second, because they were only 1st graders, I didn't think my students had been exposed that much to King.

I also wanted to look at King's life from the perspective of his early years, when he was not much older than my students, and explore how those experiences might have helped make him a warrior for justice and peace.

I asked students what they knew about Dr. King. In essence, they knew he was a black man who worked for peace and that he had died. They knew nothing of King's childhood days in Atlanta, and were excited as I read to them from *The Young Martin Luther King Jr.: "I Have a Dream."* One story, for example, told of young Martin riding the city bus in Atlanta when a white woman boarded the bus and demanded his seat. When he stood up for his rights and refused, she slapped him. My students were appalled.

"How could she do that?" one of them wanted to know.

I asked, "That wasn't fair, was it?" All emphatically said no.

I asked them to draw a picture showing what would have been fair, and they were eager to share their drawings.

"This is Martin Luther King sitting down and this is that lady standing up, because he should not have to get up just because she is white," Stephan said in explaining his picture.

Some students were able to write down by themselves what their picture said to them. For students who had not yet reached this level, I wrote what they said on a note card.

I asked my students what they would have done if they had been in young Martin's shoes. It was a difficult question for them. I also explained to them it was not until King became a grownup that he began to work to change things for African Americans in the United States.

Then I posed a question that was key to my goal for the unit: "Do you think that young children can help to change things in our world that are not fair?"

Only two of my students answered yes. This surprised me, since we had just discussed the story of young Martin. When I pressed them on why they felt that way, one student said that kids were just too young to do anything. They did not know enough to change things that were unfair.

"Even if they knew they were unfair?" I asked.

"Yes," they replied.

Ruby Bridges

Then we read *The Story of Ruby Bridges and Through My Eyes* (the autobiography of Ruby Bridges).

In 1960, Ruby Bridges became the first African American to attend William Frantz Elementary School in New Orleans, following court-ordered desegregation. In reading the books, my students heard about a six-year-old girl (the same age as many of them) who stared down angry white mobs in order to help desegregate the New Orleans public schools. They saw illustrations and photographs of this tiny little girl walking to school surrounded by U.S. marshals. They were amazed.

After reading and discussing the books, we talked about the meaning of Ruby Bridges. What did we learn from her efforts? What did her story say about the role of children in helping to create change? As a class, we brainstormed words that described Ruby.

Right away, James came up with the word "brave."

"She showed us that kids can do something to change unfair things," he said.

Nathaniel drew a picture of Ruby when she was praying over the group of white people who stood outside her elementary school everyday. "This is Ruby Bridges," he wrote. "She prayed for the people who didn't like her."

Tammy drew a "before and after" picture. In the "before" side, she had a picture of Ruby going to a school labeled "black." On the other side, she had Ruby outside a different school she labeled "black and white."

"Ruby Bridges helped to change laws so black and white (children) could go to school together," Tammy wrote.

When I saw Tammy's picture, I felt a sense of accomplishment. Somehow the unit had helped at least some of my students make that bridge from "unfair" on an individual level to "injustice" on a social level. I also felt clear progress toward one of my goals: that my students understand that young children can make a difference.

However, this is where I worked myself into a corner of sorts. Upon further reflection, I realized that the way I had approached the unit made it difficult to accomplish another key goal: to convey to my students that they could take actions in our own classroom and school community to change our environment for the better.

By emphasizing "brave" and "historical" figures such as Ruby Bridges and Martin Luther King Jr., I inadvertently gave my students the impression that only larger-than-life heroes can work for change. Yet I had wanted to convince my students that any action they take to improve our community — no matter how small — is significant. In the future, I know I must create lessons that allow students to decide on what is necessary to make changes in their own lives, and what steps they can take to facilitate those changes.

After I finished this unit, I realized how much more I would have liked to do. I wanted to bring the unit to more contemporary times and study issues of unfairness that the children face in their lives today. I also wanted to study other peoples' struggles for justice throughout the world.

> **I learned that it can be worthwhile to deviate from the standard curriculum, especially when it involves an important concept that my students face every day.**

Despite its shortcomings, I was pleased I did the unit on "fairness."

For the students, I believe the discussions provided background for even more meaningful lessons on "fairness" and "unfairness," "justice" and "injustice," as they get older. For myself, I now have some curriculum materials on "fairness" and some experience in how to approach the topic.

I also overcame my fear that I was doing something wrong. I learned that it can be worthwhile to deviate from the standard curriculum, especially when it involves an important concept that my students face every day.

This year, my students learned of young people who played a role in changing unfairness. Next year, I want my students to consider how they can play a role in changing today's unfairness. I don't expect a perfect unit, but that won't stop me. I have learned that progress in teaching, as in social justice, often comes slowly. ▪

Stephanie Walters is a Rethinking Schools *editor and most recently served as an organizing consultant to the Wisconsin Education Association Council. She is a co-editor of* The New Teacher Book *and* Keeping the Promise.

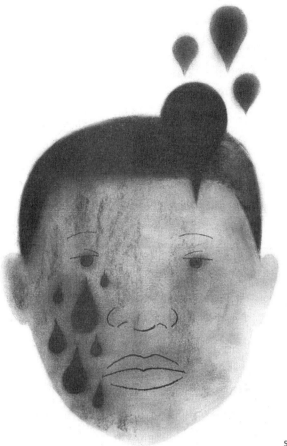

Scott Bakal

Aquí y Allá

Exploring our lives through poetry—here and there

ELIZABETH SCHLESSMAN

Allá en las montañas,	**There in the mountains,**
para entrar no necesitas	**to enter you don't need**
papeles, estás libre.	**papers, you are free.**

Adriana's steady gaze accompanies her sharing of her poem during our Aquí/Allá (here/there) poetry unit. Her words are met with silence and sighs, nods and bright eyes. She gets it, I think. In this verse of her poem, Adriana suddenly pushes beyond a contrast of the smells of pine and the cars of the city streets. She voices her critique of the world through her poem, contrasting two important places in her life—the city and the mountains.

The opportunity and space to find our voices—to see, name, analyze, question, and understand the world—is an invitation I work to create again and again in our 5th-grade dual language classroom about 30 minutes south of Portland, Ore. Labels and statistics define our school as 80 percent Latino, 70 percent English language learners, and more than 90 percent free and reduced lunch. My students spend 50 percent of their academic day in Spanish and the other half in English. Cultures, however, are not so easily equalized. The dominant culture—one in which much of my own identity was formed—can too easily shutter and silence the multifaceted, complex cultures of students' lives. My daily challenge is to pull up the details and experiences of their lives so that they become the curriculum and conversation content of our classroom.

Our Aquí/Allá poetry unit did just that. It surfaced the layers and parts of lives often overpowered by a common classroom curriculum. It created spaces where students could analyze and name the details of their lives.

In the past few years, the bilingual poetry and stories of Salvadoran writer Jorge Argueta have been an invaluable resource in my classroom. I've used poems from *Talking with Mother Earth* for homework and

> **My daily challenge is to pull up the details and experiences of my students' lives so that they become the curriculum and conversation content of our classroom.**

class analysis during a study of ecosystems, the story *Xochitl and the Flowers* to lead into persuasive writing, and *Bean Soup* to teach personification, similes, and beautiful poetic language. As I scanned books for a poem that would raise the level of vivid imagery in my students' narrative writing, I returned to this trusted source. Argueta's poem "Wonders of the City/ Las maravillas de la ciudad," from his book *A Movie in My Pillow/Una película en mi almohada*, has the potential to pull the everyday details of students' lives into a place of power. It is a tightly packed representation of the tension of bridging cultures and places, something most of my students negotiate on a daily basis.

"Wonders of the City" has a simple and accessible structure, particularly for language learners, a category that fits all of my students at one time or another during our 50/50 day. (See sidebar, next page) The introductory stanza hints at the irony of the poem: "Here in the city there are/wonders everywhere."

The second stanza surprises the reader with a puzzling observation: "Here mangoes/come in cans." As the reader wonders why someone would eat a mango from a can, the third stanza calmly counters, "In El Salvador/they grew on trees." The repetitive contrast pattern and concrete details are simple windows to the profound dissonance of longing for one place while living in another.

Breaking Down a Model, Building Up a Draft

After reading the poem out loud a few times and discussing the meaning, we read the poem again, this time as writers. I prefaced this reading with our usual writers' questions: "What do you observe or notice about the writing?"

"The author is contrasting two places."

"There is repetition, a pattern—here, there."

One Spanish language learner, Ben, surprised me by noticing the parallel language structure: "When the author talks about 'here,' he writes in present tense. When he talks about 'there,' he uses past tense."

When the responses to the open-ended question began to dwindle, I probed for more. "What does Jorge Argueta do to show the contrast? What details does he choose to compare?"

"He contrasts food." Students had a harder time naming the author's content choices. I pointed out the use of everyday details, like the comparison of the packaged wonders of the city with mangoes and chickens in a more natural environment.

We ended our discussion of the poem's meaning with the questions "What do you notice about the author's attitude toward the two places?" "What feelings does Jorge Argueta convey in the poem?" "Does he seem to like one place more than the other?"

Students noticed the irony: "He likes El Salvador more." We talked about how the culture that is labeled by the world as "more advanced" and full of technological wonders is often missing the richness and connections to the natural world that are an integral part of indigenous cultures.

After discussing the poem's irony, I asked students to think about contrasts in their own lives, suggesting possibilities that would open the assignment to all: home/Grandma's house, the United States/another country, school/nature, Oregon/another state. Miguel's eyes lit up when he received an affirmative answer to his question "Can I contrast life in school and video games?"

Once students had chosen their topics, they began using a two-column Aquí/Allá list to generate ideas for their poems. We looked back at the poem to notice how the author contrasted mangoes in both countries, how he compared mango to mango, and not mango to melon. I shared my own list of ideas comparing school with nature. Although I, too, wanted to write a poem contrasting two countries, I knew that many of my students had lived their whole lives in our community.

There is nothing "mini" about a brainstorming session in my classroom. I find that the more ideas we share during the prewrite stage of the writing process, the more excited, confident, and successful my students are as they begin their writing. We shared lists once students had a few ideas down. "Here in the United States we celebrate Halloween; there in Mexico they celebrate Day of the Dead," read Juliana. Although validating the observation (especially since we were listing ideas on Oct. 29), I realized that our challenge to show, not tell, had followed us across genres.

"How might you show the reader how people are celebrating Halloween or Day of the Dead so that the reader can see the difference? What do you see on Halloween? What do people do to celebrate El día de los muertos?" I asked. Students eagerly shared their experiences of families gathering to honor ancestors and loved ones. Ana Maria suggested, "Maybe you could say, 'Here we knock on doors in our costumes/ There families gather at the cemetery.'"

As students shared some of their ideas, I tried to push them to critique and value. I tried to explicitly value the allá: "I wish more people here celebrated Day of the Dead. What a powerful way to remember loved ones."

Students continued to share ideas: "The money is different," said Carlos. "You play different games." "The stores are different," Mayra observed. "Here I need to speak two languages to be understood, and there only Spanish." "In Florida it is hot, and in Oregon it is rainy."

I responded with questions that would generate word pictures: "What does the money look like? How

---

WONDERS OF THE CITY

Here in the city there are
wonders everywhere

Here mangoes
come in cans

In El Salvador
they grew on trees

Here chickens come
in plastic bags

Over there
they slept beside me

— Jorge Argueta

LAS MARAVILLAS DE LA CIUDAD

Aquí en esta ciudad
todo es maravilloso

Aquí los mangos
vienen enlatados

En El Salvador
crecían en árboles

Aquí las gallinas vienen
en bolsas de plástico

Allá se dormían
junto a mí

— Jorge Argueta

---

could you show the reader the difference in appearance or value?" "How are the toys different? Where and what do children play?" "How do people dress or what do they do that might show us the difference in weather?" "What do you see and hear in the market?" As students headed off to write their drafts, I reminded them to write with vivid images instead of generalities.

Some days during writing workshop you can hear pencils scratch and thoughts flow directly from the brain to the page. Not on our first Aquí/Allá drafting day. The clamor of questions and conversations continued as pencils carved thoughts in the white spaces between blue lines. "Alejandra! What do you call the toys the kids play with in Mexico?" asked David. "Which toys?" "The ones that you spin, the ones…" "Oh, yeah," I heard Roberto murmur from across the room.

Noticing, Naming, and Applying

At the end of the initial drafting session, we gathered in a circle on the floor. Students read a few of their favorite lines or their entire poem to the class. This in-progress read-around motivates students by providing an immediate audience, allows them to borrow and adapt ideas from others, and helps me develop revision mini-lessons. We all work together to notice and name what students are already doing so that others can try the technique in their own writing.

The bulk of my teaching about writing happens once students have a working draft that can be revised. Although all the students had easily applied the "here/there" structure to their poems, most students were struggling to show details instead of telling them. Their energy until this point had been focused on identifying the contrasts instead of crafting an image.

The next day began with a series of revision invitations that I listed on the board as I introduced them. "When Erica writes, 'Aquí dicen trick-or-treat,' she inserts dialogue in her poem. You might try the same technique in your own writing today."

Next, I used a student poem as a revision possibility. "Dalia uses personification in her poem when she says, 'Over there in Mexico there is brilliant yellow lightning/that cuts the sky like a cake.' Go back and find a place where you might add personification."

Later, as I conferenced with individuals, I noticed David's "Aquí dicen hello, goodbye/Allá dicen hola, adios." He also wrote that children play with "wooden tops that dance."

Eva revised her lines about paletas:

**Aquí venden
paletas dulces y sabrosas
"ay que ricas, que deliciosas"**

**Allá en México
hay paletas picosas
con chile
color fuego ardiente
"ay, ay, ay, me pica me pica
quiero agua"**

**Here they sell
sweet and tasty paletas
"oh, how yummy, how delicious"**

**There in Mexico
there are spicy paletas
with chile
burning fire color
"oh, oh, oh, it's hot, it's hot
give me water"**

Fernando moved from "They are different" to:

**Aquí los zapatos son famosos
por la marca y cómo se mira**

**Allá no les importa mucho
de cómo se mira
nomás les importan
si duran y están baratos**

**Here shoes are famous
for the brand and look**

**There it doesn't matter a lot
what they look like
it only matters
if they last and are cheap**

Luis used a subtle form of personification:

**Aquí hay trabajos de sudando
y de dolor de pie a cabeza**

**Here there are jobs of sweating
and ache from foot to head**

Toward the end of our work on the poems, students met in small response groups. They shared their poems with one another, writing down favorite lines and images, describing cultural contrasts, trying to name what they noticed. In one group we paused to think about how much more sense it makes to play with a top or a ball than it does to buy a $200 video game system. In another we marveled over the personal relationships and interactions involved in buying tomatoes and onions in the market.

Students read their favorite lines from others' poems during a whole-group share. As I passed from one group to the next, Alex exclaimed: "Wow, you should read Juliana's poem. It is really good":

**Aquí cuando llueve
sólo caen gotitas pequeñas
que bailan en el piso**

**Allá los truenos caen
y casi te desmayas del miedo
los relámpagos caen
pueden romper a la mitad un árbol**

**Here when it rains
only tiny drops fall
that dance on the floor**

**There the thunder falls
and you almost faint from fear
lightning falls
it can break a tree in half**

Taking It Beyond Our Walls

Alex wasn't the only one who thought our poetry was "really good." When I shared our poems with Catherine Celestino, a 2nd-grade teacher whose class my students knew as "reading buddies," she responded with an invitation: "Could your 5th graders teach the poem to my 2nd graders?"

The plan to teach our reading buddies to write Aquí/Allá poems blasted fresh energy and relevance into our work. "When I plan a lesson for you, I always think about the goal of expressing our lives and views through the writing of a poem, as well as the skills I want to teach you in your writing. What are our goals as we teach our reading buddies?" I asked.

Students broke into groups of three or four to create a list of the important skills they had learned while writing their poems. We shared ideas with the whole group and then, together, determined which were most important. We decided that the prewriting and revision goal would be to use a list with commas, sensory details, and similes. The students defined the most important editing goals as taking out unnecessary words and deciding where to use line breaks.

"Who doesn't have a partner? Raise your hand." As we entered Mrs. Celestino's 2nd-grade classroom, students formed pairs and settled into work.

"What does your grandma's house look like? What kinds of things do you find there?" I heard Adriana ask her partner.

I saw students develop new strategies to scaffold learning: "We've decided that I will write one line for my partner and he will write the next." "I'm writing down whatever she tells me on this paper, and then my partner is copying the words onto hers." Jessica, Michelle, and Alex were dividing the Aquí/Allá columns horizontally and adding categories: food, names, toys, activities.

"Aquí we speak Spanish, allá we speak another language," I heard 2nd grader Alma explain to Mayra. Most students who had compared the United States and Mexico focused on the English in the here and the Spanish in the there.

"Can you teach us some words in your other language?" I asked in Spanish as I lowered myself to the rug to join the conversation. Alma smiled with the confidence of an expert as she told me the words for tortilla and water. Mayra and I repeated the new words, practicing and trying to learn the sounds. I moved across the room, and Mayra helped Alma move from oral idea to a new line in her poem: "Here we say tortilla and agua, in Mexico we say 'sheck' and 'nda'," she wrote.

When we returned to the room after our first teaching session, I heard about successes and frustrations. "My partner picked Mexico and she can't remember what Mexico is like." We talked about the importance of picking a place you know and remember well, and brainstormed some possible local choices. "My partner just sits there." "We've already written a whole page!"

Stepping Back and Learning Forward

I feel fortunate each time we shake to the surface parts of students' home lives, traditions, languages, and cultures, as well as their views of the world around them. I can't completely know and understand the allá of every student's life, but I can join Jorge Argueta in his critique of the "wonders" of aquí. I can create space for students to name the details and cultures of their lives in the classroom curriculum. I can help students question the aquí and value the allá. Next year I will ask even more questions, probe for more details, and leave more spaces for talking and sharing and critiquing the contrasts of our lives.

Students often follow me as we head out to the playground, eager to share a thought or experience that they weren't comfortable enough to share in class. We head out to midmorning recess after drawing and labeling detailed diagrams of crickets during a study of ecosystems. Andrea hesitates for a moment as some of her classmates sprint off, eager to join the game of tag or secure the best swing.

"We eat crickets at home. You know, they are really good with a little bit of lime and salt," she tells me, staring off in the distance as she stands at my side. "Really?" I ask, turning to face her. "What do they taste like? How do you catch them?" Andrea continues to talk, and, as we line up to head back to the classroom, we share her cricket connection with the class.

How can I continue to open spaces so that rich moments of linguistic and cultural revelation are not chance conversations on the peripheries of the playground and hallway, but a central core of the classroom curriculum? How can I help students bridge the conflicting cultures of their lives?. ▪

Notes

"Wonders of the City," by Jorge Argueta, is reprinted from *A Movie in My Pillow/Una película en mi almohada* with permission of the publisher, Children's Book Press, San Francisco (www.childrensbookpress. org). ©2001 by Jorge Argueta.

All conversations and student work in this article were originally in Spanish. Student work was translated by the author.

The words "sheck" and "nda" come from the Oaxaca Amuzgo language, spoken in the village of San Pedro Amuzgos in Oaxaca, Mexico. The spelling of the words is taken directly from 2nd-grade student work.

Resources

Alarcón, Francisco X. *Iguanas in the Snow/Iguanas en la nieve.* San Francisco: Children's Book Press, 2001.

Argueta, Jorge. *Bean Soup/Sopa de frijoles.* Toronto: Groundwood Books, 2009.

Argueta, Jorge. *Talking with Mother Earth/Hablando con madre tierra.* Toronto: Groundwood Books, 2006.

Argueta, Jorge. Xochitl and the Flowers/Xochitl, la niña de las flores. San Francisco: Children's Book Press, 2003.

....

Elizabeth Schlessman teaches bilingual 4th grade in Woodburn, Ore. She is a teacher-consultant with the Oregon Writing Project.

Student Poem

AQUÍ, ALLÁ, MÉXICO, WOODBURN

Aquí en las escuelas
los niños se ponen
cualquier ropa
solamente que no sea
tan pequeña y que no
sean camisas de tirantes

Allá en México
se ponen una falda,
un chaleco color de una nube de
tormenta,
una camisa y medias
color de una nube blanca y esponjada

Aquí en Woodburn hay
lavadoras y secadoras
hacen un ruido feo y Ruidoso
chuk, chuk, chuk

Allá las personas
lavan a mano
tienden la ropa
afuera para que
se seque colgada con pinzas

Aquí venden
paletas dulces y sabrosas
"hay que ricas, que deliciosas"

Allá en México
hay paletas picosas
con chile color
fuego ardiente
"ay, ay, ay, me pica, me pica,
quiero agua"

— Ana

HERE, THERE, MEXICO, WOODBURN

Here in schools
children wear
any kind of clothing
as long as it isn't
too small or
a tank top

There in Mexico
children wear a skirt
a storm cloud color vest
puffy cloud color
shirt and socks

Here in Woodburn there are
washers and dryers
that make an ugly and loud noise
chuk, chuk, chuk

There people
wash by hand
they hang the clothing
outside so that
it can dry hanging on clothespins

Here they sell
sweet and flavorful paletas
"ah, how delicious"

There in Mexico
there are spicy paletas
with chile
burning fire color
"ah, ah, ah, it's hot, it's hot
give me water"

— Ana

Aquí y Allá Notes

Use the spaces below to write down notes about the two places you are comparing in your poem.

	Place #1	Place #2
People		
Food		
What I Hear		
What I See		
What I Do		
Weather/ Natural Surroundings		

AIDS – 'You Can Die from It'

Teaching young children about a difficult subject

KATE LYMAN

"This is poison ivy," indicated our guide on a walk through a nature preserve. "Now, don't touch it. It can give you a painful, itchy rash if it brushes against your skin."

"Wait a minute," interrupted Henry, a new 2nd grader in my class. "You can get AIDS from it, right?"

This year, as in the previous several years of teaching various grade levels from kindergarten through 3rd grade, I had heard the topic of AIDS brought up with increasing frequency. "OOOO, don't let her kiss you!" I would hear on the playground, "You'll get AIDS!" At sharing time, I'd hear about television programs that children had seen about AIDS. Occasionally, a child or a parent would tell me that a relative or friend of the family was in the hospital with AIDS-related symptoms. By 1st grade, most children at our school had heard about AIDS, whether from the "streets," the media, or their families. When questions arose in the classroom, I would deal with them as with any "controversial" issue, by responding in an open, direct manner, and then returning to the lesson at hand.

I had recently decided to use AIDS Awareness Week as an opportunity to expand the bits and pieces of discussions into a unit on AIDS. I was hoping not only to clear up misconceptions about AIDS and to raise the level of awareness in my combined 1st-/2nd-grade classroom, but also to enhance students' learning in all areas by focusing on a topic of high interest and relevance to their lives.

The unit on birth and reproduction that I had done with half the class the year before had provided something of a knowledge base, as well as a precedent for an AIDS unit. I also felt assured that the 2nd graders, whom I'd had the year before, could be counted on to hold the giggles to a minimum. (At this point I had been teaching in the public schools in Madison, Wis., for 19 years, and had been at Hawthorne School for seven years. About 50 percent of the students qualified for free or reduced lunch, and about 38 percent of the students were students of color, the biggest percentage being African American. About a quarter of the students lived outside the school's neighborhood boundaries, and chose Hawthorne because of its emphasis on the integration of the arts, multicultural education, and open classroom strategies.)

By 1st grade, most children at our school had heard about AIDS, whether from the "streets," the media, or their families.

After calling Madison AIDS Support Network (MASN) for ideas and resources, and asking our school librarian and nurse to help me locate developmentally appropriate literature, I was ready to begin the unit. I had decided to start with a group "web," a technique I typically use when beginning a unit to access students' interest, knowledge, and questions on a topic. I felt confident about my resources. I was quite certain that the students' web would help guide my plan.

But what about the parents? I knew that some, especially those with whom I had worked the previous year, would support this unit. But there were many families I didn't know as well. Would they go running to the principal, concerned that it was inappropriate for their children to learn about such matters? AIDS, I knew, is an especially "sensitive" topic. Learning about AIDS means dealing with those life issues that are usually avoided in early elementary school and by our society at large — sex, death, homosexuality, drugs.

I decided to alert parents by inserting a few lines in the weekly newsletter. I informed the parents:

Next week is AIDS Awareness Week. December 1 is World AIDS Day. Next week we will be discussing myths and facts about AIDS. We will be reading related children's books, seeing a video, and having our school nurse visit our classroom to address concerns and questions, and share information appropriate to 1st- and 2nd-grade students, as outlined in the MMSD Health Curriculum.

Monday, Nov. 28 started as a normal day. No pink phone message slips awaited me in my mailbox. Even though I had given the principal a copy of the newsletter, she greeted me cheerfully in the hall. I was uneasy, but eager to start.

"AIDS," I wrote with thick black marker on the purple roll paper. "AIDS — you can die from it," was the first contribution. "You get it from kissing," offered another student. "No, you don't," said Nathan, with the authority that comes from being one of the youngest of 10 siblings, "You get it from sex." Undaunted by several giggles, he continued, "Hey, it's nothing to laugh about. It's serious. Sex is how we all got here!"

I wrote quickly as the kids shared their knowledge. Soon the purple paper was filled up with lines and words that radiated from the word, "AIDS." "AIDS is a disease of the blood." "It can't jump from one person to another." "You can get it from a cut, if you touch someone's blood." "You can get it from needles. Don't pick up needles." "Magic Johnson got AIDS." "You can't get AIDS if you wear a condom." "What's a condom?" "You want to know what a condom is? I'll tell you." Tonisha, who has two teenage sisters, answered the query quickly and accurately. She added, "They stop people from getting pregnant and from getting AIDS."

"I know," suggested Emily. Her contribution to the web had been that her uncle had died of AIDS. "Let's study about AIDS."

Taking Emily's cue, I told the class that I had thought that AIDS could be our next unit, and had contacted a group called Madison AIDS Support Network (MASN) to get ideas about how we could learn more about the subject. At that point I showed a *3-2-1 Contact* video on Ryan White. The group sat absolutely still for 30 minutes, a rare occurrence. The video's portrayal of Ryan White's battle with the ignorance and prejudice surrounding his disease was followed by a moment of shocked silence.

Kendra was the first to speak. She stood up, demanding: "Hey, I have asthma. That's a disease. What if Hawthorne School would kick me out because of my disease? Would that be fair?" Her comment sparked a discussion in which students argued that students at Hawthorne would never be as cruel or as ignorant as those who ostracized Ryan White. Their indignation called for some action. I told them that MASN had suggested that they make posters to publicize AIDS Awareness Week in our school, and red ribbons to symbolize support for people with AIDS.

"Why red ribbons?" someone asked. "It's for support," explained Cassie. "It's like the yellow ribbons that my family had on our tree to show that they supported the soldiers." "But why red?" came the persistent questions. "Are they red for blood?" That idea was popular, but inaccurate, so I shared an explanation of the red ribbon that I had seen at the local university's AIDS Awareness display:

> The red ribbon demonstrates compassion for people with AIDS and their caretakers; and support for education and research for effective treatment or a cure, the many voices seeking a meaningful response to the AIDS epidemic. It is a symbol of hope; the hope that one day the AIDS epidemic will be over, that the sick will be healed, that the stress on our society will be healed. It serves as a constant reminder of the many ways people are suffering as a result of this disease, and of the many people working toward a cure — a day without AIDS.

"I know," said Jeremy, who listens carefully but rarely contributes to class discussions. "We could sell the red ribbons." That idea was an instant hit. "But whom would you give the money to?" I asked.

"My church," said two of the students. "Homeless people," suggested Nathan. "Poor people," said someone else.

Caleb looked disgusted. "You guys," he said impatiently, "we're selling the ribbons for AIDS. We have to give the money to someone who will help people with AIDS." Caleb's suggestion was accepted by the class.

I was excited, yet unsure. Yes, it was an excellent idea, a meaningful way for the students to work for a cause about which they had some knowledge and felt strongly. And I was glad that the students were not seeing themselves in the role of passive recipients of knowledge, but rather as activists. But, again, what would the parents think?

> **I was glad that the students were not seeing themselves in the role of passive recipients of knowledge, but rather as activists. But, again, what would the parents think?**

That next afternoon, Steven's parents had arranged to come in to visit the classroom. Not knowing them well, I worried about how they would react to the giant AIDS web that I had tacked up on the board. I was hoping they wouldn't notice it. Also, kids were planning to start putting together the red ribbons during their free time. Would they think I had put them up to the project? Would they feel that it was inappropriate for 1st and 2nd graders? Steven led his mom and dad into the classroom after recess.

"Look, it's AIDS Awareness Week," he announced to them, pointing to the sign on the blackboard. "We're going to study about AIDS and make red ribbons to support people with AIDS." After being introduced to the class and showing family photos and pictures of their motorcycles, and fielding questions about their Harleys, Steven's parents approached me.

"It's great, what you're doing," said Steven's mom. "Steven told me all about it. It's so important he is learning about AIDS. I'll help them make the ribbons." Later that day I received a message to call Steven's mom at work. "She's had second thoughts," I worried, as I dialed the number. "Hi, Kate," said Steven's mom, "I told the people at work about the red ribbons and they would like to buy some from the class. Tell Steven to make 10 extra ribbons, and I'll send $5.00 with him tomorrow."

Several other parents asked for extra red ribbons to sell at work. One mom brought in some ribbons she had made at home. "Sarah and I had trouble getting them just right," she said apologetically, "but I think they'll do." I was thrilled. We had trouble keeping up with the demand for ribbons to sell to teachers, custodians, family members, parents' co-workers, and neighbors. Even the principal was seen wearing one.

That week, our classroom exploded with AIDS learning experiences and projects. The school nurse did a presentation on AIDS. She read a book written about AIDS for young children, *Come Sit by Me*. She explained how the immune system works to protect our bodies from most viruses; in the case of AIDS, however, the virus attacks the immune system itself. Students listened carefully and asked questions, which she answered calmly and directly.

Suddenly, the presentation took on a different tenor when the nurse shared: "My brother had AIDS." The class was stunned. "Is he alive?"

> ## Suddenly, the presentation took on a different tenor when the nurse shared: "My brother had AIDS." The class was stunned. "Is he alive?"

"No, he died. It was hard for him and for all of his family, but the hardest part was how he was treated by some people while he was alive." She explained how badly her family felt when a neighbor wouldn't let her children use their pool anymore because of a fear that her children could get AIDS from swimming in a pool that he had used. I was grateful that the nurse had shared her personal story with the class. Her presentation, good as it was, had twice the power with the added personal perspective.

Another guest speaker was a friend of Cassie's family who came in to talk about his role as an actor in *Parting Glances*, one of the first movies made about AIDS. Cassie mentioned to me and other classmates that he was gay, information that was accepted in a matter-of-fact fashion, partly, I think because Jordan's moms had openly identified themselves as lesbians. Neither the class nor the parents appeared to perceive AIDS solely as a gay issue, perhaps because it is also of particular concern to low-income and minority communities.

I showed the class a section of the movie in which our guest was visiting his best friend and they were both struggling with the anger and frustration they felt. The students watched as the friends unleashed their feelings by breaking dish after dish. We discussed why the characters might be compelled to act so violently. Our guest shared how it felt to act out that scene, and why he felt it important to act in a movie about AIDS, including because, as a gay man, many of his friends had been affected by the disease. Children took turns role-playing the character of the friend, exhibiting feelings of sadness, helplessness, and frustration in their mini-dramas.

The students read every age-appropriate book on AIDS that I could provide. Cody, usually a reluctant reader, preferring activities like etching swear words into the woodwork to independent reading, grabbed a book called *Alex, the Kid with AIDS* and guarded it religiously, taking every available moment to read another few words. Kids filled up pages in their journals with stories, questions, facts, and feelings about AIDS. Jordan published his own book about Ryan White, who had become a class hero. Some students also made posters about AIDS Awareness Week, which they put up all around the school.

We had compiled a class book about AIDS, containing a statement and drawing from each student in the class. Someone had the idea of reading the book to another class; soon the kids were signing up to go in pairs to read to the 2nd through 5th graders. I felt some trepidation about sending off these pairs of vulnerable 1st and 2nd graders to present their information to older children. But my students' confidence in their knowledge and dedication to the task enabled them to rise above the embarrassment and presumed superiority of the older students. Rarely stumped by questions (except in one classroom, where the teacher had to help to clear up confusion about whether or not it was the spread of AIDS that had wiped out so many Native Americans in Columbus' time), and undaunted by the whispering and taunting, the 1st and 2nd graders impressed students and teachers alike.

Meanwhile, the red ribbon sales continued and the coffee cans decorated with construction paper filled up with pennies, nickels, and dimes. The delight and pride that the kids displayed in being able to raise money for the AIDS cause appeared to offset, yet not overshadow, the gravity of the life-and-death issues we were dealing with every day. The function of the red ribbon as a symbol of hope was inspiring children, staff and parents to work toward a common goal. Jeremy, the originator of the idea, was usually the first to say, after each new contribution, "Can we count the money again?" Kids sorted money, counted by fives and tens, made piles of coins equaling a dollar, used the chalkboard, Unifix cubes, and calculators; individually and in small groups they worked out strategies for counting and recounting the money.

When Larry Davis, the MASN representative, came in to receive our donation, the class was adding on the nickels and dimes donated that morning: "It's almost $100 ... It's $96.91!" the kids shouted out. After learning that Larry's job as an MASN volunteer is to work with children whose moms have AIDS

while the moms attend a support group, the class voted to give the money to the kids. Everyone was attentive to the drawings that Larry had brought, drawings in which the children had represented AIDS as a demon-like monster or had written words such as "I hate AIDS but I love Mom." The pictures that Larry brought, and his stories of how the children he worked with struggle with their situations, inspired empathy. Students in the class, many from single-parent families, tried to grapple with the idea of a parent having a terminal disease. "What will happen to the kids when their moms die?" was asked more than once. Larry left with a promise that he would let us know how the kids had decided to spend the money. A few days later we received a note from him. "We are using the money for supplies for the children's group, food, as well as a special trip. We're

going roller skating next week. Thanks very much for everything!!"

"$96.91" stayed up on the chalkboard for the rest of the school year, along with the quotation about the meaning of the red ribbon and Larry's kids' drawings. As the school year progressed, we moved to other units, skills, and projects. However, nothing else had the power, the total involvement, the sense of community spirit of our AIDS unit. On the last day of school, several parents came in to say goodbye.

"You won't believe this, Kate," said Kendra's mom, "but learning about AIDS meant so much to Kendra that every night before she goes to sleep, she pins her red ribbon on her pajamas."

Caleb's mom told me that her son was worried about going to a different school in Chicago, where they were moving. "Caleb, you'll like your new school. You'll soon make friends, and I'm sure you will have fun things to do in your new classroom," she pointed out. "But Mom," protested Caleb. "I just know they won't learn about AIDS and sell red ribbons like we did!"

Caleb's mom and I exchanged glances. Caleb was probably right, yet I can only hope that primary classrooms in his new school, and in other schools around the country, will open up their classrooms to the study of AIDS.

I now realize that learning and teaching about AIDS will be a continual process. A year after that first unit on AIDS, a teacher came into my room to give me money that he had pledged for the AIDS Walk in Milwaukee. "Why is he giving you money?" asked a student. He told them that, along with thousands of other people, I had walked six miles to raise money for AIDS support, education, and research in Wisconsin. "What's AIDS?" asked a student new to my class. The answers to her question came quickly from students who had been in my class the previous year. I realized, however, that their statements were much more sophisticated than those in our original web. "AIDS," explained Emily, "is a virus, but it's different from other viruses. The white blood cells that protect you from most viruses can't protect you from AIDS, because AIDS attacks them!" The students from the previous year's class expanded on her definition and also talked about the videos, the guest speakers, and the money we'd earned from selling red ribbons to give to the kids whose moms had AIDS. "We made a book. We should read it to them," somebody suggested.

Any questions I had in my mind about doing another AIDS unit were obliterated by the focused, enthusiastic attention of my class. And besides, Henry needed to learn that you can't get AIDS from poison ivy. ▪

....

Kate Lyman teaches in Madison, Wis. The names of the children in this story were changed.

Resources

Armstrong, Ewan. *The Impact of AIDS.* New York: Gloucester Press, 1990. This factual book on AIDS is rather complex, but it could be a good resource for teachers and older children.

Fassler, David. *What's a Virus, Anyway? The Kids' Book About AIDS.* Burlington, Vt.: Waterfront Books, 1990. This book uses children's drawings and writings to present basic facts about AIDS.

Girard, Linda Walvoord. *Alex, the Kid with AIDS.* Morton Grove, Ill.: Albert Whitman and Company, 1991. A photo essay book that explores the daily life of a 4th-grade boy with AIDS.

Jordan, MaryKate. *Losing Uncle Tim.* Morton Grove, Ill.: Albert Whitman and Company, 1989. A boy struggles with the experience of his favorite uncle dying of AIDS.

Merrifield, Margaret. *Come Sit by Me.* Toronto: Women's Press, 1990. A girl in a primary classroom wonders why some children are afraid to play with a classmate who has AIDS. Misconceptions about AIDS are cleared up. A video of the story also is available.

Moutoussamy-Ashe, Jeanne. *Daddy and Me.* New York: Alfred A. Knopf, 1993. In photo essay form, Arthur Ashe's daughter describes her relationship with him and her understanding of AIDS.

Sanders, Pete. *The Problem of AIDS.* New York: Gloucester Press, 1989. This book contains information about HIV and AIDS that is suitable for older children.

Schilling, Sharon and Jonathan Swain. *My Name is Jonathan (and I Have AIDS).* Denver: Prickly Pair Publishing Co., 1989. This is a photo essay book that uses the words and drawings of a preschool-age boy to describe how he lives with AIDS and how he explains it to his classmates.

Starkman, Neal. *Z's Gift.* Seattle: Comprehensive Health Education Foundation, 1988. A fictitious classroom story about AIDS.

Verniero, Joan C. *You Can Call Me Willy: A Story for Children About AIDS.* New York: Magination Press, 1995. An 8-year-old girl who has AIDS deals with discrimination when she joins a baseball team.

Weeks, Sarah. *Red Ribbon.* Hong Kong: HarperCollins, 1995. An 8-year-old girl wears a red ribbon to show her concern for a neighbor who has AIDS.

White, Ryan. *I Have AIDS: A Teenager's Story.* 3-2-1 Contact Extra, 1988. Often available from local AIDS support organizations, such as the Madison AIDS Support Network.

Howard Chandler Christy

Rethinking the U.S. Constitutional Convention

A role play

BOB PETERSON

The U.S. Constitution has been called one of the great documents of human history. In my own schooling, however, I recall the study of the Constitution as a source of great boredom. Sterile descriptions of the three branches of government dominated much of the study of that period each time I was cycled through American history—in 5th, 8th, and 10th grade. U.S. history textbooks gave the Constitution considerable space and probably share blame for the lifeless rendition of what was undoubtedly a very exciting time in our nation's history.

It was only years later when I returned to the classroom as a teacher that I realized the Constitution's importance and its potential as a learning tool. In fact, the study of the American Revolution and the struggle over the Constitution in my 5th-grade classroom helps set the basis for the rest of the year. I pose questions such as: Who benefited most (and the least) from the American Revolution? Who wrote and ratified the Constitution for the new nation? Who benefited most (and least) from the Constitution? Since the Constitution was finally ratified in 1787 how have people struggled to expand the democratic impulses of the American Revolution?

This article describes a role play that I use as part of my U.S. history curriculum on the American Revolution and the Constitution. It brings the above questions to life, energizes the class, and helps me assess my students' knowledge and skills. The structure of this role play and some of the parts are taken directly from a role play written by high school teacher and *Rethinking Schools* editor Bill Bigelow. (See Bigelow's "Constitution Role Play: Whose 'More Perfect Union'?" at the www.zinnedproject.org site.)

I do this role play after my students have studied early European colonialism in the Americas (using many materials from *Rethinking Columbus*) and also the American Revolution. It could, however, be part of a government class, or just a stand-alone lesson, depending on students' background knowledge.

Students like this role play of the Constitutional Convention because it is done with a twist—we include many groups who were not invited to the original one in Philadelphia in 1787. In the role play, I divide the class into seven social groups, and have students focus on the key issues of slavery and suffrage. The groups negotiate among themselves to get others to support their positions, and then hold a debate and a final vote at a mock Constitutional Convention. The issues that students address in the role play are:

• Should slavery and the slave trade be abolished, and should escaped slaves be returned to their owners?

• Who should be allowed to vote in our new nation, especially what role should gender, race, and property ownership play in such a decision?

I have several objectives for students:
• To learn about the social forces active during and immediately following the American Revolution.

• To explore two burning questions that confronted the new American nation: slavery and suffrage.

• To develop strong oral presentation skills, including both persuasive and argumentative skills.

• To develop critical skills of examining arguments and social reality.

Setting the Stage

I start this mini-unit by showing a poster of a painting that depicts the Constitutional Convention (the one by Howard Chandler Christy on the previous page works well, and in a pinch "The Signing of the Declaration of Independence" by John Trumball is a passable substitute, given that the same types of people are represented). We then make a composite list of our observations. Students observe everything from the men's long hair, to "funny" pants, to most of them looking old, to the participants being white and male. I ask why they think only those people were involved in the writing of the Constitution. I explain the importance and the difficulty of the task of writing a set of laws that would govern a new nation, especially considering that this was the first time in human history that a revolution had been won with the express purpose of having the governed—or at least some of them—involved in determining how they were to be governed. I explain that these people were wrestling with the difficult issues of slavery, taxation, suffrage, and how much power the federal government should have compared to the states.

I tell students that we are going to have our own constitutional convention to discuss some of these issues, but that we are going to invite groups of people who weren't invited to the real convention. I tell them that in addition to the southern slave owners and the northern merchants who attended the first Constitutional Convention, we will invite white indentured servants, women of different nationalities and social classes, free African Americans, enslaved African Americans, and Iroquois. I describe the two issues we will focus on—slavery and suffrage.

I also mention that there are key vocabulary words for the role play. I go through the list and then have students, working in groups, write out individual definitions. For homework that night they finish their vocabulary sheets and practice the words. (The words include: unfair, just, justice, wealthy, property, merchant, trader, suffrage, Constitution, abolitionist, fugitive, convention, Bill of Rights, taxes, abolish, prohibit, resolve, indentured servant, slavery, Iroquois, and plantation owner.)

Explaining Each Group

The following day I review the words by having kids first in pairs and then in foursomes explain the words to each other. I observe how well the kids do and then as a whole group go over a few words that seem the most confusing. I then give mini-lectures on each of the seven groups and encourage students to take notes. I use the handouts and other materials as background. We discuss these roles drawing on what they've learned in our previous study of the American Revolution.

At the end of the lesson I explain the role play format. I then re-list the seven groups on the overhead and ask students to write down their top three choices. Then I divide the class into seven groups, trying to balance each group with strong readers, speakers, thinkers, and a racial and gender diversity. (In my classroom I also mix children by language dominance.) I attempt to place students in one of their top three choices.

Brainstorming in Groups

I post the categories in the morning so that if any changes need to occur, they can be negotiated by that afternoon. In the afternoon I review the format and explain what the groups will have to do to prepare for the role play. Each group is to read over the explanation of their positions and then decide how they are going to argue their case on slavery and suffrage. I explain that my expectation is for each group to brainstorm a list of arguments they can use during the role play. I give them a folder with enough copies of the "position" paper for each group member, one copy of a brainstorming sheet, and additional reading materials. I explain that one person should write down the group's ideas, but that soon each person will have to write his or her own speech. I encourage them to use other sources to find additional background information about their group.

If there is time, I bring students back together as a whole group and ask for an argument that they think can be used either to support or oppose slavery or the right to vote for a certain group. I write that argument down on the overhead and ask if anyone can think of a counterargument. I then ask for a counter-counterargument. In this way I try to get

children to think more critically about their positions and anticipate opposing arguments. For example, in the past students have argued that slavery is necessary to produce cotton and tobacco, two items essential to the well-being of the nation. Countering this, students have argued the "well-being" should include everyone; and that even if the nation as a whole benefits it doesn't warrant enslaving a whole race of people. At the end of the lesson I collect the folders.

Alliance-building

As a prelude to the role play, I have the students engage in an "alliance-building" session in which they make arguments and try to win groups over to their positions. I explain that the purpose of this session is to sharpen their arguments and thinking skills and to seek alliances with other groups. One or two designated "negotiators" from each group travel to other groups to seek alliances around the issues that will be debated at the convention. The negotiators wear 4-by-6 cards identifying their group and their role as a negotiator. The other students sit grouped together with signs identifying their group. This exchange of ideas whets students' appetite for more conversation and further encourages them to start thinking about arguments and counterarguments. It should also help them become clearer as to what they want to put in their speeches. The length of this alliance-building session varies according to each class. Sometimes I bring people together and we briefly discuss how the session went. Other times I go immediately into the next activity of creating speeches.

Preparing Individual Speeches

I review what we did previously and tell the students that in their groups they will each write a speech about one or both of the two key questions: "Should slavery be abolished?" and "Who should have the right to vote?" I say that they must first introduce themselves (as either a fictitious or real historical figure), tell a little about who they are, and then present their arguments. I prepare a formatted sheet with headings for each student to help facilitate this process. I model writing one speech for one individual in the class. I encourage them, when possible, to choose real people who fit the category of their group, reminding them that examples (both fictitious and real) are contained in the original statements that they received earlier.

Students then work in groups writing their individual speeches. I circulate to help where needed. After about a half hour I have one or two people present their speeches in front of the class. We give positive feedback and constructive suggestions. For homework that night the students are to finish writing their speeches, rehearse them, and ask an adult for feedback and suggestions.

Practicing Speeches and Final Preparations

I usually have the students practice their speeches in pairs or in their entire group once or twice before the final role play. Sometimes I have students make signs or posters for their group, highlighting their main concerns. I ask them to develop questions to counter arguments that they anticipate will be made against their positions. At the end of this session I call the groups together and have a few people present at least part of their opening statement. I also pull out my drama box and show some possible hats and vests that students might wear, which usually animates kids to think of what they might bring from home to dress the part. (Using props in role plays is tricky—on the one hand it can stimulate genuine student interest, on the other hand it can distract them from the real purpose of the project, and may even contribute to stereotyping.) I explain how the class will be rearranged so that delegations sit together. I also tell students that I will assess their work by the content of their opening statements, their interactions, and their behavior. I explain that I won't permit any put downs or insults of individuals or groups, but that one can be very critical of the ideas of individuals or groups. Homework is to practice their presentations and to think up two arguments and counterarguments for at least one of the two issues.

The Role Play

During lunch time the day of the role play I have some students rearrange and decorate the room (with red, white, and blue crepe paper). We group the desks according to the number of students in each delegation and affix the group's sign. We decorate the school podium and hang a banner "Constitutional Convention—Philadelphia, 1787." I have students go to their places and put on their costumes if they have something to wear.

I introduce the role play and act as chair. I start by thanking everyone for attending this historic convention, quickly introduce the delegations and then repeat the two burning questions:

- Should slavery, as well as the entire slave trade, be abolished, and should escaped slaves be returned to their owners?

- Who should be allowed to vote in our new nation, and especially, what role should gender, race, and property ownership play in such a decision?

I explain that the meeting will consider each question separately, and that we'll debate one after another. I restate the first question and then ask for comments. Once a representative has spoken, I allow feedback in the form of questions and counter-statements. When I feel that students have thoroughly debated the slavery question, I cut it off and ask for a group to make a formal proposal for what our constitution should say about the issue. Sometimes we vote on the issue right then; other times, I wait for all the voting to take place at the end of the convention. I then pose the second question. At the end I ask for another formal proposal. I allow for closing arguments.

During the role play I take notes—including a tally of who speaks and key arguments and rebuttals. At the end, I distribute written ballots for everyone to vote—in character. While two people count the ballots in the hall, the rest of the students reflect on the experience by writing on questions such as: What did you learn from your participation in the role play and the preparation? Given the different social groups in the United States at the time what do you think might have happened if other people were really given a voice at the convention? In what ways did the arguments at our class convention remind you of controversies in our community, nation, or world today? I also encourage them to write additional reflections in their journal during the next journal time.

Follow-up

On the day following the role play I have students reflect in groups and as a whole class. We focus on two aspects: content and process. In terms of process, we talk about how such role plays could be improved; how we can encourage broader participation; how arguments can be more effective. In terms of content, we compare our convention with what really happened in 1787. Students naturally think it is not fair that such an exclusive group of people crafted the Constitution. (See the handout by Bill Bigelow, "Who Wrote the Constitution?" available at www.zinnedproject.org, for a listing of who actually attended the Constitutional Convention and their social positions.) I point out that it has been precisely these conflicts of exclusion and power that make studying U.S. history and learning from the past so important. I explain that throughout the rest of the year we are going to examine other exciting conflicts in which those who have been excluded and oppressed throughout history — working people, women, enslaved African Americans, Native Americans, and others — fought for their freedom. ▪

....

Bob Peterson (REPMilw@aol.com) was a co-founder and 5th-grade teacher at La Escuela Fratney in Milwaukee for 22 years, a founding editor of Rethinking Schools *magazine, and serves as president of the Milwaukee Teachers' Education Association. He has co-edited numerous books including:* Rethinking Columbus, Rethinking Our Classrooms, Rethinking Globalization, *and* Rethinking Mathematics. *He would like to thank Bill Bigelow for many of these ideas and his feedback on earlier drafts of the article.*

White Workers/Indentured Servants

You are shoemakers in the city of Boston, Massachusetts. Before this, you were indentured servants for seven years. (At the beginning of the Revolution there were 200,000 indentured servants in the colonies.) You came to the 13 colonies from England because you were promised a good life. In order to pay for your boat trip here, you agreed to work for a wealthy person for seven years for no pay. It was a hard seven years. You were almost like slaves, although your white skin allowed you freedom. Because of your experience as indentured servants, you understand more what it must be like to be enslaved. You don't think anyone should have to be a slave or servant to anyone else.

You have families with small children. You barely make enough money to live. You want the right to vote so that you can make sure that the government represents people like you, and not just rich people. The rich are the ones who should pay more taxes, not poor and working people.

You fought in the Revolutionary Army, unlike the rich plantation owners or the bankers who either sent their sons or paid someone else to take their place. You didn't do it for the money. In fact, the government didn't pay you in money. They gave you IOUs, which weren't worth anything.

Now that there is talk about writing a new constitution, you're concerned about how the new government will deal with people like you who are poor and own no property. You've also heard that some people at the Constitutional Convention don't even want to allow people like you to be able to vote in elections. No property, no vote, they say. Who do they think they are? When people were dying in the war, it was the farmers and workers who did most of the bleeding, not the rich plantation owners, bankers, and merchants.

QUESTIONS FOR THOUGHT
1. How do you make your living?
2. What are some of the similarities between being an indentured servant and being enslaved? What are the differences?
3. If a runaway slave appeared at your home, what would you do? What is your position on slavery?
4. Who should have the right to vote?

POSSIBLE HISTORICAL FIGURES:
Very few have been recorded in historical records. Please make up your own name.

Enslaved African Americans

The year is 1787. Eleven years ago the Declaration of Independence stated that, "all men are created equal." And yet because your skin is black, and you were born in slavery, you still remain enslaved. Obviously the American Revolution didn't mean freedom for everyone. In fact the man who wrote those words in the Declaration of Independence, Thomas Jefferson, is himself a Virginia slave owner. And the man who led the Continental Army, George Washington, is also a slave owner. There are about 700,000 enslaved people in the new United States.

Your life in slavery is harsh. Up when the sun rises, you must work until it is dark. Then there are more chores when you return from the fields. You are under constant control by your master, though with your family you have tried to make the best out of your life. However, you know that the owner could sell you far away from your family, if he felt like it.

The Constitutional Convention raises the possibility of freedom. Slavery might be outlawed. A number of states in the North have already abolished slavery, and there is much talk about abolishing the slave trade — the bringing of new enslaved Africans into the country. Thousands of enslaved people have been allowed to buy or earn their freedom in Virginia in recent years. Maybe slavery will not be outlawed in every state, but perhaps enslaved people would be allowed to keep their freedom if they escaped into a free state. True, the Revolution didn't really free you, but the talk of liberty and justice makes you want your fair share.

QUESTIONS FOR THOUGHT

1. What things worry you?
2. What do you hope the Constitution will do for you?
3. Who do you think should have the right to vote?

POSSIBLE HISTORICAL FIGURES

Enslaved people who fought for the Americans became free after the war, so there are few records of slaves in 1787. Please make up your own name.

Free African Americans

You are free African Americans. There are over 59,000 of you in the 13 colonies. (Unfortunately, there are nearly 700,000 enslaved African Americans!) You know that African Americans — both free and enslaved — make up 20 percent of all the non-Native American people in the colonies. And yet you have virtually no rights:

- You are not allowed to own property in many of the 13 colonies.
- You are not allowed to vote.
- You are not allowed to speak in court.
- You are not allowed to serve on a jury of any kind.
- You are not allowed to attend most schools.

Even though you are free, if a slave catcher catches you and takes you back to the South or sends you to the Caribbean, it would be very difficult for you to prove that you are free. Some people argue that the Constitution should allow slave owners to come into Northern states where there is no slavery and take runaways back South. The "runaway" may be you — even though you are free. If slavery exists anywhere in the United States, it is a threat to free African Americans, such as yourselves.

Over 5,000 African American men fought in the Revolution. They were promised their freedom if they fought. After the war, some of them were not given their freedom and had to fight their former owners to get it. Remember that the first American killed by the British in the War was Crispus Attucks — whose father was African and whose mother was a member of the Massachuset (Indian) tribe. He was killed in the Boston Massacre in 1770. African Americans have petitioned the government to end slavery. And between 1780 and 1786, the states of Pennsylvania, Massachusetts, Connecticut, Rhode Island, New York, and New Jersey passed laws against slavery.

QUESTIONS FOR THOUGHT

1. Did most Africans want to be brought to the United States?
2. What role did Africans — enslaved and free — have in creating the wealth of the 13 colonies?
3. What arguments can you use to convince people to oppose slavery?
4. Who do you think should have the right to vote? Why?

POSSIBLE HISTORICAL FIGURES

Phyllis Wheatley, Peter Salem (fought at Bunker Hill), William Lee (aide to General Washington), Oliver Cromwell (with Washington at Delaware).

White Women

You live in Boston. Some of you are married to men who fought in the Revolution. Some of you are widows because your husbands were killed in the war. You and your women friends organized in favor of the American Revolution. Women built the organization "Daughters of Liberty," which organized campaigns to refuse to buy British products. Abigail Adams was one leader of such activities. During the war many women continued their support of the Revolution through "Ladies Associations." They donated clothing and medical supplies to the Continental Army led by George Washington. In Philadelphia alone, the Ladies Association collected about $300,000 in Continental money. The money was used to buy shirts for the soldiers. The women organized sewing circles throughout the colonies to spin, weave cloth, and make clothing for troops. They also passed resolutions supporting the rebel cause and pledged not to do business with merchants who imported British goods or didn't support the Patriots' cause. On one occasion 500 Boston women held a protest against a merchant found to be hoarding coffee.

The women also kept the country going. While their husbands were off fighting the war, the women kept small businesses open, kept the farms running, and took care of the children. You know that some women actually fought in the Revolution. Deborah Sampson and Molly Pitcher fought in the army. Others like Lydia Darragh acted as spies. Why shouldn't women benefit from the Revolution if they helped with it?

You also know that you pay taxes when you buy certain things. Wasn't one of the main issues of the Revolution "no taxation without representation"? Right now in many ways you are little more than the property of your husbands or fathers. Even a decade after the Declaration of Independence you don't have the right to do many things, just because you are a woman:

- You do not have the right to vote.
- You do not have the right to own property.
- You do not have the right to speak in court.
- You do not have the right to be a member of a jury in court.
- You do not have the right to be a government official.
- You do not have the right to go to most high schools and colleges.

In 1776, Abigail Adams wrote the following to her husband, John Adams:
Remember the Ladies and be more generous and favorable to them than your ancestors. Do not put such unlimited power into the hands of the husbands. Remember all men would be tyrants if they could. If particular care and attention is not paid to the Ladies, we are determined to foment a rebellion, and will not hold ourselves bound by any laws in which we have no voice, no representation.

QUESTIONS FOR THOUGHT

1. Should you have the right to vote? Why?
2. How is the position of women in our nation similar to that of being enslaved? How does it differ?
3. What do you think of slavery and the slave trade?

POSSIBLE HISTORICAL FIGURES

Abigail Adams, Deborah Sampson, Lydia Darragh, Molly Pitcher.

Male Southern Plantation Owners

You live in Virginia and are tobacco planters. Your family owns about 30 black slaves and you are quite wealthy. Your wealth, however, depends on your slaves. Slaves do all the hardest work. They plant, harvest, dry, pack, and load the tobacco to get it off for sale. You wouldn't know where you'd get people to do the work if you had no slaves.

From time to time a slave will run away. You hire a slave catcher and usually the runaway is brought back. Sometimes the slaves get up into the North before they're caught. But slaves are your property, and fortunately you usually get them back.

The American colonies defeated Great Britain in the Revolution but there are still problems. One problem is that there is a lot of protest from the common people, the "rabble"—the poor farmers, the unemployed, and workers in the towns and cities. Up in the state of Massachusetts, Daniel Shays led a rebellion against the government and large property owners. As property owners yourselves, when these people talk about "equality" you wonder whether they mean to take away your property so you'd be equal to them! These people scare you. In some places they're even allowed to vote and run for office. Sometimes they make laws that threaten the safety of private property: your property.

QUESTIONS FOR THOUGHT

1. How do you make your money?
2. How do you feel about slavery?
3. Do you think that you should have the right to go to northern states and get your property (slaves) if they try to run away?
4. How do you feel about the common people?

POSSIBLE HISTORICAL FIGURES

George Washington, Thomas Jefferson, James Madison.

Northern Merchants and Bankers

You are rich. Some of you own ships, some own mills, and some own banks. You were strong supporters of the Revolution because the British didn't let you trade and make deals with countries other than Britain. Now you can trade with the French, the Dutch, the Spanish, and Portuguese. You are getting richer and richer. While you didn't fight directly in the battles, your son served as a leader in the Continental Army (George Washington's army).

While you are not as set in your ways as the southern plantation owners, you still have many questions regarding who should vote and how slavery should be handled. While slavery may not be OK in Boston, the South is different. The slaves in the South harvest the tobacco you smoke and the cotton that comes to your mills. If it wasn't for them you wouldn't be so well off.

Very upsetting things have been happening recently. Many state legislatures have passed laws allowing "debtors"—people who owe money—to pay their debts "in kind" with corn, tobacco, or other products whether or not they may be of any value. In other words, a banker might lend $100 and get paid back two cows and a bushel of corn. That's outrageous! There is very little respect for property anymore. The state legislatures have entirely too much power. Maybe if all those poor people didn't vote, this kind of unfairness would not happen.

You were educated in school and speak English and French. You believe in democracy and the right to vote, but really only for those who have the schooling and money that give them the knowledge and time to understand the issues.

QUESTIONS FOR THOUGHT

1. How do you make your money?
2. Why might it be against your interests if lots of people could vote?
3. How do you benefit from slavery and the slave trade?

POSSIBLE HISTORICAL FIGURE

John Hancock.

Native Americans: Iroquois Nation

You are members of the great Iroquois League of Nations. You live with your families in a Seneca village on the Genesee River in New York. You live in a longhouse with your families and grandparents. You have attended the Grand Council — the meeting of leaders from the original Five — now Six — Nations of the Iroquois. At that council the leaders tried to solve their differences peacefully. The American War of Independence changed all that. Some of the Iroquois — the Oneida and Tuscarora Nations — generally supported the Americans. But many Iroquois — under the leadership of Mohawk Chief Joseph Bryant and Seneca Chief Red Jacket — fought on the side of the British. They were so angry at the Americans for taking their land that they hoped that the British would win, and that the Americans would no longer be able to steal Iroquois land. Even though you fought on the British side, you feel people at the Constitutional Convention should listen to you and your ideas for several reasons:

- Some members of the Iroquois Nation met Benjamin Franklin many years ago when Franklin was a young journalist who made a study of the Iroquois governmental system. Franklin admired the fine workings of democracy among the Iroquois — with its checks and balances among different "branches" of government. The Iroquois' "League of Nations" has six tribes or nations. The government of the Iroquois includes three parts — executive, an assembly, and a judicial system. That's the same as the proposal that the new United States government have a President (executive), a Congress (an assembly), and a court system (the judicial system). A key difference is that the Iroquois allow all people to vote, and in fact, women are the ones who run your court system — the ones who make the final decision when there is a disagreement.

- The American settlers have taken much of your land. They keep breaking treaties. They say they won't take any more land and then a few years later settlers start moving in. You need the right to vote in order to get laws passed to protect Native Americans.

- George Washington was angry at Iroquois support for the British and so he ordered an army into Iroquois lands saying that it should "not merely be overrun, but destroyed." The American army was to scorch the earth, and they did — burning towns, stealing things, uprooting crops, chopping down orchards, killing cattle, and destroying grain supplies. He ordered the destruction of your villages and the killings of women and children.

- You know that your Native American relatives have suffered as slaves ever since the time Columbus came to this part of the world. The Europeans eventually decided not to use Indians for slaves because you could run away easily — you knew the land.

QUESTIONS FOR THOUGHT

1. Whose land is this?
2. Why should you have rights even though you fought against the Americans in the War of Independence?
3. Who should be allowed to vote and why?

POSSIBLE HISTORICAL FIGURES

Red Jacket, Joseph Bryant.

Barbara Miner

Writing Wrongs

Essays on justice fighters in an elementary classroom

KATHARINE JOHNSON

In the introduction to *Rethinking Our Classrooms*, the editors wrote, "Curriculum and classroom practice must be: Hopeful, joyful, kind, and visionary." So how do we, as social justice teachers, expose our students to the myriad historical and contemporary truths of injustice, prejudice and systematic cruelty while still being hopeful, joyful, kind, and visionary? One way is to share examples of how people have organized to fight injustice throughout history. With a little digging, I am confident there is a corresponding movement for justice that accompanies every example of injustice in our history.

With this in mind, I designed a unit of study about people who have fought for justice. I taught the unit as one of several writing lessons in an intensive writing summer school serving struggling 5th and 6th grade writers from across Portland Public Schools. All of the students came from Title I schools and all qualified as academic priority, meaning they were below grade level according to teacher grades and standardized tests. A group of teachers who had all attended the Oregon Writing Project came together to develop writing lessons, community building activities and reading experiences for this summer school. It was essential to me and the other teachers developing the curriculum that the lessons be engaging and grounded in social justice principles, and that the lessons also develop some concrete writing skills these students deserved to have.

Jumping off Bill Bigelow's article, "Teaching about Unsung Heroes" and Linda Christensen's "Honoring Our Ancestors," I had some clear goals in mind. Beyond learning about essay format and research, I wanted my students to develop close connections to one or more of the people we learned about. I wanted students to have choice inside the unit, so they would have a better chance of developing that connection and of producing higher quality work. And I wanted to ground all the people we learned about inside movements for justice. I was wary of the lone wolf myth that often becomes the way we remember the faces of movements. I assembled possible justice fighters and thought about essays or poems students might write.

> **I was wary of the lone wolf myth that often becomes the way we remember the faces of movements. I assembled possible justice fighters and thought about essays or poems students might write.**

Because many summer school teachers taught the unit at the same time, we couldn't get enough copies of the beautiful picture book biographies available to teach them about various justice fighters. (See Elizabeth Schlessman's resource list on p. 145.) Instead, I began what my husband and fellow teacher, Mark Hansen, calls web spelunking. With help from other teachers working on the summer school curriculum, we searched for videos about movements for justice and famous justice fighters. We found several that were developmentally appropriate for 5th and 6th graders, then narrowed the list to ones that did not reinforce the lone wolf myth and finally tried to make a broad and balanced collection of movements.

I narrowed it down to six short videos about six important justice fighters and their movements. The list of possible people included women and men, people from various parts of the planet and people involved in different types of justice movements: environmental, human rights, workers' rights, etc. I included Wangari Maathai, Dolores Huerta and César Chávez, and Aung San Suu Kyi. I designed the unit in the spring of 2011, the 50th anniversary of the Freedom Rides, so the Freedom Riders made the list

as well. In hindsight, I would have changed the role of the Freedom Riders. It was misleading to have the only African American justice fighters in this lesson as a composite of several people rather than an individual. Additionally, focusing on college students as the faces of the Civil Rights Movement marginalizes the vital role played by working people, the elderly, and others rarely seen as the fierce warriors for justice they were. These videos became the content we used to springboard students' learning and writing. Under normal teaching circumstances, I wouldn't use a single source and I wouldn't use just images to teach students about movements for justice and their champions. But given the time constraints of summer school, the videos gave an effective and efficient access to enough meaningful content to move forward with the writing.

I knew the content would be challenging for students, even when it came from fairly accessible videos. Rather than jump into research and writing, I decided to open with a tea party. I told the class that our assignment for the week was a research essay about people who have fought for justice. Then I had students talk in table groups to share the names of people they already knew about who fought for justice. Sharing these names after a few minutes as a whole group, the most familiar names came up time and again.

"Martin Luther King."

"Rosa Parks."

"Harriet Tubman."

Instead of a long list of names on the board, we had those three with lots of stars next to them to denote that multiple groups had thought of the same names.

The Freedom Fighter Tea Party

I told students: "These people were all very important justice fighters, but there are so many more. Some of them are people we remember and write books about. Other justice fighters are regular everyday people who stand up and do the right thing. We are going to learn about some other justice fighters who are pretty famous, but who also worked as part of groups of regular people doing the right thing."

Rattling a brown paper bag filled with tea party roles, I told students that each of them would get a slip of paper about a justice fighter or group of justice fighters. Their job was to be that justice fighter, to get into character and stay in character for about 45 minutes as they moved around the room and met the other justice fighters.

Before letting students pull a role out of a bag, I modeled the types of information students should read for in their groups.

"What do you need to know in order to be able to be this person?" I asked.

"What's their name?" Jaylen called out.

"Is it a man or a woman?" Deja added.

"Are they alive?"

"Where do they live?"

"Did they use violence?"

I recorded students' ideas on the board as they called questions out. Then I added my own questions: "To really know about these people you also need to know: What were they fighting for and who were they fighting with?"

With the questions listed on the board, students were ready to get into small groups and read the roles.

Each student pulled a role out of a bag then found the other students who received the same role. I had copied the roles onto colored paper to make it easier for students to get into small groups based on which justice fighter they pulled for the tea party. One corner of the classroom had Chris reading the role of Wangari Maathai aloud to the rest of his group. Another corner had Danielle, Lizbeth and D'Angelo highlighting important facts about the Freedom Riders while Jaylen and Aisha compared notes they had written at the bottom of their role of Aug San Suu Kyi. These were all strategies for understanding the roles that my teaching partner and I had suggested. Students read and talked intently.

Once students met and discussed their roles with other students who had the same role, it was time to mix. So they remember and refer back to what they learn in the tea party, I find it helpful to have students take notes on important information they learn. To ensure students' success, my summer school teaching partner, Blake Robertson, and I modeled for the class how to stay in character and go off to meet another justice fighter.

Walking up to Blake, I offered my role slip of paper and said, "Here's the information on César Chávez. Gimme your paper."

Blake exaggerated his shocked response and said, "I think we're supposed to act like our person, not swap papers."

"Oh," I answered and took my paper back. I extended my hand and said, "Hello, I am César Chávez. I worked for the rights of farm workers."

"Hi, I am Wangari Maathai," Blake responded.

Looking back at the class, Blake asked which way seems more like a role play: swapping papers or acting in our roles? Roles was the obvious answer.

Pointing back at the questions we had listed on the board to guide students as they read their roles, I reminded them that the answers to those questions are the types of things they should write on their note-taking sheet.

The room hummed with talk as students moved around, taking notes and introducing themselves over and over. Friends went to each other immediately, but soon had to move on and meet all of the justice fighters. Near the end of the mixer, Ricky played match-maker, helping Jesús find an Iqbal Masih and Angelique find a César Chávez. After about 30 minutes, almost everyone had met and taken some notes on each justice fighter. We called everyone back to seats and had them write what else they wanted to know about these justice fighters.

Seeding the Research with Questions

"So now you have a little taste of who these people were and what movements for justice they were part of," I said. "What else do you want to know? What are you curious about? Write down one or two questions or things you wonder about these people and these movements. The videos might answer your questions, but they might not. Having questions helps you focus as a researcher, even if those questions are hard to answer."

These questions are important for a couple of reasons. We needed to calm everyone down after a very high-energy, high-interaction lesson. More than that, we wanted students to know that writers have questions in mind before they start to research. And even more than that, we wanted students to chase their own questions, to follow their own curiosity.

Fueled by their new knowledge and new questions, students seemed eager to watch and take notes from the videos. I developed a note-taking chart to guide students as they collected information. (See resources at the end of this article.) I wanted them to learn a few common pieces of information about each justice fighter because this would ultimately make organizing the essay easier. They needed basic biographical information like the person's name, but I wanted to steer them toward the struggle for justice and the idea that these people did not work alone, so I added a note taking section for "allies." The notes included an important section for the injustice the person was fighting and one for questions and reactions. I also wanted to include a section for drawing a key scene so students would tap into that imagery both for long-term memory and for writing compelling essays. I created a large chart on the wall that matched the ones students were taking notes on. In order to buoy the passion students generated during the tea party and to model how to take notes from a video, I used only the wall chart at first. This helped give all students access to information.

> **We wanted students to know that writers have questions in mind before they start to research. And even more than that, we wanted students to chase their own questions, to follow their own curiosity.**

We first watched the video about Iqbal Masih. For the initial viewing, I wanted students simply to watch and get out of the video anything they could.

"Let's watch this video. See what you can learn about Iqbal Masih. Try to find out why he is thought of as a justice fighter."

Students were sad, then furious to learn at the end of the video that he had been killed. As soon as the video was over, comments popped up all over the room.

"Why'd they kill him?" Paige fumed.

"That's so sad," added Natty.

"Yeah, but look at how much those other kids looked up to him," Claire reminded the class.

I let students freeform discuss their emotional reactions for a few minutes, then asked them to watch the video again. This time I passed out sticky notes to each student and asked them to write down

something important about Iqbal as we watched. They could write anything that they thought was important. In small groups, students read one or two of the facts they wrote down to each other. Then I asked for volunteers to share one note.

Justine raised her hand and read, "Iqbal wanted to help kids get out of working in the carpet factory."

After she read, I pointed to the wall chart and asked, "Where would you put that on our chart?"

Justine thought it belonged under what injustice he was fighting. The class agreed through a show of thumbs up. I invited Justine to come up and put her sticky note on our wall chart where she thought it belonged.

Quiara threw her hand in the air. "He got killed for fighting for justice."

"So where should we put that?" I asked.

Quiara narrowed her eyes and studying the categories on the chart: "Result?"

"What do you think, class?" I asked. "Does his murder belong under the category result?"

Thumbs up from most everyone.

Quiara came up and added her note to the chart.

"Was his murder the only result of his work for justice? Did anything get better because of Iqbal and the Bonded Labor Liberation Front?" I asked.

Chris remembered that some kids in the United States had been inspired by Iqbal and the Bonded Labor Liberation Front to raise money to build schools for children recovering from child labor. I gave him a new sticky note and asked him to write that idea and add to the chart.

A few more kids offered to share their ideas. Then I invited everyone to place their sticky note on the chart where they thought it belonged.

Once our class chart overflowed with sticky notes and ideas, I distributed the individual note-taking sheets. We continued to add to the class chart—sometimes through discussion, sometimes with sticky notes, sometimes just when a student felt compelled to add something. Some students recorded lots of information on their own note-taking sheets, others relied more heavily on the class chart.

Writing the Essay: One Step at a Time

Once we viewed the videos and students collected notes, I helped students narrow the focus of their research. I developed a synthesis sheet for students as one more step in the process of moving from research to writing. (See resources at the end of this article.) The "research" students had done was cursory due to the condensed nature of summer school. There was much more I wished they could know about these movements for justice, but the videos had provided enough content for them to practice their skills of synthesizing information—soon to be incorporated in an essay. Another aspect of being a social justice teacher is taking responsibility for fueling students who have been historically underserved by school, namely poor students, recent immigrants and students of color, with the academic skills they need to find success in school in meaningful ways. The synthesis sheet was a chance for students to take the entirety of what they had learned and zoom in on what was most salient for each of them.

"Writers, we have a lot of information here," I began, pointing to the class note-taking chart covered with sticky notes of many colors, and filled with lots of different handwriting. "If I tried to write all of this in an essay, I think it would end up reading like a list of facts. I want to write an essay in praise of justice fighters. I want it to be good."

I displayed the synthesis sheet on the document camera and asked students to read through it.

"Does this sheet have as much space to write as your note-taking sheet?" I asked.

Students responded with no's and shaking heads.

"That's because all your facts don't need to go into your essay. Today you are going to narrow your focus to what matters to you the most. Just like when we wrote our narratives and we zoomed in on the small details instead of writing and then and then and then stories, essays need a zoomed in focus as well."

I passed out the synthesis sheets (see p. 149) to everyone, then asked them to close their eyes.

"What scenes or images about these justice fighters are clearest in your memory? Try to see a movie in your mind, try to remember a moment we learned about."

After a silent minute with the lights off and eyes closed I got students ready to start the synthesis sheet.

"When I turn on the lights, I want you to pick up your pencil and draw one scene that really stuck in your memory. When you finish that scene, try to draw a second scene. Feel free to rest your head and close your eyes again if you lose the picture in your mind."

Students drew, then shared images at their tables. A few students brought their scenes to the front of the room to show on the document camera and tell the class what the scene was and why it mattered to them. The scenes would serve some students well as a way to enter the essay through a scene introduction.

Next, it was time to complete the advice section. I wanted students to see themselves as potential justice fighters as well. While we did not have a chance to do an activist project with the summer school group, I still wanted them to at least have a sense of their own potential as agents of positive change. By asking for advice from the justice fighters we studied, students had a chance to imagine themselves carrying on the work. Again, I modeled imagining what César Chávez

> **By analyzing the style and structure of several student model essays, students were able to generate a set of criteria as a class for what makes a good justice fighters essay.**

or Aung San Suu Kyi would say to me if I asked them for advice on how to fight for justice. When I asked for help thinking of what they might say, students offered ideas like, "Never give up," "Stay strong even when others try to stop you," and finally, "Get other people to help you." Working with a partner, students completed the advice section of their synthesis sheets. Finally, each student thought about their opinions and feelings.

Students had now winnowed their ideas and research down to the pieces they were most likely to need for writing the essay. It was time to write. By analyzing the style and structure of several student model essays, students were able to generate a set of criteria as a class for what makes a good justice fighters essay. I started by simply reading a model essay and asking the class to highlight something they thought was good writing. Students shared highlighted sections with partners or table groups, then with the whole class. As they shared the parts they noticed were good writing, I highlighted a copy of the essay displayed with the document camera. Then we read a second essay and highlighted its strengths as well. Once we had read two essays, I guided the students to notice commonalities: both essays had paragraphs, both essays told facts about justice fighters, both essays had introductions. I listed these common elements on a chart paper and they became the criteria for the essays my students would write. I added thesis to the list of what they noticed because I wanted them to know what a thesis is and to include one in their own essays. In developing what I wanted to be a hopeful, joyful, kind, and visionary unit, the last thing I wanted to do was to leech the passion from students by confining them to a formulaic essay template. The criteria offered enough of a frame to guide students' writing so they understood how to structure, pace, and plan an essay, but did not limit them to a formula.

Finally, to write effective and impassioned essays, I had the students study examples of introductions and conclusions from other student essays. Based on the models, students chose a type of introduction they wanted to try. They tried it, shared it and decided if it would work or not. If not, they tried another type.

I have taught justice fighters units to 2nd through 6th graders pretty much every year since I began teaching. Every year students are inspired by and connected to one or more of these people and the movements they represent. But there was something special about introducing the videos of justice fighters. While students had always been engaged when reading about and discussing justice fighters, the energy and excitement filling my room during summer school was palpable and satisfying. I anticipated that students would like the videos simply because images and sound are engaging. What I had not thought about before we started watching, taking notes and discussing was how much closer the students were able to get to the justice fighters we studied because they saw them in real time, moving, talking, and tapping into some internal source of courage.

Given more time than our short summer academy, I would use the videos in tandem with picture book biographies and articles about each person to broaden and deepen students' understanding. But I would not teach this unit again without the videos.

When I teach this unit again, as I surely will, I want to be sure to include more understanding of the context for each movement for justice. While students saw that César Chávez marched with thousands, I am not sure they understood the link between the success of the United Farm Workers struggle and the sheer number of people involved in the marches and strikes. They saw Wangari Maathai planting trees with hundreds of other women, but did not understand the forces behind the original deforestation. As much as social justice education is grounded in being hopeful, joyful, kind, and visionary, it must also be transparent about who benefits from injustice and who orchestrates it. Every time I teach a unit on justice fighters, it gets better. The need for this type of work with students is clear. Unfortunately, we will continue to be faced with old and new forms of injustice. Fortunately, countless people will continue offering themselves to organize, to stand up, and to fight for justice. ■

References:

Au, Wayne, Bill Bigelow, Stan Karp. "Introduction: Creating Classrooms for Equity and Justice." *Rethinking Our Classrooms, Volume 1*. Milwaukee: Rethinking Schools, 2007.

Bigelow, Bill. "Teaching about Unsung Heroes," *A People's History for the Classroom*. Milwaukee: Rethinking Schools, 2008.

Christensen, Linda. "Honoring Our Ancestors: Building Profile Essays." *Teaching for Joy and Justice*. Milwaukee: Rethinking Schools, 2009.

Justice Fighters Resource List Compiled by Elizabeth Schlessman

BOOKS

These narrative non-fiction books tell stories of people working for justice—creating change—in libraries, villages, factories, fields, restaurants, schools, and streets.

Biblioburro: A True Story from Colombia
Jeanette Winter
Beach Lane Books, 2010.

The Carpet Boy's Gift
Peggy Deitz Shea
Tilbury House Publishers, 2006.

Harvesting Hope: The Story of César Chávez
Kathleen Krull
Harcourt Children's Books, 2003.

The Librarian of Basra
Jeanette Winter
HarcoSeeurt Children's Books, 2005.

Mama Miti: Wangari Maathai and the Trees of Kenya
Donna Jo Napoli
Simon & Schuster, 2010.

Mendez vs. Westminster: For All the Children
Michael Matsuda and Sandra Robbie
Blue State Press, 2006.

Sit-In: How Four Friends Stood Up by Sitting Down
Andrea Pinkney
Little, Brown Books for Young Readers, 2010.

Through My Eyes: Ruby Bridges
Ruby Bridges
Scholastic Press, 1999.

Wangari's Trees of Peace: A True Story from Africa
Jeanette Winter
Harcourt Children's Books, 2008.

VIDEOS

César Chávez
http://www.youtube.com/watch?v=wRPLZC7woUo&feature=youtube_gdata_player

The Freedom Riders
http://www.democracynow.org/2010/2/1/the_freedom_riders

Dolores Huerta
http://www.youtube.com/watch?v=Hpi1-Yrp668&feature=related

Wangari Maathai
http://www.alternativechannel.tv/blog/en/comments/video_nobel_peace_prize_green_belt

Iqbal Masih
http://myhero.com/go/films/view.asp?film=courage

Aung San Suu Kyi
http://www.youtube.com/watch?v=841B0X8aRdQ&feature=email&safety_mode=true&persist_safety_mode=1

http://www.youtube.com/watch?v=j1ZlLd1fnxU&feature=email&safety_mode=true&persist_safety_mode=1

Mixer Roles

WANGARI MAATHAI

I won the Nobel Peace Prize for 2004 for my contribution to sustainable development, democracy, and peace. I went to study in the United States and when I returned to my country (Kenya) I was shocked that many trees had been cut down. I founded the Green Belt Movement where, for nearly 30 years, I have mobilized poor women to plant 30 million trees. My methods have been adopted by other countries as well.

DOLORES HUERTA

I am a tireless organizer for farmworker rights in the United States, a leader in the United Farmworkers of America. My father was a farmworker and my mother a waitress. I became a skilled union organizer and, people tell me, a fantastic speaker. I became especially active in working against the use of pesticides (chemicals) in the fields that were poisoning workers and our children. In a 1988 San Francisco rally, I was beaten so severely by police that I had to have emergency surgery.

CÉSAR CHÁVEZ

I was the son of farmworkers, who were some of the most mistreated people in the United States. I organized the United Farmworkers of America to fight for the rights of migrant farmworkers, many of them from Mexico. My union led boycotts of grapes and lettuce. I also fought against the use of so many pesticides (chemicals) in the fields because I knew the pesticides were bad for workers and bad for consumers, the people who buy and eat the fruits and vegetables.

IQBAL MASIH

I was born in Pakistan in 1992. When I was four years old, I was sold as a child slave to a carpet factory for a peshgi of U.S. $12. I was forced to work on the looms, making carpets until I ran away from the factory at age 10. I was freed from slavery by the Bonded Labor Liberation Front (BLLF). After I learned about my rights and the laws in my country, I refused to go back to work in the carpet factory. I worked with the BLLF to help free other children from child slavery.

Mixer Roles *continued*

FREEDOM RIDER

I am a young college student and, like other people all over the country, I am outraged by segregation. It is wrong and unfair for people to be treated differently and told to use different spaces based on the color of their skin. The Supreme Court decided in 1960 that it is illegal for bus companies to have a separate section for blacks. But still, the bus companies segregate the buses, the waiting rooms, even the drinking fountains.

I have decided to join the Freedom Ride leaving Washington, D.C. in May 1961. The ride will have blacks and whites riding buses together. We will travel into the deep South where segregation is strong and powerful.

I am frightened because I know some people will resist us with violence. Even though I am afraid, I feel I must do what I know in my heart to be right. I will join the Freedom Ride. We will sing to keep up our spirits. We will stand together to fight for what is right.

AUNG SAN SUU KYI

I was born in Burma but went to school in India and England. My father was famous for helping gain independence for my homeland, Burma. I lived far away from Burma for a long time. I went back when my mother was dying. What I saw when I went home made me so sad. The government and the army were brutal to the people fighting for their rights. I joined the people. I started speaking out and ended up in jail. I have spent years and years in jail for using my voice. I have never given up my belief in non-violence. In 2010, I was released from many years of house arrest.

Justice Fighters Tea Party Notes

Name _____

Name of the justice fighter you read about _____

Try to meet all of the other justice fighters.

Name	Details about that person

Write down one or two questions you hope to get answered as we learn more about these justice fighters:

Synthesize

Combine a number of ideas into one whole new understanding.

Name ⸻⸻⸻⸻⸻⸻⸻⸻⸻⸻⸻⸻⸻⸻⸻⸻⸻⸻⸻

Synthesize what you have learned about justice fighters using pictures and words.

SCENES

What are two scenes about the lives of justice fighters that have stayed clear in your mind?
Draw those scenes here.

ADVICE

Imagine meeting one of these justice fighters. What advice do you think this person would give you about fighting for justice?

FEELINGS

What are your opinions or feelings about one or more of these justice fighters?

Justice Fighters Introductions

Every essay opens with an introduction, but every introduction is unique. You have some choices about how to write your justice fighters essay introduction. Here are some ideas to get you started. You can always invent your own type of introduction.

SCENE INTRODUCTION

This type of introduction describes an event or a moment that is important in the justice fighter's work and life. Be as descriptive as you can with this type of introduction.

Chloe used a scene to introduce her essay:

> *Imagine you are at home reading the newspaper. A big job ad catches your eye. It reads: Looking for a job with no bathroom breaks, little money, dirty drinking water, and no lunch breaks? Then this is the job for you. Call 1-800-UNFAIR to be a farmworker today. Ages 8 and older can apply. Doesn't sound like a good job does it? César Chávez, Dolores Huerta and the United Farm Workers didn't think so either. So like justice fighters all over the world, they worked hard and worked together to make it better.*

HISTORICAL OVERVIEW INTRODUCTION

This type of introduction tells the reader a little bit about the history of the fight for justice.

Marcel used a historical overview for his essay about the Freedom Riders.

> *The year is 1961. The Supreme Court decided a year earlier that it was illegal to stop black people and white people from riding buses together. But the bus companies didn't listen. They still practiced segregation. So large groups of black and white people got together to make that change. They got onto buses together and headed into the deep South where segregation was strongest. They must have been so scared, knowing they could be beaten or sent to jail. These people were brave. These people were the Freedom Riders.*

"JUST THE FACTS" INTRODUCTION

This type of introduction gives the reader a few important facts that will make the rest of your essay make more sense.

Olivia introduced her essay with some key facts about Iqbal Masih.

> *Iqbal Masih was a brave justice fighter. He was only four years old when he was sold to the carpet factory for $12.00, 10 years old when the Bonded Labor Liberation Front helped him escape, and 12 when he put his own life in danger to help other kids.*

Student Essay: Iqbal Masih

NATTY (5th Grade)

In 1992, a legacy was born. His name was Iqbal Masih. Even though he died as a kid, his legacy is still alive today. This is the story of Iqbal Masih.

Iqbal Masih was born in Pakistan in 1992. When he was just four years old, he was sold into slavery to a miserable carpet factory for $12. The factory was horrible. The kids were barely fed because hunger would help keep their fingers small. Smaller fingers can weave better. They didn't have a bathroom and they were often tied to a chair. If they did any little thing wrong, they would be severely punished.

When Iqbal was 10 years old, he ran away from the carpet factory. With the help of the Bonded Labor Liberation Front (BLLF), he escaped. After that, he completed six years of school in just two years. After his release, Iqbal decided that no kids should ever be slaves. He started to help the Bonded Labor Liberation Front work against child slavery.

Iqbal fought against child slavery by doing many things. He went to schools around the world, informing other kids about the terrible things some people did to children. He also asked for donations. He started marches where people would walk through the streets protesting. But sometime that would have to end.

Iqbal went back to Pakistan and was murdered right outside of his grandmother's house. It was 2004. He was just 12 years old. He was just a kid when he was killed, yet he had made such a big difference to the world.

A lot of people have decided to follow in Iqbal's footsteps. Some school kids raised enough money to build eight schools for children freed from slavery. They followed Iqbal's example. Maybe someday you will, too.

Justice Fighters Conclusions

You have written a powerful essay about powerful people. Make sure you end your essay with power.

Here are a few examples of how other writers wrote a conclusion for a justice fighters essay.

LEGACY CONCLUSION

Lupita ended her essay by describing how Iqbal's work goes on even after his death.

> *That is the sad and wonderful life of the incredible justice fighter, Iqbal Masih. He was treated unfairly and he suffered terribly most of his life. But it is his courage and his kindness that we remember. Even though his life was so hard, his dream did finally come true. Many kids are freed from carpet factories and sent to school. Sadly, Iqbal did not get the chance to see it.*

Try writing a conclusion that describes the justice fighter's legacy.

EMOTIONAL CONNECTION CONCLUSION

Saivon ends his essay by connecting to the pride he imagines the Freedom Riders feeling.

> *Imagine being a Freedom Rider, knowing you helped to end the terrible effects of segregation, knowing how brave you were and how you refused to give up. You would be proud to think of how many people you helped. The Freedom Riders were truly amazing people.*

Try writing a conclusion that tells how you feel about the justice fighter(s) or how you imagine they feel about themselves.

COMPARE AND CONNECT CONCLUSION

Lincoln wrote a conclusion that compared and connected the justice fighter he wrote about with other justice fighters.

> *Wangari Maathai did not work to end segregation and she didn't fight for farmworkers' rights like some other justice fighters. But like other justice fighters she brought the most prized and precious thing to people: hope. If you pass it along, a spark of hope can grow into a flame. This is what Wangari Maathai did with her spark.*

Try writing a conclusion that compares and connects your justice fighter(s) with others.

Justice Fighters Essay Criteria Sheet

Use this sheet to make sure your essay sounds as good as possible. Make sure to make AT LEAST 3 changes (adding sentences, crossing sentences out, changing sentences around).

INTRODUCTION:

What type of introduction did you use?

Did you try at least two versions of your thesis?

Is it clear which justice fighters you are writing about?

BODY PARAGRAPHS:

How many body paragraphs do you have?

Does each body paragraph have a main idea?

Does each body paragraph have details?

Did you add or cut out at least one detail? Copy it here:

CONCLUSION:

What type of conclusion did you use?

Does your conclusion make it obvious you are done with the whole essay?

CHANGES:

Write about one change you made in revision that made your essay better:

Justice Fighter Research Notes

	Wangari Maathai	César Chávez & Dolores Huerta	Aug San Suu Kyi	Freedom Riders	Iqbal Masih
Who?					
What injustice were they fighting?					
What were their strategies? How did they fight for justice?					
Draw a scene or copy a quote.					
Who were some allies or helpers in the fight for justice?					
What was the result of the fight for justice?					
What are your thoughts? Questions? Opinions?					

Name _____

PhotoAlto / James Hardy

My Mom's Job Is Important

MATT WITT

"My mother is a cashier. She works at Zayre's. My mom said to be a good cashier you should be punctual, courteous, broad-minded, honest, and accurate."

So begins 5th grader Antonia Guzman's account of her mother's job at a discount department store. But Antonia's account does not stop with the usual recitation of the skills and attitudes that people need to fit into the world of work that so often emerge from classroom units on employment. Instead, Antonia goes on to explore her mother's dreams and reflects on the importance of her mother's contribution:

> My mom said that the job she wants if she could change her job right away is to become an entrepreneur. She would like to own a retail business like a gift shop. She would like to be an entrepreneur because she would like to be her own boss, and your income is not limited and you can work at your own pace.
>
>   I think my mom's job is important because if there's no cashier no one would keep track of the prices when a customer buys an item or a product.

Antonia is a student at Oyster Bilingual Elementary School in Washington, D.C., a public school whose students come from a wide variety of racial, ethnic, and economic backgrounds. Parents and teachers at Oyster organized a yearlong "Program on Work," which demonstrated some exciting approaches to teaching and learning about work.

In the Oyster program, children critically examined slides of work situations, interviewed their parents, explored probing questions, entertained controversy, invited parents and other adults into the classroom to talk (and in one case, sing) about work, and constructed a display for parents featuring stories, poems, and drawings they had created. An understanding and respect for their parents' jobs was combined in the unit with the exploration of legal and historical issues.

Why study work? First, because it is a central aspect of our lives and our society.

Why study work? First, because it is a central aspect of our lives and our society. If a goal of education is to teach students to think critically about how our society is organized, their study of work-related issues cannot be limited to learning the difference between "goods" and "services," memorizing a few names like Samuel Gompers or George Meany, and soaking up donated corporate propaganda that paints an incomplete picture of the country's economic life.

Second, studying work is a good way to encourage interaction between students, parents, community residents, and teachers — either by bringing people from the community into the classroom to talk about their work or by sending students out to investigate.

Third, studying work provides stimulating subject matter with which to develop skills such as writing, interviewing, debating, drawing, and singing.

The program at Oyster School began with discussions about work in each class from 2nd grade through 6th, conducted by teachers and parent volunteers. To begin with a subject that students could relate to easily, they were shown slides of child labor taken in the United States in the early years of this century.

"What are these children doing?" students were asked. When they established that the children in the slides were working — in coal mines, cotton fields, textile mills, and other industries — students were asked, "Why are they working and not in school?"

Exploring Child Labor

Through further discussion, students discovered that as recently as when their grandparents were children, many young people were employed in child labor. This led to many questions: "Why did child labor exist? Who benefited from it, and who opposed it? What did working people do to get it outlawed?"

Slides of modern-day child labor in other countries provoked comments from students from recent immigrant families. "They still don't have any laws against children having to work," said a student who came to the United States from Guatemala. "Children have to do a lot of hard work, especially on the farms."

Students were then asked whether children have a right to get an education instead of going to work, which provoked a discussion about who decides what is a right and what is not.

They were shown slides of people of different races, ages, and genders, and were asked whether they thought it would be legal for an employer looking to hire someone to pick among those people based on those differences. They also saw a slide of a pregnant woman and were asked whether it would be legal to fire her if she refused to do a task that might threaten the health of her unborn child.

After students gave their views, they learned that laws establishing what they considered to be obvious rights had been passed just since their parents were born. Asked how they thought workers got those laws passed, students drew on what they learned during a schoolwide program honoring Martin Luther King Jr. and the Civil Rights Movement.

"Boycotts," they suggested. "Sit-ins. Strikes. Marches."

Historical slides showed some of these tactics being used, including sit-down strikes in the 1930s and equal rights rallies in the 1960s. Rights, students learned, are not given but won, and change with time as new social movements emerge.

Next, students saw slides of men doing traditionally "male" jobs — doctor, factory worker, coal miner — and women doing traditionally "female" jobs such as secretary, flight attendant, and homemaker. That prompted a discussion about whether both men and women could do those jobs.

The next slides showed men and women doing the jobs that are stereotyped as being only for the opposite sex. Discussion followed on whether all people should be able to choose jobs that suit them, or whether, as a few boys in each class would argue, "the only work women should do is at home."

Another discussion in all classes, including pre-K, kindergarten, and 1st grade, was based on slides of various Oyster parents doing their jobs. Construction workers and housekeepers are more common among the school's families—but the range is wide including a lawyer, a reporter, a dancer, a furniture maker, a cab driver, and aides to government officials. The occupations were discussed from many points of view. "What does the person shown actually do in his or her job? What would be satisfying about the work, and what would make it difficult, stressful, or dangerous? What makes the job important to society?"

In all classes, students were able to identify a number of reasons that each job is valuable to society. In some cases, that led to new questions, such as, "If each job is important, why are some jobs paid more than others?"

What Do You Do at Work?

When shown slides of homemakers and asked what job these people were doing, a few students answered: "They don't have a job. They just stay home." This provoked lively discussions about the duties of homemakers and both the strains and satisfactions of childrearing.

With these classroom discussions as background, students were assigned to interview their parents or

Drawings by students from Oyster Bilingual Elementary School

other adults about their work. "What do you do while I'm at school? What do you like about your job? What would you change if you could?"

What they learned from these interviews was as varied as the jobs their parents did. Many children learned that what their parents liked most about their jobs was a chance to meet or help people, while a common complaint was that customers or employers did not treat them with respect.

Some of the recent immigrants told their children they wished they had jobs like they had had in their native countries, instead of the less skilled work they were confined to in the United States.

Other parents talked about problems with shift work, mandatory overtime, and being denied benefits that were due them.

All classes from pre-K to 6th grade had discussions about what they had learned. In the pre-K through 1st-grade classes, a parent brought in a guitar and sang with the children, "What does your mama (or papa, grampa, etc.) do? What does your mama do? What does your mama do when you're in school, you're in school?" The song would stop as a student explained what she or he had found out, and pick up again when it was time to give someone else a chance.

After all students did drawings and the 2nd- through 6th-grade classes wrote reports or poems using what they had learned, their work was put on display at the school and compiled in a booklet. Parents were invited to the school one evening to see the display, get copies of the booklet, and take part in a community forum about work along with teachers, students, local union leaders, and local labor scholars.

Problems and Lessons

In carrying out the "Program on Work," teachers and parents at Oyster School encountered a number of problems. For example, when the program was first proposed, some of the white middle-class parents active in the PTA objected that "the poorer families are not going to want the fact that they are a housekeeper or a janitor plastered all over the walls." As it turned out, the opposite was true: Parents with lower status jobs greatly appreciated both the recognition they received and the open discussion of issues of equity in the work world.

Another obstacle was the desire of some teachers to narrowly define the program as "career education." It took a great deal of discussion to convince some that the role of the school was to prepare students not merely to fit into the world of work as it exists, but to be able to analyze it and critique it.

Parents with lower status jobs greatly appreciated both the recognition they received and the open discussion of issues of equity in the work world.

In adapting the program for other schools, certain omissions would have to be corrected and some program elements could be developed further. For example, children of the few parents at this particular school who were without work were simply told to interview them about jobs they used to have or would like to have, or to interview an older sibling, neighbor, friend, or worker at the school.

In retrospect, more time should have been spent in classroom discussion on unemployment, disability, retirement, and other issues related to people without work. Students could have been asked to think of all the reasons why someone might be unemployed or unable to work, to consider what obligation society has to such people, if any, and to discuss possible solutions. Perhaps someone active in a community organization working to win expanded jobs programs could have been invited to talk with students about the causes of unemployment and proposed remedies.

Particularly for older students, the chance to experience or at least observe one or more jobs would be an obvious complement to discussions and interviews about adults' views of work. Parents from a 4th-grade class at Oyster demonstrated the potential for "work experience" activities by arranging for students to work as teachers' aides in a nearby nursery school. When each had had a turn, the students had a lengthy discussion about what they had learned, and prepared an oral report that was given to the rest of the school during an assembly.

Workplace visits are also recommended. They are most fruitful if a worker visits the school first and prepares students to think about the working conditions they will see, how conditions have changed over the years, how decisions are made when problems come up, and so on. Otherwise, such visits tend to focus almost exclusively on what tasks a worker performs at his or her job.

One final suggestion: Schools that need extra funds for materials, transportation, or other expenses to incorporate the world of work into the curriculum might consider asking local unions for help. They also may be able to help set up workplace visits. ∎

Matt Witt was coordinator of Oyster Bilingual School's "Program on Work." He is director of the American Labor Education Center and its website, www.TheWorksite.org, which provides downloadable resources.

Janis Litavnieks

3.

Minding Media

Our lives are immersed in commercial media and our schools are saturated with commercial curriculum. There aren't many places you can look without glimpsing an advertisement or a logo, so keeping a critical perspective on consumerist messages is a full-time job. Teachers can help students see how print and electronic media affect their sense of themselves, their communities, and the world by taking up media as a topic of study. We can help students reflect on how our media environment shapes their vision of the world as we empower them to articulate their own.

Barbara Miner

Six Going on Sixteen

Fighting 'age compression' and the commercialization of childhood

GERALYN BYWATER MCLAUGHLIN

"I saw you on Myspace!"
"Yesterday after school Trina and Shayla got in a catfight over Brandon!"
"My butt is hot!"
"I got his phone number!"
"She thinks she's cuter than me."

These comments may or may not raise an eyebrow in any middle school classroom, but the year they became a common occurrence in my kindergarten and 1st-grade classroom threw me for a loop. It was just a few years ago, and at that time I had been teaching for 18 years. My combined kindergarten and 1st-grade classroom was in a small, urban K-8 school serving about 165 students from a mix of cultures and classes. The student population was about 45 percent black, 27 percent Latino/a, and 23 percent white. That particular school year was one of the most challenging I have experienced. The social dynamics were a constant source of stress and strife for my students, my families, my assistant teacher, and for me. At the end of a particularly frustrating day I described the situation to my principal: "We have two 'middle schools' in our school. The middle school and the K-1!"

In a nutshell, that is how the year felt. The problems I encountered, mostly around the over-sexualization of my students, caught me off guard and utterly unprepared. I had 5-year-old girls vying for the attention of the "coolest" 1st-grade boy. They would push to be near him at the sand table, and groan audibly if I didn't place them in his book group. Students in the class thought of each other as "boyfriend" and "girlfriend." Freeze dance and soul train, which are usually a big hit and lots of fun, had a new dimension as students danced out the social scenarios they had seen in music videos. My 5-, 6-, and 7-year-olds played out and talked about "being in the club" and "drinking Heineken." They wrote about the music world in their journals and turned the block area into a radio station. Sometimes they used the hollow blocks to build a stage to perform on. Small cylindrical blocks were their microphones. This type of play was OK with me, except who was "in" and who was "out" was a constant social battle.

There was another aspect of this that negatively impacted our classroom community, and that was the idea of certain kids wearing the "right" sneakers. This was among a group of boys, but the rest of the class was affected. It was something we had class meetings about, and tried to minimize the negative effects of, but it was a continuous struggle. One morning, as they walked up the stairs to our second-floor classroom, a kindergarten boy and a 1st-grade boy got in a pushing and hitting fight because the younger boy said he was wearing "Carmelo Anthonys" and the older boy said, "No, those are Jordans." Another boy, whose mom refused to buy expensive sneakers, had repeated meltdowns (crying, throwing things, yelling) when other boys arrived at school with new sneakers, stylish shirts or outfits, or big plastic gold rings.

One day in June, things crystallized for me as the three K-1 classes rode a big yellow school bus on our annual trip to The Farm School, in Athol, Mass. The Farm School is an important part of our school culture. Everyone in the school visits the working farm at least once a year, and starting in 4th grade students get to sleep over. The K-1's were excited. The school bus was happily buzzing with kids talking to each other about the farm, the animals they would see

and hold, what they had in their lunchbox — general happy kid talk. Then, the bus driver decided to put on the radio. I was very near the back, so I had a good vantage point. The music pumped for just a few seconds, but the mood in the bus changed dramatically. All of a sudden kids popped up in their seats and checked out who else heard the song. They knew the song, but I didn't. I saw and felt the change in energy. They were looking for other kids who were "in the know" and related to that teenage/grown-up world of popular music. They weren't talking about the farm anymore. My assistant teacher and I exchanged knowing glances and sighed. We understood this is what we had been struggling with the whole year, the negative effect of mainstream media on our young students — the way it was taking away their chance to just be little kids excited about a day at the farm.

Throughout the year, I tried many strategies to counteract the negative impact that all of these complicated factors were having on our ability to live, learn, and laugh. We had class meetings and made rules. I partnered students with classmates they didn't usually work with; had lunch meetings with the powerful core group; set up a series of lunch meetings for my most involved girls to meet with our counselor; talked a great deal to moms and grandmothers; devoted some of my weekly newsletters for families to this topic; brought back some of my former students to help create a positive counterculture; brainstormed with families and colleagues; cried and yelled. Some strategies helped, but it was an ongoing, uphill battle.

We made it through the year. That June I remember meeting with the rest of the staff at our end-of-the-year retreat. I shared my struggles and my determination to get a better handle on what felt to me like a crisis in the early childhood realm. I had consulted with colleagues throughout the year, and some of them knew what I had been up against. Others were amazed, shocked, and saddened. One friend and colleague made a suggestion that ended up being the best and most transformative advice I've received in a long time. She told me about Diane Levin, a professor at nearby Wheelock College, and she suggested I enroll in the two-day summer media institute, called Media Madness: The Impact of Sex, Violence, and Commerical Culture on Children and Society.

It was from Diane that I learned how the corporate world deliberately targets vulnerable children. I learned how child development experts now work with marketing firms to optimize the impact of commercials according to the developmental stage of the target audience and how the toy market has dramatically changed since children's television was deregulated in 1984. I also learned about "age compression." In Levin's recent book, *So Sexy So Soon*, she describes age compression this way:

> "Age compression" is a term used by media professionals and marketers to describe how children at ever younger ages are doing what older children used to do. The media, the toys, the behavior, the clothing once seen as appropriate for teens are now firmly ensconced in the lives of tweens and are rapidly encroaching on and influencing the lives of younger children. In addition, there is a blurring of boundaries between children and adults, as demonstrated by the similarities in clothing marketed to both groups by the fashion industry. Age compression is especially disturbing when it involves sexual behavior. Children become involved in and learn about sexual issues and behavior they do not yet have the intellectual or emotional ability to understand and that can confuse and harm them.

Here's a true story that helps illustrate my experience with age compression. It was the first day of kindergarten, fall of 2005. I had brought my class to the cafeteria for lunch. The students were assigned seats at one of our 10 round tables. I sat down next to a 5-year-old girl who was beginning to eat her lunch. "That's the popular table," she said matter-of-factly as she gestured over her shoulder. I was taken aback, but followed her finger to see where she was pointing. I looked again at her and asked, "Popular? What do you mean by that?" "Oh, you know, they have nice clothes," she explained. I thought about that for a moment, and since it was the first day she'd ever been in school, I asked, "Where did you learn about that?" Without a moment's hesitation she answered, "The Disney Channel."

On the upside, my school is a pilot public school, so we have autonomy over curriculum. Despite No Child Left Behind and the current high-stakes testing frenzy that have sadly turned many kindergartens into heavily academic 1st grades, our 5-, 6-, and 7-year-olds still get to play with blocks and play-dough. They love to dress up, play with puppets, cuddle the baby dolls and draw hearts. And they have time to play. Even the "coolest" kids will sing "The Pizza Song" and "Make New Friends." "Can we sing it in a round?" they'll ask. Also, I have students for two years, so I have time each summer to think more about them and what they need and what I can do. I was determined to have a better handle on the issues, find more strategies for the classroom, and extend my small one-on-one conversations to begin a broader community conversation.

One huge goal was to find ways to bring back childhood—making even more time in the day for creative and imaginative play.

As the new school year began, I knew that one huge goal was to find ways to bring back childhood—making even more time in the day for creative and imaginative play. I also wanted to encourage kids to turn off their screens and become more connected with the natural world, their classmates, and their own selves. To this end, I titled my fall curriculum unit Garden Friends: Taking Care of Each Other and Taking Care of the Earth. I had studied gardens with young children before, but this time I had an added goal of lessening the influence of screen messages. I knew from experience that one excellent antidote to screen addiction is nature. Children are fascinated by it. It's also affordable and available, even in our urban school. We got our hands dirty and looked closely at snails and spiders. We also spent time in those first few weeks explicitly practicing positive problem-solving skills. At the media institute, Diane had described "problem-solving deficit disorder" and "compassion deficit disorder," two critical social problems affecting our children as a direct result of current media and popular culture. These terms described beautifully the issues that I had felt firsthand in my classroom. I realized I needed to be even more explicit and deliberate in my problem-solving lessons, activities, and discussions. For example, I needed to teach some of my young children how to look at each other's faces and interpret others' reactions and what words to use to solve conflicts. Throughout the school year I used my weekly letter to families to let them in on our struggles, conversations, and solutions. Families are on the front line in the battle against corporate encroachment into children's lives and I wanted them to stay connected with our work at school. I knew their support was one important factor in our growing success. Here is an excerpt from a November letter to families:

> I added baby dolls to the dress-up area, and watched and listened as the week unfolded. Monday and Tuesday had children claiming baby dolls as their own, and conflicts and tears arose. On Wednesday morning, with 8th-grader Darren's help, we did a skit about the baby dolls. Darren pretended to play with a doll and our student teacher pretended to snatch the doll so she could play. I pretended to add fuel to the fire, making the situation even worse by yelling and stomping my feet. The students laughed at how silly we looked, then helped brainstorm ways to be safe and take care even when we disagree. For example: stay calm; take a deep breath; count to 10; use nice words like "Can I please use that?" or try playing Rock, Paper, Scissors.
>
> By Friday, our project time was more satisfying and productive. John pretended his baby needed surgery and Jared was the skillful doctor. Keisha pretended she was a childcare worker taking care of a few babies. I overheard Jennifer listing the symptoms of her baby as Louisa (the doctor) listened closely, nodding her head and asking questions about the baby. When conflicts arose, I saw students trying our techniques.

In the spring my curriculum theme was Imagine, Pretend, and Play. I designed the unit to celebrate and highlight children's ability to be in charge of their own learning as they create stories, invent problems, and evolve as powerful individuals. I wanted all students to know that pretend play is important and to practice making choices that involve imagining, pretending, and playing. They would learn how to create their own entertainment and that many things can be used for play—rocks, sticks, dirt, cardboard boxes, scraps of fabric, and unmatched socks, for example. We focused our literacy work on reading stories that celebrate imagination, such as *Amazing Grace,* by Mary Hoffman, *Gilberto and the Wind,* by Marie Hall Ets, and *Roxaboxen,* by Alice McLerran. I found related poems to recite and songs to sing. The students had special journals to record and reflect about their play. I had students practice describing how they felt while they were engaged in their chosen activity. We invited our families for a special breakfast and exhibition as we displayed our accomplishments. I shared with families a quote from a wonderful book to help illustrate my curriculum decisions: "The ability to play is central to our capacity to take risks, to experiment, to think critically, to act rather than react, to differentiate ourselves from our environment, and to make life meaningful." (Susan Linn, *The Case for Make Believe: Saving Play in a Commercialized World,* p. 19.)

One student stands out in my mind. In his early years, he had been exposed to a great deal of media. He was literally tuned in to the teenage/grown-up world and had trouble making friends his own age. I struggled to find ways for him to be comfortable and happy at school. During the Imagine, Pretend, and Play curriculum he found some of his happiest school moments. He used recycled materials to build his own skate park and used found objects (boxes and bottles) to make his own drum set. He worked on and perfected these projects over a number of weeks. One day, when reflecting, he said, "I was pretending I was downtown. I had the bass drum, the solo drum, and the high drum." He added that, "It was hard to get the pretending into me. Once I started, I felt good."

Along with changes I made in my own classroom, I also worked with my colleagues and the school as a whole. A few of us formed a small media work group where we could meet and share ideas and resources. We wrote front-page newsletters to the community. Every Friday our school sends a newsletter home. It includes a front-page letter, usually written by the principal, but often written by other staff members, occasionally a parent and sometimes even a student. Besides the front-page letter, there are columns written by each of the 10 classroom teachers, hot topics, and more. Our school uses our Friday newsletters as a place to share ideas, reflect, inform, pose questions, and stimulate conversations. Here are some excerpts from one newsletter:

> The trouble is that media-linked toys limit children's play. Children need to play creatively.

They need to invent. They practice problem-solving as their play evolves. Picture a child playing with wooden blocks. She builds a tower, pretending the smallest blocks are the people. As she plays, another child joins and builds nearby. Someone gets the idea to connect their two buildings, and they decide to turn them into a hotel and a parking garage. Their play continually evolves as they share ideas, make decisions and solve problems. They end feeling powerful and satisfied.

Media-linked toys, however, lead children to imitate the scripts they have seen. How often have you seen children playing "Power Rangers," "Cheetah Girls," or some other show? The boys have to be violent and the girls have to be sexy. That's what they see, so that's what they play. When children act out the scripts from TV shows or movies, they aren't in control of their play. They aren't creating, they are imitating. This isn't a satisfying kind of play.

In December, we sent home an excellent resource to all our families. It was TRUCE's *Toy Action Guide*. Teachers Resisting Unhealthy Children's Entertainment (TRUCE) is a national group of educators actively working to raise awareness about the negative effect of violent and stereotyped toys and media on children. They are supporting teachers and parents in their efforts to promote healthy play. Their free and downloadable guide is a powerful tool for parents. The guide helps parents understand healthy play and how it is a critical part of healthy development. It helps them understand how open-ended and simple toys are actually better than the glitzy electronic toys that are expensive and limiting to problem-solving and creativity. The guide lists books, articles, organizations, and websites for further support. Again, parent response was overwhelmingly positive, though a few parents lamented that it was hard to find good toys at the stores that are convenient to shop at. Even toys such as wooden blocks and generic puppets can be hard to find, and they can be expensive.

Those comments spurred me to work on opening our Toy Lending Library. I asked around for donations and found some underused materials already in the school. IKEA donated a set of shelves and bins, and even some great creative toys. I got donations from other stores and parents. The library became a hit. Once a child in one class borrowed a set of blocks,

puppets, or a marble run, other students wanted to do the same. It was a big project to undertake and organize, but it has proven to be a fun resource and conversation starter. The Toy Lending Library also helps counter our country's consuming culture, since the toys are not purchased but shared within the community.

> **Our Toy Lending Library helps counter our country's consuming culture, since the toys are not purchased but shared within the community.**

A simpler schoolwide initiative was the Family Game Night we had in January. The entire school community was invited to come for a potluck dinner and games. It was an "unplugged" night with no remote controls, video games, or electronic gadgets. Many staff members volunteered to oversee a wide range of games. We had fun playing Twister, Uno, bingo, blackjack, charades, and more. The biggest hit was a fast-paced card game called Spoons, led by our middle school humanities teacher. Even families who usually play board games at home were excited. "We usually only get to play with our small family. It was so much fun to play with so many people." "When can we have the next Game Night?" I was asked excitedly the next day by parents, students, and staff.

In February, we had a Family Council Meeting on the topic of media influences. Our media work group facilitated the evening, and more than 30 parents and staff gathered to share information and strategies to combat the media onslaught that we felt was attacking the well-being of our children and families. One idea that stemmed from the meeting was for our school to celebrate "Turnoff Week," an annual event sponsored by the Center for SCREEN-TIME Awareness.

The National Turnoff Week coincided with spring break, so we chose a week in May that worked better for us. In the weeks leading up to our Turnoff Week, we launched a campaign to build enthusiasm. For many people, it isn't easy to just turn off screen entertainment. You have to prepare for it. You have to schedule other entertainment and a plan for what you will do. Students throughout the school brainstormed alternatives. At our Friday Share (a weekly community gathering of the entire school community) we dedicated one entire assembly to the event. Teachers did funny skits about kids who played too many video games and watched too much TV. We recited poems and sang songs about turning off our TVs. In the end, Turnoff Week was a great success. Over 50 students and staff from kindergarten to 8th grade successfully turned off their screen entertainment for one week, and many others watched less than usual. However, it was the conversations that were the most important indicator of the event's success. In classrooms from kindergarten through 8th grade, classes talked about why we were having the event and how media impacts our lives. In the end, we heard from students who read more and played more outside instead of watching TV. They did puzzles, picked dandelions, got better at basketball, and helped their grandmothers. Parents thanked us, saying things such as "Turnoff Week is the best thing ever." They played more with their kids and got projects done around the house. Some parents noticed their children slept better and were thinking about keeping the screen entertainment off during the weekdays. Five days after the Turnoff Week ended, one 5th-grader said to me, "I watched my first show last night," meaning she'd gotten out of the TV habit.

More good news is that the conversations have continued. Parents and colleagues send each other links to related news stories. For example, the Feb. 2009 *Scientific American Mind*'s cover story, "The Serious Need for Play," has been making the rounds. The staff is hosting another unplugged Family Game Night this year, and the Family Council will have a follow-up meeting about media influences. In the weekly newsletter, a "Portraits of Play" column documents how our students engage in imaginative play.

A few years ago I felt hopeless. Now, armed with more information and support from colleagues, families, and key organizations, I am hopeful and empowered. The students are better supported in their efforts to learn how to just be kids. I know that I am not alone when I join successful letter-writing crusades from Campaign for a Commercial-Free Childhood, which among other successes has pressured Scholastic to remove the highly sexualized Bratz doll merchandise from their school book fairs and book clubs. I gain inspiration from the Alliance for Childhood, which works to educate policy makers about the benefits of child-centered play, and from places such as Quebec, which bans all advertising to children younger than 13 under the Quebec Consumer Protection Act. And finally, I'm inspired by parents who share stories.

Children are complex, and pop culture and media are not the sole cause of their troubles. However, protecting them from a corporate world that forces them to grow up too soon, and promoting their creative play are two giant leaps in the right direction. ▪

....

Geralyn Bywater McLaughlin helped start the Mission Hill School in Boston, where she taught for 11 years. She is the founder of Empowered by Play.

Christiane Grauert

Beyond Pink and Blue

4th graders get fired up about Pottery Barn's gender stereotypes

ROBIN COOLEY

"Pink, pink, pink! Everything for girls in this catalog is pink," exclaimed Kate, one of my 4th graders, as she walked into the classroom one morning, angrily waving the latest Pottery Barn Kids catalog in the air.

"I HATE the color pink. This catalog is reinforcing too many stereotypes, Ms. Cooley, and we need to do something about it!"

I knew she was right. And I was glad to see that our classroom work on stereotypes resulted in my students taking action: As we finished up the school year, my students initiated a letter-writing campaign to Pottery Barn, one of the country's most popular home furnishings catalogs.

Newton Public Schools is actively working to create an anti-bias/anti-racist school environment. In fact, beginning in 4th grade, we teach all students about the cycle of oppression that creates and reinforces stereotypes. I wove discussion of the cycle of oppression throughout my curriculum to help my students understand how stereotypes are created and reinforced, and more important, how we can unlearn them.

> **I wove discussion of the cycle of oppression throughout my curriculum to help my students understand how stereotypes are created and reinforced, and more important, how we can unlearn them.**

Anti-Bias Literature

I began the year's anti-bias work in my multiracial classroom by looking at gender stereotypes. As a dialogue trigger, I read aloud the picture book *William's Doll*, by Charlotte Zolotow. This is a wonderful story about a little boy who is teased and misunderstood by his friends and family because he wants a doll. When I finished the book, I asked the students the following discussion questions: "Why was William teased? What did William's father expect him to be good at because he was a boy?" I explained that the fact that William was expected to like sports and play with trains were examples of stereotypes, oversimplified pictures or opinions of a person or group that are not true.

Next, I asked the class, "Why did William's family and friends tease him because he wanted a doll? Why should only girls play with dolls? Where did this idea come from?" The students immediately said, "Family!" Through discussion, the students began to understand that they are surrounded by messages that reinforce these stereotypes. We brainstormed some ideas of where these messages come from, such as television shows, advertisements, and books.

Next, I asked the class, "Why didn't William's father listen to his son when he said he wanted a doll?" One student exclaimed, "Because William's father believed only girls played with dolls!" I explained that the father believed this stereotype was true.

One boy in my class complained: "I don't get it. I like dolls and stuffed animals. Why did William's dad care? Why didn't he buy his son what he wanted? That doesn't seem fair. Someday, I'm going to buy my kid whatever he wants!"

Finally, I asked the class: "In this story, who was William's ally? Who did not believe the stereotype and helped William get what he wanted?" The students knew that William's grandmother was the one who stood up for him. She was an example of an ally. William's grandmother bought William the doll, and she taught the father that it is OK for boys to want to hold dolls, the same way he held and cared for William when he was a baby.

Each week during the fall semester, I read a picture book that defied gender stereotypes, and we had discussions like the one on *William's Doll*. Tomi dePaola's *Oliver Button Is a Sissy* is another excellent book about a boy who wants to be accepted for who he is. Oliver really wanted to be a dancer, and all the kids at school teased him about this. Despite great adversity and risk, Oliver had the courage to do what he wanted to do, not what others expected him to do or be. After reading the book, students in my class were able to share personal stories of what their parents expected them to do, or when they were teased for doing something "different."

A few more titles that helped to break gender stereotypes were Mary Hoffman's *Amazing Grace* and James Howe's *Horace and Morris, but Mostly Dolores*. In *Amazing Grace*, Grace loves to act in plays and has been taught that you can be anything you want if you put your mind to it. When she wants to audition for the part of Peter Pan, her classmates say she can't. But she pursues her dream and gets the part.

Horace and Morris, but Mostly Dolores is about three mice that are best friends. One day, the two boy mice decide to join the Mega-Mice Club, but no girls are allowed. Dolores joins the Cheese Puffs Club for girls. She is unhappy and bored because all the girls want to do is make crafts and discuss ways to "get a fella using mozzarella." One day, the three friends decide to quit their clubs and build a clubhouse of their own where everyone is allowed, and you can do whatever you want, whether you're a boy or a girl.

Looking at Families

Next we explored stereotypes about families. The students were aware of the messages they've absorbed from our culture about what a family is supposed to look like. Ben, who is adopted, said he was upset when people asked him who his "real" mom was. "I hate that I have to explain that I have a birth mother who I don't know, and my mom lives with me at home!" he said. We discussed some different family structures and talked about how some families might have two moms or two dads, a single parent, or a guardian. Leslie Newman's *Heather Has Two Mommies* is a great picture book that illustrates this point.

After two months of eye-opening discussions, the last anti-bias picture book I read to my class was Linda DeHaan's *King and King*. This picture book does not have the typical Disney ending. In this story, the queen is tired and wants to marry off her son so he can become king and she can retire. One by one, princesses come, hoping the prince will fall in love with them. Each time, the prince tells his queen mother that he doesn't feel any connection. It's not until the last princess arrives with her brother that the prince feels something—but it's not for the princess. He falls in love with her brother. The queen approves, and they get married and become "king and king." My students loved this story because the ending is NOT what they expected at all! They also appreciated hearing a picture book that has gay characters because they know gay people exist. They wondered why there aren't more gays and lesbians in picture books.

> **Since my students were so excited about their anti-bias work, I decided we should do a project with our 1st-grade buddies and teach them about breaking stereotypes.**

Since my students were so excited about their anti-bias work, I decided we should do a project with our 1st-grade buddies and teach them about breaking stereotypes. We created a big book called "What Everyone Needs to Know." This became a coffee-table book that we left on the table at the school's entrance waiting area. The 1st and 4th graders brainstormed all the stereotypes that we knew about boys, girls, and families.

Then each pair picked a stereotype to illustrate on two different pages. On one page, the heading was "Some people think that…" with a drawing portraying the stereotype. On the next page, the heading would say "but everyone needs to know that…" with a drawing breaking the stereotype. For example, one pair came up with "Some people think that all families have a mom and a dad, but everyone needs to know that all families are different. Some families have two moms or two dads. Some families have one grandparent. All families are different."

Another pair came up with "Some people think that only girls wear jewelry, but everyone needs to know that both boys and girls wear jewelry."

I knew our work on stereotypes was sinking in because my students would continually share with the class examples of how they tried to speak up when they saw people acting on stereotypical beliefs. One day, a student told the class about how she spoke up to a nurse at the hospital where her baby brother was just born. "I couldn't believe the nurses wrapped him in a blue blanket and the baby girls in pink!" she said. "I asked the nurse why the hospital did that and she said it was their policy. I don't think I can change the hospital's policy, but maybe I at least made that nurse stop and think."

Making a Difference

The day my class decided that they wanted to write individual letters to Pottery Barn Kids catalog was the day I knew my students felt they could make a difference in this world. They wrote letters that told the truth about how they felt and why they thought the catalog was so hurtful to them. I was so proud that my students were able to explain specific examples of gender stereotypes in the catalog and why they thought the images should change. The students analyzed the catalog, front to back, and picked out things I hadn't noticed. One student wrote:

Dear Pottery Barn Kids,

I do not like the way you put together your catalogs because it reinforces too many stereotypes about boys and girls. For instance, in a picture of the boy's room, there are only two books and the rest of the stuff are trophies. This shows boys and girls who look at your catalog that boys should be good at sports and girls should be very smart. I am a boy and I love to read.

The boys in my classroom felt comfortable enough to admit out loud and in writing that they wished they saw more images of boys playing with dolls and stuffed animals. Another boy wrote:

Dear Pottery Barn Kids,

I am writing this letter because I am mad that you have so many stereotypes in your magazine. You're making me feel uncomfortable because I'm a boy and I like pink, reading, and stuffed animals. All I saw in the boys' pages were dinosaurs and a lot of blue and sports.

Also, it's not just that your stereotypes make me mad but you're also sending messages to kids that this is what they should be. If it doesn't stop soon, then there will be a boys world and a girls world. I'd really like it if (and I bet other kids would too) you had girls playing sports stuff and boys playing with stuffed animals and dolls.

Thank you for taking the time to read this letter. I hope I made you stop and think.

— From a Newton student

The day we received a letter from the president of Pottery Barn, my students were ecstatic. The president, Laura Alber, thanked the students for "taking time to write and express your opinions on our catalog. We'll try to incorporate your feedback into the propping and staging of our future catalogs and we hope that you continue to see improvement in our depiction of boys and girls."

I knew the students would expect the fall Pottery Barn Kids catalog to be completely void of pink and blue and I reminded them that change is slow. The most important thing is that they made the president of a large corporation stop and think. I pointed to two of the quotes I have hanging in my classroom, and we read them out loud together:

"Never doubt that a small group of thoughtful, committed citizens can change the world. Indeed, it's the only thing that ever has."　— Margaret Mead

"Each of us influences someone else, often without realizing it. It is within our power to make a difference."

— Deval Patrick

Epilogue

The fall Pottery Barn Kids catalog arrived in my mailbox in late August, and the first thing I noticed was the cover: There's a picture of a boy, sitting at a desk, doing his homework. Another picture shows a boy talking on the phone, not just a girl, which was something one of my students had suggested. The boy is also looking at a *Power Puff* magazine, something that is typically targeted for girls. When I asked one of my former students what she thought, she said: "Well, the catalog sort of improved the boys, but not really the girls. They still have a lot of changes to make."

One thing I know for sure is that my students now look at advertisements with a critical eye, and I hope they have learned that they do have the power to make a difference in this world. ▪

Robin Cooley teaches 5th grade in Newton, Mass.

Resources

De Haan, Linda. *King and King.* Berkeley: Tricycle Press, 2002.

dePaola, Tomie. *Oliver Button Is a Sissy.* New York: Voyager Books, 1990.

Hoffman, Mary. *Amazing Grace.* New York: Scott Foresman, 1991.

Howe, James. *Horace and Morris, but Mostly Dolores.* New York: Aladdin Library, 2003.

Newman, Leslie. *Heather Has Two Mommies.* Los Angeles: Alyson Publications, 2000.

Zolotow, Charlotte. *William's Doll.* New York: HarperTrophy, 1985.

TV Selfishness and Violence Explode During War on Terror

2nd graders discover new trends in TV since 9/11

MARGOT PEPPER

Six years into the "War on Terror," my 2nd-grade Spanish immersion students found that aggression, selfishness, and insults have exploded on national television.

For the last decade, I've had my students at Rosa Parks Elementary School in Berkeley, Calif., analyze television shows preceding National TV-Turnoff Week, organized by the TV-Turnoff Network, now called Screen-Free Week and organized by the Campaign for a Commercial-Free Childhood. I ask the 7- and 8-year-old students to collect all the data themselves. For seven days, students study a random sampling of about 35 English and Spanish-language children's television shows—and one or two soap operas or reality shows.

The first day of the study, as homework, students shade in a square on a special graph sheet each time they see hitting, hurting, or killing on half-hour segments of the shows they regularly watch, viewed from beginning to end. The second day, they focus on acts of selfishness; the third day, on instances of put-downs; and the fourth day, on the number of times a typical class rule is broken. Finally, in class, four groups of students compile the data produced by the homework, each focusing on one of the four variables in the study. But in April 2007, when I pulled out model graphs compiled by a class in April 2002 — year one of President Bush's "war on terror" — the contrasts between their graphs and those produced five years prior shocked my students.

"In a half-hour of [the cartoon] *Jackie Chan Adventures* in 2002 you would see hitting 10 times at most," wrote 7-year-old Flynn Michael-Legg in the essay I assigned summarizing the findings of our study. "In 2007, shows of *Jackie Chan* had [up to] 34 hitting scenes." For the 2001–02 season, nearly one-fourth of the television shows my students watched had one

Whenever students exhibit disruptive behavior, appearing to ape television, I ask them to please turn off the television in their head if they happen to have left it running.

or no acts of violence at all in one half-hour. Of the shows they watch, only *That's So Raven* continues to have no violence, and all other shows have at least three instances of hitting or violence in one half-hour. Nearly half the shows randomly viewed by my students contain seven to 34 instances of hitting or other violent acts each half-hour.

The maximum number of put-downs or insults nearly doubled between 2002 and 2007, going from 10 in *That's So Raven* to 18 in *Dumb and Dumber* — more than one put-down every two minutes. In *SpongeBob SquarePants*, Flynn pointed out, one would hear at most two put-downs in 2002. In 2007, it was 16. No shows had more than 10 put-downs in 2002. Now three shows did — *SpongeBob* (16), *Dumb and Dumber* (18), and *Betty la fea* (13). Very few shows have no insults at all anymore.

All the shows my students watched in 2007 showed people or characters being selfish at least once per half-hour segment. From our class rule to "be considerate and cooperative," my students interpreted "selfish" to mean any time a character did something that put him- or herself first at the expense of someone

else. In 2002, only three shows had more than three acts of selfishness in a half-hour. Now, 10 did. Half of the 2007 shows contained five to nine instances of selfishness in each episode.

Students also found that in April 2002, only one show depicted the violation of ordinary class rules — making good decisions: no hitting, put-downs, being unsafe, etc. — 12 or more times. In April 2007, the number of such programs rose to six. In 2002, the maximum times class rules were broken on a given half-hour show was 17. In 2007 the number of such shows quadrupled with the maximum number of rules broken on a given show doubling or reaching more than 35. The worst offenders, with 18 or more broken rules, were *SpongeBob*, *Dumb and Dumber*, *Jackie Chan*, and *Phil of the Future* — the latter two topping the hitting and selfishness categories as well.

Whenever students exhibit disruptive behavior, appearing to ape television — pretend shooting, arms flailing, mouth ceaselessly chattering gibberish, etc. — I ask them to please turn off the television in their head if they happen to have left it running. Students often chuckle and, following my lead, turn off an imaginary knob around their ear. Now, as we embarked on our study, many of these students seemed eager to learn more about the television implants I implied existed in their brains; others appeared enchanted with the excuse to watch the boob tube as homework. (Every year, one or two students are excused from the homework due to parental objections to television viewing or, like their teacher, the absence of a set at home. They serve as positive role models and still participate in the class data analysis.)

After sorting the completed television homework graphs into four piles, I assigned one variable or "change" (e.g., "violence") to student groups to compile into one of four large rainbow-colored graphs like the 2001–02 model I had on the board in front of them.

"Which homework graph sheet recorded the highest number of hitting or hurting instances?" I asked the "blue group" in Spanish. Students sifted through to find the greatest number of shaded-in squares.

"¡Mira! *Jackie Chan* tiene 34! (Look! *Jackie Chan* has 34!") Leah Abramsom voiced her discovery in perfect Spanish, though her multi-ethnic roots, which include African American and Jewish, do not include Latina.

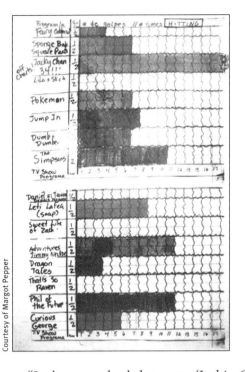

Courtesy of Margot Pepper

For the sake of easy comparison, I wrote "Jackie Chan" on our Violence Graph in the same color and position relative to its appearance on the 2002 graph. Then I had a student take a turn to color in 34 squares.

"Let's put a check by every 'Jackie Chan' you see on other homework sheets because we're done looking at that program," I reminded them. "Now which homework has the next largest number to 34 of violent acts?"

Just as my students had in 2002, the students proceeded through the pile under my supervision to record the top 16 violent shows, assigning each a particular color. Regardless of discrepancies in student perceptions of violence of up to three instances for the same program, date, and variable (the margin of error over the years), just as in 2002, students recorded the highest number of aggressive acts for each of these shows. After each group of five students completed its specific group bar graph of findings, and students saw it next to the colorful 2002 graph of the same variable, they were visibly horrified. Gisell González clasped hands over her mouth to refrain from completing an exclamation of "Oh my," while others gasped, "Ieeew!"

Ever since the first month of school when we studied opposing points of view about the so-called discovery (or not) of the Americas, I've encouraged my students to turn to other sources like library books and the internet to answer questions or prove social studies and science hypotheses and, for the most skilled, to question the sources of their answers. So

when I proposed searching the internet to support our findings, many were delighted.

The next day, I rotated each group of five through my English internet research station around a large computer. The class had decided on the preliminary Google search terms: "television violence increase." Though students controlled the mouse and keyboard, I helped weed out irrelevant sites and urged them to explore promising ones. We'd scroll through these until we found something that either the students or I thought related to our hypothesis about increased violence. Next, I'd give them time to read paragraphs on the screen to each other. "Puppies" (native standard-English speakers) would read the material to the "Kittens" (standard-English language learners), explaining if necessary. When they got to a finding, they would let me know so I could record it on chart paper in the color corresponding to their group.

Traditionally, in this way, virtually all students have been able to discover something to share with their group. Usually two students in each group alight on juicy, complex information and, perhaps because of the immersion program's need for translation, are able to simplify explanations for the rest. The overall quality of research and writing vocabulary has been extraordinary in part, I think, because of each group's heterogeneous composition ranging from one to two high-skilled students to one or two who are currently performing well below grade level. Typically, my two-way Spanish immersion classes have been composed of one-third children of college-educated professionals, while half qualify for free lunches. About a third are native Spanish speakers or Latino children; up to one-fifth African American children, and the rest European American and other minorities.

I had the "green group" explore the TV-Turnoff Network site. The students clicked on the Real Vision study. "Wow! Kids will have seen '200,000 violent acts on television by age 18...and 16,000 murders,'" Maeve Gallagher was shocked. Some wondered if the increase in television violence highlighted on the site had led to more real-life killing.

"What words do you think you might see in a report that says killing is related to television?"

They decided on "television + violence + killing."

"Oh my gosh! 'TV shows and Video Games Teach Children to Kill!' Look, down there!" Ceilidh Welsh was pointing to the screen of search results. The note turned out to be a footnote in a report from the Parents Television Council (PTC). I showed the group how important it was to trace primary sources and helped them type in the name of the author of the study, which turned up in a Senate Judiciary Report.

"This is a report by our own government!" Now I was excited, too. We typed in the report's title and got the full report titled "Children, Violence, and the Media."

"Video Games and TV are 'teaching kids to kill,' and 'teaching them to like it!'" Maeve read aloud for us from the report.

"Violence on TV is more than 300 times more than before the war!" Students in the subsequent yellow group were jumping up and down. Well, not exactly. I darted to the board and shaded parts of pizzas to explain percentages. This made the concept more understandable to some, but for most, I had to translate. Using both the internet and fact sheets, children in the "yellow group" found that according to a 2007 study by the PTC called "Dying to Entertain," since 1998, violence on ABC TV has quadrupled (a 309 percent increase — a huge rise, though not quite the "300 times" increase students had mistakenly proclaimed.)

They found that in 1998 the network had about one act of violence per hour (.93). By 2007, it was almost four (3.8) on average. CBS, according to the PTC study, had the highest percentage of deaths during 2005–06, with more than 66 percent of violent scenes after 8 p.m. depicting death (www.parents.org). Incidentally, the study points out that, in general, violence in all television shows has shifted to being more central to the story — with more graphic autopsy or torture scenes — than it was more than five years ago. It indicates that the 2005–06 season was one of the most violent ever recorded by the PTC.

After each group read its findings aloud, facts discovered by students in the "red group" persuaded the rest of the class, through a show of hands, to agree to limit their television viewing, turning it off completely during the TV-Turnoff Network's TV Turnoff Week — something they were reluctant to do when our television unit began. What this group had discovered is that there are more televisions (2.73) in the average home than people (2.55), according to *USA Today*. The average home keeps a television turned on eight hours

a day, according to Nielsen (2006). Children who watch six or more hours a day perform worse on reading tests than do those who watch one hour a day or don't play video games, reports the Center for Screen-Time Awareness. And by the time they finish high school, children will have spent more hours watching TV than in school.

I knew students would brainstorm both absurd and frighteningly astute reasons to justify the increase of violence and selfishness on television. My aim was to get these young philosopher-scientists in the habit of asking "why" about their world instead of merely consuming it — of making educated hypotheses then requiring multiple sources of supporting evidence.

My aim was to get these young philosopher-scientists in the habit of asking "why" about their world instead of merely consuming it.

During the group discussion, I learned that they were most troubled by the Senate report statement that television was teaching them to "like killing." The report also claimed that 10 percent of crimes committed are caused by violence seen on television. The study, though predating ours, related the violence they saw on television directly to their present world.

I asked students if they had noticed an increase in violence in their world with the increase in television violence. Jacobo McCarthy and several others fiercely nodded: "Three years ago, I'd only see one or two kids in trouble in the office now and then; now there's up to six or seven," Jacobo commented. I too have noticed an increase in behavior problems at the school since 2001, despite better leadership and more effective intervention. However, increasing poverty and less spending on social services leading to a rise in domestic or neighborhood violence could be equally valid contributors.

"What do you think the reason is behind the increase in television violence?" I asked.

"For brainwashing. TV advertises or sells violence. It influences us to vote for a president who uses war to solve problems," Flynn said.

"I suspect the increase in television violence has something to do with the war on terror," English-learner

Andres Ventura emulated his classmate Sebastian Anderson's elevated vocabulary in his summarizing essay. "By scaring kids and parents and pushing violence, people are more likely to vote for war. The TV makes you dumb because if you see a lot, it makes you forget things. It makes parents forget how things were when they were kids."

One of the most shocking facts my students found was that according to the TV-Turnoff Network's Real Vision project, parents spend only 38.5 minutes a day with their children in meaningful conversation. And more than half of 4- to 6-year-olds (54 percent) would rather watch TV than spend time with their parents.

This finding inspired Alejandro González's conclusion: "I think George Bush wants to make people more scared. We know George Bush likes war. And ... TV makes you like more war. What's scary is kids spend more time seeing TV than being with their dad. Since our study, I turn off the TV more and go play with my dad. Maybe the president used to watch more TV than being with his dad."

"And if Bush isn't responsible? Why would television stations or their advertisers want us to like war?" I asked after reading Alejandro's essay aloud.

"To make money, to sell things and make rich people richer like the people selling guns," Ceilidh said.

"To steal stuff from other countries to make our own country the richest!" Jacobo asserted.

What impact did the students think this increase in television violence and selfishness was having on the world around them?

"TV makes people want violence by making it seem cool," Ceilidh said.

"Then they want to be part of the army," added Sebastian. "It's a cycle. TV affects the world, then the world affects the TV, which affects world violence. It's a 'chain reaction of evil,'" he said, borrowing from a Martin Luther King Jr. quote I had them memorize for Dr. King's birthday.

"Yeah, TV leads to more fighting. Fighting leads to war," added Jacobo. He evoked Dr. King to finish his thought: "'Hate begetting hate. Wars producing more wars. ...' We need to stop or 'we shall all be plunged into the dark abyss of annihilation.'"

It was a peak teaching moment. Students were assimilating valuable things they had learned earlier in the year to shape their thinking about the world. Although some of the conclusions tended toward hyperbole, I can't argue with the soundness of my students' hypothesis that television selfishness and violence are part of a propaganda campaign to foment war and enrich certain sectors. But more importantly, my students are learning to think for themselves, to question the sources of their information.

One of my former students, Daniel Hernandez-Deras, once commented that "watching television replaces your imagination with television thinking and there's not much space left after that." Now my current students had begun to turn off the televisions in their own brains and turn on their imagination and curiosity. At last, they had begun to internalize the insight contained in Maeve's essay: "If you watch too much TV, you lose the kid that is inside you," wherein lies our higher inner wisdom. ■

....

Margot Pepper is a bilingual educator, journalist, and author. Her memoir, Through the Wall: A Year in Havana, *was a top nomination for the 2006 American Book Award.*

Daniel Garcia / AFP / Getty Images

Girls, Worms, and Body Image

A teacher deals with gender stereotypes among 2nd and 3rd graders

KATE LYMAN

"I need to lose weight," Kayla was saying. "So do I," another 2nd-grade girl chimed in. "I'm way too fat."

My students' conversation shocked me. Distracted from my hallway responsibility of monitoring the noise level at the water fountains, I listened in more closely. Linda, a 3rd-grade girl who is thin to the point of looking unhealthy, grabbed a piece of paper from Kayla. "I'm the one who needs this." "No, I need it!" insisted Rhonda.

The hotly contested paper turned out to contain the name of an exercise video that my 2nd- and 3rd-grade class had seen in gym class. The gym teacher later assured me that the student teacher had stressed that the exercises were for health and fitness, not weight loss. However, the girls were convinced that the video would help them lose weight and were frantic to get hold of it.

Issues of women and body image are certainly not new to me. I thought back to when I was a teenager struggling to make my body match the proportions of the models in *Seventeen* magazine. I had learned that the average model was 5′9″ and 110 pounds. I was the ideal 5'9″, but even on a close-to-starvation diet of 900 calories a day I could not get my weight down to 110 pounds.

But that was in the 1960s. Hadn't girls liberated themselves from such regimens? I asked myself. And even back in the 1960s, it wasn't until high school that I remembered my classmates living on coffee and oranges. Seven- and 8-year-olds ate all the cake and candy and potato chips that they could get their hands on.

I wondered how I could enlighten my 7- and 8-year-old girls who were so concerned about their body image. What follows are ways, sometimes successful, sometimes not, in which I struggled with the issue throughout a recent year of teaching.

At the time of the incident with the gym video, I had been teaching a unit on women's history, and the class had shown an interest in learning about women's struggle to get the vote. I realized the unit needed to take a new turn. It was time to move on to the gender issues they face as girls and women today.

Facts and Stereotypes

I decided to start by learning more about the students' knowledge and perceptions about gender. I divided the students into two groups and asked the girls to decide on 10 facts about boys/men, and asked the boys to do the same in regard to girls/women. Before the activity, I tried to clarify the difference between opinions and facts, but the lists of "facts" revealed the futility of my attempts:

FACTS ABOUT BOYS/MEN
(written by the girls)

1. Boys are selfish.
2. Boys are different from girls because of their body parts.
3. Men make their wives take care of the children and house.
4. Dads make the moms do the shopping.
5. Men get paid more than women.
6. Men get women just for their looks.
7. Men are mean and lazy and jealous.
8. Men are picky eaters and like their dinners when they get home.
9. Men and boys are bossy.

FACTS ABOUT GIRLS/WOMEN
(written by the boys)

1. They always complain.
2. They are too loud and picky.
3. They are sensitive.
4. Girls and women are better bakers than boys and men.
5. They are bossy.
6. Girls are always talking about boys and men.
7. Girls and women aren't as smart as boys and men.
8. Girls are more jealous than boys.
9. Girls and women spend a long time getting ready and want to look pretty.

We discussed the "facts" as a group and tried to come to an agreement about which statements were indeed facts and which were stereotypes, generalizations, or opinions. The girls protested vehemently the idea that boys and men were smarter than girls and women. They insisted, in fact, that the opposite was true.

Many students were reluctant to concede the veracity of some of the other statements. One student, Yer, for instance, argued: "I know for a fact that women are better bakers than men!" Anna countered that not only was her dad a good cook, but he also helped with the shopping and didn't insist on his dinner on time.

The other students saw Anna's dad as a single exception to the rule, but were willing to add the qualifier "most" to the statements about men and household tasks.

It occurred to me that a short story, "X," would be a good vehicle for further discussions on gender stereotypes. In "X," written by Lois Gould (1982), a couple agrees to let their baby be part of a scientific experiment in which no one is allowed to know the baby's gender except the parents and the baby him/herself.

At first, students responded to the dilemmas posed by X's situation with their own gender blinders. In the story, X's relatives cannot figure out what kind of presents to buy X—"a tiny football helmet" or "a pink-flowered romper suit." The students in my class were equally confounded.

"Maybe they could buy an outfit that was split down the middle, half blue and half pink," said one student. Another suggested that X "could wear a baseball top and pink lacy bottoms."

I asked them to look around the room at each other's clothes. To a child, they were wearing unisex outfits — mainly jeans and T-shirts. But it still didn't occur to them that there might be baby clothes that would be suitable for either a boy or girl.

After my frustrating attempts to define fact vs. stereotypes about gender and my less than successful attempts at discussion around the story "X," I again thought back to my childhood. A photo taken of me at about my students' ages shows me in a lacy dress, cuffed white socks, and patent leather "Mary Jane" shoes, my hair tightly braided and tied in ribbons. I am sitting on a bench in my yard, surrounded by my

> **A photo taken of me at about my students' ages shows me in a lacy dress, cuffed white socks, and patent leather "Mary Jane" shoes, my hair tightly braided and tied in ribbons.**

dolls. My head is turned to the side and I am smiling shyly. What would I have said about men's and women's roles? Would the story of "X" have made any sense to me? I'm not sure how that '50s girl would have fit into the gender discussion, but I do remember that under the neat, frilly dress was a girl whose heroes were TV cowboys, a girl who daydreamed about being a boy so she, too, could have adventures on horseback.

I was trapped in the much more rigid gender expectations of the 1950s, and yet I wondered if my girls in their jeans and sweats really had that many more options than I'd had. The girls in my class were right. Most women do have the major responsibility for taking care of the children and house. Most men do still get higher pay in their jobs. And the stereotypes still abound.

I was stuck in this examination of gender roles. Stuck in the classroom and stuck with my own personal history. I did not know where I was going with the unit.

A Saving Rain

But then, just as lesson plans were failing me as often as not, nature cooperated with a heavy rain that forced hundreds of worms up from the soil onto the playground. At recess the boys picked the worms up and dangled them at the girls, who ran screaming. Kayla, Stephanie, and Melissa, who will take on any drama, were leading the group with their screaming. Linda, Mandy, and other more shy, usually passive girls were joining in, following their lead.

Kayla came running up to me. "Help, help, Tony's got a bunch of worms and he's chasing me with them. The worms are going to bite me!"

Reasoning was useless. Boys and girls were too engrossed in their drama. I picked up a worm and demonstrated that it did no harm, but my attempts to educate the girls failed. The chasing and screaming continued. I was successful at stopping Tony from coming into the school with worms in his shoes and pockets, but the screaming continued into the halls and music class.

I felt defeated. Times had not changed. This playground scene could have occurred in my elementary school in the 1950s. I decided that before I moved on to more subtle aspects of gender stereotyping, I needed to deal with girls and worms.

Then, after recess, Stephanie and Kayla took a brave step forward. They came back to the classroom with rubber gloves that they had gotten from the "lunch lady" so that they could touch the worms. I suggested to the class that we could collect worms for our classroom, but that the rubber gloves were not necessary.

I put Kayla in charge of the terrarium and gave Stephanie the spoon. A group of 10 or 12 girls followed them outside to collect worms for the classroom. "Can't boys help get the worms? Only girls?" asked David dejectedly. I assured him that he could help, and several other boys joined the project, but the ringleaders were still the girls. They quickly got over their squeamishness.

"I'm not scared of worms anymore!" Anna proudly announced.

Soon we had about two dozen large, fat earthworms and several cups of dirt. The worm center was so noisily enthusiastic that I could barely hear the principal's announcement over the intercom. I think it had something to do with keeping the halls clean by not tracking the mud in from the playground.

The girls had conquered their fears of worms, but I still heard conversations — and, even worse, insults — about body image. One girl told another student that he should think about going to Jenny Craig.

Toys and Media

I decided to lead a critique on two sources of stereotypical images of women: toys and the media. I wanted to give the students an opportunity to analyze images of women that they see every day, to have some understanding how those images influence their self-concepts.

I began with a lesson focused on a Barbie doll. Most girls in my class said that they owned Barbies, but none remembered to bring one in, so I borrowed one from another classroom. I started with an open-ended question: "Tell me what you notice about Barbie."

I was somewhat nervous because there was a university student visiting my classroom and I had little confidence in what my probing would bring about. Quickly, however, the observations poured out. Kayla, who is of stocky build herself, as is her mom, was quick to point out that Barbie has a very skinny waist.

"But she has big boobs," added Stephanie. I asked Stephanie if she knew a respectful way to refer to that part of a woman's body and she nodded. "Breasts," she corrected. "She has huge breasts."

"Barbie has tiny feet," someone said. "They are made for high heels."

"She has a cute, turned up nose."

"She has a very long, skinny neck."

"She has very skinny arms and legs."

Students agreed that Barbie looked very different from the women they knew — their moms, grandmas, and teachers. The students didn't bring up Barbie's ethnicity, so I asked them to look around the circle and see how else she was different from many of them.

They looked around at each other, more than half with dark or various shades of brown faces, and only one blonde-haired child among them.

"She's white!" yelled out Shantee. "She has yellow hair and blue eyes."

"My mom will only let my sister play with black Barbies," added Steven.

"Do the black Barbies look like real-life African American girls?" I asked.

"No, they have hair like white people," concluded Shantee. "Only it's colored black."

I asked them why the toy manufacturers might make a doll for girls to play with that looked so different from real girls and women. The consensus was

> **I wanted to give the students an opportunity to analyze images of women that they see every day, to have some understanding how those images influence their self-concepts.**

that girls want to look like her so that men would like them better. The only dissenting voice was Kayla, who said that her mom's partner liked his women big.

Other comments were that women wanted to look beautiful, like Barbie, all skinny and pretty, with hair down to their waist. To further probe why that might be, I moved to the part of my lesson dealing with women in advertisements.

I hoped my students could grasp the concept that advertisers create an illusion that their product will transform a woman into a younger, prettier, more appealing self. I also wanted my students to practice looking at advertisements more critically — to analyze the hidden messages and to begin to see how women are objectified and minimized. I didn't expect them to understand all these concepts; I saw the lesson as an introduction.

I had torn out dozens of ads from women's magazines, general magazines such as *Ebony*, and other sources, showing women using products from cigarettes to weight loss formulas to cosmetics. We discussed several ads as a group. I asked my students to look at how the woman was shown, what product the advertiser was trying to sell, and what the advertiser was telling women about what would happen if they bought the product. Then I sent them on their own to choose one of the ads and write about it. After they typed and edited their writing, they made the ads and script into posters that I hung in the hall.

Stephanie chose a cigarette ad with the message "A Taste for the Elegant" and the picture of a thin, sophisticated woman in a white pantsuit and high heels. Her commentary noted in part: "'A taste for the elegant' is what it says on my poster, but it can't be a taste for the elegant because cigarettes don't taste good. Cigarettes are bad for your lungs."

Anna wrote that her ad for a perfume product was saying that "women have to be skinny and have a dress with no sleeves and if she uses this perfume then she gets a man."

Kayla wrote: "I think she's trying to get people to get the Oil of Olay to look young when they just look fine the way they are. I mean they don't have to listen to a woman that wants people to look young. That's stupid. The people look fine the way they are!!"

Rhonda interpreted the message in a shampoo ad as: "You should be cute and be skinny. The ad says that you should use Redken shampoo, and wear a lot of makeup, and wear cute clothes so you can look like a Barbie doll."

Nathan saw some humor in his ad about a weight loss product: "It is telling women that they have to be skinny, wear lipstick, and wear high heels. And from the picture of what she used to look like, I think she looks so different [now] that she should get a new [driver's] license."

Afterward, I thought of many things I should have done differently with the lesson. More background on advertising. More time for discussion and sharing. Perhaps a follow-up action project. The visiting university student, however, was impressed that elementary students could handle such a complex topic so well.

Maybe I was on the right track.

An Old-Fashioned Day

But just to make sure, I wanted to provide an opportunity for the class to experience gender discrimination firsthand, in an exaggerated yet playful setting. For the last day of our unit, I decided to have a role play of an old-fashioned school day, with an emphasis on how girls and boys were treated differently.

I sent home interview sheets in which kids questioned their parents on what school was like when they went to school, including how boys and girls were treated differently. The students shared their findings (one student noted, "My mom got hit with a PADDLE!"). My student teacher shared some old books and a slate that her grandfather had saved. Students read a book, *Early Schools,* and, using

A group of schoolchildren, circa 1941, practicing spelling and penmanship at the blackboard.

information from it, wrote first-person accounts about a day in an old-fashioned school.

Not concerned with strict historical accuracy (also knowing that schools varied regionally), we planned the morning based on the parent interviews, the book on early schools, and our own experiences. We sent home a note preparing the families for this experiment. Girls were to come dressed in dresses (not above the knees) and boys in slacks and shirts with collars. We pushed back the tables, moved the chairs into rows, and set up an "old-fashioned" schedule of handwriting, spelling bees, rote math, and textbook science. We used a variety of discipline techniques: children got sent to the corner, they had to write 100 sentences, they had to wear the dunce cap—anything short of physical punishment.

We also incorporated differential treatment for boys and girls in everything we did, from having a boys' line and a girls' line, to calling on the boys more often than the girls, to chastising the girls more for messy handwriting. The experiment went on for two-and-a-half hours, with the participation of the gym teacher and principal. The latter came in sporting a white wig and a paddle.

After gym class, we gathered back in our circle to discuss how the kids felt about the morning. I was especially interested to hear if they noticed the differential gender treatment, which was not as obvious as the differences in the setup of the room, work, and punishments. Not only did they notice the bias, but the girls were also indignant, while the boys were gleeful.

"You were paying more attention to the boys!" was the first comment. "Boys were called on more and they were getting all the answers."

My students noted that there were different rules for boys than girls. A boy had been allowed to whistle. A girl had been reprimanded for the same behavior.

"I didn't like how you said, 'That's not ladylike,'" said Stephanie.

"I liked how you didn't make us do it over when we smudged our handwriting," noted Henry.

"Yeah, you tore mine up and made me start over," said Melissa.

"And I hate wearing dresses," added Rhonda.

Girls were upset about how they had to play with Hula-Hoops while the boys played dodgeball in gym and how in science, boys did hands-on experimentation with worms while girls filled out glossary definitions from their science book.

"I know why you did this," said Anna, her face lighting up with a sudden realization. "You wanted us to know what prejudice feels like!"

Well, Anna was close. I thought that if I exaggerated the effect of gender discrimination, maybe then they would be better able to recognize the more subtle forms that they encountered within and outside of themselves. Certainly, my experience growing up had made me sensitive to gender stereotyping. But, at the same time, the cynical side of me knew that experiences with gender discussions, worms, and media critiquing paled in the light of Barbies, television, and Jenny Craig.

As I was packing up to go home after a long day, one especially exhausting due to our old-fashioned school experiment, Stephanie and Rhonda ran through the classroom to cut through the back door. As they stepped out to head for home, I heard Stephanie ask Rhonda, "So if I come over to your house, will you still be on your diet?" "Oh, no," answered Rhonda flippantly. "I don't do that on the weekend." ▪

Kate Lyman teaches in Madison, Wis. The names of the children in this article have been changed.

Who Can Stay Here?

Confronting issues of documentation and citizenship in children's literature

GRACE CORNELL

One year, the bilingual elementary school where I taught in East Oakland was subject to an attempted U.S. Immigration and Customs Enforcement (ICE) raid. Rumors began to fly early in the school day among students and teachers — ICE agents had been seen parked several blocks away from the school. The campus went into a panic, terrified that the agents would apprehend parents on their way to pick their children up from school. Office staff and parent volunteers called each family at home, instructing them to send only documented friends or relatives to get their children at the end of the day. The administration contacted the press. Soon, Mayor Ron Dellums and members of the Oakland police force were gathered outside, denouncing the fear tactics being used by ICE.

While politicians made statements outside, it was my job inside to calm down a class of 1st graders who were all too aware of what an ICE raid meant. They knew their parents could be taken away or that they themselves could be forced to suddenly leave the familiarity of their homes and schools. As my students were playing outside during recess, a news helicopter began to circle above the playground. Half of my class came running back inside, panicked, hysterical, in tears, saying that la migra was coming in helicopters to get them. It was almost impossible to assuage that fear—to tell them that they were safe here and no one would take them away. Especially because I didn't really know if that was true.

The ICE agents never actually entered our school that day. Perhaps this was because intimidation had been their only goal, or perhaps the barrage of media attention put them off. However, I later learned that several other schools in East Oakland and South Berkeley were subject to similar intimidation tactics that day—ICE agents parked nearby, watching and waiting for parents and students to leave the campus. At one East Oakland elementary school, a mother was apprehended by ICE agents in the school hallway before the start of classes. She was led away in front of her 6-year-old daughter and gathered parents and staff.

Though such a dramatic brush with immigration enforcement didn't reoccur during the two years that I worked at that school, each year many teachers, myself included, were asked by parents to write letters on their behalf for immigration hearings. And each year I knew of at least one student whose mother or father was deported.

So when I set about compiling a list of children's picture books that deal with immigration issues, the memories of that attempted ICE raid and the deportation hearings were fresh in my mind. I found books that dealt with many themes: intergenerational ties and gaps, peer pressure and friendship, and, of course, language barriers and language learning.

What caught my attention was one theme that was missing. Though many of these books dealt with border crossings, very few addressed issues of documentation and unequal access to citizenship in any meaningful way. Indeed, most skirted around the topic, leaving unexplained holes in their narratives of immigration. Others explicitly sent the message that citizenship in this country is equally attainable by all—a fact that many of my students clearly know to be false from their own life experiences.

If we want to provide literature that helps children understand their world better and realize that they are not alone in the ways they feel and the problems they face, it is important to critically analyze children's books about immigration.

It is understandable that children's book authors are reticent to address such controversial and political issues in their books, especially in the current climate. Taking a strong stance on undocumented immigration and unequal access to citizenship could limit their audience. Many might consider the issues involved—deportation, the separation of families, economic and racial discrimination—too frightening or "adult" for the children who will read their books. Yet when I think about my students' fear on the day that ICE came near our school, I can't escape the realization that many of our children deal with these issues on a daily basis. These powerful experiences and fears make their way into students' school lives, whether we want them to or not.

When we create immigration units or read picture books about immigration to our children, I do not believe we have the luxury to avoid these topics. Indeed, I believe that if we do we risk marginalizing the students who cannot choose to ignore these issues in their daily lives. Of course, children should never be prompted to share sensitive personal information or disclose their immigration status, but these topics can be discussed safely through a literary lens. If we want to provide literature that helps children understand their world better and realize that they are not alone in the ways they feel and the problems they face, it is important to critically analyze children's books about immigration. What kinds of messages do they send to students about documentation and access to citizenship?

With all of this in mind, I identified three broad categories of books according to the extent to which they explore or obscure these themes. Here are a few examples to illustrate each category. I hope that this provides a framework for critical analysis of children's literature about immigration and is helpful to teachers planning curriculum or adding to their classroom libraries.

Creating the Image that Citizenship Is Equally Available to All

The first category comprises books that choose to ignore issues of undocumented immigration and unequal access to citizenship, portraying a world in which U.S. citizenship is equally (and often easily) available to all people. The most extreme example of this that I encountered is *A Very Important Day*, by Maggie Rugg Herold, in which families from the Philippines, Mexico, India, Russia, Greece, Vietnam, the Dominican Republic, China, Egypt, Ghana, Scotland, and El Salvador all joyously celebrate as they make the trip downtown to the courthouse to receive their papers and to be granted citizenship. They happily swear loyalty to the United States of America and recite the Pledge of Allegiance, waving tiny American flags as they exit the courthouse.

This book strongly implies that each family has had an equal opportunity to apply for citizenship, whether from Scotland or Ghana. They have all followed the same equitable legal process that is described in the epilogue. For a child unfamiliar with the economic, linguistic, and political issues that make U.S. citizenship far more attainable for some than others, this book creates a false sense of security—look, our system is working well! For a student who is undocumented or whose parents are undocumented, this book raises many unanswered questions—why can't we just go down to the courthouse, recite the Pledge of Allegiance, and become citizens if everyone else can? Unless a teacher is willing to engage with these issues and discuss the author's underlying assumptions with the students, this book could do more harm than good in a classroom setting.

The second book in this category, *How Many Days to America? A Thanksgiving Story*, by Eve Bunting, does portray immigration and border crossings as difficult, but the barriers suddenly and inexplicably disappear in the end when the need arises to create a happy ending. This book tells the wrenching story

of a family that is forced to leave an unnamed Latin American country, fleeing from political oppression. They board a fishing boat to travel to the United States. Their journey is arduous—the motor breaks, the soldiers in their country shoot at them from the shore, their food and water run out, people become ill, and what little they have left is taken by thieves. When they finally arrive at the shore of the United States, they are greeted by soldiers who give them food and water but do not let them land. "They will not take us," the father comments sadly, but he refuses to explain why.

> ### Some children's literature on immigration ignores issues of undocumented immigration and unequal access to citizenship, portraying a world in which U.S. citizenship is equally (and often easily) available to all people.

Yet suddenly, the next day, the boat makes landfall on U.S. shore again. This time there are no soldiers, but instead a large crowd of people who welcome the family and usher them into a shed with tables covered with delicious food. They explain that it is Thanksgiving and tell the new arrivals about the significance of that day in the United States. The book ends with a description of how "Father gave thanks that we were free, and safe—and here." The little sister asks if they can stay. "Yes, small one," the father replies. "We can stay."

This book clearly sets up a false expectation: No matter the struggle that it takes to get to the United States, once here, you are safe and you are allowed to stay. Yet this is so clearly not the case for many undocumented immigrants, and many children recognize that, despite their family's arduous journeys to this country, they still face the dangers of deportation, exploitation, and discrimination on U.S. soil. Just as this book stays silent on the reasons why the soldiers initially refuse to allow the family to land, it all too swiftly conjures up a happy ending when many questions still remain in the mind of a critical reader. Like *A Very Important Day*, it ignores the possibility that citizenship might not be attainable for all people who set foot on U.S. shores.

Someone Else's Problem

If the first category is comprised of books that ignore issues of documentation and equitable access to citizenship completely, the second category includes books that hint at these themes but do not explore them. They imply that the aforementioned dangers exist, yet avoid putting the main characters at any real risk. The message that they send is that deportation and the separation of families does occur, but that such things usually happen to someone else.

The first of these books, *My Diary from Here to There/Mi diario de aquí hasta allá*, by Amada Irma Pérez, is the diary of a girl who immigrates to the United States from Mexico. Although her father is a U.S. citizen, the family must wait a long time near the border while her father secures their green cards. The narrator expresses sadness at how she cannot see her father and fear that he will not be able to get green cards for the rest of the family. Yet they wait patiently, the green cards finally arrive, and the family is able to cross the border legally and be reunited. Interestingly, on the bus into the United States, the police arrest a woman without papers. This incident is mentioned but not discussed, leaving children on their own to question why some immigrants have documents and others do not.

Another book, the charming *Super Cilantro Girl/La superniña de cilantro*, by Juan Felipe Herrera, tells the story of Esmeralda, a child whose mother is stopped at the U.S.-Mexico border despite the fact that she is a U.S. citizen. Worried about her mother, Esmeralda dreams that she turns green like a bunch of cilantro, grows into a giant, and flies to the border to set her mother free. Here Herrera paints a vivid picture:

> She gawks at the great gray walls of wire and steel between the United States and Mexico. She stares at the great gray building that keeps people in who want to move on.

In the dream, Esmeralda rescues her mother. When the soldiers begin chasing her, she makes green vines and bushes of cilantro grow up and erase that border, declaring that the world should be sin fronteras — borderless. However, when Esmeralda wakes up in the morning, she discovers that everything was a dream and that her mother is already safely back home.

This book hints at the terror that children experience at the prospect of their families being split apart, but it does not actually put the characters in real danger. Esmeralda's mother is a citizen and does not truly run the risk of being separated from her family. In the foreword, Herrera expresses concern about families that are kept apart by borders and shares his wish that some superhero could abolish such borders and bring those families back together. However, his choice to make Esmeralda's mother a citizen in no danger of actually being barred from returning home still sends the message that family separation, deportation, and detention centers are all part of a dream from which you can wake up. If they are real dangers, they exist only in the lives of others.

Tackling the Subject

The final category includes the handful of books I found that do deal with issues of documentation and unequal access to citizenship head on. In *Hannah Is My Name*, by Belle Yang, a family immigrates to San Francisco from Taiwan. Though they apply for green cards, they wait more than a year to hear back from the government. During this time, the narrator's parents must work illegally to make ends meet. Hannah's mother is fired from her job in a clothing factory when the boss realizes that she doesn't have papers, and her father is constantly on the watch for immigration agents as he works at a hotel. One of Hannah's friends, Janie, a child from Hong Kong, is deported because Janie's father is discovered working at a Chinese restaurant before his family receives their green cards. And one day, while Hannah is visiting her father's work, she and her father are forced to flee from an immigration raid. From then on, her father must work at night. In the end, the story concludes happily — the family finally receives the green cards and is allowed to stay. In the process, however, the author exposes several key issues, including the seemingly arbitrary nature of the immigration process (e.g., papers can be delayed for extended periods of time without explanation) and the fact that many families must work illegally to survive while applying for documents.

From North to South/Del norte al sur

By René Colato Laínez
Children's Book Press, 2010

From North to South/Del norte al sur addresses issues of family separation and deportation head-on. The story is told from the perspective of José, a young child who travels from San Diego to Tijuana to see his mother, recently deported in a factory raid. At the shelter where she is staying, José meets other women and children who have also been separated from their families. It is clear how deeply his mother's deportation affects José—and this is movingly described—but there are several reasons that his situation should not be considered broadly representative. His father is a permanent resident of the United States and can hire a lawyer for his mother, and José lives close enough to the border to visit her every weekend. His mother has been able to find lodging at a safe and welcoming shelter, and every indication is that she will soon be able to return home. Neither the other women and children in this book, nor our own students who face similar challenges, are guaranteed these advantages and resources. Thus there is much here for teachers to discuss with their students—especially the complex reasons behind José's family's separation and the different ways that families experience deportation.

The story ends with a description of José's dream as he sleeps on the car ride back to San Diego: Mamá has the right papers, the family crosses the border together, fireworks fill the sky, and José knows "that all the other children would see their parents soon, too." This is a beautiful dream, but it is indeed a dream. The real world does not deliver fairy-tale endings so reliably, and the other children at the shelter may not soon be reunited with their families. In this respect, the book seems torn between the attempt to realistically portray the pain caused to children by deportation and the desire to provide a happy ending. In choosing the latter, it may set students up with the unrealistic expectation that deportation is always temporary, and those who face it will inevitably be reunited with their families in the United States.

Despite these issues, *From North to South/Del norte al sur* directly portrays a child's struggle with family separation caused by deportation, and so is an invaluable addition to any classroom. — *G.C.*

América Is Her Name/La llaman América, by Luis J. Rodríguez, deals with many other harsh issues facing immigrant communities: neighborhood violence, unemployment, language barriers, and, importantly, racism, an issue that is not directly addressed in any of the books reviewed above. América's mother is called a "wetback" when she goes to the market. In school, América's ESL teacher, Ms. Gable, scornfully refers to her as an "illegal." América's confusion is heartbreaking:

How could that be—how can anyone be illegal! She is Mixteco, an ancient tribe that was here before the Spanish, before the blue-eyed, even before this government that now calls her "illegal." How can a girl called América not belong in America?

This is a powerful question to pose to students, one that could generate much discussion. Fortunately, América finds release from the pressures of her life through writing poetry, discovering her voice and her place in this new passion. Her family and her teacher, who are initially skeptical, finally support her, telling her that she will be a real poet some day. "A real poet," the book concludes. "That sounds good to the Mixteca girl, who some people say doesn't belong here. A poet, América knows, belongs everywhere."

Teaching Critical Thought

The books critiqued above are only a few of the many that are available. However, although there are many children's books that deal with the experiences of Asian and Latin American (specifically Mexican) immigrants, there is a paucity of literature that tells the stories of immigrants from other places in the world, such as Africa or the Middle East. I urge teachers to seek out books that do represent these populations when building their classroom libraries, especially books that choose to tackle the difficult issues surrounding immigration status and citizenship. This is especially important if we want immigrant students to recognize that they are not the only ones who face struggles in the United States—that many different groups share similar experiences and that this may in turn be due to the existence of larger systemic injustices.

I have reflected on the books above from the perspective of a teacher whose class includes immigrant students, many of whom are undocumented or have undocumented family members. However, I believe that it is just as important for teachers who do not have immigrant students to look critically at the books about immigration available in their classrooms. In all probability, children who do not confront these issues in their daily lives are the least likely to question the portrayals of immigration in the books they read.

Finally, and most importantly, I want to emphasize that none of these books stands alone, regardless of whether they choose to confront or evade the topics of documentation and inequitable access to citizenship. Read these books aloud and make them the subject of group discussions before adding titles to the classroom library for independent reading. This is to assure that the sensitive issues involved can be treated with care, given the attention they deserve, and dealt with in a safe environment mediated by a caring adult. If our goal is to develop students who think critically about their own lives and about the world around them, teachers should be integrally involved in guiding children as they discover, explore, and analyze all of these books. I have tried to provide a framework to help us, as educators, look closely at the messages sent by the books about immigration that we choose for our classrooms. Thinking critically about the books ourselves is the first step in facilitating thoughtful dialogue among our students. ▪

Grace Cornell is a bilingual educator in Oakland, Calif.

References

Bunting, Eve. *How Many Days to America? A Thanksgiving Story.* New York: Clarion, 1988.

Herold, Maggie Rugg. *A Very Important Day.* New York: Morrow Junior Books, 1995.

Herrera, Juan Felipe. *Super Cilantro Girl/La superniña de cilantro.* San Francisco: Children's Book Press, 2003.

Pérez, Amada Irma. *My Diary from Here to There/Mi diario de aquí hasta allá.* San Francisco: Children's Book Press, 2002.

Rodríguez, Luis J. *América Is Her Name.* Willimantic, Conn.: Curbstone Press, 1997.

Rodríguez, Luis J. *La llaman América.* Willimantic, Conn.: Curbstone Press, 1998.

Yang, Belle. *Hannah Is My Name.* Cambridge, Mass.: Candlewick Press, 2004.

Katherine Streeter

'Save the Muslim Girl!'

Does popular fiction about Muslim girls build understanding or reinforce stereotypes?

ÖZLEM SENSOY and ELIZABETH MARSHALL

Young adult titles that focus on the lives of Muslim girls in the Middle East, written predominantly by white women, have appeared in increasing numbers since Sept. 11, 2001. A short list includes Deborah Ellis' trilogy *The Breadwinner*, *Parvana's Journey*, and *Mud City*; Suzanne Fisher Staples' *Under the Persimmon Tree*; and, more recently, Kim Antieau's *Broken Moon*. These titles received high praise and starred reviews from publications like *Horn Book* and *Publishers Weekly*. Each features a young heroine trapped in a violent Middle East from which she must escape or save herself, her family, and other innocents in the region. Authors portray Muslim girls overwhelmingly as characters haunted by a sad past, on the cusp of a (usually arranged) marriage, or impoverished and wishing for the freedoms that are often assigned to the West, such as education, safety, and prosperity.

Young adult literature about the Middle East cannot be separated from the post-9/11 context in which these books are marketed and increasingly published. *The Breadwinner*, for instance, was originally published in 2000, but Groundwood publishers rushed to rerelease a paperback reprint of it in the United States after 9/11 (Roback & Britton, 2001). Since that time it has been translated into 17 languages and has become an international best-seller (Atkinson, 2003); in 2004 it was selling an estimated 15,000 copies a month in the United States (Baker & Atkinson, 2004). "Save the Muslim girl" stories emerge alongside a preoccupation with Islam in mainstream news media and a surge in U.S. and Canadian military, political, and economic activities in the Middle East and West Asia. The texts are framed and packaged to sell in a marketplace at a particular moment when military interventions are centered on Afghanistan and other predominantly Muslim countries.

As many teachers have found, these stories offer an enticing way for students to engage with current events, language arts, and social studies curricula. However, given that these books are written for and marketed primarily to a Western audience, what ideas do they teach young adult readers about Muslim girls, Islam, and the Middle East? In what follows, we detail three lessons that dominate the "save the Muslim girl" stories.

Our interest here is not to defend any particular doctrine (fundamentalist Christian or Islamic). Rather, in this article we identify how these books reproduce — and offer opportunities to challenge — long-standing ideas commonly associated with Islam: backwardness, oppression, and cultural decay. We believe that these novels can best be used to teach about the common Western stereotypes that are universalized in these books rather than to teach about Afghanistan, Pakistan, or Islamic cultures.

LEARNING A STEREOTYPE LESSON #1:

Muslim Girls Are Veiled, Nameless, and Silent

Young adult books about the Muslim girl usually feature a veiled adolescent on the cover. Her face is cropped and concealed, usually by her own hands or her veil. Much of her face is covered, including, most significantly, her mouth. Images serve as a shorthand vocabulary. Consider how iconic images — a white or black cowboy hat, a scientist wearing a white lab coat, a princess — set up a stock plot. The repeated images of veiled girls reinforce familiar, mainstream ideas about the confined existence of Muslim women and girls. This is the Muslim girl story we expect to read.

These kinds of images have a long history in the West. Steve McCurry's famous 1985 photo of 13-year-old Sharbat Gula on the cover of *National Geographic*

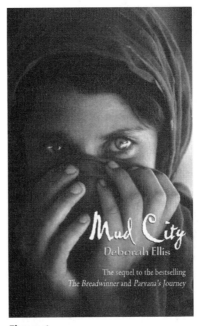

Figure 1

provides the most well known example. When we show the photo of the famous green-eyed Afghani girl in our education courses and ask students to write what they know about her, every student recognizes her image, yet few if any know her name, where she comes from, or that her photograph was "captured" in a refugee camp by a white U.S. journalist. Interestingly, the 2004 Oxford edition of *Mud City* reproduces a photo of Sharbat Gula on its front cover, taken from the same series of photographs McCurry captured in the mid-1980s (see Figure 1). The cover of Antieau's *Broken Moon* has a virtually identical image: a close shot of a young girl with a veil covering her mouth, and her hands cupping her lower face (see Figure 2). What ideas about Muslim or Middle Eastern girls — specifically Afghani girls — are we as audience invited to imagine?

Figure 2

Just about every book in this genre features such an image on its cover. These are familiar metaphors for how the Muslim girl's life will be presented within the novel. The way the girls' mouths are covered reinforces existing ideas about their silence and suggests that we in the West (conceptualized as "free" and "liberated") need to help unveil and "give" them voice. The images also invite ideas about girlhood innocence and vulnerability, and invite Western readers to protect, save, and speak for these oppressed girls.

But, is it not true that Muslim girls are oppressed and voiceless? We would argue that all women experience gender discrimination in different ways and with different consequences. The experiences of a U.S. woman (for example) will vary greatly if she is heterosexual or a lesbian, living in an urban center or a rural area.

Imagine this rural lesbian is black, or black and Muslim, or black, Muslim, and a nonnative English speaker. In this way, her experiences are determined not simply by her gender, but also by her racial, ethnic, and sexual identity. What strikes us about the books that we review here is that they are written by white Western women who author, organize, and interpret stories about Middle Eastern girlhoods for Western consumption. This raises questions about the politics of storytelling. For instance, how do (white) Western women decide for "global" women what their issues and oppressions are? Who tells whose story and in what ways?

Richard Dyer reminds us that although we may believe that stereotypes are derived from a limited truth about particular people, we actually get our ideas about people from stereotypic images. So it isn't the kernel of truth that results in stereotypes. Stereotypes are created and reinforced by the repeated appearance of particular images and the exclusion of others. Thus, the repeated circulation of the image of the veiled, sad Muslim girl reinforces the stereotype that all Muslim girls are oppressed.

Stereotypes are particularly powerful in the case of groups with which one has little or no personal relationship. Thus, for young people who get most of their ideas about "others" from textbooks or from media, we need to ask what ideas are learned when they "see" a very limited image of Muslim girls.

LEARNING A STEREOTYPE LESSON #2:

Veiled = Oppressed

Gendered violence in Middle Eastern countries, or the threat of it, organizes many of the books' plots. With few exceptions, the "good" civilized men in the girl's family are taken from her. In *Under the Persimmon Tree*, a brother and father are forced to join the Taliban as fighters, while in *The Breadwinner*, the Taliban places the father in jail because he was educated in England. *Parvana's Journey* opens with the father's funeral, and a deceased dad also figures in *Broken Moon*. This absence leaves the heroine vulnerable to the roving, indiscriminate, uncivilized "bad" men who will beat her for going out without a male escort (*The Breadwinner* and *Broken Moon*), confine her to the house (*The Breadwinner*), or beat her to preserve the honor of the community (*Broken Moon*).

In this context of an absent/immobilized parent, the girl is placed at the center of the plot, further emphasizing the danger and vulnerability of her existence. Parvana in *The Breadwinner* and *Parvana's Journey*, Nadira in *Broken Moon*, and Najmah in *Under the Persimmon Tree* each cut their hair and disguise themselves as boys. This cross-dressing draws heavily on Western ideas that girls should be unfettered by the requirement to cover themselves, and authors present this type of transformation as the only humane alternative to wearing a burqa and the only way to travel safely outside the domestic sphere.

The veil or burqa, which has exclusively functioned as the shorthand marker of women's oppression, is a much more complicated thing. To give you a sense of the range of meaning of the veil, consider for instance that in Turkey—a predominantly Muslim country—the veil (or "religious dress") is outlawed in public spaces as a means to underline the government's commitments to Kemalism, a "modern," secularist stance. In response and as a sign of resistance, some women, especially young university students and those in urban areas, consider the veil to be a marker of protest against government regulation of their bodies and the artificial division of "modern" vs. "faithful." Similar acts of resistance are taken up by feminists in Egypt who wear the veil as a conscious act of resistance against Western imperialism. As another example, before 9/11, the Revolutionary Association of the Women in Afghanistan (RAWA) documented the Taliban's crimes against girls and women by hiding video cameras under their burqas and transformed the burqa from simply a marker of oppression to a tool of resistance.

> **Although veiling has different meanings in different contexts, it exclusively carries a negative connotation in the "save the Muslim girl" texts.**

It is problematic to wholly and simplistically equate women's oppression with the burqa, just as it would be problematic to claim that once Western women stop using makeup to cover their faces, it will mean an end to domestic violence in the United States and Canada. Although veiling has different meanings in different contexts, it exclusively carries a negative connotation in the "save the Muslim girl" texts. For example, in *The Breadwinner*, the reader is educated about the burqa through the main character, Parvana: "How do women in burqas manage to walk along the streets?" Parvana asked her father. "How do they see where they are going?"

"They fall down a lot," her father replied.

Nusrat, the American aid worker in *Under the Persimmon Tree*, describes the burqa similarly: "In the cool autumn air, Nusrat forgets how suffocating the folds of the burqa's synthetic fabric can be in hot weather, and how peering through the crocheted latticework eye piece can feel like looking through the bars of a prison."

In contrast to these confined women, the heroines of these novels, like "free" girls in the West, wear pants and experience freedom of movement. The freedoms associated with Western women are further emphasized in these texts by the addition of non-Muslim characters. The French nurse in *Parvana's Journey* (who works in Pakistan for a relief agency) and the American Nusrat in *Under the Persimmon Tree* (who establishes and runs a school for refugees) each choose to come to the Middle East to help. A white woman veterinarian who "wore the clothes of a Westerner" tends to the camels in *Broken Moon*. These "choices" that enable non-Muslim women to move and to work are placed in contrast to the experiences of the girls/women in the story who are at the mercy of violent events and settings in which their mobility (not to mention their way of dress) is strictly regulated and supervised.

There is a compelling character in *The Breadwinner* who offers the potential to represent Afghani women's liberation in more complex ways. This is Mrs. Weera, who leads a women's resistance group. She also convinces Parvana's mother to join her in running a covert school for girls. It is regrettable that Mrs. Weera does not occupy a more central place in the story since, unlike any other adult woman in the "save the Muslim girl" literature, she offers a transformative representation of activism among Muslim women in Afghanistan.

Again, we want to reiterate that we are not arguing that women and girls in the Middle East or predominantly Islamic societies do not experience domestic violence. In fact, we believe that domestic violence is a global epidemic that most countries, including predominantly Christian countries such as Canada and the United States, have neglected to face head-on. Rather, we are arguing that the victim narrative that is so often a part of these young adult novels about Middle Eastern women reinforces the idea that the region is inherently violent and that women must be protected by outside forces. These young adult novels serve as de facto legitimization for the U.S.-led incursions in the region as a project of women's emancipation. As Laura Bush argued in her radio address on Nov. 17, 2001: "The brutal oppression of women is a central goal of the terrorists." In this way, the complexities of Afghanistan's history, as well as U.S. interest in the region and ties to violence, escape attention.

That girls in the Middle East are consistently at risk of gendered violence implicitly suggests that girls in the "civilized" West are immune to such threats. The education students with whom we work are very familiar and comfortable with the stereotype that the lives of Muslim women are inherently scary, that they cannot work or vote or walk around without the threat of violence. Of course there are Muslim women who live in oppressive or patriarchal regimes (in the Middle East and elsewhere). What we contend is that young adult novels written by white women and marketed and consumed in the West consistently reinforce the idea that Muslim women are inherently oppressed, that they are oppressed in ways that Western women are not, and that this oppression is a function of Islam. By positioning "Eastern" women as the women who are truly oppressed, those in the West pass up a rich opportunity to engage in complex questions about oppression, patriarchy, war, families, displacement, and the role of values (imperialist or faith-based) in these relations.

Although some might argue that an author's literary imagination is her own, we suggest that these representations of Muslim girls do not—and cannot—exist independent of a social context. That these "save the Muslim girl" stories continue to be marketed by major publishers, reviewed favorably by literary and educational gatekeepers, and/or achieve best-seller status like *The Breadwinner* suggests an intimate connection to the current ideological climate within which these stories are told, marketed, and consumed.

LEARNING A STEREOTYPE LESSON #3:
Muslim Girls and Women Want To Be Saved by the West

For many in the West, the plight of Afghanistan is framed exclusively within a post 9/11, U.S.-led "war on terror." Although radical women's organizations like RAWA have condemned brutality against women in Afghanistan for decades, their voices were absent, and are now muted, in a landscape of storytelling that is dominated by white Western women representing them. In an open letter to *Ms.* magazine, for instance, a U.S.-based supporter of RAWA notes that U.S.-centric women's organizations such as the Feminist Majority fail to give "credit to the independent Afghan women who stayed in Afghanistan and Pakistan throughout the 23-year (and counting) crisis in Afghanistan and provided relief, education, resistance, and hope to the women and men of their country." Novels like *Broken Moon* play on popular scripts in which the West saves

the people of the "East." These stories cannot be seen as simply works of fiction. They ultimately influence real-world experiences of girls in the Middle East and (most relevant to us) of Muslim and non-Muslim girls in our schools in the West.

Ellis and Staples gain legitimacy as authors because they have visited, lived, and/or spoken to real girls and women in the Middle East. *The Breadwinner* trilogy and *Under the Persimmon Tree* each include a map and an author's note that touches on the "tumultuous" history of Afghanistan and a glossary. The history offered in the end matter and in the texts themselves glosses over the history of colonization in the region. The authors dilute what is an extremely complex history that has led up to the current violence in the Middle East, particularly the role of U.S. foreign policy and military interventions that contributed to the rise of the Taliban.

The authors fail to capture the complexities of U.S. involvement and intervention in favor of stereotypical lessons about educating and saving Muslim girls. As Sonali Kolhatkar, vice president of the Afghan Women's Mission, and Mariam Rawi, a member of RAWA, argue: "Feminists and other humanitarians should learn from history. This isn't the first time the welfare of women has been trotted out as a pretext for imperialist military aggression." On one level these texts are part of a larger public pedagogy in which the United States and its allies are framed as fighting a good fight in Afghanistan and other regions of the Middle East. Readers are encouraged to continue to empathize with the lead character and the ideas that are associated with her: saving wounded children rather than critiquing U.S. policy, "pulling oneself up by one's bootstraps" rather than organizing together, fighting against all odds—ideas firmly rooted in mainstream U.S. ideals of exceptionalism and Western values of individuality.

Teaching a More Complicated Truth

We support teachers using books like *The Breadwinner* with the pedagogical goals of critical examination. We are not advocating for the one "right" Muslim girl story, nor do we suggest that teachers avoid using these books in classrooms (for we recognize that in many cases, decisions about what books teachers have access to are made by economic constraints at the school and district levels). We would, however, like to offer suggestions for the kinds of questions teachers could ask in order to use these resources in ways that are critically minded:

- How are Muslim girls visually depicted on the cover? You might ask students to generate a list of adjectives that describe the girl. The curriculum *Scarves of Many Colors* is a terrific resource for exploring the relationship between graphics and students' ideas about people. Consider questions of accuracy, context, and motivation. For example: How accurate are the details in the image? When and how will this image be "made sense of"? Who produced this image and why?

- Which parts of the novel are you absolutely certain are true? How do you know? Where did you learn this information? Students can try to pinpoint the resources they rely upon to get their "facts."

- Who is the author of this story? How do they legitimize themselves as an expert? What might be their motivations? Who are they speaking to and for?

- How is the book marketed and what does it intend to teach Western readers? Students might examine the description on the back of the book, the author's note, the map, the glossary, and book reviews to make observations about what kinds of readers are being targeted.

- How does Afghanistan (or Pakistan) fit into the region? In the author's note, Ellis points out that Afghanistan has been at war for decades. Often we study one country at a time. A more critical approach would investigate the relationships among countries. Students could explore the historical and current relationships (economic, political, cultural) between Afghanistan and other nation-states such as the former Soviet Union, Pakistan, Iran, and China.

- Whose story is missing? Students can create visual representations of the social locations (e.g., the race, class, gender, education) of each of the characters. Given these details, whose story is this? Whose stories are not here, and where might we go to learn about their stories?

Although these examples of young adult fictions do not offer much in the way of transformative education about the Middle East, they do offer the potential to educate us about our own assumptions and our pedagogical purposes when we teach the "oppressed Muslim girl" stories. It is in this capacity that we hope educators will take up these novels. ■

....

Özlem Sensoy teaches in the Faculty of Education at Simon Fraser University in British Columbia. She recently published Is Everyone Really Equal? An Introduction to Key Concepts in Social Justice Education. *Elizabeth Marshall, a former elementary school teacher, teaches courses on children's and young adult literature at Simon Fraser University. They co-edited* Rethinking Popular Culture and Media.

References

Antieau, Kim. *Broken Moon.* New York: Margaret K. McElderry Books, 2007.

Bigelow, Bill, Sandra Childs, Norm Diamond, Diana Dickerson, and Jan Haaken. *Scarves of Many Colors: Muslim Women and the Veil.* Washington, D.C.: Teaching for Change, 2000.

Dyer, Richard. *The Matter of Images: Essays on Representation.* New York: Routledge, 1993.

Ellis, Deborah. *The Breadwinner.* Toronto: Groundwood Books, 2000.

Ellis, Deborah. *Parvana's Journey.* Toronto: Groundwood Books, 2002.

Ellis, Deborah. *Mud City.* Toronto: Groundwood Books, 2003.

Kolhatkar, Sonali & Rawi, Mariam. "Why Is a Leading Feminist Organization Lending Its Name to Support Escalation in Afghanistan?" July 8, 2009. www.alternet.org/world/141165.

Miller, Elizabeth. "An Open Letter to the Editors of *Ms.* Magazine." *Off Our Backs.* September/March 2002: 59–61.

Sensoy, Özlem. "Ickity Ackity Open Sesame: Learning About the Middle East in Images." *Rethinking Curricular Knowledge on Global Societies.* Charlotte, N.C.: Information Age Publishing, 2009: 39–55.

Staples, Suzanne Fisher. *Under the Persimmon Tree.* New York: Simon & Schuster, 2005.

Realistic Reflections

Beyond the Medal

Representations of disability in Caldecott winners

CHLOË MYERS-HUGHES and **HANK BERSANI JR.**

As regular readers of Rethinking Schools publications, we have benefited from many strategies for addressing the prejudices of racism, classism, and sexism. We wondered, however, about a parallel prejudice that rarely gets attention: ableism, or discrimination against people with physical, mental, or emotional disabilities. Using a set of 10 guiding questions we developed (*Rethinking Schools*, 2009), we decided to explore ableist stereotypes in winners of the Caldecott Medal, which is awarded annually to "the most distinguished American picture book for children." Caldecott winners are often endorsed by schools and libraries, and therefore purchased by many families. Unlike books intended for older audiences, picture books rely heavily on visual art to convey meaning. Children can read these picture books on their own; they don't necessarily have meanings mediated by an adult. Books with the Caldecott seal may provide children with their first impressions of our diverse society. What hidden messages will they learn about disability?

1. Does the book promote ableism by ignoring people with disabilities?

Sometimes what is not present in a book is as important as what is included. For example, *So You Want to Be President?* makes no mention of disability in any of the U.S. presidents. After contracting polio at age 39, well before he became president, Franklin Delano Roosevelt was never able to move or stand again without the assistance of a wheelchair, braces, or another person. Yet *So You Want to Be President?* fails to depict or acknowledge his disability.

2. Do the illustrations promote ableism by addressing disability in stereotyped ways?

Look at the hidden messages in images, even among the onlookers in the text. For example, in Peggy Rathmann's *Officer Buckle and Gloria*, a young girl in the audience watches in a wheelchair, enjoying the hilarious safety duo as much as everyone else. She does not assume any major role, but is simply there, included without comment as any other child would be. Rathmann's drawing normalizes disability and reinforces a sense of inclusivity rather than ostracism. Compare this illustration with one toward the end of *Madeline's Rescue* that depicts the tiny figure of an elderly lady being pushed in a wheelchair with a neatly coiffed poodle on her lap. The illustration emphasizes dependence, for she is purely tangential, being vigorously pushed by a man in uniform, alone and disconnected in a bustling cityscape.

Throughout art and literature, people with disabilities have often been stereotyped as being less than human, as dangerous, or as eternal children.

Such negative portrayals are illustrated by the dwarf in *Saint George and the Dragon*, who is pictured in servitude, rarely referred to in the text, and never given any dialogue. Without his own agency, he is infantilized: His only eye-to-eye human relationships

> **Throughout art and literature, people with disabilities have often been stereotyped as being less than human, as dangerous, or as eternal children.**

are with children. The visuals in this text support a diminishing cliché that adults with disabilities are simple, dependent children who need to have others make decisions for them.

3. Does the story line promote ableism?

Evaluate the standard for success for characters with disabilities. The title character in *The Fool of the World and the Flying Ship*, for example, has to exhibit extraordinary qualities in order to gain acceptance and approval. Since he is so "simple," he does not have a concept of what is impossible. Only by attempting and succeeding at the impossible (flying a boat) does he gain acceptance, make friends, and win the hand of a beautiful princess. Can people with disabilities gain the right to inclusion and love only if they have superhuman powers? If they lack preternatural gifts, is society to shun them?

Also assess the credibility and three-dimensionality of characters with disabilities. For example, in Paul Zelinsky's aesthetic masterpiece *Rapunzel*, the prince secretly marries Rapunzel. When he returns to the tower, he encounters the sorceress and plunges to the ground. Although the fall is not fatal, it leaves him blind. He wanders in the wilderness for more than a year before he hears his wife's voice and runs toward her. Rapunzel's tears magically restore the prince's sight so that he can admire his wife and children and lead them all "out of the wilderness toward his kingdom."

The disability of blindness is incorporated into the story as a literary device to symbolize inner struggle, impotence, and even punishment for stealing Rapunzel's chastity. Ability (lack of disability)—the restoration of the prince's sight—signifies enlightenment, the power to lead, and forgiveness. The prince becomes blind in order to see.

In contrast, despite having lost an eye, the likeable Etienne in *The Invention of Hugo Cabret* has an instrumental and well-rounded role to play in the story. He appears in the pictures, text, and dialogue, and is a positive force in Hugo's life. After losing his job at the movie theater, Etienne studies to be a cameraman and tells Hugo that the eye patch "actually makes it easier to look through the camera—I don't have to close one eye like everyone else." He reframes his "disability" as an "advantage."

4. Do loaded words convey negative messages about disability?

Adjectives can diminish and restrict our view of people with disabilities, as we see in *The Rooster Crows*. A little girl in one of the rhymes is called Peep Peep because "the poor little thing has only one eye." Her very name is a word play underscoring her visual challenge: Peepers is slang for eyes. Provided with this diminishing description and an illustration of Peep Peep isolated on a mountaintop, the reader is likely to see her as pathetic and separated from the world.

Descriptive words can also incite our greatest fears. *Shadow*, a story translated from the French, draws upon children's fascination with and fear of shadows. The mysterious shadow "is mute…never speaks …is blind…has no voice." We also learn that it "could prick…or bite" and that it "cast[s] a spell over you…mocks you and makes a fool out of you." Do the repetitive literary associations among shadows, disability, and danger help maintain societal apprehension about people with physical and intellectual impairments?

Figurative language can underscore negative values and beliefs about disability. The very title of *The Fool of the World and the Flying Ship* is an example of overtly dehumanizing language about intellectual disabilities. An early classification of intellectual disability was "natural born fool." The image of the "ship of fools" is iconic in literature, theater, film, and art. Fifteenth-century woodcuts show depictions of people with various disabilities ("fools," "cripples," etc.) being cast off from one port and sent on to the next as

ship captains were paid to remove undesirables. This is the tragic history evoked by this figurative title.

5. Are characters with disabilities portrayed as three-dimensional people who belong or as flat, stereotyped outsiders?

When books portray disability in superficial and stereotyped ways, readers learn misleading information about the lives of people with disabilities. Pressing concerns of people with disabilities—such as employment, personal relationships, housing, transportation, and health care—that would shed light on their lifestyles and, moreover, their humanity, are largely avoided in Caldecott selections.

6. Who in the story has agency? Are people with disabilities always the recipients of the efforts of others or are they portrayed with value?

Dipping into the first pages of *Saint George and the Dragon*, we soon observe the social hierarchy and the positions of power. The noble knight, George, is followed by Princess Una, whose innocence is underscored by her steed, a little white donkey to which is tethered a white lamb. Bringing up the rear is a bedraggled dwarf hunched under the bundle of food he is carrying for the brave couple. It is hard not to interpret the pecking order: man, followed by woman, then animal, and, at the very bottom, the person with disabilities. It is the able-bodied characters who have agency. Although the dwarf remains faithful throughout the book, the reward for his own loyalty and help on the treacherous journey is more servitude. At the end of the story he is pictured carrying a decanter to the table of the royal family. Meanwhile the king tells George that his reward will be rest, Una's hand in marriage, and eventually the throne.

7. Are characters with disabilities ever in the role of hero or are they always victims to be rescued by the hero?

There were no credible heroes with disabilities among the 72 Caldecott medal winners. We believe that a hero needs to be a protagonist whom children will want to emulate. Etienne's role in *The Invention of Hugo Cabret* is too minor to be counted. *The Fool of the World and the Flying Ship* is so "simple" that we doubt many children would dream of following his example.

The prince's blindness in *Rapunzel* is fleeting, unbelievable, and connected to his "wretched[ness]" rather than his heroism. If children have aspirations to be like the prince, it seems more likely they would associate with the prince in his sighted, handsome, and commanding form.

There was, however, potential for discussing heroism simultaneously with disability in the Caldecott books. In *So You Want to Be President?*, FDR is portrayed as a hero, but his disability is never mentioned. This omission seems all the more negligent considering the discussion of difference toward the end of the book:

> Every president was different from every other and yet no woman has been president. No person of color has been president. No person who wasn't a Protestant or a Roman Catholic has been president. But if you care enough, anything is possible. Thirty-four presidents came and went before a Roman Catholic — John Kennedy — was elected. Almost two hundred years passed before a woman — Geraldine Ferraro — ran for vice president.

Were the author and illustrator to update this book in light of the results of the 2008 presidential election, this summation would have to be revised, but would it occur to St. George and Small to portray challenges based upon disability in addition to gender, skin color, and creed? Clearly, an opportunity to teach children about leaders with disabilities was missed.

8. Does the book promote positive self-image for people with disabilities?

Can children with disabilities form a positive self-image by seeing characters like the dwarf in *Saint George and the Dragon* and the "fool of the world" in *The Fool of the World and the Flying Ship*, or from hearing fear-evoking descriptions of disability in *Shadow*? Will these children develop a strong self-concept if the few characters they see who have disabilities are so undervalued? What lessons will children without disabilities learn from reading books like this? In a classroom with a student who is blind or who has a learning disability, what will these portrayals mean? Do they offer teachers an opportunity for a productive discussion on disability or do they create conditions for more fear and misunderstanding?

9. Is there something in the author's and illustrator's backgrounds that recommends them to writing about the disability experience accurately and with sensitivity?

One might reasonably expect specific insights into sexism from a woman author, and into racism from a black author. One might also expect authors and illustrators with disabilities to have a different approach to disability from others. Within this Caldecott collection, we found no information about the authors and illustrators (on the books' jacket flaps or back covers, or in their forewords) that mentioned any connections to disability.

10. Look at the copyright dates.

The copyright date is a good clue to how disability will be portrayed in very early Caldecott medal winners like *Animals of the Bible* (1937). This first Caldecott medal winner uses quotations from the King James Bible, including the passage, "Then shall

> **In place of broadening understanding about disability, most of the few Caldecott winners that portray disability do so in ways that distort perceptions and help maintain societal biases.**

the lame man leap as an hart and the tongue of the dumb sing," which connects the "lame" and the "dumb" to the "oppressed" and "afflicted." These passages from Isaiah have troubled biblical scholars and disability activists alike. Do they imply that disability is a fallen state and that people with disabilities must be redeemed? Reviewing a book from 1937, which quotes a scriptural text nearly 3,000 years old, points out the dilemma of reviewing an older work and judging it by today's sociopolitical standards.

Although copyright dates do not guarantee that disability representations will be negative or positive, they do help us place the text within a social context. The publication date may also become part of a discussion with some students, as parents or teachers attempt to put the book in context.

Conclusion

We found few representations of disability in this famous collection of picture books. Representations were limited in variety, with physical and sensory impairments most commonly portrayed. Portrayals were also limited in depth, rarely giving insight into the lives of people with disabilities, instead tending to reinforce stereotypes or use disability as a literary device. Within these award-winning books, inclusion of disability—and even the obvious exclusion of it—is generally compatible with the argument of ableism. In place of broadening understanding about disability, most of the few Caldecott winners that portray disability do so in ways that distort perceptions and help maintain societal biases.

Recommendations

These popular books have a good deal to offer young readers, but they are not perfect. As when encountering sexism or racism in children's literature, we recommend that adults consider the subtle and not so subtle textual messages contained within any children's book. We call upon parents, caregivers, and teachers to provide a lens through which the children process the images and stories; mediation by an adult can make all the difference. Only by critically engaging children in reading the world within the text and illustrations can we hope to create a more equitable society for people with disabilities. Failure to do so is getting in the way of changing our ableist society. ▪

....

Chloë Myers-Hughes, an associate professor at Western Oregon University in Monmouth, Ore., teaches literacy and diversity classes in the Division of Teacher Education. Hank Bersani Jr. is a professor in the Division of Special Education at Western Oregon University and teaches undergraduate and graduate classes in special education.

Works Cited

Bemelmans, Ludwig. *Madeline's Rescue*. New York: Viking Press, 1953.

Brown, Marcia. *Shadow*. New York: Scribner, 1982.

Hyman, Trina. *Saint George and the Dragon: A Golden Legend*. New York: Little, Brown, 1984.

Lathrop, Dorothy. *Animals of the Bible*. New York: HarperCollins, 1937.

Ransome, Arthur. *The Fool of the World and the Flying Ship*. New York: Farrar, Straus and Giroux, 1968.

Petersham, Maud and Miska Petersham. *The Rooster Crows*. New York: Macmillan, 1969.

Rathmann, Peggy. *Officer Buckle and Gloria*. New York: Putnam, 1995.

Selznick, Brian. *The Invention of Hugo Cabret*. New York: Scholastic, 2007.

St. George, Judith. *So You Want to Be President?* New York: Philomel, 2000.

Zelinsky, Paul. *Rapunzel*. New York: Dutton, 1997.

References

Hehir, Thomas. "Eliminating Ableism in Education." *Harvard Educational Review* 72.1 (2002): 1–32.

Myers, Chloë and Bersani, Hank. "10 Quick Ways to Analyze Children's Books for Ableism: Prejudice by Able-Bodied and Able-Minded People." *Rethinking Schools* 23.2 (2009): 52–54.

Izzit Capitalist Propaganda?

Free curriculum misleads children

JULIE KNUTSON

Free teaching materials intrigue me. I could spend hours perusing Curriki and TeacherTube for appropriate, antibiased resources for my 8th-grade U.S. history students. So, when forwarded a link to izzit.org—which allegedly serves 195,000 teachers, 44,000 schools, and 18 million students—I took the bait. As the basic but inviting website opened, my eyes were immediately drawn to the free DVD offerings for educators. I began scanning the list of films, entertaining the possibility that the cryptically titled *Yours and Mine: The Lessons of 1623* might provide a fresh perspective on life in the Plymouth colony.

Admittedly, after all that excitement, the DVD sat shrink-wrapped and unwatched on my bookshelf for nearly a year. I came across it again a few weeks before launching a unit on early colonial life in the Americas. Hoping it could offer some compelling details about 17th-century New England, I decided to watch it. No stranger to the world of teaching materials, I prepared myself for some hackneyed but harmless reenactments and some overly brief accounts of colonial history. Nevertheless, the DVD's description promised some "surprising facts"—such as the Pilgrims' affinity for "colorful clothes"—so I remained vaguely optimistic. Several minutes into the film, however, I realized I was watching an unabashed ode to free market capitalism and private property.

We begin with our young narrator, Priscilla, whose stated purpose is to debunk some common myths about the Pilgrims. As she prepares us to venture into the main storyline, she stresses that we should think of the Pilgrims not as brass buckle-wearing religious zealots, but rather as social pioneers whose image should be conjured "every time we use our cell phone or iPods." As if sensing my confusion, Priscilla looks into the camera with a raised eyebrow and asks, "Curious?" Not knowing where her odd digressions were taking me, I mentally replied with a cautious "Yes."

On this myth-busting expedition, our host is accompanied by her father, an economics teacher and direct descendant of the Fullers of Plymouth. Hell-bent on discussing the role of private property in the nascent years of the colony, Priscilla's father attempts to reeducate his daughter and a misinformed reenactor named Samuel about the devastating effects of sharing on the Plymouth Plantation.

Through a series of interviews with the local townspeople, we learn of the Pilgrims' trials and tribulations that first winter on Cape Cod Bay. Although the colonists managed to produce a good harvest the following fall (thanks to whom the teacher's guide calls "a friendly native"), a ship bringing 35 more colonists meant that food needed to be rationed. Malnourished and still relatively unskilled at growing food, we're told that the Pilgrims' initial attempts at sharing the labor and harvests began to unravel. "It left the opportunity for some to take advantage," a woman in period garb explains through what is apparently a Puritan accent, "and leave the work for others." To combat these "leeches," as Samuel calls them, Gov. William Bradford decides to parcel the farmlands into private individual properties and order is restored in Plymouth. Therein lies the great Lesson of 1623: that privatization and ownership provided the Pilgrims with an incentive "to work harder and be more productive in a strange land."

By placing a premium on this "lesson," *Yours and Mine* relegates all other aspects of life in the early years of the Plymouth colony to the margins. The traditional classroom "origin myth" of a peaceable Thanksgiving is supplanted by the new myth of capitalist self-determination, with both approaches problematic in that they sap history of its messiness and humanity. No need to mention boring details of the Pilgrims robbing Native American graves or raiding buried corn supplies. Anyway, those were just mistakes made before colonists learned the value of private property in the Lesson of 1623.

The traditional classroom "origin myth" of a peaceable Thanksgiving is supplanted by the new myth of capitalist self-determination, with both approaches problematic in that they sap history of its messiness and humanity.

So what's the alternative? What should be mentioned? What lessons could 1623—and the three years that immediately preceded it—offer? As James Loewen has suggested in his book *Lies My Teacher Told Me*, "The antidote to feel-good history is not feel-bad history but honest and inclusive history…allow[ing] students to learn both the 'good' and the 'bad' side of the Pilgrim tale." The Izzit team could have accomplished this through inclusion of four key but oft-neglected aspects of Plymouth's early history: European disease and the subsequent near-decimation of the region's indigenous population; the aforementioned looting and grave robbing that characterized the Pilgrims' first few months; Wampanoag leader Massasoit's strategy in entering into early peace treaties with Pilgrim leader John Carver; and land agreements and relations between the Pokanoket Tribe of the Wampanoag Nation and the Pilgrims, which served the Pokanoket well but displaced other New England tribes.*

*On the practice of grave robbing, see Karen Kupperman, *Settling with the Indians* (Totowa, N.J.: Rowman and Littlefield, 1980), p. 125; for additional references to looting and grave robbing, see also Nathaniel Philbrick, *Mayflower* (New York: Viking, 2006), p. 61, 64, 67–69. Philbrick provides additional details on early peace treaties between the Pokanoket Tribe of the Wampanoag Nation and the Pilgrims, p. 99.

These omitted realities of life in the fledgling Plymouth colony could be introduced to viewers with relative ease, but it's unlikely that such a revision would interest Izzit.

When I began investigating the "who" and "what" of this organization, Izzit's brief tribute to private property—rather than to a more truthful telling of multiple histories—became less surprising. The izzit.org website features a "Who Izzit?" page with the smiling faces of five employees. There's no mention of funding or financing. A basic Google search on Izzit yields nothing particularly substantive either; most hits that mention the site feature teacher "buzz" hyping the website's free services. Adjusting my search to "Izzit nonprofit" I'm finally led to Izzit's silent parent organization, freetochoosemedia.org. Curiously, there's no mention of "Free to Choose" on the Izzit site. At the bottom of the page, a line in fine print reads "An educational initiative of the Palmer R. Chitester Fund." Searching for information on Chitester, I find a telling profile featured at mediatransparency.org that describes an organization "created by the combative Bob Chitester, with startup money from the Bradley Foundation, to create right-wing popular media."

Disguised as innocuous learning material on izzit. org, Chitester's agenda is apparently making its way into more and more American classrooms—complete with teaching guides and prefab quizzes. According to the Chitester Fund's site, Izzit has been used by "one in four secondary social studies teachers in America." This statistic is likely inflated, but is nonetheless concerning, in that many of Izzit's other film selections and resources can be described as nothing less than comically libertarian, promoting the idea that laissez-faire capitalist economies are the answer to all social ills and that governments are universally and unequivocally bad. This philosophy is perhaps most aggressively promoted in the Milton Friedman-oriented *The Price System,* in which the narrator summarily states, "free markets, personal freedom, and political freedom—they need each other and lead to the predictable miracle of steadily better ways of life through the price system." Other Izzit features, including *Everyone's Space,* place equal faith in entrepreneurial capitalism to develop "options and solutions" for our collective future—in space. Izzit's apparently enormous reach means Chitester's cherry-picked history and radical free market prescriptions—so aptly illustrated by *Yours and Mine, The Price System,* and *Everyone's Space*—are likely finding their way into increasing numbers of classrooms.

Knowing this about Chitester, it's no wonder that *Yours and Mine* presents Plymouth's alleged "ownership society" as a fixed and immutable economic principle established in early American life. This notion not only meets Izzit's laissez-faire agenda, but also serves the more nefarious purpose of justifying inequities in our own times by suggesting that poverty and hardship are individual problems and not a social responsibility. The DVD's argument leaves little room for a broader critique of social and economic disparity, its historical roots, and its effects on modern American culture. ∎

....

Julie Knutson taught both middle and secondary school in Houston.

Susan Lina Ruggles

4.

Math Is More Than Numbers

Why are the fraction problems in the math curriculum always about sharing brownies and pizza? They *do* ask students to think about sharing in a fair way, but what happens when our mathematical teaching steps out of the pantry and takes on some more pressing issues of fairness? How are global resources shared (or not)? How can military spending help us understand large numbers? When students inquire mathematically into the economic and cultural melee swirling around them — gathering data to describe problems and make arguments — they become infinitely wiser about what does and does not add up.

Jean-Claude Lejeune

Teaching Math Across the Curriculum

A 5th-grade teacher battles 'number numbness'

BOB PETERSON

I recently read a proposal for an innovative school and it set me thinking about math. It wasn't the proposal's numbers that got my mind going, but rather the approach to structuring math into the curriculum. I disagreed with it.

The plan called for the curriculum to be divided into three areas—math/science, the arts (including fine arts and language arts), and history/philosophy. Blocks of time were set aside for a unified approach in each area. As I mulled over the proposal and thought of my experience in a self-contained 5th-grade classroom, I realized I was uneasy with the proposed curricular divisions, specifically the assumption that science and math belong together as a unified block. It reminded me of how some elementary teachers integrate the curriculum by lumping language arts and social studies together in one strand, and math and science in another.

It also raised several questions for me. Why place math and science together, and not math and social studies? What are the political and pedagogical assumptions behind such an approach? Why shouldn't reformers advocate math in all subject areas? Why not have "math across the curriculum," comparable to "writing across the curriculum?"

One reason reformers have advocated changes in how math is structured is because of the historic problems with math instruction itself: rote calculations, drill and practice ad nauseum, endless reams of worksheets, and a fetish for "the right answer." These have contributed to "number numbness" among students, and ultimately among the general population when students become adults.

But the problem is deeper than a sterile teacher-centered and text-driven approach. "Number numbness" also has its roots in how math is segregated in schools and kept separate from the issues that confront students in their daily lives. Most students don't want to do abstract exercises with numbers or plod through text-based story problems that have them forever making change in some make-believe store. The curriculum rarely encourages students to link math and history, math and politics, math and literature — math and people.

There are unfortunate consequences when math is isolated. First, the not-so-subtle message is that math is basically irrelevant except for success in future math classes, or if you want to be a scientist or mathematician, or in commercial transactions. Second, students learn that math is not connected to social reality in any substantive way. Thus students approach math in the abstract and never are encouraged to seriously consider the social and ethical consequences of how math is sometimes used in society. Third, if students are not taught how math can be applied in their lives, they are robbed of an important tool to help them

fully participate in society. An understanding of math and how numbers and statistics can be interpreted is essential to effectively enter most debates on public issues such as welfare, unemployment, and the federal budget. For example, even though the minimum wage is higher than it has ever been, in constant dollars it is the lowest in 40 years. But you need math to understand that.

The curriculum rarely encourages students to link math and history, math and politics, math and literature — math and people.

When I first began teaching, I was dissatisfied with "number numbness," but wasn't sure what to do about it. My growth as a teacher first came in the area of language arts and reading. I increasingly stressed that students should write for meaningful purposes, and read books and stories that were connected to their lives. Thus I had children read and discuss whole books, conducted writing workshops, and had students read and write in science and social studies. My math, however, remained noticeably segregated from the rest of the curriculum, even though I increasingly emphasized problem-solving and the use of manipulatives.

With the help of my teaching colleague Celín Arce and publications from the National Council of Teachers of Mathematics, I started to view math as akin to language. I believe that math, like language, is both a discipline unto itself and a tool to understand and interact with the world and other academic disciplines. Just as written and oral language helps children understand their community, so can written and oral mathematics. Just as teachers stress the need for "writing across the curriculum," I believe it is important to advocate "math across the curriculum." Just as students are expected to write for meaningful purposes, they should do math for meaningful purposes.

Plans to integrate math into science are a step in the right direction. And assuming that the science curriculum is "meaningful," the teaching of mathematics will improve. But linking math with science is only a beginning, and should be followed with integration of math across the curriculum. I have found that my 5th graders, for instance, are particularly interested in social issues. Thus integrating math with social studies is an effective way to bring math alive for the students.

Before I go any further, I want to make two important clarifications. First, I don't mean to imply that distinct math "mini-lessons" aren't important. They are, just as such lessons are necessary in reading and writing. I also want to make clear that integrating math with social studies does not necessarily make the teaching more student-centered or the content more concerned with issues of social justice. Those important components depend on the teacher's philosophical and pedagogical beliefs.

In the past few years I have tried in a variety of ways to integrate mathematics—from the simplest understanding of number concepts to more complex problem-solving—with social studies. In the interests of clarity (my classroom life is never so neatly ordered), I outline these approaches as Connecting Math to Students' Lives; Linking Math and Issues of Equality; Using Math to Uncover Stereotypes; and Using Math to Understand History.

Connecting to Students

The starting point of many teachers is to build on what students bring into the classroom, and to connect curriculum to students' lives. Math is a great way to do this. I usually start the year with kids exploring, in small groups, how math is used in their homes and communities. They scour newspapers for numbers, cut them out, put them on poster paper, and try to give sense to their meanings, which at times is difficult. They interview family members about how they use math and write up their discoveries. As part of a beginning-of-the-year autobiography, they write an essay, "Numeric Me," tying in all the numbers that connect to their lives, from height and weight, to the number of brothers and sisters they have, to addresses, phone numbers, and so forth. I also ask them to write a history of their experiences in math classes, what they think about math, and why.

This process starts a yearlong conversation on what we mean by mathematics and why it is important in our lives. As the class increasingly becomes sensitive to the use of numbers and math in news articles, literature, and in everyday events, our discussions help them realize that math is more than computation and definitions, but includes a range of concepts and topics—from geometry and measurements to ratios, percentages, and probability.

As part of the autobiography project we also do a time line. We start by putting the students' birthdates and those of their parents and grandparents on a class time line that circles the outer perimeter of my classroom (and which is used throughout the year to integrate dates that we come across in all subject areas). The students also make their own time lines—first of a typical day and then of their life. In these activities, students use reasoning skills to figure out relations between numbers, distance, time, fractions, and decimals.

I also use another beginning-of-the-year activity that not only builds math skills but also fosters community and friendship. The whole class discusses what a survey or poll is and brainstorms questions that they would like to ask each other. After I model one survey, each student surveys their classmates about a different topic. Kids, for example, have surveyed classmates on their national origin, their favorite fast-food restaurant, music group, or football team, or what they think of our school's peer mediation program. Each student tabulates his or her survey data, makes a bar graph displaying the results, and reflects in writing on what they have learned. Later in the year they convert the data into fractions and percentages and make circle graphs. I encourage the students to draw conclusions from their data, and hypothesize about why the results are the way they are. They then present these conclusions orally and in writing.

This activity is particularly popular with my students, and often they will want to do more extensive surveys with broader groups of people. The activity lays the basis for more in-depth study of polling and statistics around issues such as sampling, randomness, bias, and error. For extensive curricular ideas on the use of polls and statistics in social studies, see *The Power of Numbers* curriculum published by the Educators for Social Responsibility.

Math and Inequality

To help my students understand that mathematics is a powerful and useful tool, I flood my classroom with examples of how math is used in major controversies in their community and in society at large. I also integrate math with social studies lessons to show how math can help us better understand the nature of social inequality. Kids are inherently interested in what is "fair," and using math to explore what is and isn't "fair" is a great way to get kids interested in all types of math concepts, from computation to fractions, percentages, ratios, averages, and graphing.

> **Kids are inherently interested in what is "fair," and using math to explore what is and isn't "fair" is a great way to get kids interested in all types of math concepts.**

For example, during October and November, there is often lots of discussion of poverty and hunger in my classroom, related either to the UNICEF activities around Halloween or issues raised by the Thanksgiving holiday. This is a good time to use simulation exercises to help children understand the disparity of wealth in the United States and around the world. In one lesson (explained in detail in "World Poverty and World Resources," on p. 92 of *Rethinking Our Classrooms*, Volume 1) I provide information on the distribution of population and wealth in the six continents, and then have children represent that information using different sets of colored chips. After working with students so they understand the data, we do a class simulation using a map of the world painted on our playground. Instead of chips to represent data we use the children themselves. I tell them to divide themselves around the playground map in order to represent the world's population distribution. I then use chocolate chip cookies, instead of chips, to represent the distribution of wealth, and hand out chocolate chip cookies accordingly. As you can imagine, some kids get far more chocolate chip cookies than others, and lively discussions ensue. Afterward, we discuss the simulation and write about the activity.

Not only does such a lesson connect math to human beings and social reality, it does so in a way that goes beyond paper and pencil exercises; it truly brings math alive. I could just tell my students about the world's unequal distribution of wealth. But that wouldn't have the same emotional impact as when they see classmates in the North American and European sections of the map get so many more cookies even though they have so many fewer people.

I also use resources such as news articles on various social issues to help students analyze inequality. In small groups, students examine data such as unemployment or job trends, convert the data into percentages, make comparisons, draw conclusions, and make graphs. This is a great way to help students understand the power of percentages. Because they also use a computerized graph-making program, they realize how the computer can be a valuable tool.

One group, for example, looked at news stories summarizing a university report on the 10,000 new jobs created in downtown Milwaukee due to commercial development. According to the report, African Americans held less than 8 percent of the new jobs, even though they lived in close proximity to downtown and accounted for 30 percent of the city's population. In terms of the higher-paying managerial jobs, Latinos and African Americans combined held only 1 percent, whereas white residents who are overwhelmingly from the suburbs took almost 80 percent of the new managerial jobs. Using these data, students made bar and pie graphs of the racial breakdown of people in different jobs and in the city population. They compared the graphs and drew conclusions.

They then did a role play, with some students pretending to be representatives of community organizations trying to convince the mayor and major corporations to change their hiring practices. What began as a math lesson quickly turned into a heated discussion of social policy. At one point, for example, a student argued that the new jobs should be split one-third black, one-third Latino, and one-third white, because those are the three principal ethnic groups in Milwaukee. Others, however, disagreed. Needless to say, this led to an extensive discussion of what is "fair," of reasons why minorities had so few of the jobs created downtown, and what it would take for things to be different.

Math, Stereotypes, and Voice

It is important for students to be aware of whose voices they hear as they read history books or the newspaper, or watch a movie. Who gets to narrate history matters greatly, because it fundamentally shapes the readers' or viewers' perspective. We can analyze these things with kids and help them become more critical readers of books and other media. In this process math plays an important role.

I usually start with something fairly easy. I have students analyze children's books on Columbus, tabulating whose views are represented. For instance, how many times do Columbus and his men present their perspective, vs. the number of times the views of the Taíno Indians are presented? The students, using fractions and percentages, make large graphs to demonstrate their findings and draw potential conclusions. Large visual displays—bar graphs made with sticky tape, for instance—are good points of reference to discuss and analyze. Math concepts of percentages, proportions, and comparisons can be used to help kids discuss the statistics they've uncovered and the graphs they've made.

A similar tabulation and use of percentages can be used to analyze popular TV shows for the number of "put-downs" vs. "put-ups," who is quoted or pictured in newspapers, stereotypes of females in popular cartoons, who is included in textbooks, and who is represented in the biography section of the school library.

Numbers and History

As we study history, we pay particular attention to dates and data. I try to highlight numbers that relate to social movements for equity and justice. For example, as we look at women's struggle for equality we try to imagine what it was like for Susan B. Anthony to go to work as a teacher and get paid $2.50 a week, exactly half the salary of the previous male teacher. Lots can be done with such a statistic—from figuring out and graphing the difference on an annual or lifetime basis, to looking for wage differentials in other occupations and time periods, including the present. I have found children particularly interested in looking at wages paid to child workers—whether it be in coal mines or textile mills. We compare such wages to the price of commodities at the time, to wages of adult workers, and to wealth that was accumulated by owners of industry. Such historical connections can be easily linked to present-day concerns over U.S. child labor and minimum wage laws or to international concerns over multinational corporations ex-ploiting child labor in Asia or Latin America to make consumer goods for worldwide markets.

One math/history connection that can range in sophistication depending on the level of the students is to look at who is represented in different occupations and areas of power in our society, and how that has changed over time. For example, students can figure out what percentage of the signers of the Constitution were slaveholders, common working people, women, wealthy individuals who held bonds, and so forth. A similar exercise would be to analyze U.S. presidents, or the people our country has chosen to honor by putting their faces on currency and coins. Such historical number crunching can take a contemporary turn if the students analyze the gender and racial breakdown of the U.S. House and Senate, the editors of major newspapers, or the CEOs of the Fortune 500.

I have found children particularly interested in looking at wages paid to child workers—whether it be in coal mines or textile mills.

It's important for students to understand that such numbers are not permanent fixtures of our social structure, but have changed as result of social movements such as the Civil Rights or women's movements. To demonstrate this, a teacher might have students tally the current percentage of African Americans or women in selected professional occupations and compare it to the 1960s, before the rise of affirmative action.

Another area is to teach the history of math, pointing out the contributions of various non-European cultures and civilizations to mathematical thought. Greek mathematicians, for instance, were heavily influenced by their predecessors and counterparts in Africa and Asia. Arab mathematicians inspired European Renaissance scholars. The Mayans were one of the first peoples to develop the concept of zero and make sophisticated mathematical calculations. I have used a unit on the Mayan counting system of a base 20 with my 5th graders to demonstrate such sophistication and to help students expand their understanding of place value.

Conclusion

The level of sophistication and complexity of the math we use in our classrooms naturally depends on the developmental level of our students. Teachers, however, too often underestimate what students are capable of doing. To the degree that I provide quality instruction, clear modeling, and purposeful activities, I am usually pleased with the enthusiasm with which my kids take on such math-based projects, and the success they have in doing them.

I have found that as a result of trying to implement "math across the curriculum"—and in particular, integrating math and social studies—my students' interest and skill in math have increased, in terms both of their understanding of basic concepts and of their ability to solve problems. Furthermore, they can better clarify social issues, understand the structures of society, and offer options for better social policies.

Kids need every tool they can get to make this world—their world—a better place. Mathematics is one such important tool. ▪

....

Bob Peterson (REPMilw@aol.com) was a co-founder and 5th-grade teacher at La Escuela Fratney in Milwaukee for 22 years, a founding editor of Rethinking Schools *magazine, and serves as president of the Milwaukee Teachers' Education Association. He has co-edited numerous books, including* Rethinking Columbus, Rethinking Our Classrooms, Rethinking Globalization, *and* Rethinking Mathematics.

Percent as a Tool for Social Justice

BOB PETERSON

An understanding of percentages is essential to know what's going on in the world. Unfortunately, in some math programs the concept is not even introduced in elementary school, and even when it is taught, textbooks and teachers tend to downplay its social and political significance.

Whether one wants to learn about issues of wealth, power, gender, culture, race, or discrimination, it's very difficult without the basic understanding of percent and the ability to understand and manipulate certain types of data.

Helping Kids with the Basic Idea

It makes sense to teach percent along with fractions and decimals, as they are all ways to describe parts of a whole or part of a set of things. I start by having my 5th-grade students list all they know about how people use fractions, decimals, and percent. For an initial homework assignment, they find examples of the three things at home in newspapers, magazines, and household items. (I stress they must bring in enough information so that we know the context of the number.) I provide newspapers for those students who don't have them at home. I also encourage them to ask an adult member of their household why they think percent is important. We make a bulletin board focusing on the power and omnipresence of these kinds of numbers.

I start by noting that the word "percent" comes from the Latin "per centum," meaning "per hundred." We talk about how many cents are in a dollar and I put 100 pennies in a plastic jar and keep it handy for percentage activities. I talk about "100" being that "special percent number" that allows us to easily compare one thing to another. I usually start out with something in the students' lives—like how many of them have a pet in their household, or how many homes have computers and then ask them how we might be able to compare whether our class is similar to kids across the nation or world.

It makes sense to teach percent along with fractions and decimals, as they are all ways to describe parts of a whole or part of a set of things.

Eventually I explain that the math concept of percent allows us to do that. We use that "special" number 100 and think, for every 100 kids, a certain number have whatever thing we are talking about. I then explain that if our class had 100 kids we could make an easy comparison by just counting the number of kids who had a certain thing. But since we don't have 100 kids in our classroom, I ask, how can we make it seem like—or more accurately, equivalent to—100?

I remind the kids we have my special jar of 100 pennies and with minimal discussion soon someone suggested that we divide the 100 pennies among us to see how much each of us is "worth." We pass out the pennies and each student usually is worth about four pennies—or four percentage points. We write this as an equation and see that 100 divided by the number of students in my class is about four. Each student is equivalent to 4 percent. Thus if nine kids have a grandmother or an elderly relative living with them, we multiply nine by 4 percent and we realize 36 percent of the students in the class have an elderly relative

in their household, compared to 25 percent of households nationwide. After several more polls of the class and group calculations most of the students have a rudimentary understanding of this aspect of percent. Through a variety of exercises we compare these values to fractions and decimals, attempting to get the students to understand the meaning behind the concepts and not just a rote algorithm of how to figure out percent.

To deepen students' understanding of these math concepts and their social significance I encourage kids to continue to find news articles and write about what the percent numbers mean to them—and put all that up on the bulletin board. Here are a few examples of "facts" that have spurred thinking, writing, and discussion:

1. During our school's annual "No-TV Week" my students survey the students in our school and use percentage and pie graphs to show among other things the number of kids who have TVs in their bedrooms, have cable, who can watch TV whenever they want, and who would rather spend time with parents than watching TV.

2. We use information from UNICEF (www.unicef.org) to compare our lives with those of children from around the world. For example, 20 percent of the children in "developing" countries are not enrolled in primary school, 71 percent of households in developing countries have access to safe water, and 42 percent have access to adequate sanitation. Like any other description of poverty, it is important for students to look at root causes and to ask the hard questions of why affluent governments, corporations, and people aren't doing what is necessary to change such situations.

3. In looking at discrimination and prejudice percent is key. As explained in "Teaching Math Across the Curriculum: A 5th-grade teacher battles 'number numbness,'" I have used local reports on discriminatory hiring practices as a way to bring math alive and delve into this difficult issue. After the students graphically portray such issues on circle or bar graphs, I set up impromptu dramatizations where some students are advocates for those being discriminated against and others are those in authority.

4. We look at online news services as quick sources of this kind of information (wire stories from several services are available at http://dailynews.yahoo.com). As an example, an AP story reported that the Geneva-based Inter-Parliamentary Union found that of all the parliamentary representatives in the world, only 12 percent are women, and only 7 percent of the parliaments are headed by women.

Of course the bottom line is what students do with this information that they discover. How can we best help them use that information to pose problems for further study, and share what they learn with others, and ultimately work with others to make the world a more equitable and just place? ■

....

Bob Peterson (REPMilw@aol.com) was a co-founder and 5th-grade teacher at La Escuela Fratney in Milwaukee for 22 years, a founding editor of Rethinking Schools *magazine, and serves as president of the Milwaukee Teachers' Education Association. He has co-edited numerous books, including* Rethinking Columbus, Rethinking Our Classrooms, Rethinking Globalization, *and* Rethinking Mathematics.

Michael Duffy

'I Thought This U.S. Place Was Supposed to Be About Freedom'

Young Latinas engage in mathematics and social change to save their school

MAURA VARLEY GUTIÉRREZ

I sat and talked with a group of 5th-grade Latina girls, their voices filled with urgency and excitement. We were gathered for our twice-weekly meeting of the after-school girls' mathematics club at Agave Elementary School* in the U.S. Southwest. I was the facilitator of the group, conducting participatory research as a part of my graduate studies.

---

*All names are changed to protect anonymity of research participants and research site.

The seven Latinas represented a range of mathematical abilities and confidence, as well as language skills (some bilingual in Spanish and English, some English dominant). On this particular January day, our usual opening activity of sharing stories from our lives turned to the subject of the school's potential closure, which had been proposed by the school district the week before.

At a community meeting attended by several of us the evening before, the district officials laid out their argument for closing four schools, claiming that they used an objective, neutral, mathematical procedure for determining which schools to close. The girls' discussion covered a variety of concerns about the potential impact of the closing on their community. "It's not fair, though!" Zara insisted, drawing attention to what the school district left out of its arguments: the social impact of the school closings. This led to a heated discussion that included sharing personal stories and knowledge about the community, voicing concern for others, expressing disagreement with the district's arguments, and suggesting ideas for how to save the school.

> **Our math-based participation in the community movement proved to be a powerful experience for both the girls and for me as an educator.**

After a semester of building community within the group and investigating topics such as prison vs. education spending in our state, we had planned to explore school safety. However, given the news of the school closures, we shifted the club's focus because, as Margarita reasoned, "What point is there to do school safety if there's gonna be no school?"

Between January and the final school board vote in April, the Agave community mobilized to defend their neighborhood school—a school that had been attended by generations of primarily Latino families. Zara's assertion that the closure was "not fair" seemed an ideal place to begin to push our conversation to how we might specifically use mathematics as a tool for participating in this mobilization. Our math-based participation in the community movement proved to be a powerful experience for both the girls and for me as an educator.

The Mathematical Investigations

The district argued that Agave was a good candidate to be closed because of its proximity to the proposed receiving school (1.3 miles) and its "underperforming" label based on standardized tests. When the girls questioned these arguments, I helped them shape their ideas into mathematical problems that they could solve. This evolved into a unique contribution to the community movement to save the school. We focused on alternative analyses of test score data and the school's achievement label, and on the walk students would have to take to the new school.

During our discussion, the girls asked, "How can they say we are un[der]achieving?" I helped the girls break this broad question into smaller parts that could be solved by students with a range of mathematical experience. I provided the students with details about the district's argument and introduced the girls to a district website with several years of test scores.

Zara decided to analyze test score data over time. She saw a trend toward improvement despite the school's failure to meet NCLB goals. She also disaggregated the scores by gender in order to show a trend of higher test scores for girls. Then she and Alma worked together to represent these trends in a double bar graph. In a letter to a board member, Zara wrote, "As you can see, every year we keep going up or are almost the same. For example, 40.4 percent of the girls passed the AIMS test three years ago, and two years ago 54.3 percent of the girls passed the test. Three years ago 26.5 percent of boys passed the test, and two years ago 40.4 percent of boys passed the test. Please think about these things when you vote on Tuesday." Margarita asked the board to put the test scores into a larger context. Referring to the strong partnership between Agave and the local community center, she noted that some schools "are really high [achieving on tests] and all, but do they have things that prevent kids from going to bad places, from doing bad things? Here [at Agave] we do."

After finding alternative ways to evaluate Agave's achievements, we examined the impact on the community of students attending a different school. The fact that all of Agave's students would be transferred to a single school (Samota) was described by the district superintendent as "seamless." The voices of community members and conversations in the girls' group revealed that the move would be anything but seamless for the families of Agave. Although busing would be provided for elementary-aged students who lived more than 1.5 miles from their school, most of the students who lived close to Agave would be left without school-sponsored transportation.

The girls and I decided to investigate the walk to Samota in several ways. We took the walk between the two schools ourselves, timing our journey and documenting it with videos and photos. We walked 13 blocks in 40 minutes. Then we created a map to determine our rate for walking. Most of the girls began to test whether two minutes per block was a reasonable estimate. Some solved this by multiplying two times 13. Others used repeated addition by drawing a series of 13 connected rectangles to represent the blocks; they put a two in each rectangle to represent the minutes. When a rate of two minutes per block resulted in a total walking time of only 26 minutes, the girls tried three minutes per block. They found that rate resulted in a total walking time of 39 minutes, only one minute less than our actual time. Zara decided that the extra minute was accounted for by the time used to take pictures. Drawing on her experience, Zara argued that her solution was sensible.

Having been exposed to survey work related to the 2008 presidential primary elections, Margarita suggested we ask students "what they think about the school closing." She then predicted, "I bet you it's gonna be a high number" and suggested that "if you just ask a whole bunch of people, then we can say how much people agreed that it shouldn't close."

Alma suggested a second survey question: "How about we [ask about] the number of kids who walk to school, take the bus, and have their parents drive them to school?" The survey revealed that approximately half of the students who attended Agave walked to school, and walking was often their only available form of transportation. For many families, walking to Agave worked because it was a neighborhood school, while walking to the new downtown school would involve additional dangers and a significantly longer walk. Michelle described the walk by saying, "When we went to go take the walk it seemed pretty dangerous because of all the construction sites. And some kids might go through there, and it might not be a pretty picture."

We decided to also include a question that collected data on the location of students' homes in order to calculate the average walking time it would take students to walk to the new school, using the rate we had determined from our walk. Michelle created a list of the intersections where students reported their homes were located. Then Margarita and Vane located these intersections on our wall map of the neighborhood, and all of the girls determined distances and calculated potential walking times to Samota based on the estimated walking rate. Following my suggestion, they used a line plot to represent the spread of all of the walking times.

The structure of the mathematical problems involved multiple entry points and could be solved in a variety of ways, which invited participation from girls with varying levels of understanding of mathematical concepts.

In general, the structure of the mathematical problems involved multiple entry points and could be solved in a variety of ways, which invited participation from girls with varying levels of understanding of mathematical concepts. The mathematical skills included quantifying, determining rate, calculating percent, analyzing data, and determining an appropriate representation. The problems encouraged collaboration because of the many skills necessary to complete our complex tasks, including designing surveys and collecting, organizing, and representing large amounts of data. Vanessa described the importance of this collective mathematical activity: "When you work together and you find out what [a peer's] strategy is, you might be interested in that one and you might find a new way to do it." Having the whole group contribute to the counterarguments allowed for a collective sense of arguing against the closures. This supported the participation of all of the girls, rather than only those who tended to be successful in the traditional classroom.

"People Together Make Such a Big Difference"

The girls participated in and contributed to a variety of aspects of the movement, including writing letters to board members, speaking at community forums, and attending board meetings. We shared the results of our mathematical investigations in a digital story that we produced and presented at a forum attended by 600 community members, including students, teachers, parents, business owners, and city and state officials. Although the district conducted this particular forum, the community organized a rally prior to the meeting that involved singing, speeches, and forming a human chain around the entire school. Having participated in events as a part of the larger community movement, the girls learned about the arguments of both sides. They saw community members participate, they spoke in front of the board members, and they saw how decisions were made. In effect, the girls learned about the system they sought to change.

It was apparent from the community forces that organized to defend this primarily working-class, Latino community school that a vote to close the school could have negative political consequences for the elected board members. In April, despite intense pressure from the district superintendent, the board members ultimately voted not to close the schools. Margarita described what she learned from the project: "I learned that if you work together you can do something—you can make a difference.... I would say teamwork is important because people together make such a big difference, not just one person."

Throughout their reflections and conversations, the girls expressed a sense of responsibility to give voice to younger students who might not otherwise have a say in the process. Once again, Margarita explained:

> As 5th graders they say we're role models and [as] role models, we should be able to help and speak up. It's like you're being a role model for so many people. And you're showing them that if you speak up you can make a difference.... And then if [the possibility of school closure] ever comes across when we're not in this school anymore and it happens again, they know what to do.

"A Chance to Speak Your Mind"

Because this was one experience in these girls' lives, I can make no claims of lasting influence; because it did not happen within their mathematics classroom, I cannot verify shifts in classroom learning. However, I am convinced that, as educators, we must continually find ways to give students experiences of this sort within classrooms and other educational settings. If the primary goal of education is to engage students to become active citizens prepared to participate in social change, then connecting classroom learning with community movements becomes essential.

Despite the implementation challenges in our increasingly restrictive educational environment, Margarita's voice offers a window into the possibilities of critical education. She came to me one day in the middle of this journey and said that she needed to get her ideas out, writing the following: "I finally am in a group that gives you a chance to speak your mind when something very important is happening (which everyone should feel like they spoke their mind, but not everyone has experienced that yet. I finally have after nine years). I thought this U.S. place was supposed to be about freedom and people speaking what they felt."

....

Maura Varley Gutiérrez is the director of teaching and learning at Elsie Whitlow Stokes Community Freedom Public Charter School in Washington, D.C. As a graduate student at the University of Arizona and with the Center for the Mathematics Education of Latinos/as (CEMELA: NSF grant ESI-0424983), she worked with young Latinas on critical mathematics.

Jean-Claude Lejeune

Who Do We Hear?

Language is power. And this is as true in the mathematics classroom as in the English classroom.

JESSIE L. AUGER

The language of mathematics is considered "scientific"—free of opinion, emotion, and personal connection, a language of truth and facts. But the relationship between math and language is far more complicated.

A student's ability to use "academic" words can be misheard as proof of mathematical knowledge, and the absence of these same words can be misheard as a lack of knowledge. Thus a child raised in the dominant culture is often heard as "smart," "articulate," and "mathematical" even though his ability to use the conventional words may mask confusion and uncertainty. A child whose way of speaking differs from that of the "academic" world, meanwhile, is at risk of being unheard. Her mathematical ideas are likely to go unrecognized.

In my classroom I have shaped my practice with the goal of trying to truly hear all of my students' own voices. As a white teacher, I have to be aware that society has trained me to recognize white voices most easily.

Because I grew up as a working-class female and have developed feminist and class consciousness, I also have experiences that help me to recognize voices outside of the dominant culture. I strain to become aware of language and the powerful role it plays in school success and failure. I try to see and understand the complex relationship between knowledge and language.

> **I strain to become aware of language and the powerful role it plays in school success and failure. I try to see and understand the complex relationship between knowledge and language.**

What follows are three examples of students' mathematical discussions from my classroom of 1st and 2nd graders in a public school in Cambridge, Mass. This particular year, about two-thirds are students of color, mostly African American, from working-class or low-income families. About one-third of the students are from white middle-class families.

In math class, I routinely ask students to develop their own problem-solving strategies and to record their ideas in their own ways. Students explain their thinking and questions as they discuss problems and construct mathematical understanding together. During these discussions, I point out connections between students' ideas, maintain high expectations for listening to each other, and model how to ask for clarity. In this way, the students learn that their own ideas are always the starting places for problem-solving.

Real-Life Fractions

On one particular day we had been discussing fractions, and we had worked on a number of problems from real-life situations that involved the fractions one-half, one-fourth, and one-third. I then gave the students some problems to work on their own. Jahmai asked me for help on the following problem: "Fabienne had $6.30. She spent one-third of it on a gift for her baby brother. How much money does she have left?"

"What do you know about this problem?" I asked.

"I know Fabienne has $6.30 and she spent one-third of it for a present," Jahmai said.

"What would one-third of $6 be?" I asked.

"I don't get it," Jahmai said.

"What does one-third mean, one-third of something?" I asked.

"I forget."

"What does one-half mean, one-half of something?"

"It's when you split it in half so each person gets the same."

"So, what does one-third mean?" I pressed.

"Oh yeah! It means when there are three people and you split it in half. Like we each get the same."

"So if you have to figure out one-third of six dollars…?"

"Yeah I know," said Jahmai. "We would each get two because it would be split up so we each got the same."

Jahmai used the words "split it in half" to express his understanding of the mathematical idea of dividing something up into any number of equal parts; what was important was not the number of parts but that they are consistently equal. His understanding became clear when he further explained what it would be to "split up" $6 into thirds.

However, if I had stopped Jahmai when he originally explained his understanding of one-third as "it means when there are three people and you split it in half," I might have thought that he had no concept of one-third and that he only understood halves. I probably would have corrected him that one-third does not mean "split it in half."

By continuing to listen to his ideas, though, I discovered that Jahmai knew exactly what he was talking about, and that he did understand what one-third meant. I decided that I did not need to go back to what he had said in his explanation and say, "So you didn't mean 'split it in half,' you meant 'split it equally.'" I decided to allow Jahmai's meaning to exist in his own words. I knew that in subsequent discussions about fractions, other students would help him to clarify the term.

As the teacher, I had to keep listening and asking questions to try to get at Jahmai's understanding. An easy mistake is to retell students what we thought they really meant in our own words. I try to always be aware that language can both mask and reveal knowledge.

Graphing Temperatures

Another example comes from a discussion between two students over a math problem I had assigned. We had been taking the temperature and recording it on a graph every day, and comparing the different temperatures. The problem was: "The temperature was 28 on Monday, 37 on Tuesday, and 27 on Wednesday. What is the difference between the temperature on Monday and the temperature on Tuesday?"

Joshua: "I don't really get it."

Fabienne: "I can help. OK, you know, like how are they different?"

Joshua: "I don't get it. I mean, I know they're different. But I don't get how are they different."

Fabienne: "OK. Tuesday's warmer, right?"

Joshua: "Yeah."

Fabienne: "So how much is it? Like how far from 28 to 37?"

Joshua: "Oh you mean like what's in between?"

Fabienne: "Yeah, like to get to 37."

Joshua: "Oh I get it. Like you mean you go 28 to 37 and how much is it."

Fabienne: "Yeah, like they're different, that's how much they're different."

Not only is Fabienne's explanation not the expected mathematical language of "take 37 and subtract 28 and that's the answer," but it shows that her thinking about the problem is much more complex in terms of the real relationships between the temperatures 28 and 37. She is able to express a sophisticated understanding of number relationships in terms of quantity

and direction, a more algebraic understanding of subtraction rather than simply the arithmetical idea of "take-away."

Joshua, meanwhile, is able to engage with her immediately because they are peers and because there is the expectation in the classroom of listening for understanding. Students know they should take all the time they need to try to say just what they mean in their own way. Thus Joshua and Fabienne expect that their language will be identifiable to each other.

> **Because of the way that they are talking to each other, Joshua is also able to express his idea of "what's in between," a remarkable understanding of the wholeness and complexity of number relationships.**

Because of the way that they are talking to each other, Joshua is also able to express his idea of "what's in between," a remarkable understanding of the wholeness and complexity of number relationships. He becomes more solid in his own understanding by articulating his ideas and having them recognized by Fabienne. Consequently, they both further their understanding of the problem and the mathematical relationships involved and they expand their ability to express their ideas mathematically.

Owning Language

A final example has to do with teaching my students a word that is recognized as a standard mathematical term and the ways in which they worked on making the word their own.

We had been working on geometry for about six weeks. During these weeks I had asked the students to describe in their own words different shapes they noticed in their physical surroundings, to draw different shapes and to make them out of various materials. After many discussions and sessions where students worked together as a class to create mutual understandings of geometric descriptions, I had taught them some of the standard mathematical names for specific shapes such as "pentagon," "hexagon," and "trapezoid."

I asked them to create and compare different kinds of shapes within the same categories. The day before the one described here, I had asked the students to work in partners to make four different hexagons on a geoboard and then copy and cut each one out on dot paper. During this discussion, the idea of "sameness" of the shapes came up again, as it had in previous discussions. I taught them the word "congruent," explaining that it is a word that mathematicians use to describe the idea of "sameness" that they had been describing. The students tried out the word in different ways.

The next morning as we were all sitting down for classroom meeting, Manny said, "What me and Eli had for dinner last night is congruent because we both had spaghetti." Many students responded with excited agreement that that situation of "sameness"— spaghetti dinners — could be a possibility of congruency.

During math class later that morning I asked the pairs of students who had worked together the day before to choose two of the four different hexagons that they had made to share with the class. We gathered in a circle on the rug and I called on pairs of students to put their two hexagons in the middle of the circle and share about them — how they made them, what had been difficult, and what they had noticed in the process. They then took questions and comments from the group.

Manny put his shape out, which was exactly the same as Christopher's, who had shared before him. From the group came excitement, whispers: "That's the same." "That's like Chris'." Many hands went up. Manny called on Jelena who had her hand as high up as she could make it go.

Jelena: "That's...it's...it's...ca–ca–gru–int with Christopher's! Because, because it's the same...because it's ca–gru–int...because...they got the same sides and it's ca–gru–int 'cause...it's the same."

Everyone was listening to Jelena. No one interrupted the pauses.

Manny (listening, looking at Jelena with respect)**:** "Are you done?"

Jelena: "Yeah."

Joyce: "I agree with Jelena because it is ca–gru–int. Because it has the same sides and same corners and it's the same, like the same size. It is ca–gruent."

Jelena was using the word "congruent" for the first time. She was making her understanding of the word and of the relationship between the two hexagons as she spoke it.

She used the word to get her mathematical idea out, at the same time that she used her mathematical idea to try out and make the word hers. Her pronunciation, her emphasis, her body, the pauses in what she said, made it clear that this was happening. And the attentiveness of the other students made it clear, too. They knew it was important—mathematically and linguistically—the moment she said it. They were all in it with her, together.

In order to participate in discourse—to understand and to be understood—there must be common ground between participants. When teachers, particularly white teachers, fail to understand what students of color, girls, and low-income students know, it is not just because there is a lack of common ground. Rather, it is often because the teacher fails to recognize that the ground is not common. This unrecognizing, though usually unconscious, is purposeful because it comes from the ideas that society has ingrained in us about intellectual inferiority based on class, gender, and race. Teachers are taught to teach from the place of these dominant beliefs about "intelligence."

We must learn to recognize the diverse language that our students use to express their mathematical understandings as specifically mathematical language.

Too often, teachers do not acknowledge our students' ground as different and, in schools, unwelcome. We simply expect them to step over onto the school ground. Because they don't match the place that we have learned to teach from, we refuse to recognize their ground. And then we cannot hear their words or recognize their intellect.

To make a change, our job as teachers is twofold. First, we must expand the idea of what constitutes mathematical language. We must push out the constricting and exclusive walls that enclose the authoritative words as the only real mathematical language. We must learn to recognize the diverse language that our students use to express their mathematical understandings as specifically mathematical language.

Second, we must ensure that students of color, girls, and low-income students — all those to whom the "authoritative" language has not traditionally belonged — have access to the traditional, standard, academic mathematical language. All students need to learn, use, and come to own the dominant academic language. Students must have the experience of learning and using these words in order to see that they came from human ideas and processes of expression. Only then can students demystify the academic language and learn how it came to be known as official and standard in the mathematical world. ▪

....

Jessie L. Auger teaches 1st grade at the Rafael Hernandez Bilingual School in Boston. She was part of the 2005 USA Today Teacher Team of the Year and was the 2007 Massachusetts Teacher of the Year.

A Social Justice Data Fair

Questioning the world through math

BETH ALEXANDER and MICHELLE MUNK

The gym roars with 50 different conversations. Around the walls, and throughout the room, students stand before their projects. Most are pasted on poster board, others on reused pizza boxes. Over the din, the girls describe their work to fellow students, teachers, and a handful of "willing listeners"—volunteer adults (parents, mostly) who have come to find out what the kids have learned.

Along the back wall, the 5th- and 6th-grade classes present their findings from the school waste audit. The 1st- and 2nd-grade students have studied how hard it is to live on the "welfare diet"—the contents of the average food bank recipient's weekly allotment— and have created graphs to show what they, and their families, have eaten that week. The older girls have prepared individual projects. Melanie, 7th grade, wondered if children with autism received the same amount of funding as children with other disorders, and her results are strikingly demonstrated on a bar graph. Mi-sun, 9th grade, used a line graph to demonstrate that Korean students, among all nationalities, are most likely to commit suicide. Andrea, 7th grade, used a scatter plot to investigate the correlation between GDP and carbon dioxide emissions. On a table, the results of the 6th-grade class's collective research is illustrated, with labeled bags of rice offering a three-dimensional representation of what the world eats every day: China has a huge pile; Iceland just a few grains.

The lights flicker on and off, and the conversations die down. "We're halfway finished," Michelle calls out. "It's time to switch! Those of you who were presenting should now listen, and those who were listening should now present!" The noise picks up again.

The Social Justice Data Fair has been held at the Linden School in Toronto for the past several years. It is an opportunity for our math students to use data management skills to study issues they're concerned about. The fair is an example of how our independent, girl-centered school for students in grades 1 to 12 tries to include topics of social justice in our curriculum. Compared with other Toronto-area private schools, our school is quite culturally diverse, and we enroll students from many nontraditional families. Most of our families support learning math through the lens of social justice. (Parents have commented how much they enjoy having their daughters bring math class conversations to the dinner table.)

There is increasing evidence that case studies enable students to form meaningful connections with their mathematics and lead to greater learning—especially for girls.

We, like all teachers, feel the pressure to cover a packed curriculum in a limited amount of time. In Michelle's case, data management accounts for only a few expectations in her 7th-grade curriculum—what one would expect to cover in a few classes. Preparing students for the data fair takes several weeks, putting the crunch on other important topics. There is increasing evidence, however, that case studies enable students to form meaningful connections with their mathematics and lead to greater learning—especially for girls. The Ontario curriculum, which we follow, also encourages making real-life connections, and this helps justify our program.

The Social Justice Data Fair really came into its own by its second year. For the first year, not all classes participated. Some teachers needed to see how it worked before committing to participate. This type of initiative requires all the participating teachers to create meaningful course content beyond their textbooks. It has been exciting to see how each teacher supports students to make those connections in age-appropriate and grade-relevant ways.

Start by Asking Questions

We teach girls, and girls have historically received messages that they are not good at math. These messages are often self-fulfilling. A social justice pedagogy, in addition to introducing social justice topics into the curriculum, must reduce barriers to learning for all students. It must engage students as agents of change in the world, and encourage them to view their skills—in math and elsewhere—as tools for enacting that change.

The traditional school curriculum takes today's social and environmental conditions mostly for granted. The world just is; students are not encouraged to approach it with a curiosity about how it got to be this way. Social justice math, on the other hand, begins with our curiosity about the world and especially about the world's unfairness. Thus a key part of the curriculum at the Linden School is promoting the habit of thoughtful questioning. In math classes, we use the inquiry process to reinforce the idea that knowledge is built from evidence that the students collect themselves. For example, we teach principles of geometry by conducting experiments.

"What do you know about triangles?" Beth asks her grade 5/6 split.

"They have three sides," blurts out one student.

"And three angles," adds another, "and if all the angles are the same, it is an equilateral triangle."

After this, the students find it harder to come up with ideas.

"Are there any other rules that triangles have to follow?" Beth prompts. "For example, do the angles have to be a certain size?"

The students are not sure about this. Slowly, Brianna raises her hand. "It depends on how big the triangle is. If it is bigger, the angles can be bigger."

"Well, let's find out. Today, I want each of you to run an experiment on triangles. Just like you would in science. Think of a question you wonder about triangles, then find an answer. How will you do that?" Beth turns and writes four words on the board: Question, Hypothesis, Observations, Conclusion. "Those are the steps you'll need to follow today."

"Not 'Procedure'?" asks Natane.

"No, not today."

"Yes! That means less writing." Natane pulls out a piece of paper.

The students are familiar with the scientific method. Through years of in-class investigations and annual science fair projects, we hope they see that the process of science allows anyone at all to ask a question and to find an answer. Experiments, run by people from all walks of life, formally and informally, form the basis of everything we know about the world around us. It is not a stretch, then, to apply this idea to math. Later, when we prepare for the social justice data fair, the girls are primed to use math to answer their own questions.

Keisha is constructing different triangles to see what will happen when she adds up the angles.

On her third triangle, she shouts, "Hey, do they always add up to the same thing? I'll try a bigger one." She does, using her ruler to draw a triangle that covers the whole of a new page. Double-checking with her protractor, she writes down the size of each angle. "Again!" she shouts. The girls around her laugh.

"So," says Beth, "why do you think that happens?"

By the end of the class, Keisha isn't quite sure why her angles always add up to 180 degrees. That's not important, at least not yet. What's important is that she asked a question and found an answer. And the answer, most importantly, didn't come out of the textbook or from the teacher. Social justice education is not just about recognizing problems; it's also about helping students recognize their own power to find answers. They need to trust in their own authority—not just ours.

> **What's important is that she asked a question and found an answer. And the answer, most importantly, didn't come out of the textbook or from the teacher.**

Something similar is happening in the 7th-grade classroom, where students are learning about percent. Michelle is encouraging students to present different strategies for solving problems. This reinforces the idea that questions can be approached in different ways, that the person doing the inquiry doesn't uncover the answer so much as she constructs it.

"Who can calculate this percent?" asks Michelle, referring to a problem on the board.

Mahera comes up to the board and writes her solution.

"Is this correct?" Michelle asks the class.

"No, you did the steps in the wrong order," suggests Marla.

"Yes, it's right, but I do it a different way," says Nicole.

"What do others think?" prompts Michelle.

A lively conversation follows, where students discuss the validity and merit of different ways of approaching the problem.

After Michelle gets the students' attention again, she continues the lesson. "Now it's your turn. Come up with your own percent questions."

Making Meaning Out of Numbers

The Social Justice Data Fair takes place in April, after nearly a full year of practicing inquiry skills in math and in other classes. To prepare for it, the girls start, once again, by asking questions. The 5th/6th-grade class started with a question that had bothered some of the students: Why do the garbage, recycling, and compost get all mixed up in the school containers? After gathering the contents of all of the school's containers, we took the waste up to the roof—the location of our urban school's playground—and, amid some squealing, began the messy, smelly task of sorting and weighing it. The girls were particularly interested in locating "forbidden" trash like disposable Starbucks containers, which are no longer allowed into the school. They also wanted to know how much of the total waste was food packaging, which is discouraged under our Litterless Lunch program. After determining the total masses of categories of waste (like paper and aluminum), as well as measuring the amounts of waste that were sorted incorrectly by the school community, we had an interesting set of primary data. We added this information to the results of our school survey, which gathered information about our population's habits and attitudes when it came to generating and dealing with their garbage. From there, the students used further questions and a variety of graphs to answer them. Which floor generated the most waste? Were we producing more waste than in previous years? Did the location of bins have an effect on how well sorted they were?

The upper grade students, who work independently on their projects, start by selecting an appropriate topic. Some girls find it easy to come up with their topic; they arise out of issues they're passionate about. The 7th-grade class had learned about national and per capita carbon dioxide emissions when we studied scientific notation, and many students were affected by the Copenhagen Climate Conference, so we had quite a few projects on this topic. Alina and Brigit were both concerned about species extinction, so Alina focused on tigers and Brigit chose elephants. We help students who have trouble choosing something by brainstorming topics as a group, looking in the newspaper for ideas, and describing projects from previous years. The goal is for each girl to be excited about using math to dig deeper into a topic that interests her.

> ## The goal is for each girl to be excited about using math to dig deeper into a topic that interests her.

Once the students have selected a topic and have had it approved, the next step is to develop a thoughtful research question. We discuss as a class what makes an investigable question, and then students work to hone their questions into ones that are clear, specific, and can be answered using quantitative data. The students keep in mind that they must produce at least two different types of graphs, and this affects the questions they pose. Sometimes the question development process takes some time, since students must do some preliminary research to find out what kind of data are available. After some research, 7th grader Nicole's concern about homelessness in Toronto turned into two questions: What diseases most commonly affect Toronto's homeless population (bar graph)? And what reasons do homeless people have for not sleeping in a shelter (pie chart)?

The next step is collecting data. Students decide whether it is more appropriate to gather primary or secondary data for their topic and question. For example, Helen, a 7th grader who loves green sea turtles, worried about their declining population. Michelle, her teacher, suggested some online resources, and

Helen learned about the age distribution of turtles in the Pacific. Then she analyzed her data to determine what types of graphs would best represent it. From there, she looked for trends and outliers, and was ready to start compiling her work for presentation.

Fair Day Arrives

The day before the fair, we have a dress rehearsal. The students practice presenting their projects to their classmates, and get feedback. Michelle had planned to act as facilitator for her class, to prompt discussion and to ensure that the space was safe for students to risk asking questions and risk making mistakes. To her delight, no facilitation is necessary: She just sits back and watches math happen.

Heidi stands by her bear-shaped project board. "I learned a lot from this project, but I still want to know if stopping climate change would help the polar bear populations grow again, and I also wonder if polar bears will adapt to having less ice by changing their habits," she concludes her presentation. "Are there any questions?"

A half-dozen hands shoot up. "I really liked your presentation, by the way. I love your board! I was wondering, why did you decide to use a bar graph to represent the populations?" asked Melanie.

"Why did you focus on those regions?" Alina wants to know.

"It's neat how you made the bars different colors," comments Alisa.

"Do you know how they find those numbers?" asks Nita.

Michelle sees students proudly sharing the product of several weeks of hard work, including background information, graphs, and analysis. She is familiar with the projects, and she has worked with the students to develop good research questions, find data, and use spreadsheet software to create graphs. But what impresses her are the discussions that follow the presentations. Students engage each other on the topics they researched, and on the math they used to analyze their data. They use their data management skills to justify their choices and defend their conclusions. We want students to feel that they have legitimate questions and comments to share about the math, about the thinking that their classmates were sharing.

Before students leave the gym on the afternoon of the fair, they are asked to hand in their "passports"— a brochure in which they've answered a series of questions about the student presentations they attended. The last question is "What did you learn?"

Kayla: "There are more females than males living with low incomes."

Madison: "Black men are more likely to be executed than white men."

Georgia: "8th graders from Singapore have the highest test scores in mathematics."

Meirion: "Green sea turtles are going extinct."

Zaketa: "The average North American purchases 4,000 calories of food each day, but throws 30 percent away."

Nita: "There is too much social justice to fit in this box!" ▪

....

Beth Alexander teaches at the Linden School, an independent girl-centered school in Toronto. Michelle Munk teaches at City View Alternative Senior School, a social justice-focused middle school in Toronto.

Bob Peterson

5.

Laboratory for Justice: Science Across the Curriculum

Sometimes students make sense of scientific concepts and theories in surprising ways. The global ecological crisis our students are inheriting will require that they apply their personal understanding of complicated scientific ideas to devising solutions and acting for change. Teachers must offer students plenty of time to relish the natural world in the intimate space of their classroom and to act on their learning in their communities. Both critical thinking and scientific understanding emerge from curiosity and imagination. Science is not just a body of received knowledge, but a way to inquire about the world and address its problems.

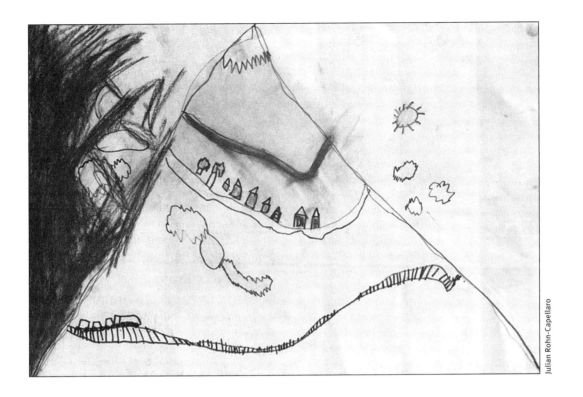

Julian Rohn-Capellaro

Exploring Our Urban Wilderness

A 2nd- and 3rd-grade teacher helps his students discover the natural world in their urban environment

MARK HANSEN

My students' home terrain consists — at least on the surface — of houses, streets, schools, and stores. Like many urban kids, the bit of unpaved, unfenced nature my 2nd and 3rd graders have access to is the domain of blown trash, sewage treatment smells, and "stranger danger."

But even the most beleaguered of cities have hidden and not-so-hidden pockets of natural resilience. In Portland, Oregon we have the Columbia Slough, a once-heavily polluted ancillary channel of the Columbia River that most of my students have been warned to stay clear of. It's not a pristine wilderness, but it's a wild space within our city that has provided many opportunities for my students to connect with their environment.

Several years ago, I set out to explore both the concept of watersheds and the wild spaces in the slough with my students.

I wanted to bridge the gap between science curriculum and local communities. Ask students what they know about the impact of deforestation on animal habitats and if they offer any answers at all, I'd wager they are more likely to bring up the Amazon than the impact of urbanization and industrial agriculture on the songbird populations in their own communities. This lack of grounding may help explain why critical ecological issues like global warming, groundwater pollution, and deforestation seem so remote to most children.

I wanted to help my city kids gain an organic connection to questions of environment and a concrete understanding of how ecosystems work. In previous years I felt I had squandered the learning potential of my school's patch of urban wilderness and reinforced my students' dislocated and disconnected sense of their natural surroundings. By studying the slough and the Columbia River watershed, my students have gained a sense of their impact on the world and how the choices they make — literally — trickle down.

Exploring "Place"

During my first years of teaching, I walked with students around the community, exploring the public housing project where many of them live. I wanted them to get a sense of their part of the city and how it fit into the larger urban landscape. I wanted them to have a very local and personal understanding of the forces that had shaped the community. I had them draw maps and write the stories of the busiest corners.

I wanted them to find the links between their own stories — of moving into a new house, of climbing trees with their baby cousins, of getting into trouble, of arriving from a different country, of finding new friends — and the stories they read about the history of Portland. This kind of connection across time can be daunting for most 8-year-olds, but my students made startling connections between the recent arrival of some students from Mexico and the African American families who moved to our neighborhood during World War II.

We made 3-D plans of what our part of the city would look like if they were in charge of the massive Hope VI urban renewal project now under way. They composed poems to their favorite plum trees and fire hydrants and wrote letters arguing for their preservation when the bulldozers came through. They paid homage to their favorite places and voiced what they thought was lacking (accessible shopping, a library, a clinic, rooftop gardens). Teams designed ideal neighborhoods, which we presented to city planners and families in the community. I wanted them to think rigorously about the constituent elements of a healthy and happy community. What does a community need to function? Which features are absolutely necessary?

> **I wanted to help my city kids gain an organic connection to questions of environment and a concrete understanding of how ecosystems work.**

I evaluated them on the plausibility of their communities, whether or not people actually could and would want to live there. I invited architects and planners from the housing authority to explain the criteria they were using to redesign local public housing. My students debated whether a redesign was even necessary if it would mean that local residents would be displaced while the reconstruction was happening. Fantasy plans for large houses with swimming pools began to give way to more community-centered features like parks, "old folks houses," and "a bigger school!"

Cecil* even convinced his group to pare down the size of housing, because "you don't want to have to clean all that."

Mapping Flora and Fauna

As I rode my bike around the neighborhood one day, I remembered LaTia arguing for "more nature, like wild animals," in our neighborhood. I'd agreed with her notion, but her planning team had ultimately dismissed nature as a low priority. Our focus was steadfastly "urban."

I decided that we would map the flora and fauna of our neighborhood. I wanted students to start identifying the wild features where they live. We walked the neighborhood again, noting the kinds of trees that grew in parks and in people's yards, looking for wildflowers in the brambles by the railroad tracks. We revisited work they had done in 2nd grade on the animals that inhabited the neighborhood. I had them return to their maps and add places where plants grew untended and where animals might live. The crucial development in our ecological study of the area came when a little blurb in the newspaper tipped me off that a new bike trail had opened a few blocks from our school, allowing access to the Columbia Slough.

I had taken for granted that my school lacked access to natural and wild settings. Early in my career, I had worked with suburban 5th graders monitoring a stream near their school, but it seemed impossible to expose my urban students to hands-on field science. I realized that there was no excuse for keeping my students cooped up in my class reading about the workings of some fictitious, abstracted watershed when they could walk five blocks to the wetland that drains our own watershed and get their hands dirty.

I wanted my students to learn about the ongoing negotiation between the world of trucks, houses, and pipes and the world of trails, nests, and sloughs. I wanted them to see that they lived in both of those worlds whether they stepped into the latter or not. I wanted them to apply their scientific and civic understandings of their world in complex ways to address the notion of sustainability. I wondered if a sense for the ecological processes taking place in the watershed would broaden and tie together their sense of the processes at work in our "built" neighborhood.

I wrote a letter/permission slip explaining to our families that there was a paved and frequently used path we would use, that we would not be in the water, and that children would be under direct supervision at all times. I also took the opportunity to invite them to join us in becoming slough scientists. Every single family responded positively, and a handful of brave parents said they would do what they could to come along.

Before our first trip I tried to explore what my students already knew about the slough. They thought that it was stinky and polluted because it is so close to the sewer treatment plant in our neighborhood. They thought the water was poisonous and that there were a lot of weeds there. All of what they said was negative. It was clear that part of our project needed to focus on rehabilitating the reputation of this little patch of wild space. I wondered how kids whose only immediate experience with nature was so grim could

possibly maintain an optimistic outlook for the future of the environment. I wanted to foster an ecological sensitivity and concern while staving off the pessimism that your average unit on the prospects of global rainforests can instill.

I asked what they wanted to know about the slough and they offered: "Is the slough safe?" "What will we see there?" "Do people live there?" "What animals live there?"

I added my own questions, letting them know that I was learning here, too: "How is our neighborhood connected to the slough?" "How does it feel to be there?"

The Urban Wilderness

Following the little map in the newspaper, we crossed the busy trucking lane that separates my school from the slough and entered a thriving urban wilderness. It's a complicated terrain, unlike any notion of wilderness I had ever entertained, completely consistent with the contradictory landscape I described above. Some kids were still reluctant to go, writing in their science notebooks that they anticipated it being "smelly and nasty."

The slough drains our watershed, and contains a curious mix of occupants. It is home to both Portland International Airport and endangered western painted turtles. There are small mountains of stacked shipping containers and low, marshy islands that hide Great Blue Heron rookeries. Coyotes and deer skulk along the railroad tracks, passing thick stands of cottonwood trees and acres of Subarus and Toyotas fresh from their berths in tanker ships.

The slough was also home to Vanport, Oregon's first large African American community, which was destroyed by a massive flood in 1948. I was aware of the enormous contradictions of the Columbia Slough's landscape, but I had yet to connect them to my school's neighborhood or to my own curriculum.

On our first few trips, fears about bad smells and danger abated as we spotted red-tailed hawks, woodpeckers, and raccoon tracks only a few yards from the railroad. We noticed tall Douglas firs that had a mysterious vine creeping up them and evidence of beavers chewing on some of the willows near the water. We saw a city landscaper working in a dirt field near the train tracks and asked him what he was doing. He explained that he was seeding the area with native

J. Amesbury

in no rush to answer these questions, because I believe healthy disequilibrium is at the heart of critical and scientific thinking. And frankly, the kids were not prepared to think that way without a lot of science instruction and time to mull over the issues.

I first asked kids to reflect in their journals about how they felt when they were in the slough. Some answers were negative:

"I was bored and I don't like walking so far," wrote Matthew.

"My mom said I can't get my clothes dirty, so I'm not going next time," Attiana wrote.

Some could not find enough exclamation points:

"I was really happy! I'm going to take my brothers there on our bikes!! And maybe I will show them the coyote scat!" wrote Angel.

Some students began to connect their actions to the state of the watershed. Tiana wrote the following:

Today it was raining and I am mad because Mr. Hansen said if it rained we can go back to school, but he lied. But I am having fun. Five minutes ago we saw some frogs and for now we saw one lizard. ... Now Mr. Hansen is talking to those kids about our toilets, saying whatever you do in the toilet will go down to the slough sewer place. I didn't like it here [at] first but now it is like part of an interesting place. I think we should find a way to make sure the water stays nice, not toilet water. I think the slough shouldn't be so dirty from the city and the cars. These trucks are too loud. Where are they going? Where do all these animals come from? They better stay away from the trucks. We could clean this up. Bye.

Tiana's answer wanders, but I hear her trying to find herself in this new environment.

My students were beginning to understand the relationships that structure our environments, both

grasses to keep the soil from washing into the slough when it rained. On the bridge over the slough we noticed an interesting bird in the water that "looked like a stork," according to Laney. Camille wasn't convinced so she consulted the bird guide her dad had stowed in her backpack. It turned out to be a great blue heron. Jabari and some others discovered coyote scat with evidence of rabbit fur. Mallard ducks swam away as we tromped down toward the shore one day, trailing some startled ducklings. Students began to fill their journals with lists of our sightings.

Was the area really even part of our "neighborhood" if it had so many animals in it? We were, after all, residents of a city.

I was as astonished as the students were at the abundance of animal life. I started to ask them to reevaluate their connection to the watershed: What did it mean that there was an ecosystem in our area healthy enough to support predators like coyotes? Was the area really even part of our "neighborhood" if it had so many animals in it? We were, after all, residents of a city. I was built and unbuilt. They were beginning to think in terms of systems, a skill they can then apply to other frameworks, as Ibrahim did in his science journal:

The reason I like nature is I like to collect information and details when we go on trips. I think that the city is our habitat but instead of rabbits there are cars. The cars need gas for their food and they need the streets and parking lots for their shelter. That's why there are gas stations in every part of the city.

Ibrahim was thinking of the city as a place with features that can be explained by the connections between them. I doubt he would have made those connections if he hadn't gotten so close to the rabbit warrens in the brambles of the slough.

As the year drew to a close and we went on our last trip, I asked the kids to return to our original questions about the slough and reflect on how their thinking had changed. Some had little to say. A few said a little about seeing animals, which was fine, but didn't say much about themselves or the connections that they found. Many kids echoed Marta, who wrote:

I changed a lot. I like nature a lot. I learned about plants and birds and the city environment. I used to hate to get dirt on me, but now I don't mind. I will be a scientist.

I was most touched by Cortney, a girl who had been initially reluctant to explore our watershed and had shown little interest in finding her place within it. She wrote, "I learned that nature is not just a thing. It is something that you discover."

I wish Cortney had written more, because I was heartened to hear that she was more engaged than she had appeared. And she was right on target: Nature is not just a thing that can be learned in a year, and neither is a city. They are both about discovering relationships over time, many of them very personal and very local. ▪

Mark Hansen teaches in a combined 3rd- and 4th-grade classroom at Peninsula K-8 in Portland, Ore. He is a co-director of the Oregon Writing Project. The names of the children in this article have been changed.

David McLimans

Polar Bears on Mission Street

4th graders take on climate change

RACHEL CLOUES

In June, when my students and I reflected on the highlights of their 4th-grade year, I was moved to learn how deeply the class was affected by our Polar Bear/Global Warming Project. They felt a strong sense of accomplishment about this community service project, which for me had been a big lesson in activism and hope.

"The project was a lot of work, but it was fun too," one student told me. Several of them asked, "If we want, can we keep working on it over the summer?" One of the students,

Cecilia, explained that at first her dad did not believe in global warming, but by the end of our project she felt she had convinced him it's an important — and real — problem.

It all began with "Feeling the Heat," an article in *Time for Kids* magazine about the sad plight of the polar bears as they face melting summer ice. I read the article out loud to my class, hoping to familiarize them with the issue of global warming. Not surprisingly, the text brought up many complex concepts for my 9- and 10-year-old students, all English language learners, some of them newcomers. (My school, Sanchez Elementary, is located near San Francisco's Mission District and is comprised of 63 percent English language learners, predominantly Spanish-speaking.) I struggled to find clear ways to answer their questions and respond to their comments, realizing that although I understand the basics of climate change, I

> **I didn't feel like I had the tools or the inspiration to tackle the issue with my students. However, it kept coming up in my classroom, over and over during the next several weeks; my students were fascinated by the polar bears!**

wasn't prepared — emotionally — to talk about it with children. I felt completely hopeless about the possibilities of slowing global warming or doing anything that could help the polar bears.

"I know!" one student, Maria Luisa, offered enthusiastically. "Let's collect money to save the polar bears!"

"This isn't really the kind of problem money can just fix," I responded curtly. I admit that I was overwhelmed by the immensity of the problem and my students' earnest, yet understandably naive, desire to find a quick solution. How could I explain to 4th graders that the world, especially this country, has a literally life-threatening addiction to fossil fuels? Or that the oil industry dominates government decisions? Or that policy change moves slowly and often backward? I couldn't figure out how to convey hope to my students, or in any way be positive about the looming crisis of global warming.

Of course we had a brief discussion of simple, proactive steps offered in the article (turn off lights, drive less) but after that, I pretty much dropped the topic of global warming. I didn't feel like I had the tools or the inspiration to tackle the issue with my students. However, it kept coming up in my classroom, over and over during the next several weeks; my students were fascinated by the polar bears!

"Polar Bear SOS"

In the springtime, my principal asked all of the teachers at our school to carry out a community service project with our classes to honor César Chávez, whose birthday is a state holiday in California. He suggested simple possibilities such as cleaning the schoolyard, working with younger students, or collecting garbage at a local park. Our timeline: one week to carry out the project and present it to the school for César Chávez Day.

Around that same time, a friend forwarded me an email from the nonprofit Natural Resources Defense Council asking for contributions to fund an educational advertisement for national television. NRDC's "Polar Bear SOS" campaign was supporting a proposal by the U.S. Fish and Wildlife Service to list the bears as "Threatened" under the Endangered Species Act, and it was also raising awareness about global warming. The poignant ad, narrated by children, showed photos of polar bears struggling to survive in their melting habitat. Viewers would be encouraged to submit comments online at NRDC.org in support of the Endangered Species Act proposal. If the bears become officially recognized as "Threatened," then the government will be required to take steps to protect them. And since melting arctic ice is now indisputably linked to global warming, this opens up possibilities for legal support requiring car manufacturers and industries to reduce carbon emissions. I decided to tell my students about the campaign, retract my statement about money not being helpful in solving the problem of global warming, and see if they wanted to raise funds to send to NRDC.

There were a few other ideas for community service projects, but the 4th graders voted unanimously to take on a fundraiser for the newly named Room 18 Polar Bear Project. They really liked the idea of doing something in response to the article we had read, which seemed to have created significant empathy for the polar bears. Taking into account that my school's families are generally poor (71 percent of students receive free or reduced lunch), I adopted a very modest attitude about the project. "If you want to ask your parents for a couple of dollars to donate, that would be great," I told them. "Bring in what you can." I also told my students that we would be spending the next few days learning as much as we could about global warming.

That evening, I spent some time thinking about and planning a few lessons to get us started. I was aware of the short timeline, but I felt like breaking away from our nominally scripted curriculum and desk work and focusing on an issue relevant not only to our school community, but to the global community as well. In the spirit of César Chávez, who confronted injustice directly and thought out of the box, it seemed worth tackling. A key point I wanted to help students comprehend is that the polar bears are in danger of losing their unique habitat due, in large part, to the actions of humans. By understanding and teaching others about the causes and effects of global warming, we could begin to help solve the problem. A different part of this project, I realized, was teaching students that another way to create change is by financially supporting organizations that work toward the same goal on a larger scale.

I found helpful resources on San Francisco's excellent Department of the Environment website (sfenvironment.org). I downloaded and copied short, kid-friendly articles with graphics in both English and Spanish. I asked students to work in small groups and use highlighters to pick out and discuss interesting facts and concepts. Then, as a large group, we talked about what questions had come up. I tried to clarify confusing sections, for example those involving the atmosphere, by drawing pictures and making diagrams on the whiteboard. The next day I took my class to the computer lab where we explored NRDC's website, including the polar bear ad. We read about how cars and industries overload the atmosphere with carbon dioxide, exacerbating the greenhouse effect. Because we live in an urban community, it was easy for my students to see how too many cars on the road create air pollution, and understand the benefits of public transportation. My students underlined these

important facts and other information in their copies of the articles, and each of them went home that day with the information in Spanish. I asked them to share what they were learning with their families.

In an attempt to better convey the concept of the greenhouse effect, which was difficult for my students to grasp, I designed a simple, age-appropriate model. I used a small, stuffed cloth earth ball and put it inside a plastic ziplock bag. In front of the students, I blew air into the bag and sealed it, to show them how the atmosphere is a thin layer of air around our planet. I took the earth ball out, dampened it with water, and put it back inside the bag. We put the model in the sun for an hour or so, and while the water heated up, evaporated and condensed on the inside of the bag, the children began to see how the earth stays warm enough to sustain life.

"It's just like the windows on our car," one student said. "When it's sunny outside, it gets really hot inside!"

"Exactly," I replied. "Some heat feels good and is important so animals and plants can live on Earth. But pollution in the atmosphere, like carbon dioxide, traps heat and makes the planet too hot."

"That's why glaciers and ice caps are melting!" My students seemed to make the connection back to the polar bear article. The plastic bag did, indeed, function as a real greenhouse. It was a rough model, but it was better than nothing.

I suggested that the class figure out a way to share their learning with other students in the school, so that our project might have a bigger impact. An artistic group, the students quickly decided to make bilingual posters to put up around the school, in the shape of polar bears, with tips to stop global warming. All over the school we posted these messages: "Take the bus instead of driving," "Ride your bike and walk more," "Turn off your lights when you're not using them," and "Donate money to NRDC.org in Room 18 to help the polar bears!" If we had had more time, it would have been great to send pairs of students from our classroom to visit each classroom in the school. As it was, a couple of students wrote a letter to distribute to every teacher, to be read out loud to their classes. The letter explained our project and asked for contributions to our campaign for the polar bears. "Dear Teachers and Students," it began.

"We are learning about Global Warming in Room 18. You can help by not using your cars because the pollution is going into the atmosphere. ..."

Esteban's Success

On day three of our project, an amazing thing happened. One of my students, Esteban, arrived with his parents at our classroom door, holding fistfuls of money, which he eagerly thrust toward me — crumpled dollar bills and coins, all spilling onto the floor. Excitedly, he explained to me that the previous evening he had walked down Mission Street — the bustling, lively center of the predominantly Latino

> **When I looked around at my class — 100 percent engaged in making posters, writing letters, reading more information, and counting money — I also realized they were getting an authentic taste of activism.**

Mission District where he lives — and talked to passers-by about our Polar Bear Project. Esteban had carried around his copies of the bilingual articles, which explain the basics of global warming, and he shared them with the strangers who stopped to talk with him on the street. "If they spoke English, I showed them the article in English, and if they spoke Spanish, I used the one in Spanish," Esteban explained to me when I asked him how he had approached the passers-by. "I just told people about why it's important to help the polar bears, and how we can stop global warming. I told them our class is raising money to send to NRDC."

When we counted out Esteban's money, it turned out to be more than $100, and nobody could have been prouder than Esteban (though his parents were very proud, too). His classmates and I were amazed and impressed, and everybody was energized to try to raise more money. "I'm going to ask everybody in my apartment building to donate money!" shouted several students.

By the end of the week, Room 18 had raised almost $300, and everybody in our school was talking about the Polar Bear Project. Children from other

classrooms would come to our door to drop their quarters, dimes, and nickels into our can. Teachers, volunteers, and our school principal all contributed money.

What thrilled me the most, however, was the way the term global warming was rolling off the tongues of my 4th graders. They were able to articulate, to anyone dropping by, concepts like what produces greenhouse gases; how the atmosphere traps heat; why polar caps and glaciers are melting; and, most importantly, many of the simple ways we can all help curb the problem. I was relieved to realize that the project had moved beyond a "Save the Polar Bears" campaign and toward genuine understanding of a complex global problem. When I looked around at my class — 100 percent engaged in making posters, writing letters, reading more information, and counting money — I also realized they were getting an authentic taste of activism. Esteban, who is a smart but sometimes socially awkward kid, was the obvious leader and hero of our campaign.

César Chávez Day

The Polar Bear Project culminated on the day before César Chávez Day, when our school welcomed Rita C. and Lydia Medina, the sister and niece of César Chávez, who spoke to students and staff. These women, along with other family members, have established nonprofit organizations to promote and apply the legacy of César Chávez. Rita Medina, well into her 80s, continues to march each year in support of farmworkers. After some inspiring words from these great activists and leaders in the farmworkers' movement, each class presented their community service project.

My students were visibly proud. Together as a class, they stood holding their posters and talked about the issue they had taken on and the money they had raised to help the polar bears, who, they explained, are part of our global community. "The ice where polar bears live is melting, and we want to help save them. We need to stop global warming," they told our school community. Rita and Lydia Medina congratulated me and my students and told us how impressed they were with our example of activism. They said their brother and uncle, César Chávez, would be proud. They pulled out their pocketbooks in front of everybody and contributed their own donations to our can of funds. It was an incredible honor to be recognized publicly by two such inspiring social justice leaders.

That evening, I sent our donation to NRDC. My attitude toward teaching about global warming had completely changed. I still feel overwhelmed by the problem, of course, but the feeling of hopelessness has

> **By deciding to walk down Mission Street and talk about global warming, Esteban inspired many of his classmates to go out and talk about what they were learning.**

been replaced with a real sense of hope. I am inspired that a classroom of kids cared enough to go out and ask for money to help save the polar bears. By deciding to walk down Mission Street and talk about global warming, Esteban inspired many of his classmates to go out and talk about what they were learning. Their ability to speak two languages was clearly an important tool.

The children felt empowered by the information they learned from reading and discussing, as well as the sizable fund they collected. Everybody, including

myself, seemed energized after stepping away from textbooks, workbooks, and standardized tests and focusing on a hands-on project. They acted, spoke, and felt like activists. Then, fortunately, they had the opportunity to be recognized by adult activists who look like them and share their linguistic and cultural background.

I also realize that I can and should teach students about global warming, whether it is overwhelming to me or not. It is a community service project—in the largest sense of the word community—to which all teachers can contribute by sharing information with their students. NRDC sent polar bear bookmarks and a handwritten thank-you card to my class. They ran their ad on television and thousands of people responded in support of placing polar bears on the Threatened and Endangered Species list.

There is growing publicity and, perhaps, a shift in consciousness regarding global warming in our communities. The example of César Chávez and his family reminds me that turning knowledge into action is powerful, and creates the potential to overcome what at first seems impossible. ▪

....

Rachel Cloues is a teacher-librarian at a K-8 school in San Francisco.

AP Photo / John McConnico

Measuring Water with Justice

A multidisciplinary lesson that explores water issues

BOB PETERSON

"Who actually owns the water?" one of my students asked me as I introduced a mini-unit on water to my 5th graders.

"Well, who do you think does?" I responded.

"The government!"

"Nobody!"

"Bill Gates!"

"The fish!" were among the chorus of replies.

I wrote the question and responses on a wall chart that listed what the kids knew about water.

The students already knew many basics: About 70 percent of the earth is covered with water; most of it is salt water; it exists in three different forms; most of our bodies are composed of water; and more.

Their questions included: Who contaminates water? What country has the most water? How much does water cost? Does the chlorine put in the water in the state's largest water park hurt animals?

I told students that they could add more questions throughout the day and I would type and categorize them for us to discuss the next day.

I had decided to do a water unit for several reasons. I wanted the "data and statistics" unit in the math curriculum to be engaging and socially relevant; the school science night loomed a couple weeks ahead; and I had learned some fascinating things about water on a recent trip to the Tijuana border area during a Rethinking Schools "From the World to Our Classrooms" curriculum tour. I had been particularly amazed at how much water cost in the impoverished community of Chilpancingo, just outside of Tijuana.

I had more specific goals as well. I wanted students to not only learn the importance and power of data in understanding significant scientific phenomena and problems, but also to get some practice in representing that data and communicating it to others. And I wanted students to learn more about water—the availability of which they take for granted—and the central role water plays in our lives ecologically and socially.

After school I categorized the students' questions, pulled relevant books from our school library, and downloaded images from the internet to make a short PowerPoint presentation. The presentation included the students' questions, images of people from Africa and Asia collecting water, and the aftereffects of oil spills.

The next day we reviewed a couple of key math concepts and skills. I had each student draw and label a circle graph of the percentage of the earth's surface covered by water. In the process we reviewed equivalent fractions and percent. We looked at a chart of a person's average water usage in the United States and calculated how much water a person would use over the course of a week and year.

Then I showed them the PowerPoint presentation and some books I planned on sharing with them. We concluded by sharing the students' previous day's questions, which I had divided into four categories:

- Water basics—fresh and salt water; how much do we use?
- Who can get clean water?
- How much does water cost?
- Oil spills

Images of oil-soaked birds and seals generated the most interest, and I realized that if had let the students indicate their preferred areas of study, all would have chosen oil spills. I decided to postpone the choosing until the next day, and instead read to them the picture book *Prince William*, by Gloria and Ted Rand, a fictionalized account of the rescue of a baby seal during an oil spill.

For homework that night I asked students to record every time they used water and estimate how much water they consumed.

That evening I decided to divide the oil spills category into two: oil spills of the world and the Exxon Valdez oil spill. That would allow more students to focus on oil spills and their consequences. I also decided to have all the students do a science/language arts activity on oil spills to tap their interest.

The following day I explained in more detail the five topics, the questions they would try to answer, and some suggested activities they might engage in. I asked students to list their top three choices on a piece of paper.

I told the class that since many students were interested in oil spills I had changed my plans to allow for that: They would all conduct a science experiment using feathers, oil, and water, and write diaries from the perspectives of ocean animals harmed by oil spills.

Science Experiment

Working in groups, the students examined the simulated impact of oil on a feather and how easy it is to wash off. One student in the group poured a mixture of vegetable oil and cocoa (added to give the appearance of darker crude oil) into a glass of water. The groups made observations of what happened to the oil, such as "The globs of oil went to the top."

Then I gave each student a seagull feather that I had collected from the Lake Michigan shore. The students dipped the feathers in a cup that had the oil and water mixture and made more observations:

"The feather gets heavier and skinnier," said one student.

"It got messy and oily," another added.

I encouraged them to imagine how the oil might affect a water bird. "It probably became so heavy that it couldn't fly or find food," Jose said.

They then tried to clean the feathers by dipping them into three different solutions: cold water, warm water, and warm water with detergent.

"It's hard to clean off a feather," Aliza said.

"Detergent and warm water work really good together to clean feathers, maybe a whole bird too," Zuleyeda concluded.

Afterward, we cleaned up and I made sure everyone washed their hands.

Writing on Oil Spills

I read aloud and we discussed another picture book, *Washing the Willow Tree Loon*, by Nancy Carpenter and Jacqueline Briggs Martin. The book describes how a bird is rescued from an oil spill, cleaned, and returned to the wild. I also gave each student a two-page fact sheet on water and pollution from the National Oceanic and Atmospheric Administration (NOAA) website. (See end of article for URL.)

After reading both materials we brainstormed all the different animals that might have been affected by the spill and what aspects of their lives would have changed. I had each student choose one animal from the list and asked him or her to write from that animal's perspective. Before writing, we talked about what might be in an animal's "diary"—how it first saw the spill, how the oil affected its food supply, living situation, members of its family, etc. The students worked on their animal diaries during writing workshop and continued them for homework. The next day they worked with their peers to write second drafts.

The writing on the oil spills grew naturally out of the science experiment and the books we read. Over the next couple of days all the students completed their diaries. Eventually, the students glued their final drafts to construction paper, added either a drawing or an internet photo of an oil-soaked animal, and displayed them on the bulletin board. The writings were uneven. Some students used lots of details about how the animals might have reacted to spills, and a few had the animals die immediately.

Aliza wrote from a duck's perspective:

I was swimming until blackness filled the water. A beautiful day it was, until it started to get very cold. I thought I was a Popsicle, frozen, couldn't move, could hardly breathe. I tried to clean myself but the taste was unbelievable. So disgusting like black coal, thick, hard to swallow. I tried to escape, I tried to fly but I couldn't. I was trapped. That whole day I thought I was going to die.

Another student, Margarita, described the thoughts of an otter:

Then some black ooze came toward us. It was smelly, thick, slimy, and smelled gross. It covered all of me except my head. It was like glue, I couldn't move. The black ooze was everywhere. I thought what is this? Will I die, are these the last days of my life? Then suddenly this person took me to a place that had a sign saying "Rescue Center for Animals." Of course I didn't know what it meant. I was wondering where I was. I couldn't see any water.

When we were inside, they put me into water and it was so relaxing. They cleaned me off and it felt great. I heard them say, "We got the oil off and she looks great." I wondered what oil was. One thing was for sure I was cleaned off. I was saved. I was so content these were not the last days of my life. I was the happiest otter ever.

Although the writings were basic, they encouraged the students to look at human-made phenomena from the perspective of other species. I think in this country we not only take too many things for granted—like the availability of water—but we rarely stop to think about the impact of our actions on nonhuman species, as well. Perhaps this exercise pushed students a bit in the direction of what some call ecological literacy.

Water Basics

I posted the research groups at the beginning of the day so students could finish complaining about who they were or were not with before math time started. At the beginning of the math period I reviewed my expectations for group work, especially the requirement that all students need to be engaged and that students need to stay in their assigned groups. I also presented a list of activities that I expected each group to complete during the next four math/science periods. I reminded students to show their math work, to use their own words in presenting information, and to put their final work on a trifold poster display board.

The "water basics" groups worked on graphically showing the role of water in everyday life. They graphed the percentage of water covering the earth's surface, the amount of water in a human being, and the amount of water that a typical person from the United States uses every day. One of the group members exclaimed: "Water is everywhere. Inside you and you use it all the time. It's almost like we are fish. Well, not really."

Students in the group working on who has access to clean water were among the most startled. Reading the book *For Every Child: The U.N. Convention on Rights of the Child in Words and Pictures* and a selection from the Universal Declaration of Human Rights,

Students in the group working on who has access to clean water were among the most startled.

they found that access to clean water is considered a human right by various international conventions. They were surprised that despite this, 18 percent or 1.1 billion people don't have access to clean water. Using data from the UNICEF website they wrote, "Every day 5,000 kids die because of dirty water and poor sanitation — that means 242,000 kids die in a year because of water." Using the book *What's a Million?* they wrote, "More than 1 billion people don't have clean water in their house. Can you imagine how many zeros 1 billion has? One billion has nine zeros! If you started counting to 1 billion it would take you 95 years."

The group spent considerable time printing photos from the Internet depicting how different people get water. I insisted that they write a caption describing each picture and identifying its location. Two of the group members wrote a dialogue poem between two girls — one with clean water and one without clean water — contrasting two very different lives. (See poem on p. 247.)

The group wrote "Clean Water Is a Right!" in huge letters on their poster board.

Water Access and Cost

The group researching water costs had a hard time tracking down data because of differences in how water costs are reported, and rates that vary on the amount of water use. Students ended up comparing the costs of water in Milwaukee, Chilpancingo, and Cochabamba, Bolivia.

The data that the group used were varied and interesting. The water costs from Milwaukee were based on my water bill. Some students were surprised to learn that we pay for water at all. The information on water prices from the community of Chilpancingo I had collected as part of the curriculum tour I had taken. We found water costs in Cochabamba on the web. We even found scans of actual water bills for individuals, showing a spike in prices once Cochabamba officials privatized the water, contracting with Bechtel, the giant transnational corporation.

The students made a chart that had information on the cost of water per gallon and per 100 gallons, the minimum wage in the area, and percentage of daily minimum wage to pay for 100 gallons of water. The contrasts were startling. They found that "in Milwaukee people pay $1.18 for 748 gallons of water. One hundred gallons of water cost only 15 cents. The minimum wage in Milwaukee is $5.15 per hour and $41.20 per day. The percentage of the daily minimum wage to pay for 100 gallons of water is about one-third of 1 percent. In Chilpancingo the people pay 15 pesos, about $1.50 for 44 gallons of water that a truck delivers to their homes, which lack running water. So 100 gallons cost about $3.00. The minimum wage in the area is $5 per day. The percentage of the daily minimum wage to pay for 100 gallons of water is 60 percent!"

The group filled a plastic milk jug with water and labeled how much it would cost in Milwaukee and Chilpancingo.

The group didn't make a direct comparison for Bolivia because the pricing varied depending on the number of cubic meters. They concluded, "The cost went high because some new people — the Bechtel Company — bought the water company. They doubled the prices or in some cases raised them by 50 percent. After lots of protests in which people got killed, the government took back the water company from Bechtel."

Ivory, one of the group members, wrote:

In Chilpancingo, Mexico, people pay three cents for a gallon of water. That's about 20 times more than what people pay in Milwaukee. In other words, we can get 20 gallons for what they pay for one, and people in Milwaukee make more money in the first place.

In conclusion, we think everybody should pay the same prices for water as in Milwaukee. It's not fair that in Chilpancingo people have to pay so much money for so little water, especially because it takes up about half of their salary. For the amount of money that people in Tijuana pay for 44 gallons we in Milwaukee could get 1,000 gallons. We learned that water is expensive in some places and in some places it is cheap. In Bolivia the people protested to keep price of of water lower. Next time I drink a cup of water I am going think to how much it is going to cost in other places.

In retrospect, I probably should have raised the impact of the possibility of people limiting consumption in these places — in the United States because of a tendency to waste water, and in Mexico and Bolivia because of its expense.

Oil Spills and Exxon Valdez

The students studying oil spills graphed the number of oil spills, starting in 1970, and then marked the location of the 50 largest ones on a large world map. They also made circle graphs that showed the causes behind large oil spills (more than 100 tons) and smaller ones, noting that "the larger ones usually are caused by collisions (28 percent) or grounding (34 percent), while the smaller spills usually happened during loading and discharging." They were surprised that the Exxon Valdez oil spill, which we had all read about, was not the largest spill ever.

The group looking at the Exxon Valdez had the most information of any group — in the form of children's books and websites. They wrote a brief history of the spill, drew a map of the affected area, and included photos of oil-soaked sea animals.

To show how much 11 million was — the number of gallons of oil dumped in Prince William Sound by the Exxon Valdez — students filled a plastic one-gallon milk jug with water dyed with food coloring to make it look like oil. Then they set it next to a math sheet with 5,000 dots that the class had used in a previous math assignment. The group calculated that it would take 2,200 pages of paper, each with 5,000 dots on it to equal the amount of oil spilled by the Exxon Valdez. "Just imagine all that dirty stuff going out into the water," said one student after finishing the calculations.

The group reflected on its research:

We learned that 11 million gallons of oil spilled when the Exxon Valdez ran aground trying to avoid icebergs off the coast of Alaska in Prince William Sound. The water was polluted and it killed millions of animals like seabirds, otters, seals, whales, eagles, and millions of salmon and others. The carcasses (the dead bodies) of more than 35,000 birds and 1,000 sea otters were found after the oil spill but since most carcasses sink, this probably is only a fraction of all those who were killed. The best estimates are 250,000 seabirds, 2,800 sea otters, 300 harbor seals, 250 bald eagles, up to 22 killer whales, and billions of salmon and herring eggs.

Science Night and Reflections

Each group made an oral presentation to the rest of the class. The presentations were somewhat anticlimactic because they were laden with data, and the students hadn't carefully thought through the best way to present the material. The two most engaging parts of the presentation were the dialogue poem and the students' new knowledge about the large numbers of people who do not have access to clean running water in their homes. I challenged students to not use the faucets in their homes for the entire next day.

I intentionally asked the group reporting on oil spills to present immediately after the one on the *Exxon Valdez*. In helping the students research, I was shocked to learn that from 1972 to the present there were 19 oil spills larger than that of the Exxon Valdez, including three that released seven times as much oil.

The final connection students made was when they looked at the pictures of the street demonstrations in Bolivia, where people protested the privatization of their water supply: "That's just like in the Civil Rights Movement," said one student. "The women's fight to vote movement, too," added another. "Geesh, just for clean water," added a third. "That's amazing."

The afternoon before science night, the students set up their displays close to the bulletin board that had the animal diaries. When parents arrived, they read the diaries as well as the information on their display boards. Several expressed surprise at some of the information students had gathered, including the amount of oil spilled throughout the world and the number of people without access to clean water. A number of the parents had grown up in rural Mexico where they had to spend lots of time fetching clean water, so they told students they heartily agreed that water should be a basic right for all.

Unfortunately, not all the groups had a student member attend science night, so not all the children heard the positive feedback from the parents.

One indication that the students valued the project is that they all wanted to take the final project home. In addition, students regularly asked me if they could start working on their water projects. The project suffered, however, from some of the same problems group projects often suffer from: In a few cases a couple of people did more than their share of the work, which led to some feelings of resentment. I tried to address this through the individual writing assignments and by assuring students that I was observing who was doing what work. Next time, I will have students reflect in writing on both their roles as group members as well as what they learned overall from the project. I also plan to give individual feedback to each student.

I also realize that we never answered the crucial question: Who actually owns the water? Or a related question that we uncovered while researching oil spills: Why is there such a thirst for oil?

That's one of the benefits of teaching. There's always next year. ▪

....

Bob Peterson (REPMilw@aol.com) was a co-founder and 5th-grade teacher at La Escuela Fratney in Milwaukee for 22 years, a founding editor of Rethinking Schools *magazine, and serves as president of the Milwaukee Teachers' Education Association. He has co-edited numerous books including* Rethinking Columbus, Rethinking Our Classrooms, Rethinking Globalization, *and* Rethinking Mathematics.

Websites

http://response.restoration.noaa.gov/index.html
Office of Response and Restoration, National Ocean Service, National Oceanic and Atmospheric Administration. Includes age-appropriate background information and descriptions of science experiments.

www.democracyctr.org/
The Democracy Center, located in Cochabamba, has lots of information on water struggles in Bolivia.

www.unicef.org
Do a search for "water" on the site and find many useful articles.

Books

For Every Child: The U.N. Convention on Rights of the Child in Words and Pictures, by Caroline Castle (text adaptation) (Phyllis Fogelman Books, 2001).

How Much Is a Million? by David Schwartz (Scholastic, 1985).

Prince William, by Gloria and Ted Rand (Holt, 1992).

Sea Otter Rescue, by Roland Smith (Dutton, 1991).

Spill: The Story of the Exxon Valdez, by Terry Carr (Franklin Watts, 1991).

Troubled Water: Saints, Sinners, Truths, and Lies About the Global Water Crisis, by Anita Roddick with Brooke Shelby Biggs (Anita Roddick Books, 2004).

Washing the Willow Tree Loon, by Jacqueline Briggs Martin and Nancy Carpenter (Simon & Schuster, 1995).

Mike Trokan

Water Dialogue Poem

We are 11-year-old girls.

I get my water in my house.

I go to the sink in my kitchen
and turn on the faucet.

When I turn on the faucet I can drink
hot or cold water right away.

I can take a shower or bath in my house
for as long as I want.

My mom puts our dirty clothes in the washing machine
and the washing machine does all the work.

I am happy to have clean water in my house.

We are 11-year-old girls.

I get my water from the river.

I have to walk a mile to the river
and scoop it up with a bucket.

I have to boil my water because
it is contaminated.

I have to take a bath in the river.

I have to wash my clothes direct in the river
and I have to do all the work myself.

I wish I had clean water in my house.

— *Alejandra Guevara and Brenda Villanueva*

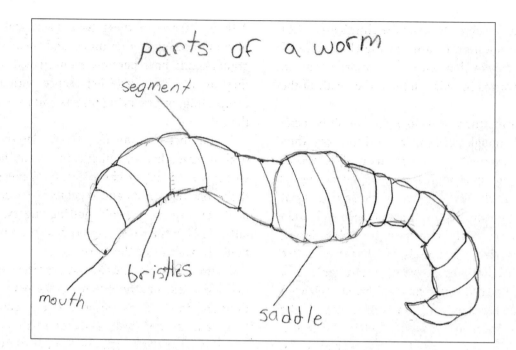

Learning from Worms

RACHEL CLOUES

Each September the reaction in my 4th-grade classroom is predictable: "Worms? Gross! Why can't we have a real classroom pet, like a rabbit or a guinea pig?"

Rabbits, guinea pigs, turtles, and other more conventional pets are fine, but there are many reasons why I prefer setting up a redworm compost bin in my classroom each year. Worms require much less daily care and they provide endless opportunities for learning about cycles, systems, decomposition, food, soil, science inquiry, and basic ecological connections.

More important, I find that having a worm bin helps children develop empathy, combat stereotypes, and gain respect for all forms of life on earth.

Our classroom "vermicomposting system," which is simply a five-gallon plastic box with a lid and holes drilled in the bottom, sits off the floor a few inches over another lid that collects drips. The bin provides a home for more than 1,000 California redworms, a variety of earthworm that can be ordered online from a number of different worm farms (see resource list) or purchased at a local plant nursery.

During the first week or two of school, the students and I prepare the bin for the worms and make predictions about what will happen in the worm bin. I ask students what facts about worms they already know, and I make a chart for the wall. I also write down what they are interested in finding out. Inevitably, someone states that worms can be cut in half to make two new worms; I respond by saying I have heard cutting worms kills them, and we agree to write the child's statement instead in the question column of the chart. Later I will bring in books that teach the children that, in fact, cutting worms in half results in the death of the worm.

The day I bring the worms to school we sit in a circle and shred enough newspaper to fill the box. Then we add water, mixing with our hands until it feels as moist as a damp sponge. This serves as bedding for the worms and also as a source of carbon. In front of the students I create the first nitrogen-rich food supply—a "worm sandwich"—with moldy bread, wilted spinach, cucumber peels, old bananas, coffee grounds, apple cores, and anything else suitable for a compost pile. Later, the students will bring their own fruit and vegetable compost from home or supply the worms with leftover lunch scraps, but at the beginning I model what is appropriate for the worms to eat.

Adding the worm sandwich to the bin is a dramatic prelude to introducing the redworms. The children wonder out loud whether or not the worms can see and smell, how they eat, and if they have teeth. They generate other thoughtful questions like "How do the worms find the food if they don't have eyes?" and "Can you tell the difference between a male and a female worm?" I add their questions to our wall chart.

At this point, we also discuss respect. I ask them what they already know about respecting people and how that translates to respecting other living things. I tell the students that worms are sensitive to noise, vibrations, and bright light. We talk about how the worms will be living in our classroom community and how we should respect them. I ask students how they think the worms should be handled and together we make a commitment to hold them gently. Most of the children are curious about the worms, and their initial reactions range from revulsion to fascination.

Once everyone has had a chance to observe the worms, to hold one if they wish, and to comment, we carefully place them in the worm bin and gently cover them with the newspaper bedding. In six years of having worms in my classroom, I have never observed a student mistreating a worm.

Most of my students come from low-income families and live in apartment buildings. They are the children of immigrants—and often immigrants themselves—from Mexico and Central America.

Although many of them have spent scattered time in rural farming communities, and their parents and grandparents have perhaps even farmed, I find that they usually have little experience with gardening, composting, or observing insects and invertebrates in the soil.

I find that the worms in our classroom model healthy eating habits, which is important because my students eat a lot of cheap fast-food meals. Worms thrive on fresh fruits and vegetables. I teach the students that we must avoid putting sugary, salty, and fatty foods in the worm bin because they are not particularly healthy for the worms.

Redworms work quickly, and over the course of the first few weeks of school they eat the newspaper bedding and food scraps we provide and convert them to a dark, nutrient-rich, and odorless compost (this is called "vermicompost," or "worm castings"). The children are amazed when the first worm cocoons appear—tiny but visible lemon-colored globes, half the size of a grain of rice. With patience, we begin to examine baby worms hatching from the egg cases.

When we add food to the worm bin I bring up the concept of recycling. We begin the conversation, which will last all year, on what recycling means both for people and in the natural world. Cycles, in general, are an important curricular theme in 4th grade, and we look critically and in depth at the process of recycling commodities. We examine the water cycle and life cycles of familiar animals and plants, including humans. There are many connections to our worm bin and endless opportunities for comparing and contrasting cycles.

Changing Attitudes

At the beginning of the year many students are reluctant to touch the worms or even look closely at them, but by June the children have come to respect, care for, and sometimes even love our classroom worms. I find that the worms provide an ideal opportunity for teaching about animal stereotypes. Like snakes, spiders, or bats, worms have a negative image. At first, many children refer to the worms as "gross," "ugly," "disgusting," and "slimy." But after they learn about the hard work worms do in the natural environment, they come to appreciate them.

"Did you know," I ask my students, "that earthworms are constantly digging through and eating dead plant material, like leaves, so that all of that stuff doesn't pile up and rot around us outside?" I also tell them how the vermicompost is full of nutrients for the soil, and we can even add it to our classroom plants or schoolyard vegetation. One student wrote about the worm bin:

> When we first got the worms I thought ICKY and I also thought that it was going to be stinky and slimy! But my teacher proved me wrong. She said that [the worm bin] was not smelly or gooey or mushy. She also said that it was damp and a decomposing habitat. So now we still think it is strange but cool at the same time!

On our classroom wall, the students post a colorful construction paper mural they made that shows worms in their underground tunnels. The students are quick to explain to visitors that outside worms dig tunnels underground, allowing water and air to reach the roots of trees and other plants. The children have examined different components of soil like sand, gravel, clay, and decomposing plant material, and they have learned about minerals. They demonstrate a new framework for thinking about soil, what makes it healthy, how it supports life on our planet, and the critical role worms play in that process by breaking down organic matter.

> **I incorporate our worm bin into lessons ranging from science and math (how does one measure a worm?), to nutrition and health, to language arts.**

In this era of intense testing and increased desk work in public schools, as well as excessive television and video watching at home, it is becoming more and more difficult to endow students with any ecological understanding or sense of place. In my classroom I try to integrate these concepts into the curriculum as much as possible. I worry that if they are left out, we may end up with a generation of kids completely disconnected from the natural world, and from each other. There is incredible opportunity for hands-on learning about ecology when a worm bin is part of a

classroom. It naturally motivates children to be interested in science and to think critically.

A book by Mary Appelhof, *Worms Eat Our Garbage*, is a wonderful classroom resource for all ages with non-harmful worm experiments, observation ideas, and reproducible worksheets. But I incorporate our worm bin into lessons ranging from science and math (how does one measure a worm?), to nutrition and health, to language arts. A challenging assignment is to ask students to describe in detail what they see, smell, and hear when they observe the worm bin closely. A group of students one year wrote, "The worm bin smells like soil, wet wood, the ground after it rains, and pinecones."

Foss and Science Ethics

My worm curriculum contrasts in some important ways with the packaged science curricula supplied by the school district. For example, the Foss 2002 edition of the insects curriculum aims to teach 1st and 2nd graders about the life cycles of mealworms, waxworms, milkweed bugs, silkworms, and butterflies. The curriculum instructs teachers to order the insects from a science supply company, create habitats for them in the classroom, teach students about the respective life cycles, and then discreetly kill the insects at the end of the unit.

In the "Plan for the End of the Life Cycle" instructions, the teacher's guide states: "The humane way to end the cycle of waxworms is to put the culture in a freezer overnight and then dispose of the medium in the trash." Although I understand that the curriculum and the instructions within are intended to be an easy method for busy teachers to teach students science concepts, I believe educators have a responsibility to teach more authentically. It is hypocritical to pretend to establish a "real" life cycle for students to observe, and then to put an end to that cycle artificially. Not only do students and teachers gain a false impression of the life cycle of that insect, they learn that the lives of insects are disposable. The unspoken result of the lesson is that the teacher, in fact, controls the life cycle.

The Foss unit on painted lady butterflies is also disturbing, for a different reason. The teacher's guide makes a weak attempt at addressing the problem of introducing nonnative species to an environment, but it then instructs the teacher to do just that:

Noah Clayton

After a month the [butterflies] will die, not because of any ill effects caused by captivity, but because that is their normal life span. Even though it is never advisable to release study organisms into the environment, if a painted lady butterfly "escapes," it will not be an environmental disaster—painted ladies are already well established throughout the country.

I recently learned that most species of earthworm are not native to the temperate deciduous forests of the Northeastern and Midwestern United States; the native worm population was killed off by glaciers during the Ice Age. European species were later brought over by settlers and have, in fact, been harmful to the forests in that part of the country—especially to some maple trees. This could be an interesting and important issue to bring to the attention of students, particularly in the states where invasive worms are affecting forests. The causes and effects of nonnative species introduced to new ecosystems can be explored in any bioregion, and certainly could be incorporated into a unit of study about earthworms.

Within the classroom, a worm bin is a harmless model for studying many kinds of life cycles, including plant, worm, and a diverse variety of decomposer organisms. The worms continue to live year after year, producing egg cases and dying in the worm bin. I always take my bin home for the summer months, but someone uninterested in that possibility could easily find a family or co-worker to adopt the worms, even someone who lives in an apartment. Another benefit of raising worms is that the resulting compost provides an outstanding natural fertilizer for classroom plants or a school or community garden plot. I have even sent vermicompost home with students in resealable bags, with a note to parents explaining its use for houseplants.

Although a weekly farmers market is set up within a mile of the school, none of my students' families shop there. The local, organic produce is too expensive. With our worm castings from the classroom bin, we have been able to start our own vegetable seedlings at school. Last year, for the first time, we began a small classroom garden in some available soil in the courtyard. In the springtime, we harvested and ate organic snap peas, radishes, carrots, and broccoli. The farmers market may still be too expensive for my students' families, but they have gained an awareness of how food can be grown, and what "organic" means. They have begun to learn about sustainable agriculture.

I have found that a worm bin is a simple and powerful learning tool. Balanced vermicomposting in the classroom requires that teachers and students work together as a team. Along with my students, I find myself challenged to think deeply about the connections between our daily lives—especially what we eat—and the earth that provides our food. The worms help my students examine stereotypes, biases, and fears, as well as to confront their own actions and how they affect the planet. Each year, the students stop asking for a pet rabbit or guinea pig. Instead, they put their ears close to the worm bin and listen carefully to hear the worms eating.

. . . .

Rachel Cloues is a teacher-librarian at a K-8 school in San Francisco.

Resources on Worms

CHILDREN'S BOOKS:

Worms Eat My Garbage, by Mary Appelhof.

Worms Eat Our Garbage, also by Mary Appelhof. Classroom teaching guide for all ages with reproducible worksheets and activity ideas.

The Worm Cafe: Mid-Scale Vermicomposting of Lunchroom Wastes, by Binet Payne.

Wriggling Worms, by Wendy Pfeffer.

VERMICOMPOSTING FOR KIDS:

www.niehs.nih.gov/kids/worms.htm

REDWORM SUPPLIERS

Earth Angel Worm & Garden; www.buyworms.com

www.happydranch.com

www.wormswrangler.com

Courtesy of Kate Lyman

Rats!

Students take action to defend their classroom pets

KATE LYMAN

Maggie stepped up to the podium, clutching her friend Isa's arm. Looking up at the seven school board members on the stage, she spoke into the microphone. "My name is Maggie and I'm going to share a letter that I wrote."

My name is Maggie and I think we should have pets. We already have two rats, Templeton and Max. They are my best friends and they could help kids all over Madison Metropolitan School District. We have to clean their cage and feed them and give them water in a water bottle. We play with them at quiet reading. If we did not take them from the Humane Society, they would have died. So please don't take them away from us.

Maggie was one of six of my 2nd- and 3rd-grade students who spoke to the school board in Madison, Wis., that night. Clara came, but backed out. "There's a million people here," she said, "I can't talk in front of all these people!"

The other students were nervous, too, choosing to go up in pairs for support. But I was proud of them for speaking out in that daunting setting, in front of at least 100 people, including school board members, the superintendent, and the school district lawyer.

It had been an extra challenging year. Due to overcrowding in our school, two classrooms were combined into one room. In addition, our classroom was an "ESL cluster," which meant that more than the school's average (29 percent) of English language learners were assigned to our class. Of our 32 students, 25 spoke a first language other than English—mainly Spanish and Hmong, but also Fulani, Urdu, and Vietnamese—and were working toward proficiency in oral and written English.

Because of language, and also because of differing background knowledge, a handful of students dominated classroom discussions. We had had some success in involving the students in a "get out the vote" action, but activities that I had found successful in the past, such as the "Inequality in World Resources" activity from *Rethinking Our Classrooms, Volume 1*, fell flat.

But the campaign to get our classroom animals back engaged the kids in a direct and relevant way that discussing local, national, or world issues had not.

The Classroom Adopts

Several months before the school board meeting, our class had joined the Humane Society's "Adopt a Teacher Program," which allowed classroom teachers to borrow animals that had been surrendered to the shelter. After notifying parents and investigating potential problems with allergies, Richard Wagner, the Humane Society's education coordinator, came in with the rats to demonstrate proper care and handling.

Initially, not all students were enthusiastic about having rats as classroom companions. "Rats!" said Isa. "Disgusting!" Richard and I explained that these animals were not the same as the rats who become household pests. Domestic, or "fancy rats," as they are called, are bred to be companion animals. The word "fancy" comes from "fancied" or "liked," unlike wild rats that are generally despised. Fancy rats can be as smart and as cuddly as dogs or cats. They are also clean, with no offensive odor, as long as their cage is kept clean. They become attached to people and can recognize them by their smell. They can be taught to come to their name and to do tricks. There are even rat clubs, rat newsletters, and rat shows.

In the following days and weeks, I brought the rats out of their cage for short, supervised sessions. The students held the rats in their arms and watched them explore on the student tables. I read daily from the book *My Pet Rat* by Arlene Erlbach, which combines the experiences of a girl who acquires a pet rat with fascinating facts about domestic rats.

Through the reading and discussions related to the book, as well as daily observation and interaction with the rats, the students came to better appreciate and understand them. The students voted to name them Max and Templeton, and once they saw them as individuals, their personalities became clear. Templeton enjoyed being cuddled and petted by the children, and Max was more active and tended to climb and explore. Max and Templeton also seemed to favor the children who handled them calmly and confidently. Both rats would climb up into Mai Nyia's arms and even hyperactive Max would settle down on Mai Nyia's fleece sweatshirt.

Tim, who hadn't written more than two sentences that year, worked cooperatively with a partner to write two pages about the rats for our class news.

Max and Templeton inspired students to write. Tim, who hadn't written more than two sentences that year, worked cooperatively with a partner to write two pages about the rats for our class news. Other students wrote stories in their draft books and illustrated books about the animals. Students argued who would get the privilege of cleaning the rats' cage. They diligently followed all of Richard's directions as they added fresh food and water, washed the bottom of the cage, and then added clean layers of newspaper and bedding. They brought in carrots, strawberries, grapes, and other treats for the rats from home and they donated small boxes and paper towel rolls to provide stimulation and variety to the rats' living quarters.

As new students joined our class, their classmates taught them how to handle and care for the rats. One of my new students, a Hmong girl from a refugee camp in Thailand, entered our class with no previous schooling and no English. She hung back, rarely smiling or even interacting with the other children. No one, not even the Hmong bilingual specialist could get her to open up. But as she held Templeton, a rare smile would creep on her face. She would even laugh as Templeton crawled up on her shoulder and tickled her neck.

A District Mandate

A few months later, when Max and Templeton were well established as important members of our classroom community, we received a call from Richard that the district had ordered him to remove all animals from classrooms by the following Monday. The district was apparently responding to a parent complaint concerning allergies by banning all animals from the schools. The information we received was confusing. Reference was made to a school board policy prohibiting "dogs and other animals" from school premises, a policy contained in a section about playground rules. "Air quality" was cited as a concern and, in some schools, all plants and even the goldfish in the school office had to be removed.

Isa overheard Connie, my teaching partner, and me talking about the mandate. "Maggie, Maggie," she cried out, rushing over to her friend, "I have really bad news! They're taking the rats away!" "What? Taking away Max and Templeton?" responded Maggie, and soon everyone had heard.

"We need to tell the principal not to let them take away the rats!" someone said. I tried to explain that it wasn't the principal's fault. Quickly I sketched out the hierarchy of the school district, explaining the role of the school board and the superintendent, who is the principal's "boss." I told the students that they could tell them their feelings through a letter or email, which many students chose to do the next day.

We didn't have time to spare, so the next morning we quickly brainstormed reasons to allow animals in the classroom. We talked about what it meant to try to persuade someone to do something, and about a possible format for a persuasive essay. We didn't spend much time planning or prewriting, because we only had a few days to try to stop the action. But the students' voices came out strongly in their writing, perhaps all the more authentic because their comments came from the heart instead of coming from a modeled writing lesson.

Although some students wrote about the educational benefits gained from having animals in the classroom, most of them stressed the emotional impact of the experience. "We want to keep the rats because they are our friends," wrote Josie. "They help us learn and cool off when we are mad. And they love us as much as we love them!"

"I think it's not fair because what if you needed an animal to do science and also what if you needed a friend?" asked Carmen. "I think if somebody was doing the same thing to you, you would be feeling sad. Why don't you first think about it?"

The students practiced a lot of writing skills in those few days. They edited their letters, typed them on the computer, and learned how to send them via email to the school board members and superintendent. Maggie suggested they send letters to the local newspaper. The *Capital Times* published four of their letters the following week, along with a photograph of Mai Nyia holding the rats in her arms. "Hawthorne Pupils: Let Us Keep Our Rats!" was the headline.

> "Maggie, Maggie," she cried out, rushing over to her friend, "I have really bad news! They're taking the rats away!"

After reading the letters to the editor, a producer from Wisconsin Public Television contacted me to see if he could include my classroom in a program they were developing called "Democracy it is!" The program featured elementary students working through the system to create change. I asked my students, who agreed that this was an exciting prospect, and then asked my principal if we could have the rats back for a day for the filming. She forwarded my request to the assistant superintendent, who granted my request, but only if I received permission from all the parents (which I had intended to do) and if I "developed a plan that notes how much instructional time will be used and how the activities will relate to curriculum standards." I stayed late that night annotating all the relevant standards—14 social studies standards, six science standards, and the entire section on writing in our 2nd- and 3rd-grade language arts standards.

All but one of the parents granted permission for the filming, but several students, particularly three Hmong girls, were reluctant. Mai Nyia, Lisa, and Pa told me that they didn't want to say anything. I assured them that they wouldn't have to be interviewed or participate in anything but the large-group filming. I was surprised, given the reluctance of so many of my students to speak up in class discussions, how many of them did volunteer to read their letters in front of the camera. Mai Nyia, Lisa, and Pa, who hadn't chosen initially to write a letter to the school board, decided to get to work. They proudly showed me their essays. "Did you want to read them in front of the camera?" I asked. They looked at each other and said, "Yes!" Hand in hand, they went over to the cameraman and read their letters.

Student Role Play

Since some students had indicated interest in reading their letters at the school board meeting, I decided to stage a role play in which students would debate the issues as school board members. I realized that we hadn't spent much time talking about why school board members might be opposed to having animals in the classroom, so I asked the students to help me generate a list of pros and cons. Since none of my students had allergies to the rats, they could not understand why the allergy issue might be such an important issue. When we first got the rats, Clara said that her eyes were tearing when she was near their

> **Since some students had indicated interest in reading their letters at the school board meeting, I decided to stage a role play in which students would debate the issues as school board members.**

cage. I moved Clara's table place to a spot farther from the rats and asked her daily how she felt. At first she didn't hold the rats, but after a while her eyes stopped watering and she was able to hold the rats without a reaction. Either she got accustomed to their presence or she'd had a cold, not an allergy. If anyone in the classroom had allergies, I would have asked another teacher to take the rats or I would have sent them back to the Humane Society. The following are the lists the students generated:

Reasons we should have animals in our classroom:
- They are like friends to us
- We use them to learn about science
- They might help you calm down

- If you don't have a friend they might be your friend
- If you're sad they can help you cheer up
- If you have no one to play with, you could play with them
- When we're lonely we need friends
- Children like pets because they are fun
- Rats are good pets
- You learn about the animal and then you won't be scared of them
- You learned how to clean their cages, give them food and water, and take care of them
- Maybe because you need friends
- If you are being bullied by someone, they will make you feel better
- You might not be scared of them
- They don't have owners

Reasons you might not want animals in the classroom:
- They might chew on something that is near their cage
- Kids might be allergic to them
- Kids might not like them
- You might not concentrate on your math
- You might be scared of them
- They might eat your homework
- They might bite you
- They might get out of their cage
- They might eat something near their cage and might be poisoned
- They might make a mess
- They might be scared of you
- They might get out and hide somewhere, like in the cubbies

Predictably, given their passion about their classroom pets, the group quickly came to a consensus. Maggie, the one "school board member" who held out on her "no animals" position, quickly relented. "Oh, all right, you convinced me. They can have their animals back." The class cheered.

The role play was valuable. It was a start, at least, at presenting an opposing point of view—a task that was difficult for my students, given their joy at sharing their classroom with animals and their sadness at having to see them go.

Benefits of Animal Visitors

Throughout my teaching career, I've had many different animals visit the classroom, including guinea pigs, gerbils, snakes, frogs, cockatiels, chickens, and guests with guide dogs. Each animal has inspired children in ways that boxed curriculum rarely does.

Beyond the opportunities for making science, social studies, math, and language arts connections, the animals help students who are struggling emotionally. I remember Daniel, a new arrival from Mexico. He had little previous education, would not try to read or write, even in Spanish, and was having trouble connecting with the other kids. He would pull his sweatshirt hood down over his face and crawl under a table. After weeks of making little progress, it was the experience of watching chicks hatch, caring for them, and observing them that helped him come out of his shell. Soon he was attempting his first writing about the "pollitos" and showing his drawings of the chicks to other students.

Courtesy of Kate Lyman

> **Beyond the opportunities for making science, social studies, math, and language arts connections, the animals help students who are struggling emotionally.**

Time after time, I have seen angry, disconnected students let go of their bad morning or their recess conflicts when I redirected them to care for animals. For some kids, caring for and about animals is a first step in learning to feel and show compassion for their classmates. Caring for animals also is a big step toward developing a classroom community. With an animal in the room, the focus shifts from "me" or "me and my friends" to the group.

Although I realize some people can have serious allergic reactions to certain animals, I also do not understand why what is a problem for a few children has to result in banning an experience that is so important for many others. I happen to have fairly severe allergies to cats and rabbits and would never have an animal in my classroom that was making a student suffer from asthma or allergies.

But in the 28 years that I have been teaching, I have never had to remove an animal because of allergies.

Even according to the school board member who most strongly advocated for the ban on animals, he had "less than a handful" of complaints a year. Far more children get broken limbs at recess (I've had two students who broke their legs in the past two years) and bee stings are potentially a far more serious risk to students with allergies, yet we don't (and shouldn't) ban recess and field trips.

School board members also argued that students are not safe with animals, either because of the risk of bites or because the students may be fearful. My experience is that children who learn to interact appropriately with animals are much safer than those who don't. Most of my students live in low-income housing and do not have the opportunity to have pets. They need to be taught safe behavior around them. Particularly in our community, where dogs are often bred for protection and/or trained improperly, dogs can pose a serious threat to children. A few years ago, I was taking a neighborhood walk with my class when a stray dog came up to them. They started to scream and run from the dog, behaviors that, had the dog been aggressive or skittish, could have resulted in a bite. I invited the education director at the Humane Society to come in with her dog and teach them how to interact safely with a dog. We all practiced "standing like a tree" as her dog came up to the children and sniffed them.

Unfortunately, the students did not succeed in getting the animals back, at least not that school year. A committee was formed to make a recommendation on whether or not, and under what circumstances we will be allowed to have animals in the classroom.

But my students found their voices. They learned, through writing and speaking up publicly about an issue that is important to them, that they can have an impact. Even if the school board denies their pleas, they saw their letters published in the paper and became part of a public TV production. And they were inspired to speak up on other issues. After we read a *Time for Kids* article about how global warming is endangering the arctic habitat of penguins and polar bears, they immediately wanted to take action. "We can write letters to the president, like we did when we wrote to the school board about the rats," suggested

My students found their voices. They learned, through writing and speaking up publicly about an issue that is important to them, that they can have an impact.

Maggie. We talked again about persuasive writing, and about whom they wanted to address in their letters. Some wanted to write the mayor about local factory pollution. Some kids wanted to make signs for their neighborhood telling people to carpool or ride their bikes to cut down on gas emissions. The second time around, the letters were a bit more polished, the arguments more persuasive.

And this time, everybody participated in the writing. The kids edited and typed their letters, addressed their letters, and mailed them in the mailbox down the street.

In response to the students' interest in habitat destruction of penguins and polar bears, we also decided to do an endangered animals unit. Students chose an endangered animal to research and write about. They also presented their knowledge to the class in the form of a play, puppet show, game, or poster. Then, after reading an article in *Kind News*, the students became interested in puppy mills (businesses that abuse and exploit dogs, keeping them confined for breeding purposes and then ship puppies to pet stores to be sold for large profits). Further research and then social action relating to this issue would have been the logical next step; however, we needed to finish up projects and portfolios and complete end-of-the-year assessments.

Almost every day after the rats left the classroom, Mai Nyia came up to me and said, "Kate, I really miss the rats." I miss them, too, but I am thankful to them for helping my students learn to care for other living things. I'm thankful, too, for what the rats taught me. They reminded me to be patient with my students. They reminded me that it is often the issues closer to home that spark an interest in social action. The students' experiences advocating for the rats gave them the confidence to raise their voices to speak out and protest policies they found unfair. The rats were only the beginning of a thread of animal advocacy that wove through the entire school year.

Epilogue

The year after Maggie spoke at that school board meeting, the committee met several times during the first semester. I was invited—along with several other teachers who had advocated for animals in the classroom—to attend two meetings.

We were able to speak at the meetings, but none of our suggestions were incorporated in a proposal that banned virtually all animals from the schools. (The exceptions were guide dogs, certain insects, and goldfish.) The proposal was presented to the school board, with surprising results.

The board members voted unanimously to reject the proposal and instructed the committee to reconvene and come up with guidelines that would, indeed, allow for animals in the classroom. I wanted to consider this decision a victory, but the real momentum behind the board's change of heart may have been that the board's anti-animal stance had made it the laughing stock of talk radio commentators. The board also voted 5-1 that, while the committee was working on a new proposal, all animals previously in classrooms could return. Unfortunately for us, Max and Templeton had been placed elsewhere. But I looked forward to some new animal guests. The students who were 2nd graders in my class the year we advocated at the board meeting continued to talk about their experience with the rats and write stories and poems about them a year later. ▪

....

Kate Lyman teaches in Madison, Wis. The names of the children in this article have been changed.

Barbara Miner

6.

The Classroom, the School, the World

What we teach, how we teach, and the conditions
in which we teach are constantly being restructured,
reformed, and retooled. If we want to build social
justice practice, then we have to defend our classrooms. Sometimes this means fighting against testing;
sometimes it means fighting for students' right to
their home languages; sometimes it means fighting
to keep libraries, music, and recess in our schools.
And sometimes it simply means listening to students,
so that we create classrooms where all of our
students belong.

Hanna Neuschwander

A Letter from a Black Mom to Her Son

DYAN WATSON

Dear Caleb,
    When you were almost 2, we would drop off your cousin, Sydney, at her K-8 elementary school. The ritual went something like this:

"OK, Syd, have a good day."

"OK," she'd groan as she grabbed her backpack. "Bye, Caleb."

"Bye," you'd wave and grin with your entire body.

"Bye," Sydney'd say one last time as she shut the door. I'd roll down the car window.

"Byeeeee," you'd sing.

"Bye," Sydney would laugh as she caught up with friends.

I'd roll up the window as you said "bye" a few more times, then start to whimper. "It's OK, sweetie, she'll be back before you know it. And you'll be off joining her before I know it." And it's true. Before I know it, Caleb, you will be throwing your backpack on and waving goodbye as you run off across the playground. I think about that moment often and wonder about the condition of schools you'll enter. I worry about sending you, my black son, to schools that over-enroll black boys into special ed, criminalize them at younger and younger ages, and view them as negative statistics on the dark side of the achievement gap.

Son, my hope for you is that your schooling experiences will be better than this; that they'll be better than most of mine.

For three years of my K-8 schooling, from 7:40 a.m. until 3:05 p.m., I was black and invisible. I was bused across town to integrate a white school in Southeast Portland, Ore. We arrived at school promptly at 7:30 and had 10 full minutes before the white children arrived. We spent that time roaming the halls — happy, free, normal. Once the white children arrived, we became black and invisible. We were separated, so that no more than two of us were in a class at a time. I never saw black people in our textbook unless they were in shackles or standing with Martin Luther King Jr. Most of us rarely interacted with a black adult outside of the aide who rode the bus with us. I liked school and I loved learning. But I never quite felt right or good. I felt very black and obvious because I knew that my experience was different from that of my peers. But I also felt invisible because this was never acknowledged in any meaningful way. I became visible again at 3:05 when I got back on the bus with the other brown faces to make our journey home.

Caleb, I want your teachers to help you love being in your skin. I want them to make space for you in their curricula, so that you see yourself as integral to this country's history, to your classroom's community, to your peers' learning. I want your teachers to select materials where blacks are portrayed in ordinary and extraordinary ways that actively challenge stereotypes and biases. Most of all, Caleb, I want your teachers to know you so they can help you grow.

Once a teacher was trying to figure out why I was so angry one day since I was generally a calm, fun-loving kid. She said to me: "I know you, Dyan. You come from a good family." But did she know me? She knew that I lived on the other side of town and was bused in as part of the distorted way that Portland school authorities decided to "integrate" the schools. But did she know what that meant? My mom — your grandma — got us up at 6 a.m. in order for me to wash up, boil an egg just right, fix my toast the way I liked it, and watch the pan of milk so that it didn't boil over, so I could have something hot in my stomach before going to school. You know Grandma, she doesn't play. We had to eat a healthy breakfast before going to school, and we had to fix it ourselves. Maybe

that's what that teacher meant by "good family." My teacher didn't know that we had to walk, by ourselves, four blocks to the bus stop and wait for the yellow bus to come pick us up and take us to school. It took us a half hour to get to school. Once there, I had to constantly code switch, learn how not to be overly black, and be better than my white counterparts.

> **I felt very black and obvious because I knew that my experience was different from that of my peers. But I also felt invisible because this was never acknowledged in any meaningful way.**

Caleb, I want your teachers to know your journey to school — metaphorically and physically. I want them to see you and all of your peers as children from good families. I don't want you to have to earn credit because of whom you're related to or what your parents do for a living. And I don't want your teachers to think that you're special because you're black and have a family that cares about you and is involved in your life. I want them to know that all children are part of families — traditional or not — that help shape and form who they are.

The summer before beginning 4th grade, I started teaching myself how to play the clarinet. It was the family instrument in that both of my older sisters played it when they were younger. For years I wanted to be a musician. It was in my blood. My grandfather was a musician, all of my uncles can sing very well, and my dad — your grandfather — was a famous DJ in Jamaica once upon a time. At the end of 5th grade, my band director took each member aside to provide feedback on whether or not she or he should continue music in middle school. My teacher told me that I just didn't have it and should quit. I was devastated. I had dreams of becoming a conductor and I loved playing music. I learned to read music and read at the same time before entering kindergarten, so I couldn't understand what my teacher saw or heard that made him think that I, at the tender age of 11, didn't have what it took to pursue playing in a middle school band. He knew nothing about me. Had never asked any questions about me, our family, my aspirations. He didn't seek to make me a better musician.

Caleb, I hope that you will have teachers who realize they are gatekeepers. I hope they understand the power they hold and work to discover your talents, seek out your dreams and fan them, rather than smother them. I hope they will see you as part of a family, with gifts and rich histories that have been passed down to you. I hope they will strive to know you even when they think they already know you. I hope your teachers will approach you with humility and stay curious about who you are.

When I was in 4th grade, my elementary school held a back-to-school night, which featured student work and allowed families to walk the halls and speak with teachers. In each classroom was a student leader, chosen by teachers. I'm not sure what my role was supposed to be. But at one point, a couple came in, desiring to speak with Mrs. S. She was busy so I thought I'd chat with them while they waited. As I approached them, they recoiled in fear and with a panicked look, turned away from me and said, "Mrs. S.?" My teacher looked away from the folks she was working with and said, "It's OK, she's not like the rest." I don't remember what happened next. All I remember is that this seemed to be one of the first in a long line of reassurances that I was special and not like other black boys and girls. For many years afterward, I was told on more than one occasion, "You're not like other blacks." This was supposed to be a compliment.

Caleb, I pray that your teachers will not look at you through hurtful racial preconceptions. I pray that they will do the work necessary to eliminate racist practices in themselves and in those around them. I pray that they stand up for you in ways that leave you feeling strong and capable. I pray that they will nurture your spirit, and that you, in turn, will desire to be a better you.

Son, I end this letter by sharing a story that Grandma has told me many times, that I hope will one day resonate with you. On the first day of kindergarten, many of the kids were crying and clinging to their parents. But not me. I was ready! I wanted to be like my three older siblings and go to school. So I gave my mom a hug, let go of her hand, waved goodbye and found my teacher. And remember how I told you that my oldest sister taught me how to read before I went to school? The teacher found this out and used this skill, along with my desire to be at school, to teach the other kids the alphabet and help them learn how to read. I believe, in part, that is why I became a teacher. She saw something in me and encouraged me to develop my passion—even at this young, sweet age.

That, my son, is my hope for you. I hope your teachers will love you for who you are and the promise of what you'll be.

Love,
Mama ▪

Dyan Watson (watson@lclark.edu) is an assistant professor in the Graduate School of Education and Counseling at Lewis & Clark College in Portland, Ore., and an editorial associate of Rethinking Schools.

Perry Kroll

The Power of Words

Top-down mandates masquerade as social justice reforms

LINDA CHRISTENSEN

Really what this [school reform] is about is equity and social justice," a district official told a local newspaper reporter when a new curricular change called anchor assignments was introduced to Portland Public Schools teachers. "It doesn't matter what school you're at, what ZIP code you live in, you should have the same opportunities for a rigorous instructional program like every other student in the city."

Sounds good, right? But what was the school reform? Multicultural books embedded into thematic historical units? Time for teachers to meet and construct lessons for students that integrated math, science, social studies, and literacy around a contemporary issue like immigration, global warming, or the war in Iraq? No. The school reform was an order from the superintendent that every teacher at a particular grade level give the same assignment to every student. She called them "anchor assignments." These assignments announced to teachers that equity, justice, and rigor were located in a standardized curriculum that all teachers were expected to administer.

As the director of the Oregon Writing Project and as a classroom teacher for more than 30 years who attempts to work for justice and equity, I was dismayed at the appropriation of social justice language for a top-down mandate that disenfranchised students and teachers. But this is not a phenomenon unique to Portland. As I travel around the country, I've discovered that central office administrators more and more frequently steal the language and metaphors of social justice education to push their top-down agendas.

First, let me take a moment to challenge the idea that these anchor assignments had anything to do with equity, justice, and rigor. In language arts classes starting in the 3rd grade, every student was required to write a literary analysis essay. The assignments privilege essay writing as the only genre worth teaching. As one consultant said in an elementary workshop, "The days of children lying on the carpet writing their little stories are over."

District administrators distributed anchor assignments as stand-alone work. These assignments, without benefit of instruction in the craft of writing a specific genre like literary analysis, ignored the fact that all students do not start with the same skills; some need more background knowledge in order to succeed on the task. The creators of the anchors (which teachers dubbed "anger assignments") assumed that students learn from dropped-in assignments created in a vacuum. District administrators, evidently unfamiliar with the actual terrain of teaching writing, failed to understand that it's not the writing of

Administrators hijack the language of the Civil Rights or social justice education movements to push districtwide mandates as quick fixes to complex problems.

an assignment that teaches students to write; it's learning how to write that improves student writing. Students learn when assignments are embedded in a rich curriculum, when they have grappled with big concepts in their lives and the lives of historical and fictional characters, so they can write out of a well of experience that they have rehearsed through talk and example and examination of the genre.

Equity? Well, I suppose that, regardless of ZIP code, every student will now have access to the same insipid anchor assignment.

Unfortunately, Portland is not the only place where district administrators hijack the language of the Civil Rights or social justice education movements to push districtwide mandates as quick fixes to complex problems. Of course, it's the desperate need for radical education reform that lends credence to the faux democratic prescriptions of the language hijackers.

One reason the rhetoric is compelling is that it boldly states the truth: Poor students and students of color have been historically disenfranchised and underserved by schools across the country. And some of the reforms are right on: for example, open access to honors classes for all students and funding effective in-school intervention for students who are falling behind.

Standardization Does Not Mean Equity

But the majority of the reforms, like Portland's ill-conceived anchor assignments, equate "equity" with standardization. For many districts, that translates into common curriculum, common pacing guides, and common assessments. Depending on the district, this standardization may include common textbooks with pacing guides that dictate day-by-day lessons as well as regularly scheduled common assessments that keep teachers and students goose-stepping in line to the end of the year.

As the Oakland Unified School District's "Equity Plan" states, "To ensure consistency and equity across schools, the district must put in place pacing guides and syllabi that tailor textbook adoptions to Oakland's needs and students. In addition, mandatory expectations for daily language arts and math instruction must be adopted and monitored through classroom observation, again addressing the wide variability of exposure to standards-based instruction that has historically occurred."

Translation: Because they've made such a mess out of things up to now, teachers cannot be trusted to imagine, create, or enact curricular reform. Change will come from on high. The school managers will choose materials, decide how they will be taught, and will monitor compliance. Ultimately, these changes made in the name of "social justice" lead to the deskilling of teachers.

My colleague, Mark Hansen, co-director of the Oregon Writing Project and extraordinary 4th-grade teacher, told me a story that illustrates how the domination of the textbook keeps teachers from seeing themselves as creators of curriculum. Mark is featured in an Annenberg Teaching and Learning video. The clip shows Mark and his students walking through his school's low-income, immigrant neighborhood in North Portland. Students carry small notebooks and gather ideas for a persuasive letter about their concerns: lack of traffic signals that make it dangerous for them to cross the street, mean dogs on the block, a malfunctioning tire swing. Mark's lesson is a great example of creating an authentic writing lesson situated in students' lives. The assignment has purpose, audience, and a real aim for students to see themselves as both writers and actors in their communities. On two different occasions teachers from other states asked him what writing program he used to get such good writing out of his students — an indication of the widespread adoption of scripted curricula. As Mark said: "I was stunned. Teaching was reduced to a consumer choice."

Despite the theft of language from one of the most profoundly democratic movements in U.S. history, these new educational reforms are rooted not in our country's Civil Rights Movement, but in the managerial strategies popularized by Frederick Winslow Taylor and made famous in Charlie Chaplin's dystopian film *Modern Times*. This is the classic in which Chaplin plays a factory worker whose every motion managers script and pace in such excruciating detail that he goes berserk and ends up being carted off to the insane asylum. In his discussion of corporations' adoption of scientific management and its impact on workers, Harry Braverman wrote: "[A] belief in the original stupidity of the worker is a necessity for management; otherwise it would have to admit that it is engaged in the wholesale enterprise of prizing and fostering stupidity." Substitute "teacher" for "worker" and "administration" for "management."

If school districts wanted to embrace a real Civil Rights agenda instead of the rhetoric of the movement, then they might turn to the work of Ella Baker, Septima Clark, Bob Moses, Charles Cobb, Myles Horton, and others involved in organizing the Freedom Schools in Mississippi and the Citizenship Schools throughout the South. Like Mark Hansen, these organizers believed in situating the literacy lessons in the lives of the local people, drawing on their students' interests and questions and using those materials as the basis of their lessons. As Charles Payne wrote in *I've Got the Light of Freedom: The Organizing Tradition and the Mississippi Freedom Struggle*, "The teaching style developed by Robinson and Clark emphasized 'big' ideas — citizenship, democracy, the powers of elected officials. The curriculum stressed what was interesting and familiar and important to students, and it changed in accordance to the desires of students."

These civil rights organizers/teachers saw literacy as a tool for raising people's consciousness about the race and class divisions that needed to be changed in our society. Literacy was not taught in isolation from the context of the learners like the current paced, scripted curriculum guides that encourage the belief that all students need the same lesson on the same day. If our contemporary schools are concerned about "teaching for equity," they might ask students who come from historically oppressed communities to analyze their own experiences in the ways these organizations encouraged. For example, in a memo to the Mississippi Freedom School teachers, the organizers wrote, "The purpose of the Freedom Schools is to provide an educational experience for students that will make it possible for them to challenge the myths of our society, to perceive more clearly its realities, and to find alternatives, and ultimately, new directions for action." Clearly, the kind of teaching for equity employed during the Civil Rights Movement did not advocate using the same curriculum with pacing guides and tests for students. Instead of the current method of deskilling teachers by purchasing curriculum, Myles Horton's workshops at Highlander brought local leaders together to share experiences and strategies — in much the same way that the National Writing Project does in the intensive summer institutes. According to Horton: "We debunk the leadership role of going back and telling people and providing thinking for them. We aren't into that. We're into people who can help other people develop and provide educational leadership and ideas, but at the same time, bring people along."

Channel Ella Baker and Septima Clark: Talk Back

As teachers, we need to decode the rhetoric and talk back to school districts that speak of equity and social justice, but treat us like robots that deliver education programs designed and shipped from sites outside of our classrooms.

Teachers in Portland challenged both the language and the implementation of the proposed reforms masquerading as movements for equity and rigor. Because high school language arts teachers were the first to experience the sting of anchor assignments, they led the charge against them. Teachers across the district came together and wrote a response to the anchor assignment mandate:

> As language arts teachers, we disagree with the anchor assignments. This is an example of a top-down decision that was made without any discussion with language arts teachers across the district.... We want to make it clear that although we oppose the imposition of the anchor assignments in our classes, we are not opposed to teaching writing. We want to clarify the difference. We don't assign writing, we teach it. In fact, our daily work consists of teaching literary analysis, narrative and persuasive writing, but this work is developed through the study of a work of fiction or nonfiction that builds toward the essay or narrative piece.

Teachers also disputed Superintendent Vicki Phillips' description of these mandates as a move toward "equity"; they addressed her word choice directly:

> We agree that equity is an issue, but we would like to challenge your version of it. For the past six years, language arts teachers at every high school have tackled the issue of equity in much deeper, systemic ways. We untracked our freshmen classes, so that students from diverse cultural, racial, and social economic backgrounds have an opportunity to learn together and to see themselves as capable of entering honors classrooms.... When we untracked our classes, we also challenged ourselves to learn new methods of teaching that would reach the diverse members of our classes.... Those of us who have been successful in teaching untracked classes also taught each other strategies.

When teachers across the district critiqued this "social justice reform" and wrote letters stating that they would not implement anchor assignments because they were poorly constructed, they were threatened with insubordination. The same people who claimed to work for "equity" sought to suppress discussion and critique.

Elementary teachers in Portland Public Schools also fought back. At community hearings and board meetings, teachers across the district testified against a fast-tracked curriculum adoption. In a petition, teachers embraced the equity impulse of securing more materials for poorly supplied schools, but rejected the equation of equity with sameness:

> The adoption process of literacy "core curriculum" materials at the elementary level needs to be slowed down and thoughtfully re-examined. Many of our schools do need new materials; they have for some time. However, purchasing and implementing a single set of materials across the entire district, on such a tight time line, without seriously examining the materials our schools already use with great success is an expensive gamble. We need to assess what is and is not working in individual schools. Then we can build on our strengths to remedy any weaknesses. That is how we will see real lasting improvements for all Portland students.

The teachers cited research that contradicted the district's assertions that common textbooks would lead to equity for all students:

- No research shows that purchasing a new reading program reliably raises reading achievement (Berends, Bodilly, & Kirby, 2002).

- Building teacher capacity and supporting rigorous teacher communities (e.g., study groups, teacher research) is the key factor for student achievement (Allington, Cunningham, 2006).

- Scripted curriculum deskills teachers, reducing them to deliverers of content rather than synthesizers of complex ideas (NCTE).

- The programs presented as possible adoptions do not align with the philosophies and rigorous teaching practices of many PPS schools.

- No single program can meet the needs of a large and diverse district like Portland.

- Portland's reading achievement has consistently risen without a districtwide adoption.

Portland teachers did not stop the anchor assignments, which the district renamed "common assignments," but teachers now collectively write them and worked over the summer months to embed them in curriculum units. They also collectively designed teaching strategies to avoid the stand-alone nature of the original mandates.

And elementary teachers, who found ardent allies in the college literacy community, did not derail the curriculum adoption, but one school board member added an amendment to every adoption. As the board notes read: "Board Director Dilafruz Williams won unanimous approval from the school board for an amendment to each adoption. The amendment confirms and emphasizes that the school district will continue to encourage creativity in teaching and learning, with teachers able to choose additional materials for their classrooms to supplement the district-provided materials."

In these times, when even the historic civil rights case *Brown v. Board of Education* has been reversed, teachers cannot afford to stand on the sidelines of curricular debates wringing our hands while district leaders speak in social justice sound bites and impose cookie-cutter curriculum reforms that deskill teachers, disempower local communities, and rob our students of a real social justice education. We may not win the battles, but our words and actions must demonstrate that education is contested terrain that we are willing to fight for. ▪

....

This article appeared in Language Arts, *the Elementary and Middle School magazine of the National Council of Teachers of English. Linda Christensen is an editor of* Rethinking Schools *and director of the Oregon Writing Project. She is the author of* Reading, Writing, and Rising Up: Teaching About Social Justice and the Power of the Written Word *and* Teaching for Joy and Justice: Re-Imagining the Language Arts Classroom.

Resources

Braverman, Harry. *Labor and Monopoly Capital: The Degradation of Work in the Twentieth Century.* New York: Monthly Review, 1974.

Emery, Kathy, Sylvia Braselmann, and Linda Reid Gold. Mississippi Freedom School Curriculum. http://www.educationanddemocracy.org/FSCfiles/B_08_MemoToFSTeachers.htm

Payne, Charles. *I've Got the Light of Freedom: The Organizing Tradition and the Mississippi Freedom Struggle.* Berkeley, Calif.: University of California Press, 1995.

SNCC. *The Student Nonviolent Coordinating Committee Papers, 1959–1972* (Sanford, N.C.: Microfilming Corporation of America, 1982) Reel 67, File 340, Page 1,183. Reprinted with permission of the King Library and Archives, The Martin Luther King Jr. Center for Nonviolent Social Change, Atlanta.

Alain Pilon

Defending Bilingual Education

English language learners come to school with a built-in opportunity to become bilingual. Schools should help them seize this opportunity.

KELLEY DAWSON SALAS

"Teacher, this is crazy!"

After six days straight of standardized testing in English, her second language, Ana lost it. She laughed out loud and the rest of us laughed with her. As her 4th-grade teacher I was expected to keep order and continue administering the test (which I did), but I could see where she was coming from. Perhaps it was the rigorous schedule: seven days of testing for three hours each morning. Perhaps it was the tedious format: listen as each test item is read aloud twice in English and twice in Spanish, then wait for all students to mark an answer, then move on to the next test item. Perhaps it was the random nature of some of the questions.

Whatever it was, Ana knew it didn't make sense. That moment has become a metaphor to me. There are more English language learners than ever in U.S. schools, and yet the policies that affect their schooling make less and less sense.

About 10 percent of all U.S. students—more than 5 million children—are English language learners. This represents a tremendous resource and opportunity. If schools serve English language learners well, at least 10 percent of U.S. students can have highly valued skills: fluency in more than one language and an ability to work with diverse groups of people. If communities give English-speaking students the opportunity to learn side by side with students who speak other languages, an even greater number of students can learn these skills.

But there are obstacles. Although research shows that bilingual education works, top-down policies increasingly push English-only education. To make matters worse, schools serving immigrants are some of the most segregated, understaffed, under-resourced schools in the country.

In a Winter 2002/03 editorial, *Rethinking Schools* wrote that "bilingual education is a human and civil right." I think all teachers should defend this right and demand equal educational opportunities for English language learners. It's not just about immigrant students: U.S. society as a whole will benefit greatly when all students have access to bilingual education, and when schools serve English language learners well.

Bilingual Education Works

Research shows that bilingual education is effective with English learners, both in helping them learn English and in supporting academic achievement in the content areas.

A synthesis of research recently published by Cambridge University Press showed that English learners do better in school when they participate in programs that are designed to help them learn English. The review also found that "almost all evaluations of K-12 students show that students who have been educated in bilingual classrooms, particularly in long-term programs that aim for a high level of bilingualism, do as well as or better on standardized tests than students in comparison groups of English-learners in English-only programs."

A synthesis of studies on language-minority students' academic achievement by Virginia Collier found that students do better academically in their second language when they have more instruction in their primary language, combined with balanced support in the second language.

There are more English language learners than ever in U.S. schools, and yet the policies that affect their schooling make less and less sense.

I have seen this in action at the two-way immersion school where I teach 4th grade. Spanish-dominant students who develop good literacy skills in Spanish have a far easier time in 3rd and 4th grade when they begin to read, write, and do academic work in English. Likewise, students who struggle to read and write in Spanish do not transition easily to English reading, and they tend to lag behind in English content area instruction. High-quality Spanish language instruction starting in kindergarten is essential. Without it, Spanish-dominant students do not get a fair chance to develop good literacy and academic skills in their first or second language.

More Need, Less Bilingual Instruction

Despite the evidence that properly implemented bilingual education works for English language learners, English learners are being pushed into English-only programs or getting less instruction in their primary languages.

Voters in three states (California, 1998; Arizona, 2000; Massachusetts, 2002) have passed referenda mandating "English-only" education and outlawing bilingual instruction. (Colorado and Oregon defeated similar referendums in 2002 and 2008.) Although many parents in these states hoped to get waivers so their children could continue bilingual education, they had more luck in some places than others.

In Arizona, one-third of English language learners were enrolled in bilingual education before voters passed Proposition 203 in 2000. Although Proposition 203 allowed waivers, the state's superintendent of public instruction insisted on a strict interpretation of the law that denied waivers to most parents. Eventually almost all of Arizona's bilingual programs were discontinued; the National Association for Bilingual Education noted in October 2005 that "bilingual education is simply no longer available" to English language learners in Arizona.

Prior to the passage of Question 2 in Massachusetts in 2002, 23 percent of that state's roughly 50,000 English learners were enrolled in bilingual education. By 2005, only about 5 percent were in bilingual programs. Under the new law it is easier for children older than 10 to get waivers, so middle and high school students are more likely to participate in bilingual education than elementary students. Students do not need a waiver to participate in two-way bilingual programs; in 2005 there were 822 students enrolled in two-way bilingual programs.

Resistance Saves Some Programs

In California, the first state to pass an English-only referendum in 1998, some schools were able to continue offering bilingual education. The law required all districts to inform parents of their option to continue in bilingual education by signing a waiver; some schools and districts succeeded in getting a very high percentage of waivers and continuing their programs. But by 1999, researchers at the University of California Linguistic Minority Research Institute found that only 12 percent of English learners were in bilingual programs, compared to 29 percent before the law changed.

Researchers also found that districts that had a strong commitment to primary language programs were able to hold on to those programs after Proposition 227 passed, whereas districts that were "not especially supportive of primary language programs prior to 1998" were more likely to do away with primary language instruction altogether.

The "English-HURRY!" Approach

Even in places where bilingual education is still permitted (by law or by waiver), top-down pressures threaten to weaken it. Since the passage of NCLB, standardized testing in English has put pressure on schools to teach English earlier and to do it faster.

Bilingual education is still legal in Wisconsin, where I teach. Milwaukee has a districtwide developmental bilingual (also called "late-exit") program. This means that children learn to read and write first in their primary language (in our case, Spanish), and in the

early grades they are taught all subjects in Spanish. Once they have gained a strong footing in Spanish, they transition to English and start to receive a larger percentage of literacy and content area instruction in English. Even after making the transition to English, students can continue to get a significant portion of their literacy and content area instruction in Spanish for as many years as they choose to stay in the bilingual program.

> **In 2002, Wisconsin did away with all of its Spanish-language standardized tests and began requiring almost all English language learners to take standardized tests in English starting in 3rd grade.**

But since the passage of NCLB, our district's developmental bilingual program has not fared as well as one might hope. In 2002, Wisconsin did away with all of its Spanish-language standardized tests and began requiring almost all English language learners to take standardized tests in English starting in 3rd grade. (Wisconsin could have purchased and administered tests in Spanish, but chose not to do so because of the cost.)

The English tests have changed classroom instruction for bilingual students in our district. District administrators, many principals, and lots of teachers have bought into the idea that kids must learn English sooner because they must score well on English language tests. "Hurry up and teach kids to read in English! They've got to be ready to take the 3rd-grade reading test in English! They've got to be ready to take the 4th-grade WKCE in English!" Suddenly a lot of what we know about second-language acquisition has fallen by the wayside in the scramble to get kids to do well on tests so we can keep schools off the list.

At my school, the year after the law changed, I was part of a team of teachers and administrators that met for months to decide how to respond to the reality that our Spanish-dominant students would be tested in English starting in 3rd grade. We ultimately decided to transition children to English reading in the 2nd and 3rd grades. (We had previously transitioned students to reading in their second language at the end of 3rd grade and beginning of 4th grade.) Other schools in my district have also pushed the transition to English to earlier grades. Still others have reduced primary language instruction in the early grades to make room for direct instruction in English reading (for Spanish-speaking students) as early as 1st grade.

There has been little public discussion about these changes, which contradict the research because they decrease the amount of primary-language instruction and allow less time for students to establish solid literacy skills in their primary language before beginning the transition to second-language literacy. Instead of engaging in discussion about these changes, many administrators and some teachers dismiss concerns with a common refrain: "This is what we have to do to get them ready for the tests."

In a report called "The Initial Impact of Proposition 227 on the Instruction of English Learners," researchers in California described how bilingual instruction changed when English-only testing began:

English-only testing was observed to have an extraordinary effect on English learner instruction, causing teachers to leapfrog much of the normal literacy instruction and go directly to English word recognition or phonics, bereft of meaning or context. Teachers also worried greatly that if they spent time orienting the children to broader literacy activities like storytelling, story sequencing activities, reading for meaning, or writing and vocabulary development in the primary language, that their students would not be gaining the skills that would be tested on the standardized test in English. They feared that this could result in the school and the students suffering sanctions imposed by the law.

Thus, even in the classrooms that had been designated as bilingual, and where principals often contended that little had changed, teachers revealed that their teaching practices had indeed changed substantially and that their students were receiving much less literacy instruction in their primary language.

Ironically, the NCLB does not specify what language students should be taught in, nor does it even require that students be tested in English. It specifies that students must be tested "in a valid and reliable manner," and that they should be given "reasonable accommodations," including "to the extent practicable,

assessments in the language and form most likely to yield accurate data on what such students know and can do."

But states have chosen to implement the law in a variety of ways. Most states test students exclusively in English. Some states give English learners extra time to take the test. Another common accommodation is to translate or simplify the English on portions of the test. The state of California allows no accommodations for students who have been in the California schools for one year. Ten California districts have filed suit claiming this violates the NCLB's provision that students be tested in a valid and reliable manner with reasonable accommodations.

Segregation and Unequal Resources

These recent changes in language and testing policies are making a bad situation worse for English language learners, many of whom were already experiencing some of the worst educational conditions in the country.

A study published by the Urban Institute in September 2005 noted that the majority of English language learners are "segregated in schools serving primarily ELL and immigrant children." The study found that these "high-LEP" schools (defined as

> **Ironically, the NCLB does not specify what language students should be taught in, nor does it even require that students be tested in English.**

schools where Limited English Proficient students comprise 23.5 percent or more of the student body) tend to be large and urban, with a student body that is largely minority (77 percent) and largely poor (72 percent). In addition, "high-LEP schools face more difficulties filling teaching vacancies and are more likely to rely on unqualified and substitute teachers," and teachers are "more likely to have provisional, emergency, or temporary certification than are those in other schools."

Researchers at the University of California, Davis in 2003 found similar disadvantages for the schooling of English language learners, saying they faced "intense segregation into schools and classrooms that place [English learners] at particularly high risk for educational failure."

Advocacy for Immigrants

As conditions and policies worsen for English learners, there is an urgent need for teachers, families, and language-minority communities to speak up in favor of immigrant students and bilingual education.

As federal courts challenge and strike down large parts of immigration laws in Arizona, Georgia, Indiana, South Carolina, and Utah, new legislation continues to fester fear and distrust. In Alabama — where a federal judge upheld an immigration law requiring schools to document immigration status of students and their parents upon enrollment — state education officials reported that some 2,000 Hispanic students (about 7 percent of the state's Hispanic student population) did not show up to school the week after the ruling.

It is important for English learners to succeed academically and to become bilingual, especially now. Many U.S. cities have majority-minority populations, and more and more people in the United States speak languages other than English. To be able to successfully live in and lead this diverse society, people need to learn how to value and accept others. All children need to learn how to communicate with people whose language and culture are different from their own.

These abilities are highly valued, and many teenagers and adults spend years trying to develop them. Children who are raised from birth speaking a language other than English have a unique opportunity to cultivate these abilities from a young age. Our schools must help them seize that opportunity. ▪

....

Kelley Dawson Salas teaches 3rd grade at the Milwaukee Spanish Immersion School in Milwaukee, Wis., and is an editor of Rethinking Schools *magazine.*

Stephen Kroninger

A Librarian in Every School, Books in Every Home

A modest proposal

BOB PETERSON

In the spring of 2010, within a week's time, two things happened that made me angry. The first was the release of scores from the National Assessment of Educational Progress (NAEP) that showed African American 4th graders in Wisconsin (most of whom live in Milwaukee) had the lowest reading scores in the nation. Despite the limitations of such tests, the results confirmed what many educators already knew: Way too many Milwaukee children are not reading at an acceptable level.

The second was the district's announcement of major cuts to local school budgets for next year. At the 400-student elementary school where I work, the projected cuts meant that, despite a modest increase in student enrollment, we had to cut an additional staff position. Given that in the past few years budget cuts had forced us to eliminate the music teacher, gym teacher, program implementor, half a secretarial position, and all of our regular classroom teaching assistants, we had little choice but to eliminate our librarian position. Similar cuts occurred throughout the Milwaukee schools, so it's likely that next year the nearly 100 elementary and K-8 schools in the district will have only five full-time librarians.

The local media and policy makers expressed "outrage" on the first matter but ignored the second. The *Milwaukee Journal Sentinel* called for "greater accountability," "firing bad teachers," "linking teacher pay to performance," and a number of other proposals. Local talk show hosts and columnists echoed the paper's calls. Ignored was any recognition that the nearly 55 percent jobless rate in parts of the black community might impact children's lives.

But, most tellingly, there was not one mention of libraries or librarians, or the need for children to have books in their homes. Such silence is unconscionable. According to researcher and linguistics expert Stephen Krashen: "Research shows school libraries are related to better reading achievement. The reason for this is obvious. Children become better readers by reading more, and for many children, the library is the only place they have access to books."

Moreover, research by Jeff McQuillan has confirmed that access to books is strongly related to performance on the NAEP exam for 4th graders, even when researchers control for the effects of poverty.

During spring break I met with my principal and a parent who is on the school governance council, and we agreed to call a public meeting about the lack of librarians. Although we are concerned about our librarian position, we recognize that all children deserve a librarian in their school. Thus our call for the meeting talked of the need to work for a "librarian in every school."

The day after spring break, the 4th- and 5th-grade teachers explained the potential loss of our librarian to our students. We invited them to form a club to address the issue. I met twice with 12 students in the week before the community meeting. After a brief discussion of why librarians are so important, the students decided to call their club the Rescue Our Librarians Club.

I explained that our school budget was $51,000 short of what we would need to have a librarian. We then moved into the "What can we do?" section of the meeting. A couple of children suggested writing letters to the president and the governor, but most focused their attention on raising money. Olivia, a 4th grader, confidently explained that on a good day she can make $20 at a lemonade stand. As others rushed to start planning the sale, I asked the question, "How many lemonade sales would that take us?"

"Lots," another student responded. I suggested we figure it out. After some group long division we

realized we would have to run 2,550 lemonade stands. The lemonade idea was shelved.

I suggested that as many students as possible stay after school on Friday to attend the community meeting (six did) and see what ideas the parents had. The group wrote out a statement with which to start the meeting, and Jalen, a 4th grader, volunteered to read it:

> We are the future of America. We are students at La Escuela Fratney who formed the Rescue Our Librarians Club—the RLC. We want the budget cuts to stop so we can keep our library and librarian. Some adults say 'Read a lot, don't watch TV,' but then they take away our library. That's not good.... It's not fair if a school doesn't have a librarian. And it's not fair if some schools have a librarian and others don't. We want to help other students and schools to have their own librarians, too.

The children from several classes made posters and the club members wrote a poem that explained why having a library doesn't work without a librarian.

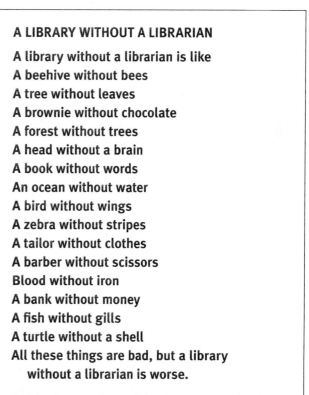

A LIBRARY WITHOUT A LIBRARIAN

A library without a librarian is like
A beehive without bees
A tree without leaves
A brownie without chocolate
A forest without trees
A head without a brain
A book without words
An ocean without water
A bird without wings
A zebra without stripes
A tailor without clothes
A barber without scissors
Blood without iron
A bank without money
A fish without gills
A turtle without a shell
All these things are bad, but a library
    without a librarian is worse.

Written by members of the Rescue Our Librarians Club at La Escuela Fratney, Milwaukee, Wis.

The community meeting, attended by 75 people — including librarians, parents, students, university faculty, and concerned community members — discussed an array of possible immediate, medium, and long-range actions.

"Some adults say, 'Read a lot, don't watch TV,' but then they take away our library. That's not good."

The most interesting proposal, from my point of view, was the idea that we should demand that the federal government — as part of its planned ESEA reauthorization — include funding for a full-time librarian in every public school with 200 children or more, plus outreach librarians in city and county library systems to work with religious and community organizations to increase the use of community libraries.

Back at the Rescue Our Librarians Club, we did some calculations. Assuming that wages and benefits for a librarian average $75,000 a year, and that there are 95,000 public schools in the United States, the government would have to find $7,125,000,000 to ensure a librarian for every school.

"Wow, that's a lot!" one student exclaimed.

And it is. I directed the children to the website the Cost of War (costofwar.com), where we discovered that the United States spends nearly $300 million daily on the wars in Iraq and Afghanistan. We figured out that funding all those librarians for a year was equivalent to 25 days of war spending.

It's too early to tell where the community meetings and the Rescue Our Librarians Club will lead. But personally, I can't stop dreaming about federal funding for school and community librarians as part of the reauthorization of ESEA. Let's see. We could ask that by 2014 or so, 100 percent of all schools should have certified librarians and 100 percent of public libraries should have expanded weekend hours. Now there's a data-driven goal I could get behind. It would provide nearly 100,000 jobs, promote countless hours of lifelong learning and enjoyment to millions of people, and most likely raise those 4th-grade test scores. ■

....

Bob Peterson (REPMilw@aol.com) was a co-founder and 5th-grade teacher at La Escuela Fratney in Milwaukee for 22 years, a founding editor of Rethinking Schools *magazine, and serves as president of the Milwaukee Teachers' Education Association. He has co-edited numerous books, including* Rethinking Columbus, Rethinking Our Classrooms, Rethinking Globalization, *and* Rethinking Mathematics.

Craig Dingle

Reading First, Libraries Last

Scripted programs undermine teaching and children's love of books

RACHEL CLOUES

When I was student teaching in Denver, in the pre-No Child Left Behind years, I visited a talented bilingual literacy teacher at a low-income public school. The teacher and her students inspired me, but what I most remember is the school's library. As I walked through the front door, right in front of me—in fact, spilling out into the hallway—was the entrance to a beautiful space full of books and plants, tanks of tropical fish, and cozy, pillow-filled spaces to read (including an old English phone booth). I was drawn in. Natural light filtered in through open windows, and lamps and tiny lights strung around the room cast a warm, welcoming glow. Bright kites hung from the rafters over the shelves of science books; near the fairy tales, a potted tree arched over a puppet theater, next to it a row of pillows and a basket of puppets. All of the bookshelves were child-sized, arranged to create intimate spaces for browsing or reading. Interesting objects, like rocks and bones, graced the tops of the bookshelves alongside carefully selected books highlighting each genre. If I was this captivated by the library, what must it be like for the students at this school?

> **I wandered through this lovely library, enchanted, and noticed it was full of children — some with teachers, others clearly on their own — all engaged in reading, browsing the shelves, and checking out books.**

I wandered through this lovely library, enchanted, and noticed it was full of children — some with teachers, others clearly on their own — all engaged in reading, browsing the shelves, and checking out books. When I spoke with the librarian, I learned he had a previous career as a costume designer in New York. His artistic expression and enthusiasm for stories were gloriously married in this wonderful space. The children, he explained, loved being in the library, and they often spent their lunch recess there. The classroom teacher with whom I spent the day confirmed this: The children at their school loved to read. They also performed well on state reading exams.

I have always carried the memory of that day tucked carefully away, to remind me of the potential of a school library. Stephen Krashen, the preeminent scholar of second language acquisition, has researched and written about the correlation between communities' access to books and the reading proficiency levels of children in schools. In a 2002 *Phi Delta Kappan* article, Krashen explains, "Research on the impact of libraries over the last decade has shown that better school libraries — those with more books and better staffing — are associated with greater literacy development." I think now of the Denver school I visited and hope that library is still open, and that the librarian has managed to keep his job. In these bleak NCLB

days of regimented, scripted reading programs and financially drained school districts, I am deeply worried about the future of elementary school libraries.

Reading First, the NCLB initiative that ostensibly aims to ensure that all children will read by the end of 3rd grade, certainly does not support the library at my own school in the San Francisco Unified School District (SFUSD). Authorized by the Elementary and Secondary Education Act in 2001, Reading First provides schools with money to improve K-3 classroom reading instruction — but only through approved "scientific research and standards-based" language arts programs. Reading First grants were awarded to schools that applied. Districts around the country identified schools at risk of not making federally mandated Adequate Yearly Progress (AYP) and asked these schools to apply for the funds. Some schools democratically voted to seek and then accept the Reading First money; others were forced to accept Reading First by concerned administrators.

When I arrived to teach at one of San Francisco's so-called "Dream Schools," I noticed a sign on the front of the school boldly proclaiming College Preparatory School, but once inside, I couldn't find the library. Finally, someone unlocked the door for me, and I discovered a small, book-filled space, cluttered and neglected. There was no librarian, nor any system to check books in or out. In fact, the shelves of picture books had been pushed against the wall to make space for parent meetings, groups of children taking tests, or after-school classes. A voter-approved measure, Proposition H, paid for us to have a librarian one day each week, but it was nearly impossible to check out books because the computer was always broken. Happily, this year we have an enthusiastic new librarian for half of every week, and he is reviving the library space and beginning to teach the children some library skills. For most of this year he used his personal laptop to check out books, but he recently acquired a donated desktop computer.

"We Do HM"

SFUSD strongly advised the "underperforming" schools (read: schools with high numbers of low-income students and English language learners) to accept Reading First money. As a result, my school uses Houghton Mifflin Reading. So much does the

Houghton Mifflin reading program influence and define language arts instruction in the district that I frequently hear teachers and administrators—and sometimes even students—use the terms "Houghton Mifflin" or "HM" as synonyms for the word reading. One might hear a teacher say, for example, "We do HM from 8 to 10 a.m. on Mondays."

Like other scripted reading programs, Houghton Mifflin Reading is textbook and workbook oriented, with some leveled supplemental books—the "HM Leveled Readers." A Houghton Mifflin representative told me that teachers are not supposed to use any other children's books at all in their classrooms, only those provided by the program. This may explain, in part, why checking out books from the school library had fallen by the wayside when Houghton Mifflin Reading was adopted by my school, though my principal told me that San Francisco's school libraries have been in a state of neglect for many years. The amount of direct language arts instruction required by Reading First schools is 150 minutes per day for grades 1-3, so if a teacher follows the daily plan exactly, there is no time

Along with hundreds of other Bay Area elementary teachers, I sat through grade-level specific classes led by "experts" who refused to acknowledge any critical discussion about the teaching of reading.

for other reading-related activities such as a trip to the school library, independent reading, read-aloud, or literature circles. Of course, some teachers work these into the school day anyhow, but often at the expense of other important curricular areas like physical education, nutrition and health, social studies, or science. Always there are the looming tests (every six weeks), or visits from the "Walkthrough Team," a group of district administrators who check each classroom to see whether the teacher has the requisite Houghton Mifflin materials displayed on the classroom wall.

Much of the Reading First rhetoric, such as "Scientifically Based Reading Instruction," is familiar to teachers; the 2000 National Reading Panel (NRP) Report is the foundation of Reading First and is full of such zealous phrases. It's an unbalanced and

incomplete work, however, and misleading in facts and figures. Dr. Joanne Yatvin, a past president of the National Council of Teachers of English and the only member of the panel with a career in elementary schools, wrote a minority view expressing her concern about the potential use of the panel's results. She concluded, "I ask Congress not to take actions that will promote one philosophical view of reading or constrain future research in the field on the basis of the panel's limited and narrow set of findings." (The entire minority view can be found at www.nichd.nih.gov/publications/nrp/upload/minorityView.pdf.) In her thorough evaluation, Yatvin interprets some of the report's inflated rhetoric and exposes the inadequacy of the NRP findings as a scientific base for reading instruction. In addition, she points out that the NRP did not recommend any commercial programs or disqualify other approaches to teaching reading, such as using methods of whole language. Despite Yatvin's critique, President Bush and Congress hailed the NRP report. Houghton Mifflin, along with a few other big textbook publishers, aggressively appropriated much of the convincing terminology from the report and seduced struggling school districts to adopt its curriculum as part of the Reading First grant. When I attended the "Houghton Mifflin Institute," a five-day professional development training for educators new to Houghton Mifflin Reading, the trainer handed me a copy of the NRP report. When I asked about Yatvin's minority view, missing from the copy, I was given a blank stare in return.

I am not opposed to professional development opportunities for teachers, but I found the "institute" to be contrived and patronizing. I had been told to register for the annual summer training when I arrived to teach in California, though I later learned that districts cannot require teachers to attend because they are paid a stipend in lieu of their regular salary. The "institute" felt like a dumbed-down seminar showcasing glossy textbooks and fat, workbook-inspired binders. Along with hundreds of other Bay Area elementary teachers, I sat through grade-level specific classes led by "experts" who refused to acknowledge any critical discussion about the teaching of reading (and there was quite a lot!). My particular trainer even told me point-blank that she was not allowed to answer questions that deviated from her script.

We read articles jigsaw-style on one day; my group was assigned "Remarks by Secretary Paige to the Commonwealth Club of California." This included such banal comments as, "No doubt about it, teaching is hard work. Even our first lady, Mrs. Bush, struggled when she was a young teacher." At the end of the article, Houghton Mifflin summarized the main point they hoped we would glean from Mr. Paige's speech: "In other words: four out of five students are being taught by a teacher who is pessimistic about their future." Really?

> **I read the books to my students in their entirety and when the children reread the excerpted versions in their textbooks, they astutely notice that the stories make less sense.**

This Houghton Mifflin training program provided little inspiration for teachers. In fact, it was insulting. I walked away from those five days horrified at the blatant attempt to indoctrinate teachers into the HM world. There was a not-so-hidden curriculum to teach me not to think about what I teach. After spending almost three years with this reading program, I am now convinced that the same agenda exists for my students. As scripted, Houghton Mifflin Reading does not challenge children to think or read critically. For example, one 4th-grade-level story is a biography of Cuban-born singer Gloria Estefan; not surprisingly, the story presents a conservative and one-sided perspective of the Cuban Revolution, and of Cuba in general. Houghton Mifflin Reading is also weak on the teaching of writing, and it is not appropriate for English language learners (who comprise 100 percent of my class). The program includes books of worksheets to use with English learners but my students need full-length picture books and easier chapter books to engage them in reading. Even the easiest "Leveled Readers" are too hard for many of them to read. The skills tests, used to measure students' progress in language arts regardless of their level of English, involve multistep directions that are difficult for even the most language-proficient students. I've found that Houghton Mifflin Reading can be a good tool for some aspects of teaching reading, but

used exclusively it is not comprehensive and it is nowhere near engaging enough for my students. This, of course, is the flaw of a one-size-fits-all curriculum.

Book by Book

Instead of following the script, I attempt to make my reading and writing instruction comprehensive in other ways. I try to adhere to the specific grammar skills outlined in each theme, but I replace the textbook stories with actual picture books checked out from the public library. I read the books to my students in their entirety and when the children reread the excerpted versions in their textbooks, they astutely notice that the stories make less sense, aren't as interesting, and are missing important illustrations. Chris Van Allsburg's richly illustrated books are a good example; his drawings are crucial for understanding the mysterious undertones of the text. I also bring in other books, lots of them—stories, poetry, and articles that I know my students will relate to and want to discuss. Skipping around in the anthology sometimes allows the HM stories to be more relevant to students' lives. So, logically, we might read the wildfire story in the fall when wildfires are burning all over California or the story about visiting a library before we actually take a field trip to the public library.

Most importantly, I teach students how to recognize books that are the right level for them, and I make time every day for them to read their own selections. Each week we visit our school library so that the students can choose books to take home and read with their families. They are learning to be responsible for what they borrow. Together, we also set up a classroom library, get to know all kinds of fiction and nonfiction texts, and discuss genres and how they often overlap. We visit the public library and apply for library cards. I try to connect reading and the importance of libraries at all levels: classroom, school, public, university, and others. I want my students to understand that public libraries, the physical expression of our intellectual commons, are essential for an educated society and for a democracy.

When schools implement programs like Houghton Mifflin Reading to the exclusion of all other methods of instruction, as Reading First mandates, it threatens the profession of teaching, and the education of our society. Privatizing knowledge shuts down the mechanisms for critical thinking. The ability of students to select their own books, for example, is a powerful expression of their learning and their autonomy. In scripted programs children do not choose what they read, nor do they learn how to select reading material that suits and interests them. Students are disempowered in educating themselves and teachers are disempowered to make professional judgments about what might best help their students learn. In a school dominated by Houghton Mifflin, the library is at risk of becoming superfluous.

I am reminded of a revealing comment from a 4th-grade student I taught last year. Javier, a bright, quiet student who loves books, was listening to me read *My Name Is Maria Isabel*, by Alma Flor Ada. We got to a part in the story where the main character happily talks of spending her lunchtime recess reading in the school library. Javier mumbled wryly, "Yeah, this book's totally fiction."

Like public schools, public libraries are threatened by budget cuts and privatization all over the country. Each day on my way to work I try to remind myself that everything we do in school says something about the society we live in. The existence and maintenance of school and public libraries in our communities says much about the kind of society we want to live in — a society where reading is a powerful and accessible path to learning for all people, where books are a key part of the pursuit of happiness. ■

....

Rachel Cloues is a teacher-librarian at a K-8 school in San Francisco.

Jordin Isip

Think Less Benchmarks

A flawed test does more harm than good

AMY GUTOWSKI

I'm staring at this bulging envelope on my desk. It's a big envelope, much larger than your typical letter-sized envelope, you know, a big one, one that could fit about 15 test booklets and answer sheets. It was just dropped off by our school's "literacy coach." I put quotes around these two words because I often wonder why she was given that title. Much of what she does has nothing to do with literacy. I think we should just call her the "test passer-outer" or something like that, because that is really the bulk of what she does throughout the school year. Positions like these have been hijacked by testing crusaders in schools and districts around the country. Originally, our district adopted these ThinkLink benchmark assessments for schools identified as not making Adequate Yearly Progress (which was disturbing enough: "Our kids are failing, so let's make them take more tests.")

Then last year I learned that virtually all schools were being forced to participate regardless of AYP status.

ThinkLink tests are designed to mirror the format of our state assessments. According to the district—and to the salespeople at ThinkLink—the ThinkLink "formative" assessments would help our district better predict student performance on our state's high-stakes exams. These high-stakes tests are aligned with our state's arbitrary set of standards for each grade level, standards that tend to be incredibly unrealistic and developmentally inappropriate.

There are four benchmark tests a year. Thanks to the folks at the Discovery Channel, that TV channel with the nifty little logo of the earth spinning, my 8-year-old students have four more opportunities to stop learning and fill in the bubbles. The folks at Discovery Education have added an extension to their suite of services. They've branched into the assessment market and now produce ThinkLink formative assessments for districts across the country.

According to the catchy little press release from Discovery Education: "Discovery Education acquired ThinkLink Learning in April 2006, expanding the business unit's high-quality products and services to include formative assessment. ThinkLink pioneered a unique approach to formative assessment that uses a scientifically research-based continuous improvement model that maps diagnostic assessment to state high-stakes tests." So essentially, it's an expensive assessment program—our district spent roughly $400,000 on it in 2008—built on the assumption that repeated testing of children will help them to do better on tests. Forget about reading specialists, art, music, school psychologists, nurses, social workers, or support staff. It's ThinkLink to the rescue!

This is why the overstuffed envelope has landed on my desk. My first impulse is to chuck it in the trash. I'm sure this is the impulse of any teacher who has actually read these assessments. The first time I saw a ThinkLink benchmark I was shocked and dismayed. It was poorly written (e.g., "There was once a little peasant girl. She was pretty as a star in its season. Her real name was Blanchette. She was called Little Goldenhood because of a wonderful little coat with a hood she always wore."); riddled with errors (e.g., "I thi nk of my summers on Grandpa's farm."); and developmentally inappropriate (e.g., "Reread the title of the story *The*

Armadillo: A Shelled Mammal. What happens when -*ed* is added to the word *shell* in the title?
A. It becomes a word that tells when the mammal was shelled
B. It becomes a word that tells how armadillos move
C. It becomes a word that describes the word mammal
D. It becomes a word that is the present tense of the verb shell")

It was all completely disconnected from the curriculum I was teaching.

> **Essentially, it's an expensive assessment program built on the assumption that repeated testing of children will help them to do better on tests.**

After our first round of benchmarks, I decided to call our district's director of assessment to ask about them. It amazed me that this program was implemented so quickly. After all, hadn't Discovery Ed. Inc. just rolled out this new suite of assessments? Teachers in the district were never asked if we wanted to use such testing in our classrooms, the tests were just bought and then mandated, without any discussion. I was upset because my 3rd graders had just finished the weeklong state assessment in November (and all of the preparation preceding), and then we had to stop reading *Charlotte's Web* for two days, and instead fill in more bubbles. The phone conversation was interesting.

According to the assessment director, teachers around the district loved the ThinkLink assessments. She said that I was the only one who complained, and that teachers were amazed at the quick return of test results and data. She said that teachers told her they were learning so much about their students and their learning from these assessments. I was surprised by this response. I had just spoken to a teacher at another elementary school who told me that the entire staff had written a letter protesting the districtwide adoption of these additional tests. The assessment director even claimed that some principals were requesting benchmark assessments for their 1st- and 2nd-grade classrooms. (In our district these tests start at 3rd grade and move up all the way through 9th grade, no classroom is left unscathed, except kindergarten and 1st and 2nd grades—which may very well change if this madness continues.) I could not believe what I was hearing.

The benchmark testing questions were all over the place. Most of them were not at all related to what I was teaching in the classroom. For example, after reading a confusing passage about edible insects—in which there was no explanation of what "edible" means, nor any obvious context clues to help children figure out the meaning of "edible"—my students were asked:

> Which of the following is nearly the opposite of edible?
> A. antiedible
> B. preedible
> C. anedible
> D. inedible

Is this not insane?

I teach about prefixes and suffixes in my classroom, but come on, people. The questioning is so convoluted. My students are 8-year-olds who just started reading two years ago. I want my children to become independent learners and lovers of books. These tests make reading seem awful and tedious. An equally upsetting question asks children to identify an author's purpose (one of our 3rd grade reading "standards" in Wisconsin). My 3rd graders are often asked if a passage was written to entertain, persuade, or inform. Much of what we read in our lives does all of these. We recently finished reading *Turtle Bay*. It's a story about friends cleaning a beach so sea turtles will come and lay their eggs. The story was definitely entertaining, it persuaded my students to think about their actions (e.g., littering hurts animals), and we were informed about turtles. So, in the name of "standards," my students are expected to answer these horribly misleading questions. Why has reading been reduced to this?

At the end of our conversation, the director of assessment asked me if I wanted to participate in making the tests better. I agreed to go over the initial assessment, highlighting grammatical errors and misplaced questions. I sent the offending booklet to her office with red marks and comments. I was then asked if I would be interested in going over future ThinkLink assessments, and at the time, I agreed. But then I began to think about it. I was never asked my opinion about these assessments in the first place, and now here I was agreeing to spend my valuable time working to make these lame assessments better? These tests were mandated in our district without critical discussion and questioning. I was also told that the district would survey teachers about these assessments at the end of the school year. I have yet to see a survey.

Needless to say, I did not spend more of my time working to improve the flawed benchmarks. I have, instead, decided to advocate for my students and their learning. I have been sending opinion pieces to local newspapers and magazines. I have testified at school board meetings. I stand up at staff meetings (often alone) and express my concerns. I will not be apathetic. I'm not buying into this random adoption of mandated assessments. I am tired of this antichild, for-profit agenda in our schools and classrooms. Teachers must come together and speak out against the foolishness and absurdity of it all. Our students deserve more than this. The huge sums paid to Discovery Education Inc. could be put to much better use.

So here I sit, staring at the envelope full of Think-Link tests. The envelope conjures up conflict within me. I don't want to subject my students to this nonsense. I want to resist. I want to shred each booklet page by page, especially the top page with the cute little earth logo. But I can't. I have to pass out these tests or risk my job. Tomorrow, when I pass out the booklets and scantron sheets, I'll explain to my students that some of the questions were confusing even to me, their teacher. I'll ask them not to worry. I'll ask them to do their best. NCLB puts pressure on districts to gather more data, and testing companies get richer producing tests that guarantee large amounts of failure, thus ensuring future customers. It's a vicious, mean-spirited cycle. The way we educate our children is being driven by these test scores. We spend hours at staff meetings looking at the "data" gathered from these mass-produced assessments instead of sharing ideas about meaningful learning and what really works in the classroom.

Who needs the arts? Screw recess. Let them eat tests. I'll think about this tomorrow as my 3rd graders fill in perfect little circles on their benchmark score sheets—3rd graders who are most definitely being left behind. ∎

....

Amy Gutowski teaches 3rd grade in Milwaukee Public Schools.

Roxanna Bikadoroff

Deporting Elena's Father

MELISSA BOLLOW TEMPEL

All over the United States, formal collaboration between U.S. Immigration and Customs Enforcement (ICE) and local law enforcement under ICE ACCESS programs has deputized local law enforcement agents to enforce federal immigration law. Although no such agreements currently exist in the state of Wisconsin, the Milwaukee County Sheriff's Office has been collaborating with ICE. The result has been a significant increase (46 percent from 2007 to 2008) in the number of detained and then deported immigrants picked up on minor traffic violations in the county. The Milwaukee County Board of Supervisors heard testimony on this issue at their July 2010 meeting. Unfortunately, they sided with the sheriff's department and decided not to pursue an intensive investigation. Local community organizations continue to advocate for an end to this collaboration. Rethinking Schools Editor Melissa Bollow Tempel gave the following testimony.

I am a bilingual teacher in Milwaukee Public Schools. Over the years, I have seen many students deal with deportation. People ask me, "How does deportation affect children?" The question I'd like to pose today is "How *doesn't* deportation affect children?"

This year I had a student in my 1st-grade class. I'll call her Elena. She was a natural leader in the classroom and spoke both English and Spanish fluently. She was well liked by her classmates and always organizing games on the playground during recess. Elena's father was a model dad, the kind who worked hard and spent his free time with his family and his church. Every day he'd pick up his children from school. When Elena saw him approaching the school she'd yell, "Papi!" and run to him. They'd share a big hug and then he'd take her hand and the hand of her little sister and they'd walk home together. He helped Elena complete her homework—she is a very bright little girl—and read to her.

Elena's mother came to my classroom one morning and asked me if I could write a letter of support to the judge who would try her husband's deportation case. She told me that Elena's father, the father of her four children, had gone to work and never returned. She learned later that ICE had taken him into custody. Although she is a U.S. citizen, he was not allowed to return home while awaiting his trial. Of course, I wrote the letter for her, as did the teachers of Elena's siblings, but it did no good. Elena didn't see her father again and eventually he was deported. My own daughter was in 1st grade this year, and I couldn't even allow myself to think about the severe impact that losing her father would have had on her.

This brings me to how deportation affects my students. Elena's mother was forced to send her children to her sister's house on the other side of town to sleep every night because her husband had cared for the girls while she worked third shift in a factory. Elena's bright smile and eagerness to learn faded and she became somber, tired, and withdrawn. She stopped participating in class and often asked to stay inside instead of playing with her friends during recess. Elena stopped doing her homework because her father was not there to help her, and her mother had no time between household chores, cooking, and getting the children ready to drop off at their aunt's house every night. Her mother told me that she slept only three hours during the day while her baby was sleeping. She'd be so tired that she would oversleep and miss the pickup time at the end of the school day. We'd have to call to wake her up.

Mondays were the worst. Elena would come to school after spending some quality time with her mother and family. I'd take one look at her face and know it was going to be a hard morning. On those days I'd let her eat breakfast in the hallway with me

People ask me, "How does deportation affect children?" The question I'd like to pose is "How *doesn't* deportation affect children?"

while my teaching partner stayed with the rest of the class. Elena would sit on my lap and cry—sob, really—and tell me that she missed her father, that she wanted to talk to him, to see him. Sometimes it would make her feel better to write him letters. She would end them with "Are you coming home?" and draw two little boxes—one for him to check "yes" and one for him to check "no." Even more heartbreaking were the letters that ended the same way but with a different question: "Do you still love me?"

This summer I have spent some time with Elena and her siblings, trying to give her mother a break. Mostly I'm there because I know that Elena's having a difficult time with yet another change in her life, the transition from the school to the summer, and she's lost the regular support of her teachers for the summer.

Elena's mom told me that they will probably move in with her sister, which means that Elena will have to change schools. Her new school doesn't have bilingual classes. She'll have to make new friends and her mother will have to start over, building a support network in the community for her children and herself.

I'm using Elena as an example because this is *not* a unique story. It has many similarities to the experiences of all my students who have dealt with the deportation of a parent. There is absolutely no way that Elena and the three other children in my class who lost a loved one to deportation were not deeply affected, emotionally and academically. Our students are hurting. Some of them were born here, making them "legal," and they hope to carry out their family's dream of a better life. That dream starts with education.

These children face so many obstacles: living in poverty, lacking medical and dental care, and living in homes that landlords don't bother to repair because they know their tenants won't report them. Deporting children's parents creates just another obstacle for them, but this is the one that is the most difficult to overcome. ■

Melissa Bollow Tempel teaches in Milwaukee Public Schools and is an editor of Rethinking Schools.

Gigi Kaeser

Teaching the Whole Story

One school's struggle toward gay and lesbian inclusion

KATE LYMAN

One fall a teacher in my elementary school returned from a conference with information about the photo exhibit *Love Makes a Family: Living in Gay and Lesbian Families.* The colleague had been part of a team of four teachers at the school, including myself, involved the previous spring in the filming of the video *It's Elementary: Talking About Gay Issues in School* (see Resources).

We were coming together again to make plans to display the photo exhibit at our school. We discussed organizing activities highlighting gay and lesbian inclusion during the two weeks of the display. I fully supported the plan. But at the same time, something inside me balked at the thought of presenting it to the school district administration. I didn't want to relive all the controversy we had encountered the previous spring, when we did the filming for *It's Elementary.*

But a conversation with the lesbian parents of Paul, one of the students in my 2nd-/3rd-grade classroom, renewed my energy. We were discussing a protest to be held at a nearby church, which had invited an inflammatory antigay minister to speak. They said that they supported the actions of the protesters but that they were too tired to go themselves.

"I've gone to so many marches, so many rallies," said Jane. "There isn't a day in my life when I'm not confronted with homophobia. I'm just tired of it. I'll let the younger people do it for me. More power to them!"

I knew I wasn't any younger and was also tired of controversy. But I realized that the photo exhibit was an opportunity for me to assist in some of the struggles they faced every day.

Dealing with Student Attitudes

Although I first became aware of gay and lesbian issues through my involvement with the feminist movement in the 1970s, it wasn't until the 1980s that I began to make the connection between multicultural education, gender equity, and teaching gay and lesbian inclusion. Under our district's Human Relations Program, I had been working for several years on curriculum for Women's History Month, which included not only learning about women in history, but also challenging traditional gender roles. I began to realize that gay and lesbian inclusion should be a major part of this work, and that it also should be contained in the discourse on sexism, racism, and other types of discrimination and stereotyping that fell under the district's multicultural umbrella. "Respecting diversity" were words that frequently occurred in the district's mission statements, a commitment that I was to find out later did not fully extend to differences of sexual orientation.

Addressing homophobic name-calling, gay and lesbian stereotypes, and heterosexism became even more of a priority when I found myself teaching children with gay or lesbian parents. During this school year my classroom of 22 children was representative of the school's low-income and working-class urban population, with six African American, four biracial (African American/European American), two Asian American (Hmong), one Mexican American, and nine European American children. And, as in the last several years, one of my students, Paul, had two lesbian moms.

Although I was continuing with 15 of the students from my 1st-/2nd-grade classroom the year before, this school year had started out tense, with students challenging each other with teasing and name-calling. After several days of more minor incidents, this culminated in a fight on the playground. I read a poem with the class, "Coke-Bottle Brown" by Nikki Grimes, and facilitated a discussion about name-calling. We talked about the words that had sparked the conflict and discussed how they fell into certain categories, like racism and sexism. Kendra said, "I know a word. It's homophobia." I wrote it on the board and talked about what it meant and how it's related to words that they had mentioned, such as "faggot" and "gay bitch."

There were some negative reactions (among kids new to my class) to the word "gay." Tony said, "I hate gay people." After school he met one of Paul's moms, Anne. Paul went up to Tony and said, "Well, do you like my mom?" He said, "Yeah." Paul said, "Well, my mom's gay, so I guess you don't hate gay people."

Later, I shared with Anne what had happened. She said that she was proud of Paul's efforts to prove Tony wrong. I shared in her wonder at her child's strength and perseverance. Yet I felt uneasy. It shouldn't be up to 7-year-old kids, I thought, to defend themselves and their families against irrational fears and hatred. I felt that I needed to do a more adequate job of shouldering Paul's burden, of helping the students in my classroom to unlearn negative feelings and stereotypes about gay and lesbian people.

> **"Respecting diversity" were words that frequently occurred in the district's mission statements, a commitment that I was to find out later did not fully extend to differences of sexual orientation.**

From this initial discussion of name-calling until the last weeks of the school year, antibias education was to become a continuous thread woven throughout our curriculum. The photo exhibit opportunity seemed to be a natural conclusion to our yearlong efforts. What was clear to me and to most other teachers, however, as well as to many of our students and parents, was problematic for the district administration. As it turned out, the administration's conflicting messages and muddled tactics, along with full coverage by the local press (our school was in the front-page headlines for a week and featured on television news and radio talk shows), succeeded in creating even more of a controversy out of the photo exhibit than I had originally feared.

Conflict in the Community

At an initial meeting about the exhibit with the principal, the assistant superintendent, and a parent, we encountered little opposition. The assistant superintendent assured us, "I have no problems with this." However, after consulting with the deputy superintendent and the superintendent, she sent us a letter that implied otherwise. Along with flowery language extolling our "wonderful work" teaching acceptance of diversity and prejudice reduction was this statement: "Having a picture exhibition that highlights all the many different kinds of families would support your SIP (School Improvement Plan) goal, the larger issue of creating an inclusive school, as well as the philosophy of (our) School District. Selecting one family structure only would exclude and not be appropriate given our inclusive goals. ..." The letter concluded with a suggestion that we meet with interested parents and staff if we intended to proceed with an exhibit within those parameters.

At a hastily called meeting of 17 staff members and seven parents, it was decided that we needed to preserve the integrity of the photo exhibit by keeping it intact. People agreed that mixing in photos of heterosexual families would dilute the message: that gay and lesbian families need to be recognized and celebrated. It was felt that the exhibit would be an opportunity for gays and lesbians to be highlighted, as has traditionally been done with other groups excluded from the mainstream of school curriculum. But despite the decision of this group and letters sent to the administration from the PTO and local clergy, gay and lesbian groups, university professors, and many parents, the district maintained its stance.

A week later, however, the administrators changed tactics and delegated the decision to the school community. They set up a meeting which, according to a local newspaper, the *Capital Times*, they decided was "not one appropriate for (district) higher-ups to attend." The meeting, which was announced on television and in the newspapers as a "public hearing," was called for May 1.

Some of the photos from the exhibit, black-and-white images of racially diverse gay or lesbian families in every imaginable family configuration (extended families, two moms or two dads, single-parent families, families with stepparents, etc.), were set up in the school library for parents and other community members to preview. Discussion, however, was limited to two dozen parents who had either volunteered or been recruited by the principal to present different points of view.

The meeting, minimally facilitated by the principal and a district resource person, was described by the *Capital Times* as a "chaotic process." The story began: "A punch was thrown, a moderator lost his cool, and parents were left in an uproar. ..." Eventually a second meeting had to be scheduled to resolve the issues left unresolved.

Feelings at those meetings were indeed intense. People yelled, cried, interrupted, accused, and sometimes tried to compromise. Having an exhibit of gay and lesbian families was likened by some of the speakers to exhibiting photos of drug dealers or sadomasochists. Although many cited religious reasons ("My religion says it's a sin"), a few others gave cultural concerns ("Gays and lesbians are despised in our culture"). One of Paul's moms, Jane, who said later that she was the only gay parent who took part in both meetings, related how difficult it was for her to sit through all the insults and attacks on her family.

At the beginning of the first meeting, our home/school coordinator read a letter signed by 37 staff members supporting the exhibit. The letter said:

Dear (school) community,

If we need to be diverse in our thinking and teaching, then we need to teach and talk about gay and lesbian families. ... This is not about sexuality. This is about family structure. ... In addition, this exhibit addresses a pertinent safety issue. Children are often harassed or intimidated by other children using homophobic terms.

We, as teachers or parents, always challenge a student who is making racist comments or insults. Yet homophobic name-calling—"You're gay!" etc.—is sometimes left unaddressed. ... If we are to eliminate discrimination, we need to confront it in all forms.

We, the undersigned [school] staff, are strongly supportive of having the Love Makes a Family exhibit at our school. We believe it is educationally sound and supports our SIP goals of prejudice reduction and inclusion.

With the exception of the letter, teachers followed the advice of the union to assert our contractual right of academic freedom by refraining from debate. We joined the observers from the school and the community, who had been instructed by the principal and facilitator to remain silent. About half the parents in the discussion group expressed views similar to those presented by the teachers. They affirmed the need to be inclusive of gay and lesbian families in support of the school's and district's multicultural, antibias goals. Several stated that they wanted their children to grow up in a world in which they would be safe from discrimination, regardless of their sexual orientation.

Some parents refuted the parallels to the African American Civil Rights Movement that had been brought up in the teachers' letter, but other African American parents supported the comparison. Kendra's mother, for one, said that she had encountered discrimination many times in her life and knew it well. "I can feel it now, again, in this room," she said in an impassioned statement that received resounding applause.

> **Some parents refuted the parallels to the African American Civil Rights Movement that had been brought up in the teachers' letter, but other African American parents supported the comparison.**

Several alternative proposals were raised. They included leaving out the words "gay" and "lesbian" in the title of the exhibit, mixing in photos of heterosexual families, and moving the exhibit to the Reach room (a small classroom out of the main stream of traffic). Gigi Kaeser, the photographer who created the exhibit, and several parents deemed these suggestions unacceptable. "This is another case of forcing gays and lesbians back into the closet," Kaeser said.

Toward the end of the second meeting, it appeared that little progress had been made. The 20 parent representatives had not succeeded in narrowing the gap between their widely divergent viewpoints. Suddenly, however, during the last 15 minutes, they reached a consensus. The compromise was very similar to the teachers' original proposal: to display the photo exhibit in the school library; to provide alternatives to children whose parents requested them; and to communicate with parents. This compromise appeared to be more the result of time pressure, exhaustion, and resignation than of genuine conflict resolution. The meeting was adjourned, but the tension continued—in the stuffy and crowded library, in the halls, in the parking lot, and on the sidewalks surrounding the school.

Reactions from the Students

Meanwhile, the students in my classroom were trying to make sense of the conflict. Some children were aware of their parents' support for the exhibit; many of their parents had spoken out publicly. Cassie's dad expressed his opinions in the local newspaper: "Why don't they [the school administration] just say they don't want this in here because it is about gay people?" Jodi's dad was featured in the press as well, because he'd been involved in a scuffle with members of the "Christian Right" who were demonstrating outside the school during the first meeting. Paul's moms lent us their rainbow flag, which we displayed until the end of the school year.

Emily wrote a letter to the local newspaper, which was published.

> Dear Mr. and Ms. Editor,
> Hi. My name is (Emily). I am 9 years old and go to…the school that's fighting about gay and lesbian family posters being up in the library.
> Lots of teachers and parents think it's a good idea because it shows another kind of family than we usually see. Some school bosses that don't go to (this school) think it's not OK.
> There's some kids that live with two moms. I bet they feel pretty bad about this adult fight and I bet they want the posters up too, cuz it's like their families.
> Kids don't really know if they are gay or lesbian until they are maybe in high school. I don't think you can tell yet.
> What the people are doing when they say "no" about the photo essay is called total homophobia. I hope kids don't learn to be homophobic by listening to the adults fight about this.
> Here's a little something I can add, "Hey, hey, ho, ho, homophobia's got to go!"

After Emily read her letter to the class, the dialogue that followed was far more rational and calm than that of the parents.

Anitra: I didn't know your parents were married.

Lena: What posters are up? (*The student teacher explained the contents of the photo exhibit.*)

Cassie: I wanted to stay at the meeting, but my parents wouldn't let me. I think they should go up so people would know that being gay or lesbian isn't bad and then they wouldn't hate them.

Ian: You should fax your letter to all the schools in [our city]!

Samantha: I think two things. I do think they should go up. People can learn that they're not bad, but just the same as us. But I think that there shouldn't only be one kind of family. Just showing them gay and lesbian families looks like they're different and they're different because they're bad.

Emily: If it were Hispanic families or any other kind, they'd say it was OK. They're saying no just because they're gay or lesbian.

Cassie: I know why some people are homophobic. It says in the Bible that gay and lesbian people are bad.

Samantha: It should have been in our school first. A lot of kids tease about being gay or lesbian. Ellen came and reached over me to get something from her cubby and a kindergarten kid who was walking by our room said, "Oh, they're gay!"

Lena: Those kids probably didn't know what lesbians are. Lesbians are girls who love each other and gay means boys. Gay also means happy.

Ian: Oh, I get it. They're together so they're happy. That's why you call them gay.

Cassie: Rob and Tom [a gay couple who are friends with her family] could come and talk to our class about gay rights.

Only two families had expressed opposition to the exhibit. Joel's mom and dad wrote a letter requesting that their child not participate in the viewing of the exhibit. Ellen's mom and stepdad came into the classroom after school one day, arguing that homosexuality was against their religion and family values. I reiterated the importance of respecting everyone in the school community, regardless of whether we agreed with them or not. They left the room with assurances that their child would not be ostracized for her family's beliefs, and that alternative activities would be available for her.

The Big Day

On the Monday morning following the second parent meeting, we went as a class to view the photo exhibit. After all the discord and tension of the proceeding weeks, the actual event felt almost anti-climactic to me.

I had assigned partners and asked the students to go around the library in pairs to look at the photographs and read the dialogues that went with them. I told them to pick a favorite photo to present to the group and, if they chose, to read parts of the accompanying scripts. Gigi Kaeser, the photographer, joined us for the discussion that followed.

During the discussion, I was somewhat distracted, first by the presence of a parent from another classroom who had been very vehement about his opposing views, and second by the uneasy scrutiny of the principal. But I remember how accepting and matter-of-fact the children's reactions were. Far from seeing something exotic or sinister about the exhibit, the students were interpreting the photos and dialogues as what they were: portraits of families. When we had reconvened in a circle, I let each pair of students show the class the photo of their choice and explain why they had picked it. A typical response was, "Because it looks like a very loving, happy family."

Many members of the class chose families with a racial and/or structural resemblance to their own families. Kendra, who has had a struggle accepting her dad's second marriage to a white woman, picked a family composed of an African American mom, her two children, and her white partner. "I like how the kids didn't like their new mom at first," she said, "but then they changed their minds because she made such good cheeseburgers!"

Emily, on the other hand, laughed when she read from the dialogue accompanying her favorite photo, in which a girl said: "Teachers don't teach the whole story about families in their classrooms. Teachers need to say that most families don't have a mom, a dad, a puppy dog, and a boy and a girl." "That's exactly what I have!" Emily exclaimed. "A mom, a dad, a brother, and a dog."

Emily also said she liked the girl's story of how she had dealt with her friends' reactions to her lesbian family. In the exhibit text the girl said: "All of my friends have known about it. Anybody important to

A Kid in My Class

his house

There is a kid in my class and his moms are lesbian. He is a normal kid. There is nothing wrong about being gay or lesbian. Some people are scared of gay and lesbian people. The people that are scared of gay and lesbian people are homophobic. I am not homophobic. The kid in my class is my friend. Here is a little I can add "Hey, hey, ho, ho, homophobias got to go!!"

his other mom   his mom
kid
Bob his cat

me
my house
my bike

me has known about it and is cool about it. . . . If you can't accept my mom, you can't accept me."

Lena, who has never seen her birth father, was attracted to a photo of a woman alone with a baby. She wanted to know how she got the baby and why she didn't have any partner, male or female. "That's just like me and my mom," said Samantha, whose mom also has been her only parent since birth.

After about a half-hour of discussion, the next scheduled class, a group of kindergartners, came into the library. I invited them to join our class until we finished and they squeezed into our circle, some sitting on the laps of siblings or neighborhood friends. Interrupted only by the squeaks of the library bookracks and the voices of children from other classes checking out books, the two classes listened attentively to the remaining presentations by my students.

After the Exhibit

After viewing the photo exhibit, interest was high, so I decided to ask the class to brainstorm related activities. Someone suggested reading a class book we had compiled during the filming of the *It's Elementary* video the previous year, which was full of stories and pictures about gay and lesbian rights. "That's not fair,"

Tonisha protested. "We should write stories for a new book!" Other ideas included making pink triangle pins and designing posters for the hallway.

Such activities continued for several weeks. During their free-choice time, kids made buttons, which they proudly offered to teachers. They started out by copying a pin I had brought in that had a rainbow background and the words "Celebrate Diversity," but soon came up with their own variations in designs and slogans. They used colorful markers to make rainbows overlaid with pink and black triangles and peace symbols. Phrases like "Love one another," "It's OK to be gay," and "Homophobia gots to go!" embellished the pins.

I also read several books about gay or lesbian families to the class. A favorite was a daily "read-aloud" called *Living in Secret* by Christine Salat (1993). Since the book had been suggested by a 4th-/5th-grade teacher, I had wondered at first if it might be too advanced. The story, about an 11-year-old girl who runs away to live with her lesbian moms, turned out to be very popular. Students were relating on many levels to the story—to the element of suspense, certainly, but also to the family recombinations, loyalties, and friction that were familiar to many of them. "Read another chapter!" came to be the refrain, as our read-aloud time began to cut into recess and free time.

Adam composed a letter to the editor of a local newspaper:

I think gay and lesbian people aren't respected enough. It's not like they aren't allowed to go to the movies, or restaurants, but it's almost like legal disrespect. I don't know why people have disrespect for gay and lesbian people, because they aren't gay or lesbian so why do they care? I have some advice for you homophobic people out there, don't go out of your homes! There could be a gay or lesbian person anywhere.

On the last day of the two-week exhibit, we went as a class to have another look at the photos. Ian was fascinated by a photo of a gay family with a dog. "They have a corgi, just like I do!" was his comment. Afterward, we had a quiet writing time to reflect on issues related to the exhibit. As usual, the students chose a variety of ways to approach the topic.

Ian wrote: "I think people should all get along together. I think they should not be homophobic, because it makes gays and lesbian people feel sad. I think our school should have gay and lesbian photos in our school because lots of kids call other kids names and to educate the kids."

Jeremy related the issues of gay and lesbian rights to racist name-calling. "One time I got called a nigger and I didn't like it so I went and told the teacher because I don't like being called that name because it is bad," he wrote. "That's why name-calling is bad to say [even] when you are just playing around."

Emily wrote a science-fiction story about alien lesbians who encountered homophobia for the first time when they visited Earth. "When they got to Earth they went to an A&W restaurant and a teenager called them 'faggot.' That was the first time that had ever happened, so they said back: '*@#$%^&*!@#$ %^&*!' which means, 'We are proud to be who we are.'"

When they had finished their stories, the students worked on drawings to go with them. A crowd started to gather around Paul's table. He was drawing a picture of the Capitol building in our city surrounded by little circles that represented the 1,000 people he and his moms had joined for a gay pride march. As he drew he was counting: "…99, 100, 101…."

As I watched the children cheering Paul for trying to represent all the people who supported his moms, I thought about the progress we had made. In our classroom, gays and lesbians had moved a long way from the "other" status that they frequently occupy in school and society. Gay and lesbian families and individuals had become integral parts of our classroom dialogues and stories. Homophobia, a word now known to all, had become as serious a charge as any other form of discrimination.

On one of the last days of school, Adam and Ian came rushing in from recess, flushed and agitated. "One of the 5th graders is homophobic!" they said indignantly. "He was teasing us and calling us 'gay.'" I assured them that his teacher would want to hear about it, and, without the trepidation usually shown by members of our class when they approach the 4th-/5th-grade teachers, they confidently marched into the classroom down the hall to report the incident.

I thought back to the name-calling incidents and discussions at the beginning of the year, and all the stress and conflict surrounding the photo exhibit. Although as a class and as a school we had felt the divisions and pain, we had come through. The rainbow flag that was flying at our classroom door was a daily reminder of our struggle and testimony to our commitment. ▪

....

Kate Lyman teaches in Madison, Wis. The names of the children in this article have been changed.

Resources on Gay and Lesbian Issues Compiled by Kate Lyman

MULTIMEDIA

Different and the Same
Produced by Family Communications
Distributed by Destination Education
www.shopdei.com

This series of nine videos for young elementary children uses puppets to explore issues of discrimination and prejudice. Although it does not deal directly with issues of gay and lesbian inclusion, many of the segments could be used to spark discussions about acceptance of family differences or name-calling. It includes teachers' guides.

It's Elementary: Talking About Gay Issues in School
Debra Chasnoff and Helen Cohen
GroundSpark, www.groundspark.org

This documentary film is intended for teachers and others interested in educating elementary school children about gay and lesbian issues. It was filmed in elementary classrooms in schools in Wisconsin, New York, California, and Massachusetts.

That's a Family!
GroundSpark, www.groundspark.org

This film helps K-8 students explore what it is like to grow up with gay or lesbian, divorced, single, adoptive parents and grandparents as parents as well as parents of different races and religions. The documentary comes with a discussion and teaching guide.

Love Makes a Family: Living in Gay and Lesbian Families — a Photograph-Text Exhibit
Photographs by Gigi Kaeser
Interviews by Pam Brown and Peggy Gillespie
Family Diversity Projects, www.familydiv.org

The black-and-white photographs depict racially diverse gay and lesbian families in a variety of family structures. Included in the exhibit are written dialogues with family members and a teacher resource packet.

BOOKS

Asha's Mums
Rosamund Elwin and Michele Paulse
Toronto: Women's Press, 1990

A girl runs into a problem when her teacher doesn't accept the fact that two moms signed her field trip permission slip. This is an engaging story for young elementary students.

How Would You Feel If Your Dad Was Gay?
Ann Heron and Meredith Maran
Boston: Alyson Publication Inc., 1991

This story, geared for middle elementary children, presents the story of a 3rd-grade girl who encounters problems at school when she shares the fact that she has three dads (her mother's partner and her dad and his male partner). The book explores the reaction of her classmates and teachers, as well as the reluctance of her older brother to share his family structure.

Belinda's Bouquet
Leslea Newman
Boston: Alyson Publications Inc., 1991

Issues of body image and name-calling are explored in a story in which the fact that the child has two moms is secondary to the main plot.

The Duke Who Outlawed Jelly Beans and Other Stories
Johnny Valentine
Boston: Alyson Publications Inc., 1991

These modern fairy tales involve dragons, magic frogs, and girls who defy limitations based on gender. The characters happen to have gay or lesbian families, but only in the last (title) story is this the main issue. In the latter, an autocratic duke decrees that children who have "too many" fathers or mothers will be thrown into the dungeon.

Resources on Gay and Lesbian Issues continued

Gloria Goes to Gay Pride
Leslea Newman
Boston: Alyson Publications Inc., 1991

Gloria is excited about going to a gay pride march with her moms. She is confused, however, when they encounter protesters with antigay signs. This story is helpful in discussing homophobia with young elementary school children.

Heather Has Two Mommies
Leslea Newman
Northampton, Mass.:
In Other Words Publishing, 1989

This story about a girl with lesbian moms has raised controversy because it explains artificial insemination. However, the question "How can two women have a baby together?" is natural for students as young as kindergarten to ask. This book gives one possible answer to that question, as well as exploring the variety of families in Heather's classroom.

In Our Mothers' House
Patricia Polacco
Philomel, 2009

Narrated by an adopted African American daughter, this book tells the story of celebrating differences and love with Marmee and Meema, white moms who raise three adopted children.

Living in Secret
by Christine Salat
New York: Bantam Books, 1993

This fictional chapter book for older elementary students relates how a girl runs away to "live in secret" with her lesbian mom and her partner.

And Tango Makes Three
Peter Parnell and Justin Richardson
Simon & Schuster Children's Publishing, 2005

Based on a true story, this book tells the story of two male penguins that raise a penguin chick in the Central Park Zoo.

Wealan Pollard

Testing Kindergarten

Young children produce data—lots of data

KELLY McMAHON

I remember my kindergarten experience from 25 years ago. Way back then, kindergarten focused on letters, sounds, counting, coloring inside the lines, cutting straight along the solid black line, and learning how to get along with others. I remember looking forward to rest time, recess, snack, and show and tell. That was kindergarten before the days of No Child Left Behind. Kindergarten post-NCLB is being turned into a school experience that results in many children disliking school and feeling like failures.

I have spent the last six years teaching 5-year-old kindergarten for Milwaukee Public Schools (MPS). During this time, I have seen a decrease in district initiatives that are developmentally appropriate, and an increase in the amount of testing and data collection for 5-year-olds. Just when I thought the district couldn't ask for any more test scores or drills or practice, a new initiative and data system pops up for my school to complete. My school has not met our Adequate Yearly Progress (AYP) for the past three years. Due to our failure to meet AYP, we are now a School Identified for Improvement (SIFI), with Level Two status.

The students in my classroom during the 2008–09 school year completed more assessments than during any of my prior years of teaching kindergarten:

- Milwaukee Public Schools' 5-Year-Old Kindergarten Assessment (completed three times a year)
- On the Mark Reading Verification Assessment (completed three times a year)
- A monthly writing prompt focused on different strands of the Six Traits of Writing
- 28 assessments measuring key early reading and spelling skills
- Chapter pre- and post-tests for all nine math chapters completed
- Three additional assessments for each math chapter completed
- A monthly math prompt
- Four Classroom Assessments Based on Standards (CABS) per social studies chapter (20 total)
- Four CABS assessments per science chapter (20 total)
- Four CABS assessments per health chapter (20 total)

I recently learned that my students will also be expected to complete four benchmark assessments beginning in the 2010–11 school year.

This list does not include the pre- and post-Marzano vocabulary tests (which I refuse to have my students complete because the assessment design is entirely developmentally inappropriate) or the writing and math portfolios we are required to keep.

Last spring, the literacy coach at my school handed us a copy of the new MPS Student Reading Portfolio, which includes a list of 10 academic vocabulary words per semester that kindergartners are expected to know. My students will once more have to complete pre- and post-tests each semester. When I brought the MPS Student Reading Portfolio to the Milwaukee Teachers' Education Association's (MTEA) Early Childhood Committee, the members were surprised and disgusted. This new reading portfolio asks kindergarten students to define terms like *Venn diagram, sound out, understand, poetry, tracking, sight word, expression*, and *describe*. It also expects kindergartners to produce 20 different sounds, including the blending and digraph sounds *ch, qu, sh, th*, and *ing*, at a proficient level. This developmentally inappropriate assessment tool was designed without the input of early childhood educators. The MTEA Early

Childhood Committee submitted our comments and recommendations for proposed changes to both the MPS Reading and Early Childhood Departments. We have yet to hear a response.

Kindergartners Need to Play

One negative impact of continued assessment-crazy data collection on my school has been the total disregard for the importance of children's social and emotional development. As more and more of my students spend less time interacting with their peers outside of school, I am forced to severely limit the amount of time dedicated to play centers in my classroom. Without the opportunity to interact with their peers in structured and unstructured play, my students are losing out on situations that allow them to learn to problem-solve, share, explore, and deepen their learning.

> **One negative impact of continued assessment-crazy data collection on my school has been the total disregard for the importance of children's social and emotional development.**

As Edward Almon and Joan Miller point out in their book *Crisis in the Kindergarten: Why Children Need to Play in School*, "Research shows that children who engage in complex forms of sociodramatic play have greater language skills than nonplayers, better social skills, more empathy, more imagination, and more of the subtle capacity to know what others mean. They are less aggressive and show more self-control and higher levels of thinking."

Apparently young children stopped learning through play the moment the bipartisan NCLB bill passed Congress and was signed into law by President George W. Bush.

Sleepless in Milwaukee

The issue of allowing young children in kindergarten to rest has now become a battle all across MPS. Last year MPS issued a guideline for rest time for early childhood programs. The district guidelines proposed a maximum 45-minute rest time in the fall for all-day 4-year-old kindergarten, followed by a maximum of

30 minutes in the spring. The guidelines suggested a maximum of 30 minutes to be used for rest in the fall in 5-year-old kindergarten classrooms, and for rest to be entirely phased out in the spring.

These policies fly in the face of brain research, which suggests that sleep allows the brain to cement the learning that has taken place. As Marilee Sprenger writes in her book *Learning and Memory: The Brain in Action*:

> Through prior knowledge or interest, the new information may be added to the old and form more long-term memory. The process may have to be repeated several times before long-term memory is formed. The brain will process some of this information during sleep. Studies have shown that while rats are in the sleep stage called REM (rapid eye movement) sleep, their brains reproduce the same patterns used for learning while awake.

But MPS insists that I wake up a sleeping child who might have only gotten five or six hours of sleep each night.

My administrators have allotted my students 20 minutes of rest time each day for the 2009–10 school year. However, by the time my students finish using the restroom and get a drink of water after their one and only recess for the day, they will have roughly 10 minutes to rest. Every year I have at least one child in my classroom who is not getting adequate sleep every night.

There was a young boy in my classroom last year who went to daycare directly from school and stayed there until 11 p.m. By the time his mother picked him up, drove home, and gave him a snack, it would be 1 a.m. before he finally got to bed. This child would then be up roughly five hours later to start his day all over again. He entered my classroom exhausted and in need of additional sleep. When he allowed himself to fall asleep at rest time, it was nearly impossible to wake him.

When district officials came into my classroom, I had to defend my professional judgment in allowing this child to continue to sleep after I began afternoon instruction. I have multiple students in my classroom this year with similar sleeping schedules at home, yet they are allowed only 10 minutes for rest. I am experiencing far more behavioral problems in the afternoon this school year due to the decrease in time my students are allowed to rest.

As I enter my eighth year of teaching in Milwaukee, I'm left wondering how much more testing and data collection I might be expected to do, and how many more developmentally inappropriate initiatives I will be asked to implement. I also wonder exactly how much longer I can continue to "teach" under these circumstances. ▪

Kelly McMahon now teaches preschool in Iowa.

Works Cited

Miller, Edward and Joan Almon. *Crisis in the Kindergarten: Why Children Need to Play in School.* College Park, Md.: Alliance for Childhood, 2009.

Sprenger, Marilee. *Learning and Memory: The Brain in Action.* Alexandria, Va.: Association for Supervision and Curriculum Development, 1999.

Roxanna Bikadoroff

My Talk with the Principal

Thoughts on putting up walls—and tearing them down

ANTHONY E. IANNONE

I tried to gather myself before the meeting with my principal, but I could feel the knot in my stomach begin to tighten. "What have I done wrong now? What could she possibly want to talk about?" Her email said she had "some serious concerns...about what is and is not going on in your classroom."

I knew I had to speak to her. Halfway to her office I started to think, "This must be what students go through when they're asked to go to the office for reasons they don't quite understand."

My arrival in her office seemed to jostle her. She was consumed by a mass of paperwork on her desk. She raised her head, bleary-eyed, and invited me in. The tension in the room was palpable.

We exchanged a few awkward pleasantries. She clearly had an agenda for the meeting but seemed unsure how to begin. I broke the silence by asking what her serious concerns were about what was going on (or not going on) in my classroom.

She looked nervously down at her notes and began to talk to me about how there were things in our school that were negotiable and things that were non-negotiable. I knew exactly where she was going, but I let her continue. She explained that everyone in the school was supposed to have a word wall up in their classroom.

A word wall, I thought. Is that her problem?

A word wall—that product from the prepackaged curriculum we're supposed to use with our students when teaching them how to read. The product involves posting vocabulary from the literature anthology on the walls in our classroom. I resisted putting up the word wall because my students had no say in the words that were supposed to be there.

The words on a typical word wall are in alphabetical order, written on index cards. One of my colleagues has her word wall up only to keep our principal off her back. The only time her students use the wall is when she has them put the words on it. Under these circumstances, this word wall and the prepackaged curriculum it comes from have not only taken up precious space, but, more importantly, funds that could be used for quality literature as well.

I told my principal that I could not put up a word wall like this in my classroom. It goes against all that I believe about how children learn. I try to empower my students by teaching them how to choose what to read, providing them the opportunity to respond to the text and space to talk to others about the text. I explained to her that word walls assume that the only words worthy of our time and space in the classroom are the words from the anthology, which in turn places an artificial importance on the anthology as the source for learning to read.

At this point in the meeting, my principal looked frustrated, like she was holding something back. And, seeing her as the "enemy," the person who wanted me to have this ridiculous word wall up in my room, I wasn't prepared for the "wall" she was about to tear down.

She came clean with me. She told me that the real reason she needed me to have the word wall up was that whenever our school got "shopped" by district-level administrators with their "snapshot" observation forms, our school—and more directly my principal—was getting penalized whenever these administrators didn't see things like a word wall up in everyone's classroom. She told me that this was why she too was evaluating teachers with this "snapshot" evaluation form. She felt that by using the same form, she'd communicate to the staff exactly what was supposed to be going on (and in my case, what should be up on the walls) when others came in to observe instruction. This in turn would alleviate the extreme "heat" she was getting from district administrators. My noncompliance with the nonnegotiable items on the "snapshot" evaluation form was making my principal look weak and incapable of keeping her teachers in line.

> **At that moment, I began to see my principal as a human being caught in the same fight I find myself in each day. It's a fight between people who want the same things for children and the corporate system—which has an investment in uniformity and compliance.**

At that moment, I began to see my principal as a human being caught in the same fight I find myself in each day, a fight that usually isolates teachers and principals from one another, a fight that makes teachers decide to just put the ridiculous word wall up and move on with their lives. It's a fight between people who want the same things for children and the corporate system—which has an investment in uniformity and compliance.

Suddenly, I could hear her words differently. Strangely enough, I sensed the same thing beginning to happen with her. A new and more positive energy filled the room and as a result, I took the opportunity to talk to her about the "snapshot" evaluation form. I said that it limited her vision of what was really going on in classrooms. I told her that I thought it took away her voice and forced her to make judgments she knew were not accurate. I said that to me, as a teacher, the snapshot's authoritative nature made her seem like an enforcer. Finally, I pointed out how there was no room on that form for a dialogue between teacher and administrator. How could either of us benefit from the use of such a form?

Although she wasn't quite ready to abandon the "snapshot" evaluation form—a battle for another day—she told me that the word wall I needed to have up in my room didn't have to be the word wall from "the book." I left that meeting feeling empowered to redefine what was expected of me.

Back in my classroom, I elicited the help of my students. I told them that our Great (Word) Wall of Empowerment is a wall for the people, made by the people.

"Let's cut up multicolored pieces of construction paper in the shape of bricks," I said. "The words that go up on the wall will come from whatever you are currently reading—novels, picture books, any content area. The words can come from home, from your community, from your life."

During a lesson on multiplication, my students and I were working with words like factor and product. One of my students raised his hand and asked if we could put these words on the wall. I asked him to get two "bricks" and write them down so we could place them up later in the day. Some students in my classroom know French, Spanish, and Korean. They wrote words for us in their home languages and taught their classmates how to read these words. We also had a class blog where friends and family members could recommend words for the wall. Words also came from my students' writing. At least once a week, we did something fun with the wall. I'd come to class and challenge the students to come up with words that mean the same as cool. ("Sweet!") The students wrote the words, colored them in so they stood out on the wall and I stapled them onto the wall. I also cut up pieces of black construction paper to place in between the words to give it that wall look.

Our wall filled up two sides of my classroom and spilled down the corridor. My principal showed my wall to visitors and understood that the check-off sheet showed that she was "in control." I think we both began to see each other differently, as co-workers engaged in the same struggle to provide our students with an education that empowers. My talk with my principal simultaneously resulted in the construction of one wall—the Great (Word) Wall of Empowerment—and the deconstruction of another.

....

Anthony E. Iannone teaches 3rd grade in Charlotte-Mecklenburg Schools, N.C.

Joseph Blough

They Call This Data?

Oscar Wilde, Svab, and my students

AMY GUTOWSKI

According to the "data" collected on our fourth and final ThinkLink benchmark of the past school year, most of my 3rd graders had a hard time reading a paraphrased excerpt from Oscar Wilde's *The Importance of Being Earnest*. I was shocked. I mean, why would 8- and 9-year-olds in Milwaukee (or anywhere else for that matter) have trouble reading Oscar Wilde? The questions were so simple for a beginning reader to decode. For example:

Read this sentence from the passage. *He laid particular **stress** on your German, as he was leaving for town yesterday.* Now look at the dictionary entry:

stress *noun*
1 worries caused by difficulties in life
2 saying a word or part of a word more stongly than another
3 force of weight caused by something heavy

verb
4 to give importance to something

Which meaning of *stress* is used in the sentence above? A.1, B.2, C.3, D.4

But wait. What *is* the correct answer anyway? I'm confused. I guess I'm going to have to dust off my AP anthologies from high school if I'm going to teach to this test.

According to the "formative" assessment "data" my 3rd graders also had trouble reading a story called "The Broken Pot." In this paraphrased tale—what is it with all the paraphrasing on these tests anyway; would it be too much to ask that my students read a whole story, written for children?—there's a Brahman by the name of Svab. He has to beg for food. One day he receives a large pot of rice gruel, eats a bit, then hangs the leftovers on a nail above his bed. While full

> **What is it with all the paraphrasing on these tests anyway; would it be too much to ask that my students read a whole story, written for children?**

in his bed, his mind gets away with him, and he has greedy thoughts of selling the rice gruel, then buying goats, then trading goats for cattle, then trading calves for horses, horses have foals, he can sell the foals, etc. Then eventually he will meet a beautiful girl with a dowry. (And how many 3rd graders know what a dowry is? Just curious.) Anyway, Svab gets carried away with his thoughts, startles himself, and knocks the pot of rice gruel on his own head. Now, this is the part that kills me—the moral: "He who makes foolish plans for the future will be white all over, like Svab." Huh? Most of my students are children of color. Imagine their surprise at the ending. Some of my students laughed out loud. They didn't get it. I didn't get it either.

I don't think any of us will "get it" until this obsession with prepackaged testing ends. It's so absurd, it's almost funny, like straight out of an *Onion* article. But I'm not laughing when during a staff meeting, after a long day of working with kids in the classroom, I'm staring at a projection of a large, fancy, color-coded, computer-generated bar graph showing the dismal results of our last reading benchmark, being told my students don't know how to analyze text. I'm not laughing when we spend hours drafting our ed plan, discussing how we can bring up our test scores. I'm so very tired of wasting my valuable time discussing these so-called data. Instead, I'll continue to tell tales of the insanity of it all, hoping that one day, my 3rd graders will no longer be subjected to such nonsense. ■

Amy Gutowski teaches 3rd grade in Milwaukee Public Schools.

Resources

Beth Alexander recommends:

Peters World Atlas: [the Earth in True Proportion]. Union, N.J.: Hammond World Atlas Corp., 2002. Print.

This atlas contains a large number of thematic maps that compare different countries' access to food, electrical energy, education, etc., and is a good resource for younger students and visual learners.

Strauss, Rochelle, and Woods, Rosemary. *One Well: The Story of Water on Earth.* Toronto: Kids Can Press, 2007. Print.

This beautifully illustrated book uses graphs, statistics, and stories to explain how we use water in such diverse ways across the globe. It can start an interesting discussion about the need to conserve water, the surprising ways in which we use water without even being aware of it, and the inequities of power that lead to water shortages.

Jessie L. Auger recommends:

Moses, Robert P., and Charles E. Cobb Jr. *Radical Equations: Math Literacy and Civil Rights.* Boston: Beacon Press, 2001. Print.

Civil Rights Activist Bob Moses shows us, through his work creating the Algebra Project, how math literacy is essential to full citizenship in America.

Eleanor Duckworth. *"The Having of Wonderful Ideas" and Other Essays on Teaching and Learning.* New York: Teachers College Press, 2006. Print.

How do we understand our students' ideas? Duckworth teaches us to ask, listen, notice—to be knowledgeable about and open to the possibilities of our subject matter.

Powell, Arthur B., and Marilyn Frankenstein. *Ethnomathematics: Challenging Eurocentrism in Mathematics Education.* Albany, N.Y.: SUNY Press, 1997. Print.

An invaluable resource for all educators interested in breaking stereotypes and uncovering bias in math education.

Melissa Bollow Tempel recommends:

Boelts, Maribeth, and Noah Z. Jones. *Those Shoes.* Somerville, Mass.: Candlewick Press, 2009. Print.

This is a moving story of a boy who desperately wants "those shoes" and how he finally finds that showing kindness can be just as satisfying as having material things. The story is one that many students can identify with, from living with grandma to the box of spare clothes in the guidance counselor's office. Using it in the classroom sparks a great discussion, especially about poverty and what it means to be poor, at any level of elementary school teaching.

Leitich Smith, Cynthia. *Jingle Dancer.* New York: HarperCollins, 2000. Print.

This is the story of a Muscogee (Creek) girl who needs tin jingles to complete her dress so she can be a Jingle Dress Dancer like her grandma. Throughout the story the girl meets many strong female role models. This book helps students understand the existence of past and present American Indian traditions.

Geralyn Bywater McLaughlin recommends:

Levin, Diane E. *Teaching Young Children in Violent Times: Building a Peaceable Classroom.* Cambridge, Mass.: Educators for Social Responsibility, 2003. Print.

Especially written for early childhood educators, this book is full of practical and positive strategies for teachers who are looking to help young children feel safe and secure in a world often filled with violence and hopelessness.

Consuming Kids: The Commercialization of Childhood. Dir. Barbaro, Adriana, and Jeremy Earp. Media Education Foundation, 2008. DVD.

This powerful film for teachers and parents sheds light on how deregulation led to an explosion in marketing to children in the United States and explores the current full-scale corporate attack on childhood. The DVD includes an extra chapter on what parents can do.

Rachel Cloues recommends:

Winter, Jeanette. *The Librarian of Basra: A True Story from Iraq*. Orlando, Fla.: Harcourt Inc., 2005. Print.

Based on a true story, Winter's picture book describes how Alia Muhammad Baker, the chief librarian of the Basra Central Library, organized her friends and neighbors to move 30,000 books out of the library when the threat of war loomed. By storing the books in a restaurant, her friends' homes, and her own small house, she saved most of the library's volumes when the building was burned to the ground nine days later. This is a simply told, powerful story of the destructiveness of war, the courage of regular people, and the hope they have for a peaceful future. It is a story perfect for the elementary grades, and one that will undoubtedly provoke rich conversation if read aloud in a classroom.

Smith, David J., and Shelagh Armstrong. *If the World Were a Village: A Book About the World's People*. Toronto: Kids Can Press, 2002. Print.

Smith, David J., and Shelagh Armstrong. *If America Were a Village: A Book About the People of the United States*. Toronto: Kids Can Press, 2009. Print.

These two books are excellent for encouraging a deeper understanding of the different peoples, languages, resources, lifestyles, and cultures around the world and in the United States. By proportionally converting bigger numbers (i.e., a world population of 6.8 billion) to a scale "village" of 100 people, Smith allows children—and all of us—to more easily understand how many people speak a language other than English, how many children attend school, how many families have access to clean water, how many people drive cars, have TVs, etc. Children are captivated by the detailed drawings and eye-opening statistics that highlight the differences in how people live around the world and within our own country.

Bunting, Eve, and Ted Lewin. *One Green Apple*. New York: Clarion Books, 2006. Print.

With typical Eve Bunting style, this beautiful picture book tackles a complex societal issue from the perspective of a child. *One Green Apple* is the story of Farah, a recent Muslim immigrant struggling to fit in with her classmates. On a school field trip to a farm, Farah makes some realizations about culture and language, notices that kids generally dress and act the same everywhere, and begins to feel a connection to her new community.

Mark Hansen recommends:

Zelver, Patricia, and Frané Lessac. *The Wonderful Towers of Watts*. New York: Tambourine Books, 1994. Print.

This richly illustrated picture book tells the story of how Simon Rodia built the monumental towers of the title from scavenged bits of iron and glass and how it was saved from destruction when the community mobilized around it. I use this story to help students celebrate the unique geography of their neighborhood. What special places would they fight to preserve?

Johnston, Peter H. *Choice Words: How Our Language Affects Children's Learning*. Portland, Maine: Stenhouse Publishers, 2004. Print.

This is the only research book I've read more than once. Through vivid classroom observations, literacy researcher and teacher educator Peter Johnston explores how the language teachers use affects student learning. By noticing and naming effective decisions and thinking, teachers can reveal a sense of agency to their students—that if they act strategically they can effect change and become the authors of their own learning.

Johnson, D. B. *Henry Hikes to Fitchburg*. Boston: Houghton Mifflin, 2000. Print.

Johnson, D. B. *Henry Builds a Cabin*. Boston: Houghton Mifflin, 2002. Print

Johnson, D. B. *Henry Works*. Boston: Houghton Mifflin, 2004. Print.

These beautiful picture books, by a student of Howard Zinn's, tell the adventures of a bear named Henry who strongly resembles Henry David Thoreau. The peaceful stories reveal the hidden relationships between a love of nature, helping neighbors, and the satisfaction of working for what you believe in.

Chloë Myers-Hughes recommends:

Prater, Mary A., and Tina T. Dyches. *Teaching About Disabilities Through Children's Literature*. Westport, Conn.: Libraries Unlimited, 2008. Print.

This is a useful resource for teaching about disability through literature. It contains an annotated bibliography of children's literature, lesson plans that teach about different disabilities, and reproducible materials for activities that support the lesson plans.

Reidarson, Nina. *Outstanding Books for Young People with Disabilities*. Oslo: IBBY Documentation Centre of Books for Disabled Young People, Dept. of Special Education, Faculty of Education, University of Oslo, 1997. Print.

The International Board on Books for Young People (IBBY) is a nonprofit organization that represents an international network of people from all over the world who are committed to bringing books and children together. IBBY produces an international catalog of books that feature characters with disabilities as well as books catering to young people with disabilities. *Outstanding Books for Young People with Disabilities* catalogs are published every two years.

Anthony E. Iannone recommends:

Freire, Paulo. *Pedagogy of Freedom: Ethics, Democracy, and Civic Courage*. Lanham, Md.: Rowman & Littlefield Publishers, 1998. Print.

We live in a time when the "banking model" of teaching is merging with standardization, when being an effective teacher means making sure you have the "right" things up on your classroom walls so your principal can check it off on his list and leave thinking: "This is what school looks like." Freire's book is a constant source of inspiration. At the end of the day, I read a few pages and go to sleep thinking that, "Teaching is a human act." Knowing this helps me realize the importance of going back to my classroom the next day ready to "work against from within" alongside the 22 humans (my 3rd graders) that energize me with their passion to learn.

Stefoff, Rebecca, and Howard Zinn. *A Young People's History of the United States*. New York: Seven Stories Press, 2007. Print.

This book provides a great counter narrative to the master narratives we work against from within everyday in the classroom.

Katharine Johnson recommends:

Resources for teaching a unit on child labor with elementary school students:

Altman, Linda J., and Enrique O. Sanchez. *Amelia's Road*. New York: Lee & Low Books, 1993. Print.

Ancona, George. *Harvest*. New York: Marshall Cavendish, 2001. Print.

D'Adamo, Francesco, and Ann Leonori. *Iqbal*. New York: Atheneum Books for Young Readers, 2003. Print.

Roberts-Davis, Tanya. *We Need to Go to School: Voices of the Rugmark Children*. Toronto: Douglas & McIntyre, 2001. Print.

Freedman, Russell, and Lewis W. Hine. *Kids at Work: Lewis Hine and the Crusade Against Child Labor*. New York: Clarion Books, 1994. Print.

Jiménez, Francisco. *The Circuit: Stories from the Life of a Migrant Child*. Albuquerque: University of New Mexico Press, 1997. Print.

Youme, Selavi. *That Is Life: A Haitian Story of Hope*. El Paso, Texas: Cinco Puntos Press, 2004. Print.

Julie Knutson recommends:

Hoose, Phillip M., *We Were There, Too!: Young People in U.S. History*. New York: Farrar Straus Giroux, 2001. Print.

Hoose tells the story of U.S. history through the eyes and experiences of the young people who lived it. This collection helps students imagine what their lives would have been like in past eras.

Elizabeth Marshall recommends:

Cottin, Menena, Rosana Faría, and Elisa Amado. *The Black Book of Colors*. Toronto: Groundwood Books, 2008. Print.

First published in Mexico in 2006 as *El libro negro de los colores*, this exceptional picture book is made up entirely of black pages. The accompanying text is written in white and translated into braille. Each page focuses on a color and uses imagery to capture it. "Green tastes like lemon ice cream and smells like grass that's just been cut." The book allows sighted readers a place to begin thinking about different ways of knowing and understanding.

Bartoletti, Susan C. *Kids on Strike!* Boston: Houghton Mifflin, 1999. Print.

Written for readers in grades 5-8, this book offers a history of working conditions for youth in the 19th and 20th century and children's participation in labor strikes. The book is well researched and an engaging read. Numerous photographs throughout show children protesting as well as documenting the working conditions they faced. This is a great resource for children and a good one for adults to rethink children's ability to recognize and fight against oppression.

Schooling the World: The White Man's Last Burden. Carol Black (Director); Jim Hurst (Producer). Telluride, Colo.: Lost People Films, 2010. DVD.

This film focuses on the link between colonization and schooling. The filmmakers document the knowledge that is lost when "benevolent" educational projects are imported from the "West" into a variety of indigenous cultures.

Collins, Suzanne. *Gregor the Overlander*. New York: Scholastic, 2003. Print.

This is the first book in the five-part *Underland Chronicles* (grades 4-8) in which Gregor and his little sister Boots fall through a vent in their New York City apartment and arrive in an underland populated by talking cockroaches, rats, and other animals. Like Collins' *Hunger Games* trilogy, the *Underland Chronicles* defies gender stereotypes and offers an anti-war stance; the series includes vivid depictions of fighting and death as the results of solving problems through violence.

Michelle Munk recommends:

Gapminder. www.gapminder.org

Hans Rosling's innovative online graphical tool compares national data from numerous countries on a variety of topics. The tool is simple to use, and uses national and U.N. or World Health Organization data, making it easy to observe trends and identify outliers. Background information is also provided for some data sets, and there is also a "for teachers" section.

Radical Math. http://www.radicalmath.org/

Includes "A Guide for Integrating Issues of Social and Economic Justice into Mathematics Curriculum" by Jonathan Osler.

UN Data. http://data.un.org/

Includes data on education, employment, energy, environment, food and agriculture, health, human development, industry, ICT, population, refugees, trade.

The Data and Story Library (DASL). http://lib.stat.cmu.edu/DASL/

Elizabeth Schlessman recommends:

Kurusa, Monika Doppert, and Karen Englander. *The Streets Are Free*. Toronto: Annick Press, 1994. Print.

This beautifully illustrated book offers a picture of persuasion and empowerment in a shantytown on the outskirts of Caracas, Venezuela. Determined, organized, and persistent, the children make signs and lists to convince adults and the local government to convert an empty lot into a community park. Also published in Spanish under the title *La calle es libre*, this accessible and realistic book honors children as agents of change.

Özlem Sensoy recommends:

White, Jenny B. *The Sultan's Seal.* New York: W.W. Norton, 2006. Print.

White, Jenny B. *The Abyssinian Proof.* New York: W. W. Norton & Co, 2008. Print.

White, Jenny B. *The Winter Thief.* New York: W. W. Norton & Co, 2010. Print.

All three are novels by Jenny White, social anthropologist, professor, and author. The works of historical fiction are in the style of Sherlock mysteries with the detective being an Ottoman magistrate named Kamil Pasha. While the novels may not be appropriate for elementary readers, for teachers who want to expand their own knowledge base, White's novels are a welcome read. Because White is also a scholar, her novels are infused with academically sound details. Additionally her academic writings may serve as a helpful partnering to her works of fiction.

Kamal-Eldin, Tania. *Hollywood Harems.* New York: Women Make Movies, 1999. DVD.

A documentary film by filmmaker Tania Kamal-Eldin that examines Hollywood representations of the "oriental woman" especially in Hollywood's "classical" period.

Jhally, Sut, Jeremy Earp, and Jack G. Shaheen. *Reel Bad Arabs: How Hollywood Vilifies a People.* Northampton, Mass.: Media Education Foundation, 2006.

A documentary film and book by Jack Shaheen that examines Hollywood's representations of Arab people in movies, on television, and in cartoons.

Maura Varley Gutiérrez recommends:

Stocker, David. *Maththatmatters: A teacher resource for linking math and social justice.* Ottawa: CCPA Education Project, 2007. Print.

A teacher-created book of lesson plans and resources for integrating social justice and mathematics in the middle grades. Lesson plans provide a multitude of ideas on how to connect mathematics to real-world contexts that matter. Includes ideas for how youth can become involved in making change in their daily lives, in the local community, or globally.

Ewald, Wendy, and Alexandra Lightfoot. *I Wanna Take Me a Picture: Teaching Photography and Writing to Children.* Boston: Center for Documentary Studies in association with Beacon Press, 2001. Print.

A resource for teaching photography and writing to children filled with hands-on activities and lesson ideas. The resource is useful when implementing social justice activities, particularly involving students' own communities. The photography and writing provide children with the opportunity to document, understand, and reflect upon their worlds. The activities can also easily be adapted to creating digital stories with children.

Smith, Dan. *The Penguin State of the World Atlas.* New York: Penguin Books, 2008.

This book contains a series of world maps pertaining to topics of global significance, such as War and Peace, Wealth and Power, and Health. The maps and accompanying graphs provide an excellent classroom resource for discussions related to understanding important global issues.

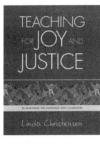

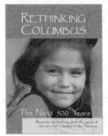

Resources from RETHINKING SCHOOLS

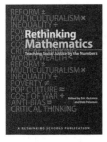

RETHINKING MATHEMATICS
Teaching Social Justice by the Numbers
Edited by Eric Gutstein and Bob Peterson
Shows how to weave social justice issues throughout the mathematics curriculum, and how to integrate mathematics into other curricular areas.

Paperback • 180 pages • ISBN: 978-0-942961-54-6
ONLY $16.95!*

RETHINKING MULTICULTURAL EDUCATION
Teaching for Racial and Cultural Justice
Edited by Wayne Au
Collects the best articles dealing with race and culture in the classroom that have appeared in *Rethinking Schools* magazine. Practical, rich in story, and analytically sharp, it demonstrates a powerful vision of anti-racist, social justice education.

Paperback • 392 pages • ISBN: 978-0-942961-42-3
Only $18.95!*

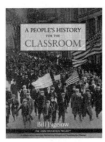

A PEOPLE'S HISTORY FOR THE CLASSROOM
By Bill Bigelow
This collection of exemplary teaching articles and lesson plans emphasizes the role of working people, women, people of color, and organized social movements in shaping U.S. history. Includes improvisations, role plays, imaginative writing, and critical reading activities.

Paperback • 120 pages • ISBN: 978-0-942961-39-3
Only $12.95!*

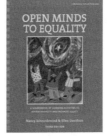

THE LINE BETWEEN US
Teaching About the Border and Mexican Immigration
By Bill Bigelow
Using stories, historical narrative, role plays, poetry, and video, veteran teacher Bill Bigelow shows how he approaches immigration and border issues in his classroom.

Paperback • 160 pages • ISBN: 978-0-942961-31-7
ONLY $16.95!*

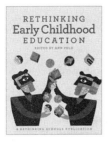

RETHINKING EARLY CHILDHOOD EDUCATION
Edited by Ann Pelo
Inspiring stories about social justice teaching with young children. This anthology shows how educators can nurture empathy, an ecological consciousness, curiosity, collaboration, and activism in young children.

Paperback • 256 pages • ISBN: 978-0-942961-41-6
Only 18.95!*

OPEN MINDS TO EQUALITY
A Sourcebook of Learning Activities to Affirm Diversity and Promote Equity
By Nancy Schniedewind and Ellen Davidson
Activities to help students understand and change inequalities based on race, gender, class, age, language, sexual orientation, physical/mental ability, and religion.

Paperback • 408 pages • ISBN: 978-0-942961-32-4
ONLY $24.95!*

*Plus shipping and handling. U.S. shipping and handling is 15% of the total (minimum charge of $4.50). Canadian shipping and handling is 25% of the total (minimum charge of $5.50).

If you liked *Rethinking Elementary Education*, then *Rethinking Schools* magazine is for you!

Take advantage of this special discount coupon to receive the country's leading social justice education magazine.

INTRODUCTORY OFFER! *Subscribe today and save!*

"A teacher's close friend—insightful, intelligent, and compassionate."

– Michele Forman, Teacher of the Year

☐ Two years (8 issues) for $22.95 *(Save $24.65 off the cover price!)*
☐ One year (4 issues) for $14.95 *(Save $8.85 off the cover price!)*
☐ Print version *or* ☐ Digital version.

☐ Please send me a free catalog of all your materials.
☐ Bill me. ☐ Enclosed is my check payable to **Rethinking Schools**.

See our website for combined digital/print subscription options. Print subscriptions to Canada & Mexico add $5 per year. Other international print subscriptions add $10 per year.

Name _____

Organization _____

Address _____

City/State/Zip _____

Phone _____

Email _____

RETHINKINGSCHOOLS
PO Box 2222, Williston, VT 05495 • toll-free: 800-669-4192 • fax: 802-864-7626   2BREEL

INTRODUCTORY OFFER! *Subscribe today and save!*

"Absolutely the best, most important education publication in the country."

– Jonathan Kozol

☐ Two years (8 issues) for $22.95 *(Save $24.65 off the cover price!)*
☐ One year (4 issues) for $14.95 *(Save $8.85 off the cover price!)*
☐ Print version *or* ☐ Digital version.

☐ Please send me a free catalog of all your materials.
☐ Bill me. ☐ Enclosed is my check payable to **Rethinking Schools**.

See our website for combined digital/print subscription options. Print subscriptions to Canada & Mexico add $5 per year. Other international print subscriptions add $10 per year.

Name _____

Organization _____

Address _____

City/State/Zip _____

Phone _____

Email _____

RETHINKINGSCHOOLS
PO Box 2222, Williston, VT 05495 • toll-free: 800-669-4192 • fax: 802-864-7626   2BREEL

BUSINESS REPLY MAIL

FIRST-CLASS MAIL   PERMIT NO.2222   WILLISTON VT

POSTAGE WILL BE PAID BY ADDRESSEE

RETHINKING SCHOOLS
PO BOX 2222
WILLISTON VT 05495-9940

BUSINESS REPLY MAIL

FIRST-CLASS MAIL   PERMIT NO.2222   WILLISTON VT

POSTAGE WILL BE PAID BY ADDRESSEE

RETHINKING SCHOOLS
PO BOX 2222
WILLISTON VT 05495-9940